Inequality and Social Structure during the Transition

Studies in Development Economics and Policy

General Editor: **Anthony Shorrocks**

UNU WORLD INSTITUTE FOR DEVELOPMENT ECONOMICS RESEARCH (UNU/WIDER) was established by the United Nations University as its first research and training centre and started work in Helsinki, Finland, in 1985. The purpose of the Institute is to undertake applied research and policy analysis on structural changes affecting the developing and transitional economies, to provide a forum for the advocacy of policies leading to robust, equitable and environmentally sustainable growth, and to promote capacity strengthening and training in the field of economic and social policy-making. Its work is carried out by staff researchers and visiting scholars in Helsinki and through networks of collaborating scholars and institutions around the world.

UNU World Institute for Development Economics Research (UNU/WIDER)
Katajanokanlaituri 6B, FIN-00160 Helsinki, Finland

Titles include:

Ricardo Ffrench-Davis and Stephany Griffith-Jones (*editors*)
FROM CAPITAL SURGES TO DROUGHT
Seeking Stability for Emerging Economies

Aiguo Lu and Manuel F. Montes (*editors*)
POVERTY, INCOME DISTRIBUTION AND WELL-BEING IN ASIA DURING THE TRANSITION

Robert J. McIntyre and Bruno Dallago (*editors*)
SMALL AND MEDIUM ENTERPRISES IN TRANSITIONAL ECONOMIES

Vladimir Mikhalev (*editor*)
INEQUALITY AND SOCIAL STRUCTURE DURING THE TRANSITION

E. Wayne Nafziger and Raimo Väyrynen (*editors*)
THE PREVENTION OF HUMANITARIAN EMERGENCIES

Laixiang Sun (*editor*)
OWNERSHIP AND GOVERNANCE OF ENTERPRISES
Recent Innovative Developments

Studies in Development Economies and Policy
Series Standing Order ISBN 0–333–96424–1
(*outside North America only*)

You can receive future titles in this series as they are published by placing a standing order. Please contact your bookseller or, in case of difficulty, write to us at the address below with your name and address, the title of the series and the ISBN quoted above.

Customer Services Department, Macmillan Distribution Ltd, Houndmills, Basingstoke, Hampshire RG21 6XS, England

---

Inequality and Social Structure during the Transition

Edited by

Vladimir Mikhalev
Oxford Policy Management Ltd
Oxford, UK

palgrave macmillan in association with the United Nations University World Institute for Development Economics Research

First published 2003 by
PALGRAVE MACMILLAN
Houndmills, Basingstoke, Hampshire RG21 6XS and
175 Fifth Avenue, New York, N.Y. 10010
Companies and representatives throughout the world

PALGRAVE MACMILLAN is the global academic imprint of the Palgrave Macmillan division of St. Martin's Press, LLC and of Palgrave Macmillan Ltd. Macmillan® is a registered trademark in the United States, United Kingdom and other countries. Palgrave is a registered trademark in the European Union and other countries.

ISBN 1–4039–0801–X

This book is printed on paper suitable for recycling and made from fully managed and sustained forest sources.

A catalogue record for this book is available from the British Library.

Library of Congress Cataloging in Publication Data
Inequality and social structure during the transition / edited by Vladimir Mikhalev.
p. cm. — (Studies in development economics and policy)
Includes bibliographical references and index.
ISBN 1–4039–0801–X (cloth)
1. Social stratification—Europe, Eastern. 2. Social stratification—Former Soviet republics. 3. Social structure—Europe, Eastern. 4. Social structure—Former Soviet republics. 5. Income distribution—Europe, Eastern. 6. Income distribution—Former Soviet republics. 7. Post-communism—Social aspects. I. Mikhalev, Vladimir, 1955– II. World Institute for Development Economics Research. III. Series.
HN380.7.Z9S63 2003
305'.0947—dc21 2002044819

10 9 8 7 6 5 4 3 2 1
12 11 10 09 08 07 06 05 04 03

Printed and bound in Great Britain by
Antony Rowe Ltd, Chippenham and Eastbourne

Contents

Part II Structural Comparison of Inequality and Social Structures among Archetypal Country Case Studies

List of Tables and Figures

Tables

Figures

Preface

The transition to a market economy in Eastern Europe and the Former Soviet Union (FSU) has been associated with greater inequality and social stratification. Living standards have fallen for the majority of people, unemployment and poverty are high, the distribution of assets and earnings has changed radically, and social benefits have decreased. The social distance between the 'winners' and 'losers' of the reforms has widened dramatically. This book prepared within the UNU/WIDER project on 'Income Distribution and Social Structure during the Transition' analyses trends in social stratification and their causes with the aim of improving social policy in the transition countries.

Social structures have been deeply affected by macroeconomic and social-sector reforms. Differences in transition strategies across countries – and thus differences in the duration and length of recessions and inflation episodes – are important determinants of changes in social stratification. Social polarization was further intensified by privatization which shifted assets towards the wealthy, and by the rise in earnings inequality associated with changes in labour markets. Moreover, the collapse of the state created an administrative vacuum leading to the erosion of the social security system and a worsening of the position of society's most vulnerable people.

Rising income inequality has been associated with profound changes in social structure. Socialist societies were stratified into 'status groups' in which social capital rather than economic capital – and social networks rather than market power – determined a person's status. These status groups have been replaced by new social classes in the transition to a market economy. People's prospects in life are now largely determined by their possession of assets, goods and income opportunities. This new pattern of social stratification is becoming clearer, although there are serious methodological and data problems in estimating the size of social classes and groups. First, there is a new elite – the product of emerging capitalism. Second, the new commercial, managerial and professional middle class has grown rapidly – despite the perception that there is no middle class in post-communist societies – though the most numerous class group consists of blue-collar workers, farmers and state-sector employees. The bottom of the social hierarchy consists of the most socially deprived and marginalized people who are in long-term poverty – their number has risen in the transition.

In summary, there are some common trends across countries. But the study also highlights significant differences. The reforming economies of the FSU have very high inequality and social polarization; Central Europe's transition countries have shown smaller increases in income inequality; and their successful reforms resulted in the early resumption of economic growth.

The findings confirm that the Central European countries did not experience extreme social polarization. The gap between the elite and the rest of society – and the size of the severely deprived group – is less than in the FSU. Many professional workers, especially the young, have successfully entered the market economy. In contrast, an extremely wealthy and powerful economic elite has emerged in Russia and some other FSU countries; coupled with the impoverishment and deprivation of many of the population. An extremely skewed income and asset distribution impedes the formation of a middle class – losers from transition largely outnumber the small and heterogeneous group of winners.

Social polarization has large economic costs. Not surprisingly, corruption and crime in the FSU is more widespread than in Central Europe where inequality has risen by less. Thus, a more active social policy – promoting better livelihoods and more investment in human capital – could have large economic returns. But there is also a need for more effective public transfers and income redistribution policies to alleviate and reduce poverty. Social cohesion cannot be ignored.

Acknowledgements

This study has been prepared within the UNU/WIDER project on 'Income Distribution and Social Structure during the Transition', directed by Vladimir Mikhalev, Senior Research Fellow at UNU/WIDER and now with Oxford Policy Management Ltd, UK.

UNU/WIDER gratefully acknowledges the financial contribution to the project by the Government of Sweden (Swedish International Development Cooperation Agency – Sida).

List of Abbreviations

B/FIGs	bureaucratic financial-industrial groups
CAR	Central Asian Republics
CE	Central Europe
CEE	Central Eastern Europe
CEU	Central European University
CIS	Commonwealth of Independent States
CSO	Central Statistical Office (Poland) (see also GUS)
EBRD	European Bank for Reconstruction and Development
EU	European Union
FSU	Former Soviet Union
GUS	*Glóway Urzad Statystyczny* (see also CSO)
HBS	Household Budget Survey
LFS	Labour Force Survey
LSMS	Living Standards Measurement Survey
LTU	long-term unemployment
NEP	New Economic Policy
OECD	Organization for Economic Cooperation and Development
PTE	part-time employment
SEE	South-Eastern Europe
Sida	Swedish International Development Cooperation Agency
SME	Small and medium-sized enterprise
SOE	State-owned enterprise
UNDP	United Nations Development Programme
UNU/WIDER	World Institute for Development Economics Research of the United Nations University

Notes on the Contributors

Vladimir Gimpelson is Director, Centre for Labour Market Studies, Higher School of Economics, Moscow.

Christy Glass is at Yale University, New Haven CT.

Jarosław Górniak is Professor in the Institute of Sociology, Jagiellonian University, Krakow.

Georges Heinrich works at the Ministère des Finances, Luxembourg.

György Lengyel works in the Department of Sociology, Budapest University of Economic Sciences.

Alastair McAuley is Professor in the Economics Department, University of Essex, Colchester.

Vladimir Mikhalev is Senior Economist – Social Policy Programme, Oxford Policy Management Ltd, Oxford.

Timo Piirainen is Senior Fellow, Department of Social Policy, University of Helsinki.

Richard Pomfret is Professor at the School of Economics, University of Adelaide.

Péter Róbert is Senior Researcher, Social Research Center TARKI RT, Budapest.

Nodari Simonia is Director, Russian Academy of Sciences, Institute of World Economy and International Relations, Moscow.

Iván Szelényi is William Graham Professor of Sociology and Professor of Political Science at Yale University, New Haven CT.

Jiří Večerník works in the Institute of Sociology, Academy of Sciences of the Czech Republic, Prague.

1
Overview: Inequality and Transformation of Social Structures

Vladimir Mikhalev

Introduction

The transition from state socialism to market economies requires understanding of the nature of new societies emerging in the course of this transformation. This book is a result of a UNU/WIDER research project, which is part of the programme of studies of economies in transition. Its objective is to understand trends in social stratification and their causes, which is important for improving social policy.

The transition to a market economy has brought about inequality and social stratification of the former egalitarian societies. The high economic and social costs of the reforms, radical shifts in distribution of assets, increases in earnings inequality, changes of welfare regimes (in many cases associated with a decline in major social benefits) resulted in reranking relative income positions and social status for many social and professional groups. One of the most important outcomes of the transition has been increasing social distance between the 'winners' and 'losers' of the reforms (Haggard and Kaufman, 1995; Hellman, 1998). The newly-prosperous elites have managed to consolidate considerable economic and political power, while the number of the poor in 18 transitional countries rose twelvefold from nearly 14 million, or about 4 per cent of the population in 1989, to 168 million, or approximately 45 per cent in 1995 (UNDP, 1998: 15).

With important similarities in the changes induced by the transition, the intensity, timing and causes of them in individual countries have been far from uniform. The Central European (CE) countries have experienced smaller increases of income disparity, lower poverty rates, and possibly less radical shifts in social structure as compared to the Former Soviet Union (FSU) and South-Eastern Europe (SEE). In a historically very short period the countries of the FSU have acquired strongly unequal patterns of income distribution similar to those of high-inequality economies of Latin America (Milanovic, 1998; Cornia, 1996, 1999).

Social consequences and outcomes of the economic transformation from centrally-planned to market economies have attracted considerable attention by policy-makers, international organizations, including donor institutions, media and academic research. Considerable knowledge has been accumulated on social costs of the transition, poverty, its incidence determinants and composition. Yet much more remains to be analysed and understood in the processes of social stratification, and their diversity in different countries. One book would not be able to bridge all existing gaps, therefore this research project had three specific tasks:

- First, to identify structuring determinants of social change (in particular, economic processes as well as institutional and political changes that cause social mobility, inequality and poverty, and which thereby shape social structures).
- Second, to map the main constituent parts of the emerging social structure using quantitative and qualitative data and group them into social strata within broadly defined new elites, the middle class and the lower classes.
- Third, to analyse diverging country developments determined by different historical trajectories and policy choices and thus obtain a more complete and more differentiated picture of emerging social structures than hitherto available.

In view of these goals, the methodology and structure of the research was designed as represented by the contents of the volume. The international team of contributors chose to present a multifaceted view of the very diverse and complex picture of social structures in transition. The authors from different backgrounds and various theoretical schools offer their own understanding of social processes. It was not the purpose of the editor to suppress certain differences in approaches or interpretations into one straight line of analysis, which would otherwise suffer from one-sidedness. Indeed, it would hardly be possible to gather a team sharing the same basic views on social stratification as this area is among the most contested in contemporary sociology. It seems therefore more productive to accept the diversity of opinions and approaches.

This chapter gives an overview of major findings and implications for policies conducive to social integration and social cohesion. The subsequent chapters provide analyses of transformation of social structures in transition economies as a whole with a view of existing diversity of these processes. Chapter 2 by Timo Piirainen summarizes a point of departure: pre-transitional social structures in centrally-planned economies and analyses new determinants of social stratification in transitional societies, in the first place the rise in income inequality as the most important new factor of emergent class divisions. Chapter 3 by Vladimir Gimpelson focuses on labour markets and changes in employment structure as a major determinant of social change. Chapters 4 through 6 discuss in depth the processes of social reranking among various groups and emerging new (or transforming old) social classes: the economic and political elite (Iván Szelényi and Christy Glass), the middle classes (György Lengyel and Péter Róbert), and lower classes and the poor (Alastair McAuley).

The second part of the book includes five country case studies (Chapters 7 through 11) of Russia (Nodari Simonia), Poland (Jarosław Górniak), the Czech Republic (Jiří Večerník), Uzbekistan (Richard Pomfret), and Kyrgyzstan (Vladimir Mikhalev and Georges Heinrich). These archetype cases with different initial conditions, reform strategies and major economic and social outcomes have been selected for purposes of comparative analysis in order to better understand the diversity of changes underway on the vast geographic space of Eastern Europe and the FSU.

Social structures prior to the transition

The focus of this study is social structures which emerge in the course of transition. Therefore trends in contemporary social structures are compared to the relatively extended period of stability prior to the transition, that is, the period of 1970–80s. *Social structure* is understood as the composition of the society of distinctive social-class or social-status groups, while *stratification* is a dynamic process of differentiation of society into these groups.

The essential characteristics of the economic organization and redistributive system which defined social structures in socialist countries before the transition included:

- state ownership of the means of production;
- full employment;
- labour wages earned at state enterprises as a principal source of income;
- an income-levelling policy which did not encourage accumulation of individual wealth; and
- a pervasive system of public transfers providing everybody with basic social services and benefits.

Under such conditions social structures were characterized by very limited private property ownership, a high labour force participation rate (including women) with employment predominantly in state-sector enterprises, and an egalitarian structure of income distribution with low levels of inequality. The control of the economy by the state essentially diminished the importance of the ownership of the means of production as the basic definitional distinction of social classes (Słomczyński and Shabad, 1997: 160). The class structure of societies under state socialism did not strictly correspond to the division of economic power. The widely shared understanding by Marxist and most other social scientists is that major classes existing in socialist societies are working class, peasants and white-collar workers (intelligentsia) (Connor, 1979: 89–90).

Szelényi and Kostello (1998) characterize the socialist economies prior to transition as redistributively integrated. The average level of cash incomes was generally low and barely above subsistence minimum, but basic food and consumer goods were heavily subsidized and essential social services including education, healthcare and housing were distributed free of charge. Even with the existence of unofficial ways of supplementing income, inequalities in countries of Eastern Europe and in the Soviet Union were much narrower than in the Western capitalist world (Davis and Scase, 1985; Lane, 1978).

Following Max Weber's approach, Piirainen in this volume further considers the pre-transition societies as stratified into 'status groups' rather than into classes. Market mechanisms there were suppressed, so that they could not develop to the extent of allowing real class divisions to emerge; relationships based on reciprocity played a more important role than that of the market. Social divisions in these societies nevertheless existed, but they were based on social networks and political power determining allocation and redistribution of resources according to a rigid system of rank and status. Status positions were associated not with market power but with being part of a group, to which access was restricted by social networks.

Social status totally depended on one's place in the power hierarchy from the top level of the party nomenklatura to ever lower levels of bureaucracy with ordinary citizens at the very bottom of social ranking. Political power was the source of privileges of the Soviet nomenklatura, which formed a clear status group, rather than class, with its distinct virtues, privileges, obligations, functions and lifestyle marking positions in society (Piirainen, 1997: 23). Nomenklatura positions were achieved according to rules, norms and policies which made these social groups increasingly closed with channels of upward mobility for the most part restricted (Starikov, 1996).

Within the overwhelming majority of ordinary not particularly well-off citizens who did not belong to nomenklatura, social distinctions were determined not so much by income or asset ownership but rather by level of education and labour qualifications. Professionals and intellectuals generally enjoyed a higher social status and occupied more prestigious positions, although their incomes were not necessarily higher than those of the working class. On the other hand, the official communist ideology attributed high importance to manual-labour workers who represented a social base of the Communist Party and were regarded as politically more reliable than intellectuals. Part of the higher-skilled labour elite enjoyed a privileged social status.

Peasantry in the former socialist societies had more distinctive class characteristics. In the Soviet collectivized system farmers occupied a clearly inferior position, being discriminated as compared with industrial workers in wage remuneration and cash transfer benefits. Even more marked distinctions of peasantry as a social class existed in countries which had preserved private land ownership (for example, in Poland).

More social divisions emerged in the last decade of communist rule when private activities on a limited scale were allowed and shadow economic activities expanded on an ever-increasing scale. Players in the second economy began to earn higher incomes considerably changing their lifestyles, including access to better housing and availability of cars and other consumer goods which used to be regarded as luxuries by the majority of the society (Szelényi and Kostello, 1998: 316). Thus prior to the beginning of radical market-oriented reforms, former socialist societies were already acquiring important elements of market economies and with them certain features of a class society.

Poverty and exclusion in the pre-reform period was limited to certain vulnerable categories of the population. These included single-parent families or large families with many children. One income in a family was often inadequate due to low wage levels and social benefits were barely sufficient to raise living standards up to the level of subsistence (Braithwaite, 1997). Pensioners on a low pension living alone were another high-risk category. Finally, there has always been a small marginalized group of homeless people and those released from the penitentiary system at high risk of poverty due to their disadvantaged position in finding jobs, getting housing and residence permits.

Determinants of social stratification in transitional societies

Transition to the market brings about distinctive social classes (as opposed to status groups) defined by economic interests in pursuit of possession of assets, goods and opportunities for income as major determinants of life chances. According to Weber (1978), in modern societies inequalities generated by markets translate into an uneven distribution of life chances and thus produce a major source of social stratification. The significance of income, type of employment and property ownership as a determinant of social status has greatly increased, while the role of state-provided welfare as well as numerous perks available to formerly privileged groups has drastically diminished or ceased to exist. With the transition to the market, life chances of working people have become more dependent on the quality of education, the level of skills and professional experience.

In reality, societies in transition continue to be mixed systems where markets coexist with redistributive mechanisms and reciprocity-based relationships (Szelényi and Kostello, 1998: 307). Essential assets (social capital) which defined social ranking prior to transition can be converted into new assets – economic capital crucial for occupying a higher status/class position in the newly-evolving social structure (Piirainen, 1997: 42–3). While undergoing transformation, social networks demonstrate strong sustainability and largely influence the processes of social mobility, particularly the formation (or transformation) of local elites. Extended family and clan relationships are deep-rooted in social structures of the FSU (particularly in the Caucasus and Central Asia) and SEE, and in some countries social networks are interrelated with the ethnic factor. Ethnicity has a strong influence on social stratification in many countries of Eastern Europe and the FSU, particularly on the formation of new elites as well as on determinants and the composition of poverty.

Political and economic liberalization is removing rigidities in social structure. The emergence of multiparty systems and freedom of personal choice in types of activity, places of work and residence, as well as lifestyle, have greatly increased social mobility. These processes have been enhanced by the opening of society to the outside world, increasing integration of local economies into the world economy. International factors have come to influence social stratification. At the upper end, elites are benefiting from their role in mediating between domestic and international economies, and are socialized into the global economic perspective as they may personally move their assets and their families abroad. This internationalization of the elite contributes to domestic social divisions. At the other end of the scale there is considerable migration of the labour force. Here, Armenians moving into Russia and Ukrainian workers taking jobs in the Czech Republic are not the only examples. Remittances make up an important part of income in poorer countries, while a new ethnic worker underclass is emerging in the more developed post-socialist economies. All of this is reinforcing the informal sector.

The expanding freedom has also had big costs in weakening the rule of law and social order. The institutional vacuum caused by the disintegration of the Communist Party has led to a decline in the state's capacity to implement consistent economic and social policies since the old administrative system could not be immediately replaced. Law-abiding societal standards and institutions need a much longer time to be built and mature, which may require a generational change. The collapse of the state is reflected by informalization of the economy, the inability of government to deliver basic public goods, and to set up and enforce an appropriate regulatory framework. It manifests itself in the accumulation of wage, tax and trade arrears, and demonetization of the economy. Underdevelopment of civil society has caused the spread of rent-seeking opportunities and practices, which in their extreme form lead to outright corruption, while weak legal systems and poor law enforcement give rise to organized crime and mafia. All these processes have a strong impact on the position of various social classes and groups.

As suggested by Słomczyński and Shabad (1997: 171) 'for some period of time the class structure of post-communist societies will be a hybrid one, shaped both by the legacy of the past political-economic order and by the requisites and opportunities afforded by emergent capitalism'. There are yet no clear social boundaries between classes and status groups, as well as no internal unity and understanding of common interests within them. Mobility between groups is high, whilst the emerging classes and social groups are themselves fragmented to the point of internal polarization (Starikov, 1996). Although the process of transition was a peaceful one, in a number of countries it had a revolutionary nature leading to disintegration of the very fabric of society. Thus social ties remain very unstable and the process of reintegration may take decades.

The collapse of the centrally-planned economic system, macroeconomic stabilization and structural reforms aimed at transition to a market economic system caused a fall in output and living standards. In most cases transformational recession proved to be much deeper and longer, and decline in welfare more profound than anticipated. The overall decline in real incomes has affected the welfare of wide groups of the population, whilst the simultaneous emergence of powerful market forces has caused a profound shift towards a more unequal income distribution. The considerable differentiation in earnings opportunities has affected both wages and other sources of incomes originating from newly-emerging forms of economic activity: profits, rent, interest earnings and dividends.

Income inequality has become a major factor of social stratification. Inequality measured by the Gini coefficient of income distribution increased on average from 24 to 33 in all countries in transition since the initiation of market-oriented reforms (Milanovic, 1998: 40–6). This change is particularly striking because it occurred in an unprecedentedly short period of time – only six years. It implies a radical transition from prereform egalitarian distributional structures to levels of inequality prevailing in OECD countries or even, in the case of the FSU, to patterns of high inequality such as are found in Latin America (Cornia, 1996: 18).

The extent, speed and direction of changes in distributional patterns were largely determined by reform strategies (big-bang or gradualist) or chosen 'target models' of a market economy (ranging from 'liberal Anglo-Saxon model' to social-democratic welfare state or 'middle-income developing country model'). However the impact of the speed and direction of reforms was significantly influenced by different initial socioeconomic conditions in transitional economies.

Macroeconomic and social-sector reforms: the impact on income distribution

Economic reforms aimed at transition to the market include such essential components as elimination of price controls, efforts to stop inflation, the process of transferring property from the state to private individuals, liberalization of labour markets, exchange rate and foreign trade regimes. All this has direct implications for economic growth, employment and opportunities to earn income and patterns of its distribution. The above policies have been the primary focus of governments implementing reforms. Other policy components which could be called safety nets – support for the unemployed, pensions for the elderly, and programmes for the relief of poverty – have received much less attention (Kapstein and Mandelbaum, 1997) because of financial constrains, or sometimes out of neglect. Unlike macroeconomic policies affecting production, social sector policies are redistributive. If rigorously pursued they would have an equalizing effect on distribution of income and wealth, but due to the their weakness their impact on income distribution and social structure has generally been very passive – they have failed to contain rapid increases in inequality.

Privatization leads directly to a redistribution of assets and hence sources of income and determinants of social status. The number of capital-asset owners has risen sharply with 'small privatization', the informalization of the economy and the removal of barriers to entry. While measurement presents a serious problem, some evidence suggests that the share of income from profits, self-employment and 'other incomes' has risen steadily, particularly in those countries where the wage economy and public transfers have collapsed. In Russia, the share of entrepreneurial and property incomes in total personal monetary income increased from 11.2 to 45.5 per cent during 1990–96 (Goscomstat, 1997: 73). It is likely that an increase in their share entails a rise in overall inequality.

A general trend appears to be a sharp rise in the concentration in larger property and capital income, and a more moderate one in self-employment income. The shift towards property concentration would likely be larger in the FSU, where the regulatory role of the state (to ensure, for instance, market competition) is less developed. So, despite a relatively modest increase in the share of property and self-employment incomes, their contribution to the overall increase in inequality seems to have been substantial in view of the rapid increase in the skewdness of their distribution.

Change in the labour-market model has led to an increase in wages differentials, and in the appearance of unemployment and underemployment as discussed in detail in Chapter 3 by Gimpelson. Earnings differentiation by skills, sector and occupation appears to be a major source of inequality, whilst wage deregulation has had an overall disequalizing effect of an increase in wage dispersion across industries (controlling for the skill intensity of each sector). In many cases this increase in interindustrial wage dispersion is explained by the monopolistic behaviour of strategic sectors (mining, energy and utilities) able to extort wage and price increases due to their political strength and influence (Mikhalev and Björksten, 1995). Greater productivity differentials, following price liberalization and productivity gains due to restructuring, appear so far to have a minor influence on wage levels.

Social stratification within the working class is determined by segmentation of labour markets by type of skills and sector of economic activity. A smaller fraction of the most competitive workers enjoys considerable advantages in higher pay levels and job security (Gimpelson and Lippoldt, 1996), which can be partially explained by the short supply of skilled workers needed for jobs entailing 'new skills', leading to overremuneration of a privileged segment of the labour force. A better position and stability in the job market is ensured not least by personal networks which may have an even greater influence in the new private than in the public sector.

The rise in unemployment is directly related to a loss of income and social status of that part of the population affected in a situation where unemployment insurance has not offered sufficient compensation. Moreover, the suppressed form of unemployment which prevails in the FSU in the form of short-time working, unpaid leave and mounting wage arrears, contributes to greater social inequality. Such hidden forms of underemployment redistribute losses from stronger (more competitive) to weaker (less competitive) workers and thus lead to further segmentation of the working class (Gimpelson, 1998).

The collapse of the wage economy, growing job insecurity and decreasing formal employment opportunities force people to resort to activities in the shadow economy. The increasing part of the working population living outside the official economy is left out of the boundaries of any legal norms and safety nets. The formation of such a dual economy, which has a potential to evolve into a pattern characteristic of economic structures of third-world countries, creates a serious impediment to the development of a socially integrated society.

Reform strategies and diverging country trends in inequality

Reform strategies and their effects on social stratification by country have been very diverse. Major differences exist between the situation in Poland, Hungary, the Czech Republic, Slovakia and Slovenia on the one hand, and countries of the FSU and SEE on the other. Generally speaking, the social situation in East-Central Europe has been much better than in the rest of the former socialist world undergoing transition. Market reforms in the FSU have been far more difficult because of much heavier legacies of the centrally-planned economy, burdened to a greater extent by massive inefficiencies and distortions compounded by pervasive militarization of production. Contrary to CE states, which managed to implement consistent fiscal and monetary reforms that brought quick stabilization and economic recovery, Russia and other republics of the FSU (with the exception of the Baltics) demonstrated failures in macroeconomic stabilization and major structural reforms (Cornia and Popov, 2001). The social costs of the lack of stabilization, prolonged inflation and recession there have been very high. The hardships of the majority of citizens and extraordinary social inequality have been made worse by very poor tax collection, pervasive corruption and rent-seeking.

From the available evidence, we may suggest the following major causes of diverging country patterns of inequality and social mobility:

- First, inequality has risen faster in the FSU because of the sharper recession experienced in comparison with CE. In the FSU, the fall in the wage share has been compounded by the huge wage arrears accumulated by most companies.
- Second, earnings inequality in the FSU rose much faster than in CE. In addition, adverse policy factors (the abandonment of effective minimum wage regulation; the more than proportional decline of social sector wages; the inability to contain wage increases in the monopolistic-rent sector) in the FSU seem to have greatly contributed to income inequality and a decline in social status of several professional and occupational groups.
- Third, social transfers in the FSU were traditionally lower, have fallen faster, and are less efficiently targeted. The decline of social welfare there can be explained by a weakening of the state capacity to implement consistent social policies. In CE, social transfers have not fallen as dramatically and helped to contain the surge of inequality over the short-term. The long-term effect of this policy is, however, questionable because of the long-term intergenerational distributive problems it may cause. In addition, even over the short term transfer policy may have been less than ideal. While family allowances, unemployment compensation and social assistance appear to have been increasingly better targeted, pension reform has contributed to a shift towards greater inequality.
- Finally, in some of these countries, the surge in inequality might have been exacerbated by the approach followed in the privatization of state assets and by a greater informalization of the economy.

Divergence between individual country development patterns requires case studies representing economies with different levels of inequality as well as different causes of the increase of inequality (depth of the recession; extent of the collapse of the wage economy; approaches to privatization; level and targeting of social transfers). These countries also often represent different 'overall archetypes' of market economies. For purposes of comparative analysis, five such archetype country cases have been selected in this study. They differ in sets of initial conditions, reform strategies, property-rights regimes, the role of the state in the economy, patterns of income distribution and evolving social structures. The countries selected include Russia, Poland, the Czech Republic, Uzbekistan and Kyrgyzstan. Four of these five countries: (i) Poland and the Czech Republic, and (ii) Uzbekistan and Kyrgyzstan, can be considered as pairs having very similar initial conditions but following different reform strategies, and/or demonstrating different macro-economic and social results.

Two broad patterns seem to be emerging from analysis of the available evidence: (1) a fairly moderate increase in inequality in CE, and (2) a rapid surge of inequality in the FSU and SEE.

Centre Europe: a comparatively moderate increase in inequality

In the CE economies the Gini coefficient of net per capita household income rose on average by 4 percentage points, an amount surprisingly similar to the 'average difference' between the market and socialist economies of Europe during the pre-transition period. At present, the CE economies (with the exception of Poland) have Gini coefficients similar to those of the UK and Canada, and higher than those of the Nordic countries and Germany. For these economies one could hypothesize a 'physiological adaptation of inequality' to levels typical of a Western market economy. However, this 'spontaneous adaptation' hypothesis does not seem to be borne out by the evidence, as in CE the sources of inequality are substantially different from those of the developed market economies.

The social structures of CE countries in transition did not experience polarization to an extreme extent. While reranking of social status of various groups is certainly taking place, the gap between the elite and the rest of the society looks less profound while the group of severely deprived people is far less massive than in the FSU. These countries have made real progress in the formation of a middle class of small entrepreneurs. A substantial part of professionals and intellectuals, especially the younger of them, have found their successful way in the market economy.

Significant differences, however, exist between CE countries, as the comparison between the Czech Republic and Poland shows. Both Poland and the Czech Republic are radical and consistent reformers that inherited more mobile economies less burdened with the military sector and over-industrialization, and which had more developed social sectors. They both experienced a modest recession and rather quick recovery. The distributional consequences of the transition, however, happened to be quite different. The Czech Republic demonstrated a persistence of the wage economy, a low earnings inequality, voucher privatization, and a strong and targeted transfer system. In Poland privatization was delayed, the wage economy experienced a decline while the social transfer system, albeit quite large, had significant distortions. Consequently, Poland has much higher levels of earnings and income inequality as well as the incidence of poverty. Social reranking in Poland also looks more significant than in the Czech Republic. It appears that the Czech Republic has preserved much more of the old social structure than Poland, where the formation of the new capitalist and middle class is among the most intensive of the countries in transition.

The FSU and SEE: a rapid surge in inequality

In most of the FSU and SEE, the Gini coefficient of the distribution of net per capita household income rose by about 10 percentage points – that is, 2–2.5 times faster than in CE. Income inequality in these countries is now substantially greater than in most OECD countries, and is gradually moving in the direction of that of the high-inequality countries of Latin America, even if the sources of inequality seem to be quite different. Even these data may give only a partial idea of the distributional earthquake underway in the region. In view of the growing underreporting of income that affects official surveys, it is likely that income disparity over the past decade has risen even faster. Smaller surveys (with fairly accurate reporting of incomes) seem to indicate that a tiny class of 'new rich' now controls an exorbitant share of total income. In Russia, the income gap between the more affluent 10 per cent of the population and the poorest 10 per cent increased from four times at the start of the reforms to 13.3 times in April 1998 (Goscomstat, 1998: 213). The former get 33 per cent of all incomes, and the latter a meagre 2.4 per cent.

The social structure within Russia and some other countries in the FSU is characterized by the emergence of an extremely wealthy and powerful economic elite, alongside impoverishment and deprivation of a broad strata of the population. Extremely skewed income and asset distribution impedes the formation of a middle class, and the losers of the transition generally largely outnumber a small heterogeneous group of winners. Corruption and crime largely influencing the processes of social stratification have acquired a far larger scale compared to CE.

South Eastern Europe (SEE) (in particular Romania and Bulgaria) is characterized by a slower progress of economic reform and high levels of social inequality and poverty. The local economy has experienced a considerable recession and medium to high informalization. Privatization and liberalization were initially quite limited, earnings inequality is high, while the social transfer system has proved rather weak. Despite growing inequality, social mobility and reranking is yet more limited compared to other countries in Eastern Europe. Delayed privatization has not allowed a significant capitalist class to evolve, and even slower is the formation of small-scale enterpreneurship. While income levels of the working class, farmers and intelligentsia have declined due to economic recession, stratification of their social status (apart from earnings differentiation) has not yet taken place on a significant scale. These processes, however, are likely to intensify after more radical reform policies are initiated.

Within this vast region significant divergence of emergent social structures by country can be observed. Russia, the largest transitional economy, had the longest history of central planning and economies distorted by large-scale inefficient heavy industries with a big share of the military-industrial complex. Russia has demonstrated a shock-therapy approach, deep recession, a collapse of the wage economy, insider privatization, and a high degree of informalization of the economy. At the same time Russia has experienced the highest level of earnings and income inequality and weakness of the social transfer system. Poverty rates are quite high, the number of losers is massive, while the might and wealth of powerful elites largely determines the economic and political scene. Corruption and crime have also reached exorbitant proportions. Russia appears to have had a considerable reranking in income positions and social hierarchies.

The region of Central Asia has considerable specificity as well as diversity, which can be seen by comparing Uzbekistan and Kyrgyzstan. These two newly-independent countries have a common heritage as former Soviet republics with similar social and economic structures. They were characterized by higher proportions of rural populations; largely distorted economies dominated by narrowly specialized collectivized farming; and a substantial portion of defence industries and high dependence on financial transfers from the metropolitan centre. Reform strategies, however, have been quite different. Kyrgyzstan introduced rather radical liberalization similar to the Russian case. Transformational recession there as well as the collapse of wages was very deep while the system of social protection proved far inadequate. Consequently, Kyrgyzstan has had pervasive informalization of the economy and very high levels of income inequality and poverty. On the contrary, Uzbekistan following a gradualist reform strategy, has had modest recession, limited informalization, moderate earnings inequality, no privatization and a strong social protection system. Social stratification in Kyrgyzstan has gone considerably further than in Uzbekistan. Kyrgyzstan has seen the formation of a noticeable group of businessmen, mainly in the commercial and banking sector, whilst a considerable part of the Kyrgyz population has moved into subsistence self-employment, ranging from shuttle-traders to farmers who received their plots of land for individual use but are for the most part unable to set up productive crop cultivation or cattle breeding. Similar changes in Uzbekistan are much more limited due to slow transition. Corruption and crime are widespread in both countries but Kyrgyzstan may be more exposed to those phenomena due to a weaker government. Drug trafficking is a particularly serious social problem, especially in Kyrgyzstan. Clan relationships and community networks have crucial influence on social structures in both these Central Asian countries.

Social reranking and emerging social classes

For purposes of analysing changes in social structure, social actors can be grouped according to descriptive typological characteristics into politicians, bureaucrats, managers, entrepreneurs, professionals, blue-collar workers, farmers and peasants. These distinguishable groups differ by such features as levels of skill and education, employment in the private or the public sector, or in informal economic activities (in particular, subsistence self-employment). They can be further ranked and ascribed to broader social status and class groups using such determinants as income, asset ownership (including land), education, political influence, lifestyle, consumption, and social prestige of the job. The above indicators can also serve to measure economic and social distance between groups.[1] In many cases a higher level of income and consumption corresponds to higher education and social prestige. However, in the specific situation of transitional societies a high educational level and socially prestigious job (for example, professor, researcher or artist) may still indicate a higher social status despite low income (declined in the course of transition) and restrained consumption.

Redistribution of income and assets and the rise in inequality in transitional societies has led to greater *social polarization* which is understood here as widening distance between groups, in particular between upper and lower levels within the social structure. Apart from an increase in 'economic distance' between groups of households, the economic transition is also associated with considerable reranking among socioeconomic groups, and sharp changes in social hierarchies. Such social reranking can be viewed as *mobility* (upwards and downwards) from one group to another, or up or down in the hierarchy. These changes have been rather rapid and the process of social stratification has not yet stabilized. The available statistics and social surveys do not allow a clear definition of newly-emergent social groups. The widespread concept of winners and losers in the course of the transition may be used, although its analytical limitations should be recognized.

In addition to the loss of income they may have experienced, many of the people enjoying high 'social status' and 'political power' during the former regime appear to have been relegated to the bottom of the social ladder. Loss of social status has been common among the former 'labour elite', that is, the middle-aged, semi-skilled workers employed in heavy industry, part of the intellectual class, and managers of state companies. A considerable part of this wide group, especially members of the nomenklatura, enterprise managers and younger professionals, seems, however, to have adjusted to the new situation and retained considerable social status. Social disorientation is acute for most of the elderly who see their values, norms and lifetime savings, vanishing. Loss of political power is obviously most acute among the older generation of party cadres and bureaucrats. The position of civil servants is also weakened by lack of funds and widespread mistrust in anything that is 'socialist', 'social' or even 'public'.

The intensity of social reranking, mobility and the extent of social distance between upper and lower classes compared to the situation prior to transition differs significantly by archetypal transitional countries as diverse as Poland, Russia or those in Central Asia. A broad pattern of social stratification apparent in transitional societies includes:

1 the new elite (it is especially important to investigate who are the new capitalists and what is the nature of emerging capitalism);
2 the middle class (despite widespread perception that there is no middle class in post-communist societies, there is evidence of a rapidly growing new commercial, managerial and professional middle class);
3 the most numerous lower class, including the bulk of the working class (blue-collar workers), farmers and peasants, lower-rank employees in research, health, education and social care institutions and government administration; and
4 socially deprived and marginalized groups.

Attempts to assess quantitative proportions of social classes in a transitional society face serious methodological and data problems. For this purpose information from various sociological surveys and income statistics is usually used, and income levels and household assets generally serve as prime criteria for ranking by social class or status. This information may be supported by self-evaluation of respondents obtained from opinion polls. Such survey by the Moscow Institute of Socio-Political Research in 1994 estimated about 6 per cent of Russians as belonging to the 'rich' or the upper class, and 29 per cent to the middle class (Khlop'ev, 1996: 99–100). The majority of the remaining 65 per cent of the population would represent the lower classes or, as Zaslavskaya (1997) identifies it, the 'base stratum' of the society. Part of this majority has been affected by poverty and includes severely deprived social groups.

Poverty measurement in transitional societies presents specific problems which preclude accurate measurement. For the analysis of social stratification a further difficulty lies in the fact that poverty for many people has a transitional short-term character. In the Russian case official estimates of the poverty rate have fluctuated within 25–33 per cent of the population. For the analysis of social structures the incidence of long-term poverty is a more reliable indicator of the proportion of the population qualified as severely deprived or marginalized, and new research by Ovcharova and colleagues based on multiple criteria revealed 8.3 per cent of Russian households in a representative sample were affected by long-term poverty in 1996 (Ovcharova *et al.*, 1998).

Implications for policy

An overview of social structures in transition reveals serious changes in a historically very short period of time. The market has opened new opportunities, created new social classes and groups and intensified upward and downward social mobility. Considerable reranking and redistribution of life chances has occurred for many social groups; new opportunities have opened to winners, but there are also many losers whose ranks may be joined by some of those who initially did well in the new market economy. While the process of transition proceeds, the social structure remains unstable and variable with intense changes in the numerical sizes of groups and strata from year to year.

Deep polarization based on income inequality has become a salient feature of social stratification marking divisions not only between social classes, but within each group, including the base stratum, due to segmentation of labour, the spread of unemployment, self-employment and informalization of the economy. Apart from economic decline, the rise in inequality of income distribution has been a major factor in the expansion of poverty with all its negative consequences for human development. This apparent social dislocation bears dangerous prospects of a loss of self-identity by part of the society, a decline in solidarity and a potential for rising social conflict. The processes of social stratification in transitional societies thus present serious challenges for policy, which is needed to promote social integration and social cohesion.

Developing a policy agenda for social integration and social cohesion requires trade-offs and hard choices. The main trade-off is not between redistribution, social justice and productive efficiency (and/or growth), rather it lies between the inherited systems of universal welfare provision and scarce resources available to maintain them, and hence the need for social policy reforms and more targeted systems of social security. Recognizing the importance of social development goals does not mean that the reforming courtiers can afford to switch back to consumer subsidies and universal welfare pledged by (if not fully provided) by the former communist governments. The capacity of local economies, especially in the CIS countries, is not sufficient to allow high living standards and costly social benefits to be maintained.

Inclusive policies leading to reductions in poverty and strengthening social cohesion require the development of institutions and civil society to empower citizens, including the poor and disadvantaged. The poor need a mechanism through which they can express their needs and influence the political process at national and local levels. Therefore a primary task faced by transitional countries is building inclusive institutions which are representative of all parts of society, including the poor, but no less importantly the middle class. A strong middle class is essential to the functioning of effective, democratic and transparent institutions; therefore its interests need to be genuinely represented.

Policies promoting empowerment of the poor and the middle class include such essential elements as (1) promoting dissemination of information on social rights and policy choices to ensure these rights, and fostering public debate on development strategies; (2) decentralization of public services to move them closer to citizens; and (3) strengthening of local communities and civil society organizations and promoting their collaboration with local governments. These tasks are not straightforward and easily achievable, especially in countries of the CIS with a longer history of centralized authoritarian rule. In many of these countries traditional bases for civil society and community cohesion are underdeveloped or nonexistent and need to be reconstructed. Sometimes this process needs to overcome local-level inequalities, built-in local power structures and clan organization. Bringing households, groups and networks together can work as an effective means of citizen empowerment through collective action towards improving community welfare.

Within broad similarities of the social policy context in transitional economies, social policy processes and outcomes have considerable country specificity. As has been shown by this and other analyses (for example, Cornia and Popov, 2001), countries in transition are moving towards very different 'archetypes of economy'. Radical variations are characterized not only in terms of export orientation, industrial policies, investment rates and prospects for association to economic groupings like the EU, or the Council of Europe. Equally important are systemic differences related to levels of 'socially-acceptable' asset and income inequality, the role of the state, polarization of social structures, and social mobility. The choice of policy options available is thus determined by alternative patterns of market economy that the countries in transition are moving towards, the constraints imposed by the economic structures chosen, and by the desire to maximize growth and poverty alleviation.

Note

1 Tatyana Zaslavskaya (1997) used ten status variables to identify the position of various groups in the social structure: educational level; self-assessment of skills; basic occupation; principal kind of activity; economic branch in which the person is employed; sector of the economy (according to type of property); size of the enterprise (firm) in terms of number of employed; professional and occupational group (determined by the nature of the work performed and the respondent's self-assessment); and the level of real income.

References

Braithwaite, J. (1997) 'The Old and New Poor in Russia', in J. Klugman (ed.), *Poverty in Russia. Public Policy and Private Responses*. Washington DC: World Bank.

Connor, W. D. (1979) *Socialism, Politics, and Equality: Hierarchy and Change in Eastern Europe and the USSR*. New York: Columbia University Press.

Cornia, G. A. (1996) *Transition and Income Distribution: Theory, Evidence and Initial Interpretation*, Research in Progress 1, Helsinki: UNU/WIDER.

—— (1999) *Liberalisation, Globalisation and Income Distribution*, UNU/WIDER Working Papers 157, Helsinki: UNU/WIDER.

—— and V. Popov (2001) 'Structural and Institutional Factors in the Transition to the Market Economy: An Overview', in G. A Cornia and V. Popov (eds), *Transition and Institutions – The Experience of Gradual and Late Reformers*. Oxford: Oxford University Press.

Davis, H. and R. Scase (1985) *Western Capitalism and State Socialism*. Oxford: Basil Blackwell.

Gimpelson, V. (1998) *The Politics of Labour Market Adjustment (The Case of Russia)*, mimeo.

—— and D. Lippoldt (1996) *Labour Restructuring in Russian Enterprises. A Case Study*. Paris: OECD

Goscomstat (1997) *Sotsialnoye polozhenie i urovyen tsizni nasyelyeniya rossi, 1997* (The Social Situation Standard of Living of the Population of Russia). Moscow: Goscomstat.

—— (1998) *Economic and Social Situation of Russia, January–April 1998*. Moscow: Goscomstat.

Haggard, S. and R. R. Kaufman (1995) *The Political Economy of Democratic Transitions*. Princeton: Princeton University Press.

Hellman, J. S. (1998) 'Winners Take All. The Politics of Partial Reform in Postcommunist Transitions', *World Politics*, January.

Kapstein, E. B. and M. Mandelbaum (1997) *The Social Safety Net in Post-Communist Europe*. New York: Council on Foreign Relations.

Khlop'ev, A. (1996) 'The Transformation of the Social Structure', in C. Williams, V. Chuprov and V. Staroverov (eds), *Russian Society in Transition*. Dartmouth: Aldershot.

Lane, D. (1978) *Politics and Society in the USSR*. London: Allen & Unwin.

Mikhalev, V. and N. Björksten (1995) *Wage Formation during the Period of Economic Restructuring in the Russian Federation*. Paris: OECD.

Milanovic, B. (1998) *Income, Inequality, and Poverty during the Transition from Planned to Market Economy*. Washington DC: World Bank

North, D. C. (1997) *The Contribution of the New Institutional Economics to an Understanding of the Transition Problem*, Wider Annual Lectures 1, Helsinki: UNU/WIDER.

Ovcharova, L., E. Turuntsev and I. Korchagina (1998) *A Reassessment of the Poor in Transitional Russia*, Moscow, mimeo.

Piirainen, T. (1997) *Towards a New Social Order in Russia. Transforming Structures and Everyday Life*. Dartmouth: Aldershot.

Słomczyński, K. M. and G. Shabad (1997) 'Systemic Transformation and the Salience of Class Structure in East Central Europe', *East European Politics and Society*, 11(1).

Starikov, E. N. (1996) 'The Social Structure of the Transitional Society (An Attempt to Take Inventory', *Russian Social Science Review* (March).

Szelényi, I. and E. Kostello (1998) 'Outline of an Institutional Theory of Inequality: The Case of Socialist and Post-Communist Eastern Europe', in M. C. Brinton and V. Nee (eds), *The New Institutionalism in Sociology*. New York: Russel Sage Foundation.

United Nations Development Programme (UNDP) (1998) *Poverty in Transition*. New York: UNDP.

Weber, M. (1978) *Economy and Society*, 2 vols. Berkeley: University of California Press.

Zaslavskaya, T. (1997) 'Social Disequilibrium in the Transitional Society', *Russian Social Science Review*, 38(5).

Part I

Market Reforms, Income Distribution and Social Stratification

2
Transition and Social Structures: General Determinants of Change

Timo Piirainen

The purpose of this chapter is to explain the fundamental changes in stratification processes brought about by transition, using Max Weber's basic concepts of social stratification. General structural features of transition are briefly dealt with in the first section which discusses the different nature of social stratification in centrally-planned and in market economies. As the principal mechanism of resource allocation changed from planning to the market, a consequent change also occurred in the patterns of social stratification and income distribution. The second section provides a brief discussion of different theoretical approaches to the study of social stratification in transition countries.

Subsequent sections deal, in principle, with social mobility during the 1990s. First we take an overview of the formation of new or the reproduction of old elites in the market environment. We then consider the formation of new middle classes and the upward and downward mobility inside the vast 'middle strata' of the pre-reform society whose access to life-chances was relatively egalitarian, before examining the losers of the transition, the new lower classes or groups of the population that have experienced a rapid downward mobility. Changes within these broad social classes are considered later in this book in greater detail in the special chapters on the elites (Szelényi and Glass), on the middle classes (Lengyel and Róbert) and the poor (McAuley).

From status to class

The ideological self-image of the former socialist countries was that of classless societies where relations between social groups and strata were harmonious and non-antagonistic. As the means of production were owned by the state that represented the interests of the working people, there could, according to Marxist theory, be neither exploiter nor exploited, neither capitalists nor proletariat.

This self-understanding contained an important element of truth, although in a sense different from that suggested by the official Marxism. First, as for the distribution of income and wealth, when measured by the ordinary indices, the planned economies were remarkably egalitarian. In the 1980s, the Central European socialist countries had, together with the Nordic welfare states, the lowest levels of inequality in the world with regard to income distribution. In 1987–88, the Gini coefficient measuring inequality in income distribution was 0.19 in Czechoslovakia, 0.21 in Hungary, 0.23 in Bulgaria and 0.25 in Poland. Because of unreliable measurement these figures should be regarded as merely indicative which is even more true for the Soviet Union where the Gini coefficient was estimated to be below 0.30. As a comparison, Finland had the lowest value, that is the highest degree of equality, in the 'capitalist world', 0.21; the corresponding figure for Germany was 0.27, for the UK 0.30, for the USA 0.33 and for Brazil 0.63 (World Bank, 1996).

Empirical observations concerning egalitarian patterns of income distribution may be interpreted to suggest the existence of a classless society in the Central Eastern European (CEE) planned economies in the 1980s. Another and more theoretical argument has to do with the mechanisms through which resources and wealth are distributed in society. Central planning, that is, political decision-making, was supposed to be the primary mechanism of resource allocation in a planned economy, and the market was not assumed to play a role, although in real life the shadow market played a considerable role for people's well-being. Planned economies were not supposed to have any significant inequality created by market forces, since resources were not allocated via the market.

According to official Marxist reasoning, state ownership of the means of production was in itself a sufficient condition for the creation of a classless society. Since the state obviously did not have the objective of extorting surplus value from workers' labour for the purposes of capital accumulation, then there simply could not be either exploiters or exploited. But classes or not, few would claim that the planned economies had managed to obliterate inequality and privileges. The figures that indicate equal income distribution are also of a more ambiguous nature than those calculated in market economies. Monetary income also had less significance in socialist countries than in capitalist ones. It was an easy task to make a political decision to deliver to all households sufficient roubles or forints for the purchase of basic necessities; far more difficult was it, however, to ensure that all these goods and services were actually available for purchase. Deficits of goods were a persistent feature of everyday life in the planned economies, a phenomenon that continued to plague the real socialist societies from their birth to the very day of their final demise.

Privileges had a fundamentally different character in market economies as compared to planned economies: whereas in the former privileged people differed from the majority in possessing more money or other market assets, privileged people in socialist 'deficit economies' were lucky to be included in specific social groups that could ensure the distribution of scarce goods and services. It was the access to channels of distribution – that is, inclusion in social groups and networks through which goods and services could be obtained – that was crucial in a planned economy, not the amount of money received. A member of the party elite or an otherwise well-connected person might have had exactly the same nominal salary as an average wage-earner, but the standard of living – or 'life-chances' – of the former were considerably higher since their membership of status groups or exclusive social networks gave them access to resources that were out of reach of the majority (see for example Srubar, 1991). This was the case not only for consumption goods that were in short supply, but for life-chances of virtually every sort – including housing, education and opportunities for good employment.

Following Max Weber, social stratification may be determined as an uneven distribution of life-chances among the population in such a manner that certain population groups are systematically privileged, while other groups are discriminated against. These life-chances include, among others, economic resources, education opportunities, employment, quality of environment and possibilities to shape and influence one's own career and life course. When basic differences in the structure and the nature of social stratification – the pattern of distribution of life-chances – between planned and market economies are analysed, it seems obvious that an adequate point of departure for the analysis are the mechanisms of distribution of life-chances characteristic of each of these social and economic systems. What are the basic factors or forces that create such uneven distributions of life-chances?

The concepts borrowed from the sociology of Max Weber (1978) are useful tools in this analysis. Weber makes a distinction between two basic principles of social stratification: class and status. He presents also a third stratification principle which he calls 'party' that has to do with political power. This additional third dimension is not, however, very relevant from the point of view of this analysis, since the concept of status already refers to the principle that is the very basis of political power: the mechanisms of inclusion in and exclusion from social groups, a source from which a multitude of forms of control and exploitation of a more specific nature can be seen to be derived.

According to Weber, it is justified to speak of a social class when a social situation fulfils the following three criteria. First, a number of people differ with regard to their life-chances from other groups in the society, and a specific cause can be attributed to this difference. Second, this causal factor has to do exclusively with the economic interests of social actors; that is, with possession of property and opportunities for income. And third, the cause and the resulting social divisions are mediated by labour and commodity markets. In other words, social stratification into classes happens through the workings of the market: life-chances are distributed unevenly as a collective outcome of the activities of individual actors who differ with regard to their power in the market (Weber, 1978: 300–10).

If we follow this definition, then we obviously cannot call planned economies class societies. The privileges and inequalities of the socialist countries had a different nature: they had their origin in the mechanisms of inclusion into and exclusion from certain concrete social groups, and not in the workings of the anonymous market. The party elite, persons employed in wealthy and influential enterprises, or otherwise well-connected citizens, did not enjoy their privileges because of their stronger positions in the market. Markets were not the basic mechanism of resource allocation. Shadow markets were, of course, a part of everyday life in the planned economies, and life could be made easier by purchasing deficit goods in the shadow market. The shadow market did not, however, have a significant impact on the systematic differences in the distribution of life-chances across the population before the late 1980s, except in the case of the few who ventured to start risky careers as professional black marketeers.

Privileges in the planned economies were acquired through inclusion in privileged social groups. Social closure, not the market, was the basic societal mechanism that created the unequal distribution of life-chances. In a society where resources are distributed not via markets but by political decisions, social groups that can influence decision-making can gain a privileged access to scarce resources and distribute these resources among group members. Weber describes the social stratification that is based on mechanisms of social closure rather than on differences in market power as stratification in status groups. Status group memberships are, in the first place, not associated with market activity; they are distributed according to traditions, rules, norms, prescriptions and public policies. In a feudal society, membership of, for instance, the nobility or the clergy was not determined by market power but was acquired via descent or through apprenticeship and initiation. The process of selection and initiation of members of the party elite in the Soviet Union was not entirely different from that applied by the medieval clergy in recruiting new members.

The party nomenklatura is, of course, the prime example of a status group that was established and reproduced through the mechanisms of social closure. It could be distinguished as a separate estate with its own norms, code of conduct, standard of living, and explicit procedures of recruitment and initiation. The division of the real socialist societies into status groups and the corresponding differences in the distribution of life-chances were not, however, limited to this divide between the nomenclatura and the ordinary Soviet people. In his renowned article on the – in Weber's sense – fundamentally antimodern character of the real socialist societies, Ilja Srubar (1991) depicts these societies as consisting of 'an archipelago of social networks', that is, as fragmented into social groups and networks that had developed through the principle of social closure and whose *raison d'être* was the acquisition and distribution of scarce goods and services among their members. In Srubar's opinion, these networks were the main cohesive force in socialist societies: the mosaic of networks, that is exclusive status groups, was in fact one of the main constituents of the social order in these societies (see for example Lonkila, 1999)

Kinship networks, work collectives and neighbourhood groups were prime examples of social groups of these kinds, but the total picture was far more complex. For the networks effectively to fulfil their function to acquire scarce resources and distribute them among their members, the tentacles of these exclusive networks usually had to extend far beyond the immediate primary groups such as, for instance, colleagues, neighbours or members of the same kin. Preferably, a network included persons in positions of power to make decisions regarding the distribution of resources; through the membership of these key persons, other members of the network received access to goods and services that would otherwise have been more difficult to obtain. These key persons, often members of the nomenklatura or officials in lower echelons of the party apparatus, had, as a rule, the roles of 'patrons' in the network, and relations between the network members were often structured as vertical patron–client relations. Anybody with first-hand experience of a real socialist society can confirm that patronage and the mutual exchange of favours characteristic of patron–client relationships are usually the key to purchasing an automobile, obtaining a larger apartment, promotion in one's work career, becoming enrolled as a student in a prestigious academic institution, and a multitude of other things, large and small, all to do with the distribution of life-chances of different kinds. In this way, the complex tapestry of social networks extends across the entire socialist society, fragmenting it into exclusive social groups oriented towards the maximization of the life-chances of members, that may, in Weber's terms, be characterized as status groups.

To conclude, social stratification in planned economies was, according to this logic, stratification into status groups, whereas market economies are stratified into social classes. And, correspondingly, the transition from Soviet socialism into market capitalism also brought about a major shift in the pattern of social stratification in the former socialist countries. Stratification into social classes replaced that into status groups as the predominant mode. The changes and developments that have happened in income distribution and social structure during the transition can be examined on the basis of this fundamental theoretical theme.

The advantages of a Weberian approach

Among a number of competing approaches, why is it useful to select the Weberian point of departure for a study on social stratification and income differentiation in transition countries? In principle, four major reasons can be given for this choice of basic theoretical tools. First, since from the Weberian point of view the market – and not the sphere of production and the exploitation of labour force, as Marxist theory assumes – is the fundamental source of social inequalities, the Weberian point of departure provides a more flexible set of criteria for the study of social stratification in transition societies. Second, the Weberian approach is better suited to the study of societies in transition, because alternative theoretical points of departure presuppose a society whose basic structures are relatively stable. The third argument is that a Weber-inspired approach makes it possible to pay more attention to social actors – individuals and social groups – and not to focus mainly on social structure, as the neo-Marxist approach does. The fourth, and perhaps the most important reason for the choice of theoretical point of departure is that Weber's juxtaposition between the ideal types of the status order and market order reflects, in essence, the idea of transition, the dichotomous contrast between past and present, traditional and modern – a juxtaposition that is inherent in most of classical sociology (see Holton and Turner, 1989: 184–5).

Let us briefly examine the first argument, that is, that the Weberian approach is worth adopting because it allows attention to be paid to a large variety of factors as possible sources of inequality and social stratification. The popular neo-Marxist approach to the study of social classes sees the exploitation of the labour force in the sphere of production as the primary source of social inequality and class conflict. In this theory, society is in principle perceived as divided into exploiters and exploited, the capitalist class and the working class, with different middle-class positions in between. The definition of the class or stratification structure of a society is, *in principle,* made on the basis of the positions individuals occupy in this one-dimensional field characterized by the tension between capital and labourers, who are exploited to varying degrees.

However, adopting either a basically Marxist or a Weberian point of departure does not, of course, mean the total rejection of the other approach. Theoretically sophisticated contemporary approaches to social stratification usually contain elements from both traditions. To name the most prominent example, Erik O. Wright's (1985, 1997) class analysis, while adhering to the concept of exploitation as the central theme, also incorporates the central elements of the Weberian approach. Wright does not regard the Marxist and Weberian points of view as mutually exclusive, and in his class theory both location within production relations and market capacity in exchange relations count in the definition of class positions.

Wright insists, however, that the concept of class be ultimately grounded 'in exploitation rather than simply market-based life chances' (Wright, 1997a: 32). For the central position of the concept of exploitation, Wright provides three basic reasons. First, the 'exploitation-centered class concept affirms the fact that production and exchange are intrinsically linked, not merely contingently related'. The concept of exploitation emphasizes the fact that class relations are relations of power: for example, the asymmetric relation between managers and workers is not determined only by differences in market power, but also by their respective positions and functions in the structure of the capitalist society. Second, exploitation contains the notion of class interests and thus, according to Wright, facilitates the study of social conflict:

> Exploitation is a powerful concept because it brings together an account of opposing interests with an account of the rudimentary capacity for resistance... Exploitation, therefore, does not simply predict an opposition of interests, but a tendency for this antagonism to create manifest conflict between classes. This understanding of the inherent power of the exploited classes is marginalized when class is defined strictly in terms of market relations.
>
> (Wright, 1997a: 32)

Wright's third argument is that the concept of exploitation also allows the analysis of social classes in societies where the market does not play a significant role in the distribution of life-chances, for instance in the real socialist countries, whereas the Weberian notion of class is applicable only to market societies.

Wright's first argument is that the neo-Marxist exploitation-centred class analysis is better suited to the study of the structural determinants of social stratification than the Weberian analysis that is grounded in 'simply market-based life chances' (Wright, 1997a: 32). It is easy to point to this argument as a simplification. Exploitation is by no means the only available – or by far the best, it may be argued – concept to make visible the structural determinants of power relations inherent in asymmetric social situations. Weber, for instance, assumes that there are three different patterns of social stratification – class, status and party – that all have their specific origin: market exchange, social closure and acquisition of political power. Reference to inclusion into and exclusion from status groups may reveal at least as much of the power relations in a society as references to exploitation. This is especially true for contemporary industrial, or post-industrial, societies that do not in the first place consist of workers and managers, but increasingly of experts of different kinds occupying middle-class positions. The archaic concept of exploitation is not very helpful in grasping the structural preconditions of inequalities in modern developed countries. In the study of social mobility within the middle class, the concepts of market power and social closure are likely to be much more fruitful. The same is even more true for social mobility in transition countries: for instance, it would be next to absurd to try to explain the sudden increase of differences in the distribution of income and other life-chances in the countries of the Former Soviet Union by referring to exploitation. Social closure and market power are obviously far more relevant factors.

Moreover, when dynamic societies are studied – and this book is essentially about social mobility in transition countries – one of the basic objectives is to seek causes for the changes under study. Exploitation would not be a particularly apt causal factor to explain change. In other words, it would not be very illuminating to conclude that the new affluent classes have gained their position by 'exploiting' others, and that the cause of the poverty of the new underclass is a result of 'exploitation' by the upper classes. On the other hand, to say that the new upper classes have gained by profiting from their strong market position while simultaneously protecting that position through membership of exclusive status groups is more interesting and, more importantly, prepares the conceptual ground for empirical research.

As regards Wright's second argument concerning the concept of exploitation and class interests, the objections presented above are even more relevant. As Wright's own studies (1985, 1997a) show, persons in middle-class positions are less likely to have a distinct class identity than members of the working class or the managerial elite. And as the proportion of this middle-class workforce grows, and correspondingly that of the shopfloor working class diminishes – a tendency that has been stable in all OECD countries during past decades – the more blurred the class identity of the majority of the population becomes. 'Exploitation... does not simply predict an opposition of interests, but a tendency for this antagonism of interests to generate manifest conflicts between classes', writes Wright (1997a: 32). This postulate concerning the existence of class interests looks, however, increasingly like archaic theoretical ballast hindering the neo-Marxian researcher from seeing the contours of the new society. The new middle classes certainly have a market interest, but it is highly doubtful whether they have a class interest. For the neo-Marxist tradition, the lack of a class consciousness of the workforce in developed industrial societies and transition societies, documented by a host of studies, presents a dilemma. From a Weberian point of view, by contrast, no dilemma exists: the members of social classes may or may not be aware of their class position or class interests, and the question is not relevant for the study of social stratification. The 'tendency for the antagonism of interests to generate conflicts between classes' has failed to become manifest in contemporary developed countries. And as regards social conflict in transition countries, it has neither had the character of a class conflict between workers and managers nor has it been ignited by class interests of those groups. The conflict has had the character of strife between mutually exclusive status groups, and nationality, religion, language and kinship ties – that is, *Blut und Boden* and not abstract class interests – have been the denominators of the antagonism.

Since this is a book on income distribution and social inequality in transition countries, Wright's third argument – the notion that an exploitation-centred class analysis is better suited to the study of non-market societies such as planned economies – deserves a little more attention:

> The exploitation-centered class analysis implies that classes can exist in nonmarket societies, whereas Weberian class analysis explicitly restricts the relevance of class to markets. For Marxist class analysis, the relationship between slave master and slave or lord and serf are instances of class relations because they all involve exploitation linked to property rights in the forces of production. The relationship between bureaucratic exploiters and producers in command economies can also be considered a form of class relations since the capacity of the state bureaucratic elite to appropriate surplus rests on their effective control over the society's productive resources. For Weberian class analysis these are not class relations, but rather examples of castes or estates or some other form of inequality of power, since the differences in 'life chances' of the slave and slave master, the lord and the serf, the bureaucratic appropriator and the producer, are not the result of their meeting within a market. The Weberian restriction of the concept of class to market societies, therefore, directs our attention away from the underlying commonality of these relations across different kinds of social systems.
>
> (Wright, 1997b: 158–9)

In all societies, people and social groups have sought to maximize their well-being. In striving towards increasing their life-chances, stronger population groups have frequently benefited at the expense of weaker groups, that is, the powerful have exploited the disadvantaged. When systematic differences in life-chances have developed between population groups, we may speak of social stratification. The mechanisms of exploitation that produce and maintain social stratification have, as a rule, been fortified in legislation, ideology and prevailing social norms and practices. The Marxist sees that all relations between social strata that involve exploitation are class relations, irrespective of whether the question is of the relation between lord and serf, manager and worker, shareholder of an IT company and Internet expert, or Soviet bureaucrat and socialist worker. From the Weberian point of view, it is by contrast not entirely justified to bundle together all situations involving exploitation under the common label of class relations. The history of relations between population strata in societies both ancient and contemporary is far too complex to be grasped by a single overarching concept in a satisfactory way. Stretching the extension of a concept to an extreme always results in a loss of its analytic power.

As any history student can confirm, exploitation of weaker strata of populations by more powerful ones has happened in a multitude of ways in the course of centuries. The casteless in India are confined to carrying out the dirtiest and most despised tasks; the affluence of the lord in medieval Europe was based on the toil and obedience of the serf; millions of slave labourers perished in the labour camps of the Soviet Union and Nazi Germany; nineteenth-century industrialists accumulated large amounts of capital while their workers' life-spans were cut short by industrial accident and unhealthy living conditions; and the Soviet nomenklatura enjoyed the luxury of comfortable apartments and special stores while the everyday life of ordinary people was austere and goods shortages were a constant plague. The wealth of the world's three richest billionaires is today greater than the total wealth of the world's 600 million poorest people.

The decision to regard all these situations involving exploitation as class relations depends, in the end, on our willingness to adopt historical materialism; that is, the inclination to believe that class conflict is the prime mover of history and to adopt an ensuing conviction that the concept of class ought to be applied to all societies – in Wright's words a propensity to see an 'underlying commonality across different kinds of social systems'. It is, of course, true that most often exploitation takes place in the sphere of production, but unless we are ardent proponents of Marx' theory of surplus value, there is nevertheless no compelling reason to give production the key position in the analysis of social stratification. Instead of seeking the determinants for exploiter–exploited relations in the sphere of production, it is – especially if we are looking for causes for social stratification or studying social mobility – more interesting to question why underdogs choose to enter into exploitative production relations in the first place and what are the social mechanisms that make that exploitation possible. Is the exploitation based on mechanisms of social closure, as in the cases of the casteless in India, serfs in medieval Europe, and workers in the Soviet Union? Is it based on differences in market power, as in the case of the nineteenth-century working class and contemporary global distributions of income? Or is the exploitation based on sheer violence and coercive misuse of political power, as in the case of labour camps in totalitarian states?

In Western industrial societies, the large statistical studies that have been carried out using the neo-Marxian 'class-mapping' approach, have, despite their rigid focus, succeeded in revealing essential features of the social stratification patterns of the societies in question. In the case of transition societies, the setting is, however, more problematic. This is especially true with regard to such countries as Russia, Ukraine or Kazakhstan where there has been a drastic reduction of the life-chances of such professional groups as teachers, medical doctors, scientists and civil servants. These large groups of educated professionals, traditionally regarded as solidly middle-class, have in a short period of time become impoverished and sunk below the poverty threshold. The neo-Marxian approach with its focus on production would still regard these groups as middle-class, not detecting the rapid downwards social mobility that these important groups have experienced in the 1990s. Conversely, a Weberian approach that focuses on a market-based distribution of life-chances of various kinds would portray a completely different picture of the social reality.

The second reason for a preference for Weberian basic concepts is the fact that alternative approaches require a relatively stable society as the subject matter of their studies. The classification of a multitude of different occupational groups into classes and sub-classes in the neo-Marxian manner is only possible in an environment where labour relations are stable and where the relative positions of different professional groups *vis-à-vis* capital can be determined fairly unambiguously. This is, however, hardly the case with most of the transition countries in the 1990s. Individuals may occupy shifting and ambiguous positions in the labour market, and the difficulties in drawing a detailed map of social stratification on this basis are formidable.

A similar reservation also applies to the Bourdieuan approach to the analysis of social stratification (Bourdieu, 1979, 1980). The third reason mentioned above for the choice of the Weberian point of departure is that it also allows a focus on social actors and not only structures; this is also a strength of the Bourdieuan approach. In contrast to the neo-Marxian tradition that concentrates entirely on social structure, Bourdieu has succeeded in creating a fertile theoretical framework that enables the interplay of actors and structures to be studied; that is, the Bourdieuan approach attempts to make visible the ways social groups produce and reproduce social structures and patterns of social inequality. The range of application of Bourdieuan theory seems, however, to be limited to societies whose basic structures are stable and whose patterns of social stratification are established.

Social actors as perceived by Bourdieu strive to accumulate various sorts of capital (Bourdieu divides capital in three types: economic, social and cultural) in different social fields in order to reproduce or enhance their positions in social space; or alternatively, they may try to alter the rules of the social fields to their own advantage. The analysis of social activity thus perceived makes sense as long as the basic contours of the social fields remain clear and the value of the different types of 'capital' is relatively constant. The Bourdieuan sociologist is master in revealing how the existing social order is reproduced through such institutions as the educational systems, art or public media in 'mature' class societies such as France or England, but if the subject of study is revolution rather than the reproduction of social order – the overthrowing of old institutions and the creation of new ones – then the approach becomes problematic. The Bourdieuan observer needs, in principle, a relatively fixed and stable set of social coordinates rooted in continuity and tradition.

Iván Szelényi (Eyal *et al.*, 1998) makes an interesting attempt to combine the Weberian and Bourdieuan approaches into a coherent framework for the analysis of social structure in transition societies. Szelényi and Glass

(Chapter 5) by and large follow this approach in their contribution on elites to this volume. Szelényi's approach is sophisticated but not entirely unproblematic. In a Weberian manner, he perceives the change of social structure during transition as a shift from status-ordered society ('rank order') to a class society. Simultaneously, he postulates the three Bourdieuan types of capital plus an additional one which he calls 'political capital'. During the transition, he sees the conversion of different types of capital – in the first place the conversion of social and political capital into economic capital – as an important means of reproducing one's position in the transforming social space or achieving upwards social mobility.

From the Weberian point of view, social capital or political capital means – quite simply – inclusion into important status groups. One of the basic theses brought forth by Szelényi (Eyal *et al.*, 1998) is that while social and political capital were the most significant modes of capital in the reproduction of an individual's position in the social structure of communist societies, economic and especially cultural capital are the predominant ones in the post-communist era. But if social capital can be interpreted as an alternative way of describing inclusion into powerful status groups, doesn't Szelényi's thesis then mean that the predominance of status order has changed to that of a market order? That is, Szelényi *et al.* confirm the fact that whereas social connections were important in a status-ordered society (centrally-planned socialism), assets that have market value are important in a market-ordered one (post-Soviet capitalism).

Szelényi *et al.* understand cultural capital by and large as possession of professional qualifications. Interpreted in this way cultural capital acquires a predominant importance in post-communist society. Quite obviously, professional qualifications that are valued in the labour market are, indeed, a more important asset in a market-ordered society than in a status-ordered one.

The fourth and final reason for preferring Weber's basic concepts is that the very notion of transition, the contrast between past and present, traditional and modern, is inherent in the distinction between status and class. It would, of course, be a simplification to claim that the transition from centrally-planned communism to market order is identical with modernization of society, but, nevertheless, the pair of concepts 'status order' and 'market order' nicely reflects the essence of this process, that is the shift from a contingent and politically determined social order towards an order created by a more abstract and universal force – the market (see for example, Holton and Turner, 1989). It should, however, be noted that this analytical juxtaposition on the level of ideal types does not mean an assumption concerning a separation of these principles in the empirical world; in existing societies – be they centrally-planned socialist or market-capitalist – both these stratification patterns coexist of course, always in various and complex ways.

Old and new elites

Social stratification in planned economies was defined above as stratification into status groups, and the basic mechanism of stratification was defined to be social inclusion or exclusion, that is membership in various status groups that had unequal access to life-chances of different kinds. In market economies, market power is the decisive factor that determines a person's access to life-chances, and the market is thus also the prime cause for social stratification, that is the uneven distribution of life-chances between different population groups. If we analyse the development of the uppermost social strata during the transition in this conceptual framework, it is then essential to pay attention to how the old elites have managed to transform membership in privileged status groups into market assets, and thus to what extent have they succeeded in reproducing their former privileged status positions into privileged class positions in the new society.

In his book *Gosudarstvo i evolyutsiya,* Egor Gaidar (1995) aptly described the mechanism employed by the economic elite to convert privileged status group positions into market assets during the first phase of the transition in Russia:

> And so was formed an ideal solution for the bureaucracy: with regard to the control over the productive assets, they were in the role of owners and capitalists, but with regard to responsibility, they had neither the responsibilities of a capitalist nor those of a bureaucrat in a traditional sense... All the ways of becoming rich were open, and all the restraints that had to do with responsibility were removed. This was a situation of a servant who suddenly no longer had a master, because the master – the state – had all of a sudden been hit by paralysis.
>
> The system was, in fact, very simple. The old bureaucratic market worked in the open, while simultaneously a normal economic market was being formed. The latter had, however, only an auxiliary function: it laundered money and helped to convert the power resources of the bureaucrat into money. In principle, it was an administratively operated command system that had learned to exploit the market (or more precisely, had created 'under itself' a market, which it could exploit).
>
> (Gaidar, 1995: 147)

The process that Gaidar describes is characteristic of the first stage of transition in all former socialist countries. Bureaucrats in key positions exploited the coexistence of the old command system and the emerging market to 'convert power resources into money'. Gaidar is describing the situation that prevailed in Russia in 1990–91, that is prior to the start of the mass privatization programme of state enterprises. The privileged status groups had by then already secured their future as a privileged class in the new market economy.

Gaidar's main argument is that a rapid privatization was needed in order to halt the mass-scale stripping of assets of the state enterprises that had been left without effective owners. The outlines of the new capitalist class had already been formed before the implementation of large privatization programmes; as Frydman *et al.* (1998) put it, what emerged was a 'capitalism with a comrade's face'. But even though this might have been more or less the case in all transition societies, the method of privatization employed in Russia further strengthened the powers of the former insiders to reproduce themselves as the new capitalist class. Although the privatization of state enterprises in Russia was meant to be a voucher scheme similar to that successfully implemented in the Czech Republic, it soon deteriorated into what resembled a giveaway scheme with large concessions to the old enterprise management. The privatization scheme employed accelerated the tendency of capital to accumulate to the hands of the old privileged status groups, and is obviously among the reasons for the more unequal income distribution in Russia compared to that in the Central European transition economies.

The mechanism described above had to do with the development of the 'core' of the new economic elite. Insiders in key positions gained control of large amounts of capital in the market economy. Around this core of the top economic elite, consisting mainly of members of the former nomenklatura, there formed a stratum of entrepreneurial elite that to a large degree lived in symbiosis with this core of the new 'grand capitalists'. The privatization mechanisms employed have had a decisive influence on the formation of this entrepreneurial elite. The Russian privatization scheme that favoured former enterprise managers gave 'outsiders', for example professionals who were not former members of the nomenclatura, relatively few chances to occupy positions in the economic elite. In this sense, the privatization schemes employed in the Central Europe (CE) transition economies and the Baltic States were more open and created much more upward mobility in allowing entrance to the new economic elite for persons who formerly were not part of privileged status groups. This view receives support from, for instance, Eyal *et al.* (1998) who claim that the 'political capitalism thesis' presented, among others, by Frydman *et al.* (1998) – that is, the opinion that key groups in the old nomenclatura have, to a large degree, been able to reproduce their elite positions in the post-Soviet capitalism – is much less true for CE than for Russia and other Commonwealth of Independent States (CIS) countries.

Middle strata and middle classes

The planned economies in CEE were defined above to have been stratified into status groups or estates and not into classes. The two main estates of these societies were the party elite on the one hand, and the vast majority of the people, 'the middle strata' of society, on the other. The third estate that differed in status from the two above-mentioned was the social-marginal; groups that occupied a position at this margin of socialist society had, as a rule, a semi-legal or an illegal status. This marginal group consisted of shadow-market entrepreneurs, black marketeers, criminals and other 'non-working elements', as the official definition goes.

The elite had its clearly defined functions in society, its own code of conduct, its privileges and its consumption patterns that all differed from those of the majority. The majority of the population, 'the middle strata', led by contrast a 'socialist way of life' with a different set of accessible life-chances, supposedly distributed evenly across this entire vast stratum. The first precondition for this even distribution of income and other life-chances was full employment and a place in waged labour for every able-bodied adult member of the society. Income distribution was egalitarian, and blue-collar professions were favoured at the expense of white-collar professionals. On average, the salaries of professionally skilled workers tended to be the highest, while salaries in the services, science and culture, healthcare and public education tended to be lower. Salaries of the 'technical intelligentsia', that is technicians and engineers, were as a rule not much higher than those of skilled blue-collar workers in production. For ideological reasons, a skilled worker could often receive a larger salary than an engineer, and engineers thus often preferred to become employed as blue-collar workers (see for example Piirainen, 1997: 88–98). A gap between the earnings of men and women prevailed, however. As a rule, salaries were higher in the male professions, and in the Soviet Union the salaries of women were on average as much as 30 per cent lower than those of men (see for example Kivinen, 1994; Melin, 1997).

Another precondition for the relatively equal distribution of life-chances among 'the middle strata' of the socialist societies was the comprehensive network of social security and services provided by the state. The vast majority of the population was provided with approximately the same level of housing, similar healthcare and social services, equal access to education and the same recreational opportunities. In reality, however, there was more differentiation with regard to life-chance distribution than suggested by the official picture. Status-group membership counted, for instance, when the actual standard of living of a person or a household was determined. In the Soviet Union, workers and employees in all-Union enterprises had, as a rule, better access to consumption goods that were in shortage, because the enterprises were provided with goods directly via the respective ministries in Moscow. Also, workers in strategically important defence industries enjoyed considerable privileges with regard to standards of living and levels of consumption. Persons in social networks with members in key positions could, for instance, secure access to consumption goods, education, healthcare services and recreation that was hardly possible for others without these 'connections'.

During the transition in the 1990s, these middle strata differentiated very rapidly. For certain groups there has been rapid upwards social mobility, whereas large groups have, by contrast, experienced downwards mobility and seen a radical narrowing of their life-chances. However, country-specific patterns of social differentiation vary considerably. Countries like the Czech Republic, Poland and Hungary have, to a large degree, been able to prevent a mass-scale proletarianization of state employees; whilst, simultaneously, growing new sectors of the economy have offered chances for upwards social mobility. The pattern has been very different in countries like Russia, Kazakhstan or the Kyrgyz Republic, where a large decline in output has reduced the real incomes of the majority of the population and where the slow growth of new sectors of economy has not provided enough alternative sources for the impoverished old middle strata to find resources to maintain their previous standards of living. Country-specific patterns of social differentiation are discussed in more detail in later chapters.

The decline of output and the growth rate in the economy are among the most significant factors that explain the difference between patterns of social differentiation in CE and CIS countries. In the CIS countries, the dramatic drop in GDP after 1991 led to erosion of the tax base and a chronic budget deficit. As a consequence of the state's fiscal crisis, the real incomes of large groups of public-sector employees, for instance medical doctors, teachers, scientists and employees in public administration, declined rapidly. The salaries of professional groups that in the Western industrialized world form the stable core of the middle classes have dropped to the poverty threshold. Very often, the salaries of public-sector employees are not paid on time, and in Russia where the fiscal crisis in 1998–9 was the most difficult, delays in wage payment of six months or more were quite common. Besides the steeply declining real value of salaries and mounting wage arrears, another factor that accelerated the proletarianization of the former middle strata has been the massive shedding of employees from public administration, education and healthcare in many CIS countries, as the network of public services has been trimmed down as a result of the state's fiscal crisis. In Kazakhstan, for instance, approximately 25 per cent of medical personnel were made redundant during 1996–97 as a result of the 'optimization' of the country's healthcare system (Piirainen, 1998), and the number of employees in public administration was expected to be cut by approximately 30 per cent during 1999.

Apart from the greater decline in output in the CIS countries, another factor that explains the different patterns of social mobility in those countries and in the CE former socialist countries is the differences in the environment for small entrepreneurship. The preconditions for the development of an entrepreneurial middle class have been far better in CE. The legislative framework, taxation policies, access to credit, and the ability to guarantee the safety of entrepreneurs have made the environment for small entrepreneurs much more favourable in CE than in CIS countries. In addition, the impact of the longer history these CIS countries have had with planned economies should not be underestimated. Stalin's great terror in the 1930s managed to eradicate all the remnants of the old entrepreneurial classes from the Soviet Union, but CE and South-Eastern Europe (SEE) and Baltic countries have a considerably shorter history with Soviet socialism, and therefore also a stronger entrepreneurial tradition than Russia and other countries of the Former Soviet Union (FSU).

The decline in output, the rate of economic growth and the environment for small entrepreneurship are the most important structural factors that determine the patterns of social differentiation of the middle classes in each particular country. The most important factors that impact upon the social mobility of an individual within a given pattern of social differentiation are, in principle, the following: (1) age, (2) gender, (3) professional qualifications, (4) 'conversion' of status group membership into market assets, (5) place of residence (rural/urban, centre/periphery), and (6) position in the dual economy (domestic/international).

- *Age*. In terms of income, younger workers are more likely to gain more advantageous positions than older ones. Older workers and employees are more likely to be employed in the public sector and thus have lower salaries. The new private sector, as a rule, demands a predominantly younger labour force that is flexible and has professional qualifications required by the market economy.
- *Gender*. Besides age, gender is also an important factor. During the planned economy, differences in earnings between men and women were already considerable, but this gender-based income inequality has become aggravated in the market economy as women seldom have access to well-paid positions in the private sector, and real income in the traditional female professions in the public sector has been devaluated during the transition. In many countries, especially in the Central Asian Republics (CARs), transition has also brought about a certain traditionalization of society and a change in the status of women. Contrary to the official Soviet ideology of gender equality, women are now more often seen as responsible for the household and childcare, while men are seen as the breadwinners. The collapse of the public services, for example public low-cost childcare, has precipitated this process of traditionalization.
- *Professional qualifications* are obviously a significant factor determining the trajectory of social mobility of an individual or a household. The market power of a member of the middle strata or the middle classes – and thus the strength of his or her class position – depends crucially on the professional qualifications he or she has to offer in the labour market. The actual patterns of demand for labour vary, of course, considerably between individual countries. Whereas the Czech Republic and Poland

have experienced the development of a new and relatively stable middle class consisting of professionals, in Russia after the financial crisis of 1998–9 a common theme of discussion has been the destruction of the nascent middle class.

According to the definition set at the beginning of this chapter, class position is associated with market power. If we follow this definition, we can already trace the beginnings of professional middle classes to the 1970s and 1980s. The situation can be perceived as analogous to the *ancien régime* in France. As technology and innovation became ever more important for economic growth, the demand for professionals – technicians, engineers, research scientists – grew in the planned economies as well as in the Western industrial countries. Aware of this growing demand and of the strategic importance of their labour force, professionals in the planned economies grew increasingly dissatisfied with the egalitarianism that was imposed on them by the socialist order. It was plausible to expect that marketization of the economy and a decentralization of decision-making would serve, in the first place, the interests of professionals and strengthen their relative positions. Young professionals were therefore the most important social force that backed *perestroika* in the Soviet Union that led to the dissolution of the socialist camp and finally of the Soviet Union itself. It is uncertain whether *perestroika* could have gained momentum without this growing 'class consciousness' of Soviet professionals. Two hundred years before, the pressure from the French bourgeoisie destroyed the old estate society, and in a similar manner the pressure from the professional groups unleashed the forces that brought about the dissolution of the Soviet Union – another society that consisted of estates organized in a hierarchical order (Piirainen and Turuntsev, 1998).

- The '*conversion*' of status group memberships into market assets was described above to be one of the main mechanisms of elite formation, that is the mechanism by which certain groups of the old elites reproduced themselves in the course of the transition. For the members of the middle strata, these mechanisms have been less significant but by no means unimportant. For instance, starting a small business and gaining access to the capital and equipment needed for entrepreneurship often requires membership in social networks and engaging in patron–client relationships; these status group memberships can then be converted into market assets needed for successful entrepreneurship. Gaidar's description quoted above dealt with the stripping of the large state enterprises of their assets by top management. Asset-stripping of a similar kind happened, however, also on lower levels, and it was carried out by ordinary members of the 'work collectives'. Group power was used also on the level of ordinary workers and employees to gain productive or marketable assets.

- *Rural–urban cleavage* is the fifth factor to influence the social mobility of members of the former middle strata. In the major cities and urban areas, the developing new sectors of the economy have created opportunities for upward mobility or at least for maintaining the former social positions in relative terms. In rural areas and in declining industrial towns, however, these opportunities are much more limited. The actual stratification patterns with regard to the rural–urban divide differ very much depending on the country in question. The differences between rural and urban areas, between the centre and the periphery, are the most striking in Russia and other CIS countries where the collapse of collective farming and the difficulties of single-enterprise towns have created a rural proletariat that lives to a large degree outside the monetary economy. The inability of the state in CIS countries to maintain the heavily subsidised collective farms or to continue the operation of non-competitive industrial giants has in a short period of time led to the creation of a dual economy that is in certain respects similar to that observed in developing countries. Similar trends are apparent in Poland and Romania where rural residents were disadvantaged in the course of the transition as shown in case study by Gorniak (Chapter 8).
- *Finally, position in the dual economy* is a factor that has importance for income and social mobility, and profession and professional qualifications have been mentioned as the most important market assets of the middle classes. In the transition countries, the sector of the economy where these qualifications are marketable is, in addition to the nature of the qualifications, very important from the point of view of life-chances of an individual. Wage differences between the private and public sectors are very large, and are most marked in Russia and some other CIS countries where salaries of professionals such as medical doctors, teachers or scientists fall below the poverty threshold, if they are paid at all (for example, see Simpura *et al.*, 1999). Besides the public–private divide, another income gap exists between the domestic economy and the international sector. Those who receive their salaries from the international 'dollar' economy, that is persons employed by Western companies that operate internationally, may usually count on much higher salaries compared to those employed by domestic enterprises. Especially in Russia and the CIS, the striking difference between these enclaves that are integrated in the international economy and the domestic sector resembles the divide characteristic of economies in the developing world (see, for example, Levada, 1998; *Bednost*, 1998).

New lower classes

In general, middle classes in the transition countries may be defined as social classes that differ from others in the sense that their market power, albeit much lower than that of the elite, is sufficient to ensure a set of life-chances – that is, income level, housing, education, culture, recreation and so forth – that may be defined as distinctly middle-class, and which match certain values and aspirations. The middle classes are able to secure these life-chances through activity in the market and the monetary economy. A distinction can be made between the entrepreneurial middle class and the wage-earning middle class; the former gains access to this set of life-chances by selling goods and services in the commodity market, the latter by selling its labour power in the labour market.

The market does not yield the same set of life-chances to the lower classes, who, in transitional economies, do not have a market power strong enough to lift them above the poverty threshold. The better off among them are, however, able to compensate for this lack of market power to some extent by activities in the informal and non-monetary economy. Such activities range from subsistence agriculture to exchange of goods and services in kinship and community networks. Common to these activities is that the economic exchange involved is usually non-monetary and also not market-based. In this sense, the formation of these social classes whose life-chances are either partly or entirely acquired through activities in the informal economy can be regarded as a traditionalization of the societies in question. When the market and the state fail to secure decent life-chances, people resort to traditional means of subsistence.

Again, the stratification patterns vary greatly across countries. In CE and the Baltic countries, the resort of workers and employees to traditional means of subsistence has not been mass-scale, and the share of the population dependent on the informal economy is diminishing as economic growth creates new opportunities in the official economy. The size of these traditionalist classes is far larger in the SEE transition economies and in the CIS countries. The share of the population employed in agriculture is large in Bulgaria, Romania and especially Albania, and a large part of this employment consists of subsistence agriculture that is to a large extent outside the monetary and market economy.

Collective farmers in the CIS countries are the most obvious group that has been subject to this traditionalization. State financing of collective farming has been cut, and only a relatively small percentage of the large collective farms have proved to be commercially viable. As a consequence, unpaid wages in agriculture are the rule rather than an exception, and a large share of farm workers has thus been virtually driven out of the official monetary economy. Subsistence agriculture is the main means of livelihood for the majority of farm workers. Due to the extreme shortage of money in circulation in rural areas of Russia, Ukraine and the Central Asian countries, economic transactions take the form of barter or exchange of gifts rather than money-based market transactions. The deterioration of roads, means of transport, telecommunication systems, electricity provision and other public services precipitate this process of traditionalization of economic activity and patterns of social conduct. As a result of this deterioration of the infrastructure, small rural communities are increasingly physically isolated and subsist as self-sufficient economic units with only limited connections with the outside world.

The situation is to a certain extent similar in small industrial towns in the CIS countries. As market prices are charged for energy and transportation in the new economic environment, and as production faces a shrinking market and competition by foreign products of superior quality, the industrial giants of the FSU have very often been forced to shed their workforce. The situation is most difficult in single-enterprise towns, that is towns that have been built around a single large enterprise and which thus offer few alternative opportunities for employment. Unemployment compensation and other social transfers are either non-existent or insufficient, and subsistence agriculture and other traditional means of economic activity are often the only means of securing a livelihood (Piirainen, 1996).

In the CIS countries and SEE, large groups of public-sector employees such as medical personnel, school teachers and cultural workers also experienced a rapid downwards mobility during the 1990s. Real salaries decreased rapidly in the public sector in these countries and, as a consequence, professionals who in Western market economies are usually regarded as occupying stable middle-class or lower middle-class positions have fallen below the poverty threshold. In the CIS countries and SEE, poverty and traditionalization of economic activity and social conduct are not phenomena restricted only to the unemployed or people in rural areas; a large percentage of urban wage labourers are also forced to supplement their insufficient incomes from the official economy by activities in the informal and unofficial economies.

The position of those at the lowest end of the social spectrum is determined, in the first place, by their limited capacity to operate in the informal economy in order to supplement their insufficient official incomes. Exploiting the informal economy requires certain resources, for instance a network of kin members and friends, land that can be used for gardening and small-scale agriculture, and family members who have the time and energy to invest in subsistence farming and other similar activities. Without these resources, supplementing insufficient incomes through activity in the informal economy is hardly possible.

Thus at the very bottom of the social structure are people dependent on inadequate incomes from the public sector, either on small salaries or income transfers. These groups form a potential poor underclass (McAuley, Chapter 6). The elderly with low pensions and without relatives to help belong to this group, as well as the working poor, for instance public sector employees with many children to support and without any alternative means to augment their incomes through activities in the informal economy. In Russia and other CIS countries, families with several children are the main group that falls below the official poverty line (see for example *Bednost*, 1998; Piirainen, 1997). Pensioners in Russia have been observed to be somewhat better off than the working poor with families to support, with the majority of pensioner households being slightly above the official poverty threshold which has been set at the level of minimum subsistence.

In Russia, the poor whose income and level of consumption is below the subsistence minimum – that is the share of households living in absolute poverty – comprise, according to a nationwide survey by Goskomstat, the state statistical agency, approximately one-third of the total number of households. In CE, by contrast, the percentage of the poor in this category is much smaller. In the Czech Republic, for instance, the new system of social assistance is designed, in principle, to guarantee every household an income equal to the official subsistence minimum (Castle-Kanerova, 1997).

Conclusion

Following Max Weber, social stratification has in this chapter been defined to be the systematic unequal distribution of life-chances – not only of income – between different groups of the population. With regard to social stratification, Weber makes an important distinction between stratification into social classes and that into different status groups. Market forces are, in principle, the social mechanisms that function as a cause for social stratification into classes, whereas stratification into status groups is caused by social inclusion or exclusion. Since market forces – at least according to the official self-understanding of the pre-reform 'real' socialist societies – did not play a significant role in the distribution of resources and life-chances, these societies evidently could not, by this definition, be class societies. Differences across population groups with regard to life-chances – that is, social stratification – evidently had the nature of stratification into status groups. Consequently, the transition from planned economies to market economies also brings about a fundamental change in the pattern of social stratification, that is a shift from the predominance of stratification into status groups to that of social classes.

The ability of an individual to transform his or her status group memberships into market assets is one of the central determinants of his or her social mobility during the transition. To what extent an individual is able to reproduce their previous social position in the new market economy depends, in the last instance, on the strength of his or her position in the market. In all transition countries, the formation of the new economic elites happened, to a large degree, through a process of 'conversion' of status group positions into market assets; that is, certain sub-groups in the old nomenklatura could exploit their strategic positions and social networks to obtain considerable amounts of assets that used to belong to the state.

For 'ordinary' people, the ability to transform status group memberships into market assets played a less important – albeit still a significant – role. The most important market asset for a member of the middle classes is his or her own workforce, and this is equally true for the entrepreneurial middle class as well as for the part of the middle class that consists of wage-earning professionals. The former employs his or her own workforce in order to produce goods and services for sale, and the latter sells his or her labour power in the labour market. The market demand for this workforce, or in the case of the small entrepreneur, for the goods and services provided, is obviously the main precondition for upward social mobility. Nevertheless, the ability to transform former social group positions into market assets has also been an important factor contributing to upward social mobility or the maintenance of prior social positions for members of the middle classes. Furthermore, if the market demand for labour is weak, the more important do status group memberships become.

The mechanisms employed in the privatization of large enterprises are the most important factors that explain the differences in patterns of elite formation. By contrast, labour market demand is the most important factor that explains the large differences in the size of the middle classes and the patterns of their formation across transition countries. The difference is especially marked between the CE transition countries and the CIS countries. In the former, the initial drop in output was much smaller and economies are growing, with the result that new employment opportunities are created for the middle class. In the CIS countries, the large drop in output and stagnating economies has implied weak labour market demand and downward social mobility for large groups of the former middle strata of the society.

Weak labour market demand is also the basic cause in the formation of the lower classes. In the CE transition countries, redistributive social policy regimes have been established to alleviate the poverty of those disadvantaged in the market. This has obviously been an impossible option for the CIS countries, given the mass-scale impoverishment of the middle strata and the erosion of the tax base.

The poorest transition countries have experienced a large-scale shift of economic activity from the official economy to the informal one. As the market demand for the labour force is weak, and as a consequence a sufficient set of life-chances cannot be acquired on the basis of market activity alone, people seek to compensate for this gap by retreating to informal and traditional forms of economic activity, for example subsistence agriculture. In the CIS countries, this often means either a partial or full retreat from the market economy into a traditional non-monetary economy. It is, however, important to note that to be successful, this traditionalism requires membership of such important status groups as kinship or community networks or patron–client relationships. Traditional and non-monetary forms of economic activity are, as a rule, based on exchange and division of labour between status group members, and therefore not everybody has the opportunity to exploit the informal economy to compensate for market shortcomings.

Distinct social classes differing greatly with regard to their life-chances can be observed to have emerged in the transition countries. The relative proportions of these classes vary greatly across the countries, and can be named as: (1) the elite, (2) the middle class, and (3) the lower classes with a poorest segment forming a potential underclass. The elite consists of those who have successfully 'converted' their former prestigious status group memberships into strong market power. The market power of members of the middle class is sufficient to give them access to a satisfactory set of life-chances, and former or present status group memberships may to a varying degree have contributed to the development of this relatively advantageous market position. The market power of the lower classes is, by contrast to the two upper classes, not sufficient to yield a tolerable set of life-chances. Relying on the informal economy and taking advantage of membership in community and kinship networks can, however, to a certain degree compensate for insufficient market power. The defining characteristic of the poorest social class – a potential underclass – is by contrast that it has neither the market power to yield a sufficient set of life-chances nor membership of status groups to compensate for this insufficiency.

References

Bednost (1998) *al'ternativnye podkhody k opredeleniu I izmereniu,* Nauchnye doklady Vypusk no. 24. Moscow: Carnegie Endowment for International Peace.

Bourdieu, P. (1979) *La distinction. Critique sociale du jugement.* Paris: Éditions de Minuit.

—— (1980) *Le sens pratique.* Paris: Éditions de Minuit.

Castle-Kanerova, M. (1997) 'Social Security and Social Insurance in the Czech Republic', in J. Clasen (ed.), *Social Insurance in Europe.* Bristol: The Policy Press.

Eyal, G., I. Szelényi and E. Townsley (1998) *Making Capitalism Without Capitalists. The New Ruling Elites in Eastern Europe.* London and New York: Verso.

Frydman, R., K. Murphy and A. Rapaczynski (1998) *Capitalism with a Comrade's Face. Studies in the Postcommunist Transition.* Budapest: CEU Press.

Gaidar, E. (1995) *Gosudarstvo i evolyutsiya,* Izdatelsvo 'Evrasiya', Moscow.

Holton, R. J. and B. S. Turner (1989) *Max Weber on Economy and Society.* New York: Routledge.

Kivinen, M. (1994) 'Class Relations in Russia', in T. Piirainen (ed.), *Change and Continuity in Eastern Europe.* Dartmouth: Aldershot.

Levada, Yu. A. (1998) '"Srednii chelovek": fiktsiya ili realnost?', in T. I. Zaslavskaya (ed.), *Kuda Idyot Rossiya? Transformatsiya sotsialnoi sfery i sotsiyalnaya politika,* Pyatii mezhduradnyi simpozium, 16–17 yanvarya 1998 g., Izdatelstvo 'Delo', Moscow.

Lonkila, M. (1999) *Social Networks in Post-Soviet Russia.* Helsinki: Kikimora Publications.

Melin, H. (1996) *Suunnitelman varjossa. Tutkimus yritysjohtajista valtiososialismissa.* Tampere: Tampereen yliopisto, yhteiskuntatieteellinen tiedekunta.

Piirainen, T. (1996) *The Death of the Iron Mother. A Study of an Industrial Town in Post-Soviet Kazakhstan.* Brussels: Tacis Publications.

—— (1997) *Towards a New Social Order in Russia. Transforming Structures and Everyday Life*. Dartmouth: Aldershot.
—— (ed.) (1998) *The Privatisation of the Social Sphere in Kazakhstan*. Brussels: Tacis Publications.
—— and E. Turuntsev (1998) 'Ottalkivayas ot Maksa Webera: k ponimaniyu protsessov sotsialnoi transformatsii v Rossii', *Voprosy ekonomiki*, no. 7.
Simpura, J. *et al.* (1999) 'No Limits to Patience? Economic Crisis and the Everyday Life of Middle-class Families in St. Petersburg', *The Finnish Review of East European Studies*, no. 2.
Srubar, I. (1991) 'War der reale Sozialismus modern? Versuch einer strukturellen Bestimmung', *Kölner Zeitschrift für Soziologie und Sozialpsychologie*, 43(3).
Weber, M. (1978) *Economy and Society*, 2 vols., Berkeley: University of California Press.
World Bank (1996) *From Plan to Market. World Development Report 1996*. New York and Oxford: Oxford University Press.
Wright, E. O. (1985) *Classes*. London and New York: Verso Classics.
—— (1997a) *Class Counts*, student edn. Cambridge: Cambridge University Press.
—— (1997b) 'Class Analysis', in R. F. Levine (ed.), *Social Class and Stratification. Classic Statements and Theoretical Debates*. New York: Rowman & Littlefield.

3
The Impact of Labour Markets: Social Mobility, Segmentation and Reranking

Vladimir Gimpelson

Introduction

The role of labour markets in the transition can hardly be overestimated. The role is much broader than just a market for one of the factors of production, labour markets 'mediate the transition' channelling outcomes of macro- and microeconomic reforms into the everyday lives of households, affecting their economic and social well-being. The allocating and reallocating of jobs and earnings opportunities to the various segments of the population perform such mediation.

There are at least two broad and fairly different sets of mechanisms channelling the effects of labour-market adjustments. On the one hand, transition brought a polarization of job opportunities resulting in a decreasing share of the population remaining in employment (and economically active). Most of the transition countries have seen a decline in employment and a subsequent rise in unemployment and long-term unemployment (LTU). The likelihood of unemployment varies significantly across social space, with some social groups (for example unskilled workers) suffering more than others (the university educated, or those with occupations in particular demand). The same dispersion and concentration of risks across groups is also true in the case of the LTU.

On the other hand, retaining labour market status *per se* does not guarantee retaining the same social status previously enjoyed. Those employed in the transition economy have been exposed to growing wage and earnings differentials, with the rise in inequality due, among other causes, to structural changes in employment itself, diverging patterns of returns to human capital, and the growing likelihood of short-time and occasional (contingent) employment. Some of those in previously low-priority sectors and occupations may have gained enormously, but many former beneficiaries have been as likely to have lost. The emerging market economies change patterns of return, while 'post-socialist' workers are not always well-prepared for living in the new capitalist environments. Their human capital can be one-sided; even if fairly well-endowed with, say, skills and education for winning, they may end up as losers due to their lack of market experience and slow learning (Rychard, 1996). In many CIS countries, some workers in formerly permanent jobs have not received wage payments for months.

Newly-emerging social stratification brings new losers as well as new winners. It changes relative distances between different social positions through mobility and reranking, and increases inequality. These shifts stem from various macro- and microeconomic factors relating to both demand and supply. Structural changes in the economy – including rapid growth in the service sector, expansion of private ownership, economic growth and rates of inflation, and the demise or reform of the social protection system – are well-documented in other chapters of this volume. Another group of effects comes from the political transition, since the importance of political power in social status and earnings determination has been vanishing. Family circumstances are also important due to redistributive effects within households such as intergenerational compensatory support, or simultaneous losses/gains by two or more members in the same household.

Labour markets are extremely important here, but they are just one factor among many; they cannot explain all causes and dimensions of social reranking. Moreover, many labour market outcomes correlated with social dynamics are caused by exogenous factors. Take, for example, the rise in unemployment. This results from a number of macro- and microfactors including GDP trends, fiscal and trade policies, privatization, the pace of restructuring, the design and generosity of social protection system, dominant social values and demographic structures. Some of these effects are indirect in the sense that they are mediated by labour markets, others may evolve in a more straightforward way. Even the most developed and well-tuned labour markets are helpless when the whole economy is stagnated and new jobs are not created. Another example of social mobility and restratification is associated with new business development and self-employment which can lead to a remarkable rise in the middle-classes that only indirectly results from the labour market.

Social stratification and labour markets are, therefore, in a complicated relationship. On the one hand, labour markets are the main engine of social stratification, allocating available employment. On the other hand, individuals interacting with the labour market are not homogeneous; they differ *ex ante* in many dimensions, being unequally endowed with education, skills and other social resources. These endowments translated into labour market behaviour generate important signals according to which the market treats them. Therefore, we may expect considerable path dependence in social stratification and career histories for the same individuals taken over time. Of course, this is not an iron rule; however, under transition in times of incredibly large exogenous shocks and structural shifts, the expected inertia of a smooth career path is likely to be broken.

Major labour market outcomes vary significantly across former socialist countries, but significant labour market mobility and segmentation can be seen almost everywhere. Patterns of return to education and skills have been changing affecting both job security and earnings mobility. Under transition, the more secure jobs are often associated with better earnings opportunities due to their location in particular sectors of the economy, or due to occupations which are in demand by emerging markets. Certain social groups face a higher risk of unemployment, and are also more likely to experience downward mobility or to find themselves locked in underemployment. Among these groups are youth, women, unskilled and less-educated workers.

Social stratification and social mobility are among some of the most popular issues in sociology, and reviewing even the most important theories would go far beyond the scope of this chapter. Here, I refer mostly to a set of labour market segmentation theories[1] which consider labour markets as consisting of a few different and disconnected clusters or segments. In such theories, segmented labour markets are discontinuous, with segments differing between themselves in terms of what kind of jobs they consist of (job security, career opportunities, required skills and education, and so forth). The simplest case of such segmentation is a divide into a core (or primary labour market) and a periphery (secondary labour market). Workers outside the core are doomed to insecure, low-skilled and poorly paid work, whilst workers in the core may enjoy opportunities for fairly secure and well-paid employment. As technological and social distance between the core and periphery increases, chances of mobility or jumping into the better world vanish.

Labour market segmentation in the transition countries, however, is somewhat different. First, there are probably more than two segments and they are rather continuous. Second, segmentation is based not on technological factors but on differences in adjustment capacities of various sectors and enterprises. It results from different speeds of restructuring and corresponding changes in labour market selection. Third, the segmentation manifests itself not so much in job insecurity as in low wages, underemployment and wage arrears, among others. These factors result also from labour hoarding, oversupply of labour and shrinking demand, growing differentiation and changing requirements of human capital.

It therefore follows that the issue of how labour markets affect social structures in countries under transition is large and multidimensional and variations in initial conditions and pursued policies do not make the problem easier. The following sections cover the major labour market trends in seven transitional counties (some of which are presented in country chapters later in this volume). We discuss how labour markets affect relative positions of various social groups, but we confine ourselves largely to extended labour market statuses.

General country characteristics and data sources

The transition countries taken as a whole comprise a cluster of 26 countries. Although sharing a fairly similar socialist experience, they have rapidly diverged since the early 1990s. Different transition regimes have involved different labour market outcomes. The CEE countries faced a rapid surge in unemployment soon after the beginning of the transition; this path involved higher one-time costs, but the costs were shorter in duration and more concentrated in particular social and demographic groups. As Commander and Tolstopyatenko (1997) argue, the FSU countries explicitly chose to limit unemployment, whilst, in contrast, policies to ensure employment smoothing have been far less prominent in CEE. This brought about a very gradual employment decline (and gradual unemployment rise), one-time costs were smaller but total accumulated costs were much larger and of longer duration. Additionally, a larger part of the population has been negatively affected but in different ways than in CEE. A significant decline in real wages, a rise of underemployment and expansion of wage arrears are components of this model.

Of course, this typology describes just a very rough tendency and there are obvious exceptions. For example, the Czech Republic, Romania and the Kyrgyz Republic represent more complicated and less clear-cut cases. A lack of comparable data also limits the scope of this study. In many of the transition countries social statistics are still awaited, which is not a surprise as efforts to reform statistics are part of the transition in general.

The Czech Republic, Poland and Hungary, which are already OECD members and are in the process of EU accession, have the most advanced labour market statistics among all transition countries. They regularly conduct representative labour force surveys (LFS) and lots of information is available from various alternative sources.[2] The Kyrgyz Republic and Uzbekistan are at the opposite extreme in the quality and availability of data. Official data that are available are still very limited and scarce in detail; their quality and reliability also raise doubts. These countries, so far, have not launched regular representative LFS and rely mostly on bureaucratic procedures of formal applications to local offices of national employment services. However, both countries have on occasion conducted household surveys. Russia, Romania and Ukraine (in this particular order) are somewhere in the middle of the range. They have significantly advanced labour statistics but still lag behind the more successful CE countries.

Further discussion in this chapter is based on a wide range of data from both official and non-official sources. For better comparability, I rely (where possible) on the OECD/CCET Labour Market Database and the corresponding definitions.[3] These data are drawn from national LFS and are standardized according to ILO/OECD guidelines. The database provides data for the Czech Republic, Poland, Romania and Russia. For countries not represented in the database (that is Ukraine, the Kyrgyz Republic and Uzbekistan) I refer to various official and non-official publications as well as studies from international organizations. For Ukraine, I refer particularly to a recent ILO report (Ukraine, 1999). Survey evidence on the Kyrgyz Republic are from the Living Standards Measurement Survey (LSMS) in 1996, and data on Uzbekistan reported by Klugman (1998) are from the European University Institute/Essex Survey (EUIES) conducted in 1995.[4] Since information on these two countries is fairly limited, we need to be very cautious in final judgements; all possible caveats should apply.

Employment and participation

Changes in aggregate employment rates very often lie behind social reranking. Shrinking employment pushes people out of jobs, while jobs themselves become more volatile. Those who end up out of employment face the highest risk of income losses and poverty, a pattern which probably extends across all countries (see for example Habich and Speder, 1998: 25, 28). Meanwhile, having a job and possessing proper human capital are crucial for becoming a winner. The losses from non-employment are so large that they cannot be compensated for by the fading welfare system, and this is especially apparent in the case of families with many dependants.

An overall decline in employment is an almost universal trend throughout the region (with Uzbekistan the only exception), though it varies in size. Prior to transition the employment rate was very high, inflated by the economics of shortages as well as by politically motivated and mandatory employment. Macro- and microeconomic policies conducted in the transition period caused a general contraction in the labour market forcing some individuals to leave it, voluntarily or involuntarily. On the other hand, political and economic liberalization broadened the choice of whether to stay in the market or to leave it, to search for job or to become self-employed. Therefore, some formerly employed left the labour market voluntarily or involuntarily, while others entered the unemployed pool.

In the CEE countries, employment rates have shown a remarkable decline (Boeri *et al.*, 1998: 12). Poland (together with Hungary) leads the trend with an employment rate of 56–60 per cent down from about 80 per cent, depending on the data (Boeri *et al.*, 1998: 13). Within this cluster of countries, the Czech Republic and Romania have experienced the smallest decline, but still experience relatively high employment rates. In Romania, this 'success' is due largely to hidden unemployment in the agricultural sector.

For the CIS countries, data, except for Russia, are scarce; the employment rate in Russia has declined from about 80 per cent in 1992 to 64.7 per cent in 1996 (Kapelyushnikov, 1999). The Ukrainian LFS data suggest the rate was down to 75.5 per cent in 1997 from 84.8 per cent in 1990 (Ukraine, 1999), whilst the available survey data for the Kyrgyz Republic estimate its employment rate to be as low as about 44 per cent. However, with total formal employment of 1.65 million, the Kyrgyz Republic is reported as having about 1 million workers outside the official statistics. This includes 350,000 agricultural workers, 300,000 workers in the informal private sector, and 350,000 subsistence farmers (IMF, 1998b: 12). This pool contains a huge component of disguised unemployment and underemployment. For Uzbekistan, formal employment is somewhat high but still much lower than in European countries; in 1995 it stood at about 57 per cent of the working age population (meanwhile, the female employment rate was 1.5 times lower than that for males). Uzbekistan is the only country in the sample that has increased formal employment since the early 1990s. Over 1991–97 formal employment grew by 5 per cent, while the working age population increased by 15.5 per cent (IMF, 1998a: 83). Between 1994 and 1997, 340,000 new jobs are reported to have been created, implying an annual employment growth rate of 1.3 per cent (Klugman, 1998: 101). Relying on the 1995 household survey, Klugman estimates a participation rate in Uzbekistan of 62.4 per cent compared to 72.0 per cent based on official data (*ibid.*: 107).

Table 3.1 illustrates how various factors have contributed to the employment decline. As we can see, across the countries for which data are available, demographic shifts have played only a minor role. Shrinking participation and growing unemployment accommodate the bulk of the decline. Withdrawal from the labour force accounts for almost three-quarters of the employment decline in the Czech Republic, over half in Russia, one-third in Poland, and only a small fraction (10–12 per cent) in Romania and Ukraine. Roughly speaking, the increase in unemployment is responsible for another portion of the employment decline; it accounts for up to 90 per cent of the employment decline in Romania and Ukraine.

Labour market flows: where from and where to?

More insights into dynamic relationships between employment (*E*), unemployment (*Un*) and non-participation (inactivity) (*In*) can be drawn from labour market flows. Flows between these states (*E, Un, In*) tend to change not only labour market aggregates but their social composition as well. The intensity of flows is itself an important indicator. Moreover, moving within the triangle (*E, Un, In*), individuals change employers, jobs, occupations, sources of

Table 3.1 Decomposition of the decline in employment rates, 1991–96 (%)

	Change in employment (%)	Due to			4/1
		demographic shifts	change in unemployment	change in participation	
Bulgaria	–22.2	1.8	–9.9	–10.5	0.47
Czech Republic	–9.6	1.0	–2.6	–8.0	0.83
Hungary	–22.9	0.7	–6.9	–16.7	0.73
Poland	–13.1	1.0	–9.4	–4.6	0.35
Romania	–5.6	1.5	–6.3	–0.9	0.16
Slovakia	–11.6	1.6	–8.4	–4.7	0.41
Russia*	–13.9	1.0	–2.6	–8.0	0.58
Ukraine**	–9.3	–0.3	–8.1	–0.9	0.10

Sources: Boeri *et al.* (1998); * Kapelyushnikov (1999); ** Gimpelson based on Ukraine (1999).

income and lifestyles, and in this sense labour market dynamics is an apparent engine for social restratification and reranking.

Flows can be computed on the basis of longitudinal household data as gross flows weighted by the initial number of individuals in the stock, while the statuses are defined according to standard OECD-ILO criteria (see Boeri and Bruno, 1997). Both large-scale and smaller-scale flows have their advantages and disadvantages depending on their direction and structure. Larger-scale flows may mean more restructuring, more adjustment, more mobility. Increasing flows out of unemployment means a higher turnover in the pool of unemployed and, correspondingly, fewer long-term unemployed (LTU), holding all other things equal. At the same time, larger flows out of and into employment may bring more fragility, less security and more uncertainty.

Table 3.2 gives an overview of labour market dynamics in Poland, the Czech Republic and Russia, along with some other transition countries.[5] Outflow from employment has two destinations: one to unemployment, the other to non-participation. The total annual outflow from jobs varies from 5.6 per cent (of the employment stock) in Slovakia to 16.1 per cent (this is for 9 months; the annual rate will be even higher) in Bulgaria. In most of the country cases, more individuals leave the labour force than become unemployed. The lowest outflow from employment to unemployment is in the Czech Republic (reflecting its lowest unemployment rate) with just 1 per cent of the stock. Employment to unemployment flows in Russia and Poland are similar, while outflow into non-participation in Russia is significantly larger than in Poland or the Czech Republic.

Table 3.2 Labour market flows in transition countries, % of stock

Country	*E–Un*	*E–Out*	*Un–E*	*Un–Out*	*Out–E*	*Out–Un*	*E–E*
Poland* (1994–95)	3.5	5.5	38.0	15.6	6.0	3.2	–
Czech Rep.* (1995–96)	1.0	5.6	47.1	15.6	6.7	0.4	–
Slovakia*(1995–96)	2.9	2.7	34.8	4.2	2.0	1.6	–
Bulgaria** (June 1994–March 1995)	5.9	9.2	32.3	24.4	5.5	4.4	–
Russia*** (1995–96)	3.4	7.2	39.9	32.8	10.9	6.4	15.5
% of the labour force (total = 37.4%)	3.2	6.8	2.9	2.4	4.9	2.9	14.3

Notes: *E* = Employment; *Un* = Unemployment; *Out* = Out of the employment market.
Sources: * Boeri and Bruno (1997); ** Boeri (1998); *** Author's estimate; RLSMS (1996).

Outflow from unemployment varies from 39 per cent (for Slovakia) to 73 per cent (for Russia) of the stock. In Poland, it makes up about 54 per cent. The difference between 100 per cent and these rates indicates the proportion of those who become stuck in unemployment for longer than a year. In both Poland and the Czech Republic, outflow to jobs is as much as 2.5–3 times larger than the outflow into non-participation. About half of all the unemployed cannot change their status within a year of entering the LTU group. In Russia, again, the role of inactivity in absorbing joblessness is much greater; with outflow to jobs as large as in Poland (38–40 per cent), one-third of all unemployed go into the inactivity category. Non-participation in Russia draws more people from the labour market (from both employment and unemployment) than it does in Poland or the Czech Republic.

For Romania, comparable data are not available. Earle (1998) examined flows from industry (1993) to other labour market states (1995) and found that industry and agriculture provided the most significant contribution to non-employment (both unemployment and inactivity), while agriculture was the major destination of those moving to jobs from non-employment. Predicted probabilities of the mobility suggested that university and general high education tended to raise the probability of job-to-job flows, while those with lower education tended to move into non-employment. Older workers and women had a higher probability of finding themselves in the unemployed pool.

Compared with the early 1990s, the fall in outflow to jobs in Russia was offset by growing mobility into non-participation. This helped to contain open unemployment but the growing non-participation was partially due to a larger share of discouraged workers.

The last row in Table 3.2 shows Russian flows measured as a percentage of the labour force. It illustrates the dynamic nature of the Russian labour market where a considerable fraction of the population is in permanent motion;

almost a quarter of the labour force changed status within one year (Oct. 1995–Oct. 1996). Adding those who changed employer but remained in employment gives over 37 per cent of the total labour force.

Table 3.3 shows the composition of flows across social and demographic groups in Russia. Flows are not homogenous since these groups differ in employability and propensity to work. Outflows from employment for men and women are similar; however, men are more likely to go into unemployment, while women leave the labour market. The same pattern is observed if we look at mobility from unemployment: men are more employable while women are more likely to go into inactivity. This may illustrate an existing gender asymmetry.

The age dimension provides even more dispersion. Younger groups are much more mobile across labour market statuses; for those in the age group 16–24 the probability to move from employment into unemployment is 5.3 per cent compared to only 1.2 per cent for the 55+ group. Correspondingly, young people (from the former group) have a 44 per cent chance to be rehired compared to a 27 per cent probability of going into inactivity. This

Table 3.3 Flows by age, sex, education and occupation, Russia, 1995–96

	E–Un	*E–Out*	*Un–E*	*Un–Out*	*Out–E*	*Out–Un*	*N*
Total	3.4	7.2	39.9	32.8	10.9	6.4	6167
Age							
16–24	5.3	9.7	43.6	26.7	21.4	13.4	942
25–39	3.6	3.9	43.5	26.1	34.2	15.8	1847
40–54	3.4	5.6	40.0	30.0	17.6	12.1	1651
55+	1.2	20.0	17.1	68.6	3.6	2.1	1727
Sex							
Male	3.6	7.0	44.4	31.1	13.0	7.8	2691
Female	3.2	7.4	36.4	34.1	9.9	5.7	3476
Education							
Secondary	3.2	13.6	30.8	41.0	3.8	2.9	1461
High	3.3	7.4	48.8	19.8	18.2	11.7	1339
College (high professional)	3.6	5.8	36.8	38.6	11.8	10.5	1141
University	1.8	3.2	41.9	29.0	16.5	3.8	942
Occupation							
Managers and professionals	1.8	3.0	–	–	–	–	736
Technicians and clerks	2.8	6.2	–	–	–	–	833
Skilled workers	3.5	5.5	–	–	–	–	1362
Unskilled workers	3.0	12.3	–	–	–	–	496

– denotes not applicable.
Source: RLSMS (1996).

contrasts with 17 per cent versus 69 per cent for the older group. Thus, the younger are more likely to become unemployed but also much more likely to move back into employment.

Individuals with less than eight years of schooling have a low rate of outflow to unemployment but the highest one into inactivity. This combination seems to correlate with age and reflects the fact that inactivity may accommodate a significant portion of actual unemployment. A university diploma shows itself as an important asset helping to keep an employment status intact. Among those with higher education only 4 per cent left jobs within the period under consideration.

The variation in outflow to unemployment across occupational groups is not very large, with managers and professionals having the lowest rate. Unskilled workers and clerks are the first among those going into inactivity. The structure of labour market withdrawal provides additional evidence of shifting patterns of return to education and skills, and reflects a growing discouragement of the least competitive and marketable. This pattern seems to be universal across all CEE economies, including Russia and Ukraine.

Incidence and social structure of unemployment

Unemployment affects social stratification in multiple ways; it suppresses wages and generates a special social group (the unemployed) with one of the lowest social standings. The pool contains a mix of individuals with low skills, low education, those working in particular obsolete sectors, or those in mono-product regions. Unemployment provides a negative signal to employers as a proxy of poor skills and performance. However, obsolete 'overqualification' and 'overeducation' as a legacy of central planning are not an asset either. A threat of unemployment is expected to moderate wage claims, and in the CIS countries this threat also leads to the acceptance of wage arrears as a form of earnings suppression. These general effects emerge through various particular channels, of which we shall mention just a few:

- First, some social groups are more exposed to unemployment than others. Those who are more exposed know that and this itself may generate a relative reranking forcing the acceptance of worsening terms of employment, including loss in earnings. Acceptance of less well-paid jobs, short-time work or wage delays becomes, therefore, a function of unemployment, since the latter decreases workers' bargaining power. Additionally, expectation of unemployment (or layoffs) can increase mobility as workers look to protective change from more fragile positions for less fragile ones. Thus, the threat of unemployment is an additional factor of social segmentation and occupational mobility (Blanchflower, 1991).

- Second, even low unemployment involves flows through the pool of the unemployed. Those who have gone through are often rehired for positions and occupations different from those they had previously. This alters the occupational structure even if it does not downgrade it. Unfortunately, it often does. As Gimpelson (1996) shows for Russia, displaced workers may be rehired to inferior positions compared from those they occupied prior to layoff. Longer spells of unemployment are also associated with steeper downward mobility. Given monitoring problems and the fact that workers' productivity remains private information in these countries, private employers are reluctant to hire the unemployed. This either keeps them locked in or causes larger reductions in the reservation wage (Boeri, 1998).
- Third, unemployment may segment the population outlining a sub-pool of the labour force that is disproportionately more volatile. This effect may hold the same individuals over time as well as across individuals within households. Multiple periods of unemployment in the past increases exposure to unemployment in the future.
- Fourth, unemployment is an obvious road into poverty.[6] In Romania, for example, the incidence of poverty among the unemployed is 3–4 times higher than for those with jobs.[7] Unemployment benefits are low in most of the countries;[8] in the CIS, benefits are derisory in amount, hard to get and often delayed. Unemployment may also increase inequality by driving down wages in particular sectors and occupations. An expectation of unemployment may bring the same effect.

Trends and incidence

The incidence of unemployment varies heavily across the countries reflecting variations in initial conditions as well as different policies. Figure 3.1 shows unemployment trends for the 1990s across the sample. The overall picture appears very fluid with rapid changes in unemployment rates.

Keeping in mind all the caveats, we can roughly say that more radical economic policies speed up the occurrence of higher unemployment, which then goes down sooner. A 'muddling-through' style of reforms delays high unemployment but cannot stop its arrival; unemployment emerges more gradually but remains more persistent over time. However, this is an approximation; some countries may deviate since other factors (initial conditions, human capital endowments, availability of cheap natural resources and energy, structure of economy, and so forth), if favourable, can counteract the trend. Poland on the one hand, and Russia with Ukraine on the other, illustrate this situation; all other countries in the sample deviate somewhat from the scheme. Here, the Czech Republic and Romania are apparent examples.

The main similarity across the sample is that all the countries had no open and publicly recognized unemployment prior to the transition, but

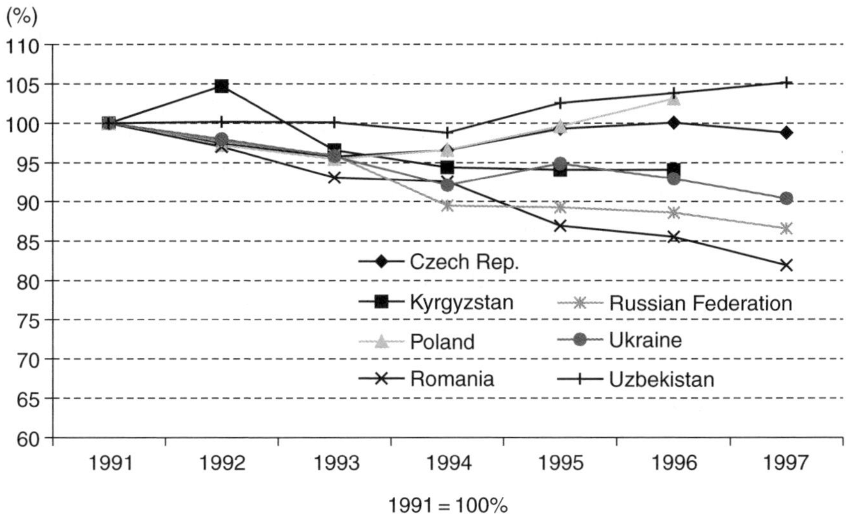

Figure 3.1 Changes in employment
Sources: EBRD (1998); national statistics.

have faced a rapid surge since. If a cross-country typology is sought, Russia and Ukraine seem to show some affinity in certain aspects between themselves, as do Uzbekistan and the Kyrgyz Republic between themselves. However, in some aspects even 'similar' countries may diverge significantly. Others differ from these patterns, as well as between themselves, even if figures for them may seem to be close.

Let us start with success stories, which Poland and the Czech Republic clearly are. The most radical reform implemented in Poland caused a drastic rise in unemployment, which started from a very low level and reached a peak of about 14 per cent of the labour force in 1994.[9] Since then, due to a sustainable recovery led by the new private sector, the rate of joblessness has been in a steady decline. The rate of surveyed unemployment fell to 11.2 per cent in 1997 and that of the registered unemployed declined to 10.2 per cent by April 1998. However, the potential for a further decline in unemployment has become almost exhausted, given the pace of job creation, structural and demographic problems.[10] Additionally, output growth stems largely from investments and productivity gains, with only a marginal contribution of the volume of labour input.[11]

The Czech Republic has enjoyed very low unemployment, and has been dubbed the Czech 'employment miracle'. Its unemployment level has been persistently low over the 1990s and remains low, though tending to rise somewhat. Among major factors have been reductions in the labour supply and considerable wage moderation. Initially in the transition, a reduction in real wages outperformed that of labour productivity, making labour even cheaper that it was before (Fleck and Večerník, 1998: 4). However, rather slow industrial restructuring and fairly favourable initial conditions in terms of human capital endowments cannot be dismissed either. This mixture of causes was also strengthened by labour market policies. Nevertheless, sustainability of the Czech employment performance is now questioned by the unemployment rate which approached 6 per cent in 1998 (*ibid.*: 10).

The relatively low unemployment in Romania might be puzzling were there not extremely high self-employment in the agricultural sector. Unemployment grew rapidly in 1990–91 following a plummet in GDP. It then declined from about 11 per cent to around 6 per cent in 1997, reflecting a temporal reversal in the GDP trend in 1994–96. However, the major reason behind fairly low unemployment is a significant agricultural sector, which, together with the huge grey economy, works as a safety cushion absorbing many of those laid off from the industry. In 1996, the self-employed (mostly in agriculture) accounted for 37 per cent of total employment, a very high rate by any standard (OECD, 1998b: 39).

Although in 1997 trends for Poland and Russia met at a level of around 11.5 per cent, in fact these countries were moving in opposite directions. While employment in Poland has clearly been recovering, Russia slides into higher unemployment gradually but steadily. Ukraine, lagging with Russia, has been following the same 'Russian way'.[12] In 1998, Ukraine almost managed to 'catch up' with Russia on this indicator. Muddling through instead of credible structural reforms feeds a gradualism which is translated into the labour market adjustment model (Kapelyushnikov, 1999; Gimpelson, 1998). A relatively slow increase in open unemployment is combined here with the significant but still not sufficient (given the actual level of unemployment and loss in the GDP) decline in wage claims, therefore leading to massive wage arrears spreading across the whole economy.

In 1992, when the first LFS was conducted, the Russian unemployment rate was 4.7 per cent. Since then it has more than doubled, reaching 8.3 per cent in 1995 and eventually exceeding 12 per cent in early 1999. Ukraine launched surveys a few years later, so we do not have comparable figures for 1992–94. As Figure 3.2 shows, in 1995–97 the Ukrainian unemployment rate moved upwards with a lag, but with a slope very similar to that of Russia. It grew from 5.6 per cent in October 1995 to 8.9 per cent in October 1997.[13] Given the actual drop in GDP and the amassed stock of wage debts, it is hard to believe that the unemployment has reached its peak; it looks to be rising.

Both the Central Asian economies have very low rates of registered unemployment. Uzbekistan keeps its register unusually clean with an unemployment figure of just 0.4 per cent. According to these data, unemployment in Uzbekistan appears nonexistent. This unbelievable performance, however, is likely to reflect a mixed effect of bureaucratic hurdles of registration with little economic incentives to register (low levels of benefits and low

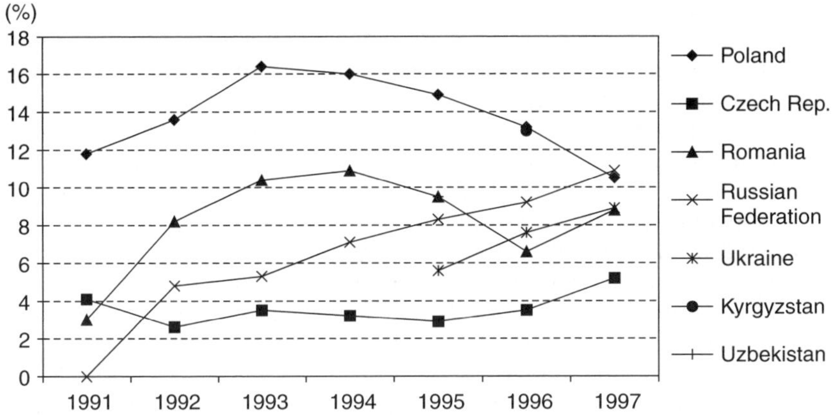

Figure 3.2 Unemployment in selected countries, % of labour force
Sources: National Labour Force Surveys; for the Kyrgyz Republic – the Living Standards Measurement Survey (LSMS) in 1996; for Uzbekistan – as reported by Klugman (1998).

duration – a feature typical for all the CIS countries and Romania). However, even in the Soviet time when labour was a scarce factor of production everywhere across the socialist world, all Central Asian Republics (CARs) (relatively less urban, more agricultural and with significantly higher birth rates) suffered from significant rural overpopulation and disguised unemployment. This is unlikely to have changed.

The 1998 IMF country report on Uzbekistan estimated the actual unemployment rate as well above 5 per cent, but gives no further details (IMF, 1998a: 80). Among possible reasons for the still modest unemployment figure could be the very slow pace of reforms associated with the lowest GDP decline, significant outmigration from urban to rural areas (ending up with self-employment in the agriculture), and emigration of the non-Uzbek (mostly Russian-speaking) population. The agricultural labour force has increased in Uzbekistan since independence, whilst output has fallen and wages have lost a third of their value. Figures on net emigration from the country differ and vary between 274,000 in 1990–93 to about 1.8 million in 1990–91, about 13 per cent of the population (Pomfret and Anderson, 1997). The emigrants were mostly professionals and technicians representing the most technologically advanced sectors but having the worst adjustment prospects. These are mainly speculative explanations. Meanwhile, Klugman (1998), using the important 1995 household survey data, estimates the unemployment rate as 9.5 per cent of the labour force (1998: 107). This is not a low rate at all.

Registered unemployment in the much more liberal and faster moving Kyrgyz Republic was 3.2 per cent in 1997 from its peak of 4.5 per cent in

1996. But this captures just a tip of the total unemployment. A representative survey conducted in the fall of 1996 estimated unemployment in the country as high as 13 per cent of the labour force.[14] Interestingly enough, internal migration in the Kyrgyz Republic is reported to have an opposite effect on the labour supply than in Uzbekistan. In the latter it is directed towards rural areas diminishing the urban labour supply, whilst in the Kyrgyz Republic the main flow is into cities from less developed rural areas, increasing the supply of urban labour resulting in higher urban unemployment.[15] This urban inflow was partially offset by emigration in 1991–96 (as it was in Uzbekistan).[16] In both countries outmigration contributed to the deterioration of the total human capital stock. Therefore, easing pressure of the labour supply in the short run can bring more losses in the long run.

The pool of the unemployed is far from homogeneous; 'Its unwelcome feature is its extreme selectivity, maybe even more ruthless than in Western Europe' (Jackson *et al.*, 1995: 4). Unfortunately, data problems do not allow us to draw a strictly comparative and detailed social and occupational profile of unemployment across countries. We are doomed to deal with rather large and heterogeneous groups defined in terms of gender, age, education and skills. Though non-negligible, these factors vary in the capacity to explain vulnerability to unemployment across the countries, and other (non-personal) characteristics may appear to be relatively more important. We can also assume that geography and community-related circumstances are important everywhere, while capitals and the most urbanized areas usually have the lowest rates.

In the three CE countries, women are affected more than men, with the largest difference (14.4 per cent versus 11.5 per cent) observed in Poland. On the contrary, in the CIS countries men are more likely to become unemployed. The largest gap here is detected in Uzbekistan with 10.5 per cent against 5.3. This contradicts a frequent observation about the 'female face' of unemployment. Of course, this fact does not mean that women suffer much less; they are just affected in a different way, being ousted into lower paid jobs or out of the labour force altogether. Thus, the relative level of female unemployment seems to be dependent on their propensity to withdraw from the labour market. Lower female unemployment rates therefore reflect a higher incidence of discouragement among women, their lower labour market power and, ultimately, their higher likelihood of withdrawal.

Gender differences may, however, look different if the picture is based on claimant count. Here, in most of the countries women form a clear majority among those applying for the status of unemployed with corresponding benefits. Taking other things as equal, this reflects different attitudes among men and women to the formal registration procedure and to potential benefits associated with it. Men are much more reluctant to take this route, since unemployment registration is considered the last resort. This again illustrates a gender asymmetry.

The gender gap in exposure to unemployment is also age-related. Generally, across the sample, youth (15–24 years) unemployment is higher than average. The difference is especially large in Poland (29.5 per cent versus 12.8 per cent in average), in Romania (16.2 per cent against 5.5 per cent) and Russia (19.1 per cent against 9.5 per cent). The available evidence for Ukraine places the 20–24 and 25–29 year groups as the most affected (Ukraine, 1999: 23). In Uzbekistan, the age group of labour market entrants (16–18 years) is the major victim, where unemployment reaches 24.3 per cent. Other groups within the 19–50 years range have figures somewhat near to the average, which drops further for those over 50 years (Klugman, 1998: 108).

In Eastern Europe female youth unemployment is almost universally higher than male. In 1997 it reached 32.3 per cent in Poland, meaning that almost every third young woman had no job and was looking for one. Male youth rates are somewhat lower but still much higher than average. In Romania school-leavers account for over one-third of all unemployed. A clear exception here is the Czech Republic with its relatively small gap between average and youth unemployment.

It would be fair to say that higher education provides the best protection against unemployment, and this is a universal pattern. Everywhere, the unemployment rate for the most educated part of the labour force is the lowest and it is 2.5–3.0 times lower than the average. On the contrary, workers with only primary (or lower) education have a notably higher likelihood of unemployment. Romania and Ukraine stand out as having the highest unemployment rates for those with intermediate – secondary – education. In Ukraine the group with secondary vocational training is especially hard hit and overrepresented among the unemployed (Ukraine, 1999: 30).

Still, workers with secondary education in all countries remain very vulnerable; besides their general education they often have only basic vocational training. In the CIS countries, where only a minor portion of all jobless applies for registration, this group (holders of intermediate education) is disproportionately represented in unemployment registers. Since application to employment centres is considered the last resort, the propensity to apply is another manifestation of low market competitiveness of this group. Across the four selected CIS countries, those with secondary (general and vocational) education make 60–80 per cent of all claimants for unemployment benefits.

Intermediate education is often associated with serious underskill (or wrong skills) for a job in the market economy. 'The professional "over-qualification" of the unemployed is a heritage of the socialist system of vocational training; the emerging market economy cannot absorb this excessive and rather specially distributed mass of skilled labour' (Jackson *et al.* 1995: 14). The combination of overeducation, preretirement age and gender (females) makes this group especially vulnerable. Data on unemployment, however, do not show the whole picture since those in the group may react by leaving the labour market or take early retirement. Anyway, the education legacy brings an additional mismatch element to the growing supply and demand disequilibrium.

Age and education-related unemployment means a break with old practices when school-leavers regardless of education and skills were welcome to take a job. Unskilled workers have been in high demand to fill slots in the soft-budget constraint economy, but this is not the case anymore. The market has started making its own ruthless selection exposing those with inferior human capital endowment to much higher risks of unemployment.

The long-term unemployed: who they are

Long-term unemployment (LTU) is a particular challenge for all transition economies (Boeri, 1994). It does not moderate wages and, therefore, has no anti-inflationary effect. Meanwhile, it increases the pressure on public finances. Its social mobility implications are negative and straightforward, the most likely being either reemployment with a steep downward shift in status, or labour force withdrawal. Entering the LTU pool is a clear mark of social segmentation and of hardly reversible downward reranking. The longer an individual stays there, the more difficult it becomes for him or her to get a new job and the more the reservation wage goes down. Unemployment benefits, which are usually low from the very beginning of joblessness, dry up quickly draining heavily on savings. All this leads the LTU into deep poverty. They lose skills (both occupational and social) as well as hope, thus inhibiting any potential upward recovery. Instead of being transient, the unemployment becomes dead-end. Labour market withdrawal in this case is often a forced option, reflecting discouragement rather than a voluntary decision to leave the market.

One of the major causes behind the increasing duration of unemployment is very slow job-creation and falling hiring rates in existing firms. These suppress turnover in the pool inhibiting exits to jobs. Therefore, even small inflows into unemployment may lead to growth of the LTU. Russia and Ukraine are exemptions from this tendency; having very low job-creation rates, Russian and Ukrainian 'old' firms have remained quite active in hiring. Despite that, however, most of this turnover is little more than churning, increasing the number of open vacancies and therefore driving up exit probabilities.[17]

The share of LTU has been growing steadily in all countries under transition since the start of reforms (see Table 3.4), with rates (as a percentage of the total national labour force) varying from 1.2 per cent in the Czech Republic to 9.4 per cent in the Kyrgyz Republic. In the European part of the sample, the long-lasting unemployed account for over a quarter of all unemployed (28 per cent) in the Czech Republic, to over a half (52 per cent) in Ukraine. In most of these countries the LTU share is on the rise, although in Poland it grew rapidly in 1992–94 but has declined since.[18]

Table 3.4 Labour market data across selected countries, national LFS (%)

		Romania 1997, Q2	**Russia 1996, Q1**	**Czech Republic 1997, Q1**	**Poland 1997, Q1**	**Ukraine 1997, Q4**	**Kyrgyz Republic 1996, Q4**	**Uzbekistan 1995, Q2**
Participation rate								
Total	Working adult population (WAP)	74.2	74.5	72.4	68.9	70.8	51.3	62.3
Males	male WAP	81.7	85.1	80.4	72.5		59.2	
Females	female WAP	68.6	70.9	64.4	65.1		43.1	
Total	total Labour Force (LF)	5.5	9.5	4.7	12.8	8.9	13.1	9.5
Males	male LF	5.2	9.8	3.9	11.5	9.5	14.0	10.9
Females	female LF	5.9	9.2	5.8	14.4	8.4	11.7	5.3
Youth unemployment								
Total	total youth LF	16.2	19.1	7.8	29.5		18.9	13.0
Males	male youth LF	14.0	18.0	7.5	27.4		19.2	
Females	female youth LF	19.3	20.7	8.3	32.3		18.5	
Prime-age unemployment								
Total	total prime-age LF	4.8	8.4	3.8	11.9			
Males	male prime-age LF	4.3	9.0	3.0	10.2			
Females	female prime-age LF	5.4	7.8	4.8	13.9			
Older unemployment								
Total	total older LF	2.1	6.3	2.5	7.2			4.0
Males	male older LF	2.6	6.6	2.5	7.5			
Females	female older LF	1.2	5.7	2.6	6.8			

Table 3.4 (Continued)

		Romania 1997, Q2	Russia 1996, Q1	Czech Republic 1997, Q1	Poland 1997, Q1	Ukraine 1997, Q4	Kyrgyz Republic 1996, Q4	Uzbekistan 1995, Q2
Unemployment by education								
Higher educ.	LF with higher	2.2	4.4	1.3	4.1		5.3	2.6
Secondary	LF with secondary	7.1	10.1	2.9	12.1		14.2	11.7
Primary or less	LF with primary	3.9	13.0	12.3	15.5		21.1	7.4
Unemployment by experience								
School-leavers	total unemployed	37.3		8.1	4.6			
Prev. experience	total unemployed	62.7	86.2	89.3	82.6			
Unskilled	total unemployed	8.9		21.1	16.0			
Long-term unemployment								
Total	total LF	2.6	3.1	1.2	3.4	4.7	9.4	
Total	total unemployed	47.8	32.8	28.1	38.0	52.3	71.9	
Males	total male unemployed	44.7	29.5	28.7	34.0		74.1	
Females	total female unemployed	51.0	36.8	27.3	42.0		68.3	
Youth	youth unemployed	41.1	26.0	17.4	29.0		–	
Older	older unemployed	55.2	33.7	–	–		–	
Unskilled	unskilled unemployed	48.6		39.3	38.1		–	
Underemployment								
Total	total LF	2.5		1.0	1.7	~6		
Total	total part-time employed	17.3		18.2	16.8	~50		

Males	male LF	3.0		0.3	1.5			
Females	female LF	1.8		1.9	1.9			
Part-time employment								
Total	total LF	14.2		5.6	10.0	12.2		
Males	male LF	11.6		2.7	8.2			
Females	female LF	17.2		9.3	12.1			
Employment								
Total	WAP	69.4	67.3	69.0	60.0	75.5	44.0	56.6
Males					64.1			67.3
Females					55.7			46.3
Self-employment								
Total	total employed	39.3	13.1	12.2	27.4	15.4		
Males	male employed	34.6	15.8	15.6	29.1			
Females	female employed	44.8	10.0	7.9	25.2			

Sources: National Labour Force Surveys: Poland (OECD, 1998a); Czech Republic (OECD, 1998c); Russia (OECD, 1997); Ukraine (Ukraine, 1999); Romania (OECD, 1997); Kyrgyz Republic (RLSMS, 1996); Uzbekistan (Klugman, 1998).

The LTU share is higher among women than men. Youth is usually less affected, while older age groups are affected more. In the Czech Republic there is no concentration of LTU in a particular age group, but unemployment of the unskilled is particularly longer-term. For example, among the unemployed without school education about 80 per cent are long-term, whilst among those with primary education the LTU make up over 45 per cent (compared with 28 per cent on average).[19] For Romania and Poland, such a strong association with low education does not seem to be the case, probably because lower educated workers may go into agricultural self-employment or underemployment.

The Kyrgyz Republic deserves special attention. It has a 72 per cent rate of LTU (among all unemployed); however, gender differences are not very pronounced. Of course, precision of measurement is questionable, but nevertheless this may mean that almost all unemployment in the country is chronic, hinting at a different nature of unemployment where a significant part is likely to have been inherited from the Soviet past rather than newly generated.[20] Here one should recall once again that before the Soviet Union collapsed, all CARs had significant disguised unemployment, which was especially high in rural areas. This was more similar to agrarian overpopulation of the third world than to the structural labour slump of industrial countries. Such unemployment could not disappear over the first transition years but had to become open. If conventionally measured it may look extremely long-term. We do not have proper data for Uzbekistan so far, but the same assumptions also seem to be valid in this case.[21]

Working shorter time

Expanding part-time employment (PTE) is another manifestation of the growing social segmentation. Even if it does not lead directly to social exclusion, it often stops short of it and directly affects earnings. PTE in its involuntary version (as short-time employment) is a clear signal to workers that they are candidates to be laid-off. Even if it does not end up with firing, PTE brings down wages. Even if it does not lead to unemployment, PTE may be quite persistent over time hitting the same people and effectively 'downgrading' them in terms of their living standards.

Here, as PTE, I consider any employment of a duration less than is standard for the particular country.[22] It includes voluntary part-time and involuntary short-time employment. Voluntary part-time work has expanded since all administrative constraints that existed in the planned economy have been lifted and this option may look attractive to some groups of employees (such as women with young children). The demand for part-time work is met with increasing flexibility of new jobs which offer more opportunities for such work. On the other hand, involuntary short-time work is also rising. This is used as a practice of disguised or delayed layoffs and a form of labour hoarding, when the total costs of keeping someone on the payroll is lower than the total costs of firing. Of course, in many cases the division into voluntary and involuntary underemployment is muted.

From being at a very low level prior to the transition, all types of short-time working have rapidly expanded everywhere. In a few countries, this employment has reached levels higher than in some OECD countries. Table 3.4 provides LFS-based estimates for some countries in our sample. PTE is relatively low in the Czech Republic (complementing low unemployment) with 5.6 per cent of the labour force, but twice as high in other countries for which data are available. Poland has a figure of 10 per cent, while Ukraine shows over 12 per cent and Romania over 14 per cent of the labour force. The table also suggests that PTE among women is higher than among men.

These estimates refer to all underemployment regardless of whether it is voluntary or not. The involuntary portion (though I should repeat here that it is very hard to separate) accounts for about one-sixth of the total PTE. This segment makes up 1–2.5 per cent of the labour force. In Romania (where it reaches 2.5 per cent of the total labour force), it affects men more than women, whilst in the Czech Republic the gender composition is opposite; in Poland, women are affected more but the gender gap is relatively small. Polish underemployment has two particular features, as reported by the OECD. First, it concerns retirees, and second it is much more widespread in agriculture where it has the form of hidden unemployment (OECD, 1998a: 86). (Agriculture-related underemployment is also expected to be high in Romania.)

We may only speculate that underemployment should be very widespread in both the Kyrgyz Republic and Uzbekistan. Both economies are largely agricultural and strongly seasonally dependent. Pomfret and Anderson (1997: 14) cite some examples of large underemployment in Uzbekistan, but I have no hard evidence of underemployment comparable with that in other countries.

Russia and Ukraine present a special case. In both countries, underemployment grew in the 1990s as output was in free-fall while countries tried to avoid open unemployment. Instead of implementing mass layoffs, firms tended to put their personnel on administrative leave or short-time work.[23] The main reason behind this was that firms considered this option economically and socially less costly than formal and legally arranged layoffs. Moreover, the governments provide implicit support to this policy, which allocated adjustment costs among a broader contingent of workers instead of concentrating the costs within a narrower group of the unemployed. However, among those affected, costs of underemployment are distributed very unevenly, being strongly skewed towards the politically less vocal and the economically less competitive.[24]

Some estimates for the scale of involuntary underemployment in Russia and Ukraine can be drawn from Table 3.4, although since they are based on administrative reporting by enterprises the estimates are at best approximate and not completely comparable. The table suggests that underemployment is more widespread in Ukraine than in Russia, but says nothing about the duration of shorter work periods for those affected. Additionally, the same people may be counted more than once. However, this pattern is widespread and deserves special attention since it inhibits industrial restructuring and labour reallocation, and also has direct negative social implications. Workers are partially or fully deprived of their wages, while they have no access to social welfare and employment programmes. Being locked-in in underemployment, they become deskilled and socially marginalized. Such workers may formally keep jobs but look for other sources of income and become involved in secondary and informal employment. It is also important to note that keeping such jobs provides wrong signals to both employees and employers. Employers tend to overestimate the rapidly degrading potential of available human resources, while employees become completely disoriented in regard of their labour market prospects. Finally, the more competitive quit for better jobs, while the less competitive either stay accepting the status quo, or quit to become unemployed or to withdraw from the labour market.

Nevertheless, short-time working on the initiative of administration has its positive side as well. It stretches the time available for adjustment to workers, decreases the likelihood of complete social exclusion and allows them to enjoy some social benefits still linked to enterprises (see Layard and Richter, 1994). This also provides employers with more flexibility. However, the advantages and disadvantages of this strategy are in a very precarious balance.[25] The positive implications are short-term, while negative ones are both mid- and long-term. As the proportion of workers affected grows, the minuses can strongly outweigh the pluses.

For Russia in 1993–96, various household surveys, which are a more reliable measurement instrument than enterprise surveys, estimate the share of those on leave as about 3 per cent and the share of those working shorter hours as 0.1–4 per cent of all employed.[26] The underemployment is concentrated in particular sectors and regions. In Ukraine, these sectors are industry, construction and transport, whilst in Russia underemployment seems to be more concentrated in machine-building and light industry. It is also more widespread in some occupational groups than in others (cf. wage arrears). Our studies suggest that while some groups are employed on a significantly reduced working load, others may suffer from overtime. Thus, highly-skilled welders, lathe operators, among some other blue-collar occupations, were in strong demand against growing underemployment of other categories of personnel (Gimpelson and Lippoldt, 1996).

Social segmentation and wage arrears

Paying wages late and/or incompletely has become a widespread phenomenon in many CIS countries, and particularly in Russia and Ukraine. Wage arrears are a kind of substitute for higher open unemployment, containing wage growth and inflation.[27] They emerge as a byproduct of tighter monetary policy, when it is not supplemented by corresponding microeconomic and legal reforms in fiscal policy, competition, bankruptcy, contract enforcement, and so forth.

From the start of reforms in the early 1990s, the most radical reformers such as Poland and Hungary were ready to accept unemployment as an unavoidable price for successful transition. In some countries, such as Hungary, enterprise arrears emerged in the early 1990s but were rapidly blocked by the new bankruptcy law adapted in 1992. Almost all CIS governments have run arrears. In 1996, the consolidated general government stock of arrears across the CIS ranged from 0.5 per cent of GDP in Azerbaijan to 11 per cent in Moldova. In our sample, this amounted to 4.6 per cent in Ukraine, 3.6 per cent in Uzbekistan, 3.0 per cent in Russia and 0.9 per cent in the Kyrgyz Republic (Ramos, 1998). Since then, wage arrears have been growing. Here could be the right place to remind ourselves that government arrears may constitute only a relatively small part of the total stock of arrears. In Russia, the government accounts for about one-fifth of the total stock of unpaid wages, while four-fifths are due to be paid by the private sector. However, the government is usually the largest single employer and wage debtor, setting norms and incentives for all others.

Interestingly, wage arrears are observed mostly in the countries with piecemeal reforms, slow growth in unemployment and poor enforcement of law. These governments may consider arrears a lesser evil than unemployment. Thus, if high unemployment is expected to moderate wage demands, in 'wage-arrears' countries the same effect is produced by arrears.

Accumulated wage debts are allocated across firms and employees very unevenly, reflecting the position of different groups in the economy, their resources and bargaining power versus other groups of workers, managers and the government. Summing up the evidence available, it appears that most of the arrears are shifted onto the least competitive and politically vocal part of the labour force. In Russia, wage arrears are widespread in sectors experiencing the most difficulty (such as machine-building or the social sector) as well as in those which are doing better (for example, oil and gas, construction, or private firms across all sectors).

In Russia, geography also appears to be a factor; the farther a region is from Moscow, the higher the incidence of accumulated wage debts. In addition, significant intrafirm variation in wage arrears suggests discrimination within firms against those with less bargaining power (Earle and Sabirianova, 1998). All this hints at a kind of efficiency wage strategy pursued by firms. Those workers who are important to the firm are always paid, while others without special skills or lower bargaining power become 'victims of sporadic wage payments'. Better-paid employees have more political clout, since they can quit and move to jobs with lower arrears and higher paid-out wages. Lower-paid workers are concentrated in sectors and jobs offering limited exit options; they are less vocal and more likely to accept payment delays with acquiescence. On the other hand, for the latter group of workers wage arrears bring a much higher probability of poverty and destitution. A similar picture of wage arrears is reported in Uzbekistan (Klugman, 1998: 348–51).

Lower paid employees are denied less in terms of the absolute amount, but significantly more in relative terms. The pattern seems to reflect a redistribution of the wage fund from the less competitive to those more competitive, or from relative losers to relative winners.[28] Suffering from wage arrears also appears to be quite a persistent phenomenon: workers who had faced arrears once, in 1994 for example, had a higher probability of experiencing them again later in 1995 or 1996. This persistent vulnerability can be explained by low personal bargaining power and/or by commitment to an ailing firm or sector.[29]

Paying late or incompletely is also a kind of tax, but it affects households in a different way than inflation. First, most employees experience no delays at all or only short ones. These people are 'tax exempt' and low inflation provides a real gain for them. Second, those who are owed back wages are taxed very unevenly. As noted, most of the wage arrears are very heavily concentrated in particular economic sectors and regions and among certain social groups. More competitive workers have higher wages and lower arrears, while less competitive workers have lower wages and higher arrears. For the latter, however, the choice is between wage arrears and unemployment and they prefer the former. Therefore, they are taxed for disinflation, while others pay little or nothing at all. In these cases, swapping inflation for wage arrears may have exposed them to even more painful hardships than high inflation would have done.

Wage arrears affect stratification differently from unemployment. High unemployment resulting from enterprise closures or mass layoffs affects those more skilled and less skilled, or more competitive and less competitive, to the same degree when an enterprise or a firm become closed or significantly downsized. The fact that the more educated and skilled workers may find another job after a relatively short spell of joblessness does not change the picture. Better placed workers are exposed to the market as well. Wage arrears, however, are much more selective since demand for different groups of workers by an enterprise which is in the red is not completely elastic. Some groups of employees cannot be downsized due to the technology or their bargaining power within the firm. If those who are not needed are still kept on the payroll in spite of a negative balance sheet, they are likely to be paid much less while those who are vital are paid much more. This drives up inequality and relative wages.

Conclusions

Although labour markets are among the major factors affecting social mobility and social reranking in the transition countries, their 'pure' impact is hard to determine and disentangle from other causes. Allocating and reallocating jobs and earnings to various segments of the population, they select individuals weighing their endowments against market demand, and therefore they stratify or restratify societies.

Labour markets change the social structure in multiple ways and through various mechanisms. This chapter has considered some of the most general influences brought by changes in participation and employment, by unemployment and underemployment in the comparative perspective of seven countries. Of course, this set of issues cannot exhaust the problem of interaction between labour markets and social stratification. Almost all countries have experienced significant reductions in participation and employment. The move out of employment reduces earnings which is echoed in downward social reranking. Though labour market withdrawal contains unemployment, it inflicts the same negative social implications. Unemployment has been increasing in most of the countries and a social group of the unemployed has emerged. Gender, age, education, skills and geography affect the probability of becoming unemployed. It is clear that up-to-date human capital embodied in good education and skills is the best unemployment protection and a factor for upward reranking.

Total losses (in terms of both incomes and social position) caused by non-employment are especially large in the case of long-term unemployment, which is a serious contributor to a growing 'underclass'. Expanding PTE is another manifestation of the growing social segmentation. Even if it does not lead directly to exclusion, it often stops short of it and directly affects earnings. If involuntary, PTE signals possible job loss bringing wages down. It can be quite persistent over time hitting the same people and effectively downgrading them in terms of their living standards.

In CIS countries, wage arrears often substitute unemployment in moderating wage claims. The effects are very selective affecting the least competitive and politically vocal part of the labour force. They *de facto* redistribute the labour compensation fund from the less competitive to the more competitive groups of workers and increase inequality.

The combination of the effects discussed in this chapter varies across the countries. One could roughly say that more radical economic policies lead more rapidly to higher unemployment, which then decreases sooner. Less consistent reforms in a 'muddling-through' style delay high unemployment but cannot prevent its gradual, steady and persistent rise. In the latter case, the effects of unemployment on social structures are supplemented by strong influences from underemployment. However, this remains a scheme with a number of outliers. These are the most aggregate conclusions on the issue, the study of which definitely deserves to be continued and enriched by updated and more detailed data sources.

Notes

1 See Kalleberg (1996) for an overview.
2 Szelényi and Treiman's (n.d.) comparative social stratification project is a good example.
3 OECD-CCET Labour Market Database 1990–97. OECD, Paris.
4 RLSMS (1996); Klugman (1998).
5 The data for countries other than Russia are based on flow charts from Boeri and Bruno (1997).
6 This is especially true in the case of LTU.
7 OECD (1998b): 119. However, low wages and pensions as a major cause of poverty dominate.
8 Benefits are relatively generous in the Czech Republic, and were fairly generous in Poland in the early years of transition.
9 In this discussion I use the ILO/OECD definition and data based on standard LFS surveys. It is additionally noted if registered unemployment data are used.
10 OECD (1998a): 81, 150.
11 *Ibid.*: 18.
12 Affinity between these two countries is apparent in many other policy instruments and outcomes; for example, wage arrears.
13 Ukranian Economic Trends (1998). See also Ukraine (1999).
14 This estimate is from RLSMS (1996). Kuddo reports the rate of 5 per cent with reference to a World Bank survey. The IMF country report (1998b) refers to a World Bank estimate that unemployment is as high as 18 per cent in rural and 21 per cent in urban areas.
15 Social Policy Strategy (1998).
16 Estimates of emigration from Kyrgyzstan are provided in Chapter 11.
17 See articles by Gimpelson and Lippoldt, and Kapelyushnikov in *Labour Market Dynamics in the Russian Federation*. For Ukraine, see Ukrainian Economic Trends (1998).
18 OECD (1998a): 82–3.
19 OECD (1998c): 79.
20 The fact that unemployment varies from 4 to 20 per cent depending on the measurement is an additional argument for claiming 'another' type of unemployment.
21 The same type of unemployment is experienced in some Russian regions located in the Northern Caucasus.
22 See OECD (1997).
23 There is much literature discussing this type of underemployment; for example, Layard and Richter (1994), Standing (1997), Kapelyushnikov (1999).
24 Here, the pattern observed is the same as in the case of wage arrears.
25 All this is valid in the case of wage arrears policy as well.
26 Cited from Kapelyushnikov (1999): 43.
27 For more on wage arrears see Earle and Sabirianova (1998), Desai and Idson (1998), Lehmann *et al.* (1999), Gimpelson (1998), Klugman (1998).
28 Actual or absolute winners are managers and entrepreneurs who do not suffer from non-payments of their wages or incomes.
29 These two reasons often coincide.

References

Blanchflower, D. (1991) 'Fear, Unemployment and Pay Flexibility', *The Economic Journal*, 101 (May).

Boeri, T. (1994) '"Transitional" Unemployment', *Economics of Transition*, 2(1).

—— (1998) 'Labour Market Flows in the Midst of the Structural Change', in S. Commander (ed.), *Enterprise Restructuring and Unemployment in Models of Transition*. Washington DC: EDI, World Bank.

—— and R. Bruno (1997) 'A Short Note on the Characteristics of Labour Turnover in Central and Eastern Europe', in Lippoldt (1997).

——, M. Burda and J. Kollo (1998) *Mediating the Transition: Labour Markets in Central and Eastern Europe*. London: CEPR-Institute for East–West Studies.

Commander, S. and A. Tolstopyatenko (1997) 'Unemployment, Restructuring and the Pace of Transition', in S. Zecchini (ed.), *Lessons From the Economic Transition*. Paris: OECD and Netherlands: Kluwer.

Desai, P. and T. Idson (1998) 'The Wage Arrears Crisis in Russia', mimeo, Columbia University.

Earle, J. (1998) *Industrial Decline and Labour Reallocation in Romania*. SITE Working Papers, Stockholm, no. 125.

—— and K. Sabirianova (1998) 'Wage Arrears in Russia: An Exploration of Causes and Consequences', mimeo, SITE, Stockholm.

European Bank for Reconstruction and Development (EBRD) (1998) *Transition Report 1998: Financial sector in transition*. London: EBRD.

Fleck, V. and J. Večerník (1998) 'Employment and Wage Structures in the Czech Republic', mimeo, Prague.

Gimpelson, V. (1996) 'Dismissed Workers in the Labour Market: Job Search and Social Adjustment', in *Creation of Labour Market and Social Mobility in Russia*. Moscow: IMEMO.

—— (1998) *Politics of Labour Market Adjustment*, Discussion Paper no. 54, Collegium Budapest.

—— and D. Lippoldt (1996) *Labour Restructuring in Russian Enterprises. A Case Study*. Paris: OECD

—— and —— (1997) 'Labour Turnover in the Russian Federation', in Lippoldt (1997).

Habich, R. and Z. Speder (1998) *Winners and Losers. Transformational Outcomes in a Comparative Context*, Discussion Paper no. 56, Collegium Budapest.

IMF (1998a) 'Republic of Uzbekistan: Recent Economic Developments', *IMF Staff Country Report 98/116*, Washington DC: IMF (October).

—— (1998b) 'Kyrgyz Republic – Recent Economic Developments', *IMF Staff Country Report 98/08*, Washington DC: IMF.

Jackson, M., J. Koltay and W. Biesbrouck (eds) (1995) *Unemployment and Evolving Labour Markets in Central and Eastern Europe*. Avebury: Ashgate.

Kalleberg, A. (1996) 'Changing Contexts of Careers: Trends in Labour Market Structures and Some Implications for Labour Force Outcomes', in A. Kerckhoff (ed.), *Generating Social Stratification: Toward a New Research Agenda*. Boulder: Westview Press.

Kapelyushnikov, R. (1999) 'Russian Labour Market: Adjustment Without Restructuring', in V. Martynov *et al.* (eds) *Issues on Theory of the Transition*. Moscow: IMEMO (in Russian).

Klugman, J. (1998) 'Wages in Transition: the Case of Uzbekistan', PhD thesis, Australian National University, December.

Layard, R. and A. Richter (1994) 'Labour Market Adjustment in Russia', *Russian Economic Trends*, 3(2).

Lehmann, H., J. Wadsworth and A. Acquisti (1999) 'Grime and Punishment: Job Insecurity and Wage Arrears in the Russian Federation', *IZA Discussion Paper* no. 65, IZA, Bonn, October.

Lippoldt, D. (ed.) (1997) *Labour Market Dynamics in the Russian Federation.* Paris: OECD.

Organization for Economic Cooperation and Development (OECD) (1997) *Short-term Economic Indicators: Transition Economies*, Supplement no. 4, Paris: OECD.

—— (1998a) *Economic Surveys, Poland.* Paris: OECD.

—— (1998b) *Economic Surveys, Romania.* Paris: OECD.

—— (1998c) *Economic Surveys, The Czech Republic.* Paris: OECD.

Pomfret, R. and K. H. Anderson (1997) 'Uzbekistan: Welfare Impact of Slow Transition', *UNU/WIDER Working Papers* no. 135, Helsinki: UNU/WIDER, June.

Ramos, A. (1998) 'Government Expenditure Arrears: Securitization and Other Solutions', *IMF Working Paper* WP/98/70, May.

RLSMS (1996) *Report on the Living Standards Measurement Survey*, Natstatcom, Kyrgyz Republic and Research Triangle Institute (Fall) (unpublished).

Rychard, A. (1996) 'In Search Of "Winning Losers"', *Social Research*, 63(2) (Summer).

Social Policy Strategy (1998) *Social Policy Strategy: Labour Market, Employment and Social Assistance.* Bishkek, Ministry of Labour and Social Protection (in Russian).

Standing, G. (1997) *Russian Unemployment and Enterprise Restructuring: Reviving Dead Souls*, ILO Study Series.

Szelényi, I. and D. J. Treiman (n.d.) Social Stratification in Eastern Europe After 1989: General Population Survey. Available from http://archiv.soc.cas.cz/SSEE.

Ukraine (1999) *Country Employment Policy Review.* Geneva: ILO.

Ukranian Economic Trends (1998) September (via website).

4

Winners of the Reforms: The New Economic and Political Elite

Iván Szelényi and Christy Glass

Introduction

The transition to capitalism in the Former Soviet Union (FSU) and its former satellites has some new – even unique – elements when compared to similar transitions on other sites and at other historic periods. One unique feature, and perhaps the most important, is that now capitalism is emerging out of state socialism, out of a socioeconomic order where individual private ownership was outlawed and where the institution of individual private property did not exist. In all other historical instances known to us, the institution of individual private property and a class of private proprietors were in place within the wombs of the old societies when capitalism emerged. A class of private owners composed of former feudal lords, *nouveaux riches* former artisans, serfs, adventurers and even outlaws, shared a material interest in fostering the institutions of a market economy. In former state socialist societies, however, no such class of individuals can be identified. For the first time in history *capitalism is being made without capitalists*.

As state socialism began to crumble, lively theoretical controversies emerged concerning the potential beneficiaries of the transition from socialism to capitalism and about the fate of the old communist elite. Issues concerning the potential for, as well as the possible origins of, a new class of entrepreneurs and private proprietors were actively and theoretically debated. In this chapter we present three competing theories offered in this debate and will offer a fourth theory that attempts to synthesize the previous three:

1 The first theory to emerge regarding the question of a new class of private owners was the *political capitalism theory*. In its original formulation, political capitalism suggested that post-communist society was likely to emerge as a form of political capitalism, in which the former

communist nomenklatura would establish themselves as a new grand bourgeoisie. This theory assumed that those who possessed the most valued form of capital – namely, political capital – under socialism, would likely convert political capitalism with ease into economic capital in the post-socialist transition.

2 This view was challenged by *market transition theory*, which posited that the power of former 'redistributors' would decline as markets expanded. A class of new entrepreneur-owners, recruited from a newly emerging group of actors – some who started businesses in the socialist second economy – would increase in size and power as the transition developed. This theory assumed that the transition to market economy would devalue political capital and that those endowed with human capital – the form of capital most likely to gain in importance with the expansion of markets – would be in the best position to accumulate economic capital.

As the transition from socialism to capitalism unfolded, both of these theories appeared somewhat simplistic – apparently not all former communists did so well in the transition and many of the proto-entrepreneurs of the late socialist epoch had great difficulties adapting to the new economic conditions:

3 Reflecting on these developments during the 1990s, a modified version of the political capitalism theory emerged, which we will refer to here as the *technocratic-managerial class theory*. According to this theory, the former nomenklatura as a whole did not emerge as a new grand bourgeoisie. Instead, it was the technocratic and managerial faction of the old nomenklatura that successfully used privatization to enrich itself. According to the technocratic-managerial class theory, this faction of the old communist elite acted as a 'cleptocratura', meaning that this group used management buy-outs in order to transform public property under its control into individual private wealth. This theory implied that political capital was indeed the source of economic capital for this group, but only under certain circumstances. Those who were well-endowed with political capital also had to be well-endowed with human capital in order to accumulate economic capital.

4 The primary goal of this chapter is to develop a synthesis of these theories. As in the theories reviewed above, our own *theory of post-communist managerialism* assumes that with the transition to capitalism a class of private proprietors is in the making. We question, however, what we regard as rather unilinear, monocausal, and teleological explanations provided by the three previous theories. We operate under three key assumptions. First, the transitions do not simply proceed from public to individual private ownership – a complex and possibly unique combination of

> property rights characterizes post-communist economic systems. Given the existence of recombinant property forms, power is not always based on ownership and, as a result, the technocratic-managerial elite often exercise power that is not rooted in any form of identifiable individual ownership. Second, as a result of the first assumption, the power of a dominant elite may be based on a combination of cultural and social, rather than economic, capital. Third, in the portrait gallery of the post-communist new bourgeoisie, more than one picture is on display. The 'cleptocratic' *nouveau riche* is undoubtedly one of them. The non-owner manager, who plays the game of recombinant property and exploits the subterranean redistribution from state agencies, is yet another. There are also 'self-made' individuals, who start with a small business that grows large, that appear among this group.[1] And, finally, there are compadre intellectuals who, rather than acquiring ownership for themselves in the businesses they manage, act as agents of foreign investors. Such individuals often seek well-paid and relatively secure managerial positions in foreign-owned companies, rather than risk their fortunes by purchasing run-down formerly state-owned enterprises (SOEs).

We conclude this chapter with a guided tour through this portrait gallery using data from the only multicountry survey of elite circulation and reproduction, collected by Szelényi and Treiman in 1993. We try to demonstrate that while each of the three previous theories offers important insights, the theory of post-communist managerialism provides the best fit to the data at our disposal.

The theory of political capitalism: from the nomenklatura to the new grand bourgeoisie

In 1988–89, Jadwiga Staniszkis and Elemer Hankiss offered an innovative set of hypotheses concerning the anticipated transformation of the state socialist social structure. Both suggested that the communist nomenklatura would use its political office to convert public property into individual private property and would establish itself as a new grand bourgeoisie. This position gained a great deal of attention and eventually became known as the theory of political capitalism.[2]

Hankiss and Staniszkis noticed that during the 1980s in Hungary and Poland, the nomenklatura began to build bridges towards a private economy. This process took place on multiple fronts. First, the nomenklatura began to accumulate capital in the sphere of consumption, mainly in the real estate market, which had experienced a major boom during the 1970s and 1980s. The nomenklatura literally sold themselves construction sites at highly subsidized prices and built private housing for themselves and for their families, all with extraordinary capital gain. As Péter Mihályi pointed out, by the time communism collapsed, substantial potential capital had already been accumulated in the non-productive sphere of the economy, and most of the convertible non-productive capital was in the hands of the former nomenklatura.[3] Thus, a major redistribution of national wealth was underway outside the productive sphere well before the fall of communism.

As early as 1982, Hankiss posited that market reform was likely to benefit the communist cadres and intellectuals much more than ordinary citizens (Hankiss, [1982] 1986; see also Manchin and Szelényi, 1987). At this time, some cadres also began to move out of the political sphere in order to create business 'niches' for themselves (Kryshtanovskaya and White, 1996: 716–21). Before 1988, the result was not the establishment of private firms *per se*, but the establishment of 'public ventures' with obscure property rights.[4] The big breakthrough in economic reform began in 1988, when the initial moves were underway to begin the 'privatization' of public firms (Windolf, 1998b: 344–50). Legislation was being prepared to create a system of 'spontaneous privatization' – a system that would enable nomenklatura and, in particular, managers to convert public property into private ownership.[5]

In summary, the theory of political capitalism suggested that the nomenklatura (a 'grand' coalition of party and state cadres and economic managers) would use political office to convert public goods into private wealth and would convert itself into a new grand bourgeoisie. The political capitalism theory predicted that:

> *Hypothesis 1* (hereinafter H1). Those who were incumbents of political office before the fall of communism were the most likely to become members of the new propertied bourgeoisie; and
>
> *Hypothesis 2* (hereinafter H2). Their political capital (as measured by party membership) will be converted into economic capital without major constraints, thus party membership in 1988 should be a good predictor of who will find themself in the command positions of the new economic system.

Market transition theory

In 1989, Victor Nee published a path-breaking article in the *American Sociological Review* (Nee, 1989) on the social dynamics and consequences of transition from socialism to market capitalism.[6] Based on data from China, Nee hypothesized that the expansion of the market would reduce redistributive power and that 'direct producers' would benefit from the transition. Nee suggested that the transition from redistribution to markets was likely to increase the return on human capital. Nee further argued that privileges based solely on the possession of political capital would decline in importance. In summary market transition theory predicted that:

Hypothesis 3 (hereinafter H3). Those in elite positions before the fall of communism were likely to be downwardly mobile during post-communism;

Hypothesis 4 (hereinafter H4). Formerly non-elite members would be overrepresented among the new propertied class in the new economic elite; and

Hypothesis 5 (hereinafter H5). Party membership was likely to be a handicap and education would be the predictor of success – especially economic success – in the emergent market economies.

The technocratic-managerial class theory: management buy-out as the road to convert public property into private ownership by the managerial elite ('cleptocratura')

During the 1990s a new theoretical approach – referred to here as the technocratic-managerial class theory – was gaining ground. At this time it appeared that the political capitalism thesis had overstated how advantageous market transition would be for the nomenklatura as a whole. In addition, market transition theory had failed to explain the advantages enjoyed by the technocratic-managerial elites. This new wave of theorizing paid closer attention to the internal differentiation within the nomenklatura (Lane, 1997, 1999) and identified the managerial-technocratic elite as the major beneficiary of the transition.

The technocratic-managerial class theory suggested that the bureaucratic faction of the nomenklatura would likely lose as a result of transition. The theory further predicted that the technocratic-managerial elite would likely succeed in appropriating vast amounts of public wealth and in establishing itself as a new grand bourgeoisie – or, put another way, as a 'cleptocratura'.

Interestingly, during the 1980s some commentators had foreshadowed the hypothesis that the technocratic-managerial elite would be the driving force behind the making of post-communist capitalism. The clearest formulation of this idea came from Erzsébet Szalai (1981, 1989a, 1991). Szalai, a scholar of the economic behaviour of large firms, noticed that management had begun to appropriate property rights. While Hankiss emphasized the collaboration between the bureaucracy and technocracy, Szalai demonstrated their conflicting interests. In her agenda-setting article titled 'The New Elite' (Szalai, 1989b), she suggested that the technocratic faction of the nomenklatura would defeat the old bureaucratic guard to become the new ruling elite. Her prediction was soon realized in Hungary where, following two decades of intense struggle between the old guard and the new elite, the new elite was free to pursue its pro-capitalist policies (Baylis, 1994: 325).

A similar analysis – although one with quite different political implications – was presented by Andrea Szegö (1983, 1985). Szegö was one of the most interesting and most controversial analysts of the 1980s, belonging to the 'left opposition' and seen by reform communists and dissidents as a 'Stalinist'. (Ironically, since she was seen as a 'left-wing deviationist' she never gained admittance into the Communist Party.) Szegö believed that the old communist guard was no longer in command and that the technocratic-managerial elite was in control. While Szegö did not to spell out the full implications of her analysis, it was rather clear that she saw the market socialism project as an attempt to restore capitalism. In retrospect, we cannot recall anyone in the East European social science literature who saw as clearly as did Szegö the way reform communism was heading.

Roman Frydman *et al.* (1993, 1996) formulated the technocratic-managerial class theory the most forcefully. This position was also supported by Akos Rona-Tas (1998) and Andrew Walder (1995, 1996), both of whom were vitriolic critics of market transition theory (Rona-Tas, 1998: 111–13). According to the technocratic-managerial class theory, members of enterprise management and other members of the technocracy would use their networks to turn public property into private wealth (Kryshtanovskaya and White, 1996: 716–21). Thus, in Frydman's terminology, they would constitute themselves as a 'cleptocratura'. Böröcz and Rona-Tas (1995) added one more qualification to this proposition: the new economic elite was likely to emerge from the middle-strata of the former socialist management.

The technocratic-managerial class theory assumed that:

> *Hypothesis 6* (hereinafter H6). Former technocratic-managerial cadres were the most likely to constitute the new propertied class and to establish themselves in the command positions of the new economic order; and
>
> *Hypothesis 7* (hereinafter H7). They will use their social networks and former political capital to achieve this rather than their human capital, thus the theory expected that the interaction term between former technocratic cadre position and party membership should be positive and highly significant.

Toward a synthesis: recombinant property and the theory of post-communist managerialism – multiple actors and multiple destinations as capitalism is made without capitalists

The theories reviewed above changed and unfolded as the history of state socialism and post-communism changed and unfolded. Before the 1980s, it was not obvious that communism would fall and, if and when it ever did, it was not clear that these societies would revert to capitalism. Even those who considered the possibility of capitalist reform did not believe that reform would converge with the model of capitalism from the advanced West (hence, the various theories of *state* capitalism). However, as socialism began to disintegrate some two decades ago, it became increasingly obvious that post-communist countries would attempt to build capitalism by design (Offe, 1991). The aim quickly turned to the creation of a carbon copy of capitalism as we know it from Western Europe or the USA, with analogous property and class relations.

David Stark, in his work on recombinant property (Stark, 1996), changed this debate in interesting ways. Stark suggested that the emergent property form was as different from socialist collective ownership as it was from individual private property. According to Stark, this form was neither 'collective', nor 'private individual' property but a 'recombination' of the two. Just as he had in his earlier work (Stark, 1992), he argued that capitalism would not be built *on* the ruins of socialism, but *with* the ruins of socialism.

The theory of post-communist managerialism is the flip side of the theory of recombinant property. While Stark offered an analysis of the economic institutions of post-communism, post-communist managerialism focuses on agents who occupy the command positions within these institutions and, hence, on class structure. Like Stark's theory of recombinant property, post-communist managerialism assumes that private property (including individual private property) and a class of propertied bourgeoisie are in the making.

Issues that remain to be explored include whether individual private property is already dominant (or whether it will ever become dominant), whether a propertied bourgeoisie already exists, and whether members of such a bourgeoisie will ever be dominant economic actors of these formerly socialist societies. More specifically, post-communist managerialism hypothesizes that the composition of the new dominant class is still a highly contested terrain; the principles governing the legitimacy of power remain to be decided. Property ownership and the possession of cultural and social capital are alternative sources of power and privilege, and those who possess these assets are still engaged in an intense social struggle over what should legitimate power in these societies. Some actors can gain power and privilege without acquiring individual private property by climbing up the social ladder on the basis of their social or cultural capital alone – exercising managerial power rather than power of ownership, for example. The new class of proprietors can come from various social backgrounds; political capital can be a vehicle to accumulate wealth, but there is no reason to assume that cultural or social capital cannot do the same. Thus, according to the theory of post-communist managerialism:

Hypothesis 8 (hereinafter H8). Cultural capital as measured by educational credentials may play an equal or more important role than political capital measured by party membership; and

Hypothesis 9 (hereinafter H9). individuals with cultural capital who were not members of any elite group before the fall of communism have equal or better chances to enter into new elite positions than those who were members of the communist elite.

Adjudicating among competing theories – some empirical evidence

Data

In 1993, we conducted extensive survey research on elites in five former communist countries: Russia, Poland, the Czech Republic, Hungary and Bulgaria. In each country we established a list of those individuals who, in 1988, were on the lists of 'central nomenklatura' positions (thus, those who were in positions that typically required the approval of the Central Committee of the Communist Party). We also established a list of analogous positions for 1993. Using these lists, we drew a random sample of the incumbents of these positions from 1988 and 1993. This sample included approximately 1000 respondents from the old and new elites (this represents approximately 10–30 per cent of all top-ranking individuals since we were focusing on the top 3–10,000 positions in each country). In other words, we have a rather clear view of the occupational destination of those who were at the very top in 1988 occupational origins of those who were on the top positions in 1993. With this database, we are in a better position than anyone else to provide answers to questions about elite circulation and reproduction during market transition.

The tables summarize our most basic findings.[7] First, we look at outflow tables, and Tables 4.1–4.5 show the occupational destination of the old nomenklatura.

Table 4.1 Occupational destinations in 1993 of people who were in economic and political nomenklatura positions in 1988 in Bulgaria

Occupation in 1993	Occupation in 1988		
	Economic elite	Political elite	Other
Economic elite	73.17	25.62	26.95
Political elite	5.50	26.74	17.68
Other	21.33	47.64	55.38
All (*n*)	100% (600)	100% (445)	100% (809)

Table 4.2 Occupational destinations in 1993 of people who were in economic and political nomenklatura positions in 1988 in the Czech Republic

Occupation in 1993	Occupation in 1988		
	Economic elite	Political elite	Other
Economic elite	85.85	22.15	61.93
Political elite	4.52	25.32	16.43
Other	9.63	52.53	21.64
All (*n*)	100% (1173)	100% (158)	100% (633)

Table 4.3 Occupational destinations in 1993 of people who were in economic and political nomenklatura positions in 1988 in Hungary

Occupation in 1993	Occupation in 1988		
	Economic elite	Political elite	Other
Economic elite	74.61	20.09	30.47
Political elite	3.77	35.90	12.68
Other	21.63	44.02	56.85
All (*n*)	100% (823)	100% (234)	100% (686)

Table 4.4 Occupational destinations in 1993 of people who were in economic and political nomenklatura positions in 1988 in Poland

Occupation in 1993	Occupation in 1988		
	Economic elite	Political elite	Other
Economic elite	79.07	23.50	23.24
Political elite	5.17	27.82	25.59
Other	15.76	48.68	51.17
All (*n*)	100% (793)	100% (417)	100% (555)

Table 4.5 Occupational destinations in 1993 of people who were in economic and political nomenklatura positions in 1988 in Russia

Occupation in 1993	Occupation in 1988		
	Economic elite	Political elite	Other
Economic elite	83.83	36.94	30.74
Political elite	9.41	48.95	15.37
Other	6.77	14.11	53.89
All (*n*)	100% (606)	100% (666)	100% (540)

Tables 4.6–4.10 show the occupational history for those who were in elite positions in 1993. In this data analysis, we focused only on those who were in political or economic elite occupations in 1988 and 1993. We did not, however, investigate those who were leaders in the field of culture or those who were in elected positions in 1988 or 1993.[8] The dataset we used does contain information on cultural elite and elected officials, but for the purposes of this chapter we excluded such individuals from our analysis and focused exclusively on political officials and economic managers. Finally, Table 4.11 offers results from a multinominal logistic regression analysis.

Table 4.6 Occupational origins in 1988 of members of the new economic and political elites in 1993 in Bulgaria

Occupation in 1988	Occupation in 1993		
	New economic	New political	Other
Economic elite	56.94	11.19	16.24
Political elite	14.79	40.34	26.90
Other	28.27	48.47	56.85
All (*n*)	100% (771)	100% (295)	100% (788)

Table 4.7 Occupational origins in 1988 of members of the new economic and political elites in 1993 in the Czech Republic

Occupation in 1988	Occupation in 1993		
	New economic	New political	Other
Economic elite	70.22	26.90	33.93
Political elite	2.44	20.30	24.92
Other	27.34	52.79	41.14
All (*n*)	100% (1434)	100% (197)	100% (333)

Table 4.8 Occupational origins in 1988 of members of the new economic and political elites in 1993 in Hungary

Occupation in 1988	Occupation in 1993		
	New economic	New political	Other
Economic elite	70.57	15.35	26.53
Political elite	5.40	41.58	15.35
Other	24.02	43.07	58.12
All (*n*)	100% (870)	100% (202)	100% (671)

Table 4.9 Occupational origins in 1988 of members of the new economic and political elites in 1993 in Poland

Occupation in 1988	Occupation in 1993		
	New economic	New political	Other
Economic elite	73.42	13.71	20.42
Political elite	11.48	38.80	33.17
Other	15.11	47.49	46.41
All (*n*)	100% (854)	100% (299)	100% (612)

Table 4.10 Occupational origins in 1988 of members of the new economic and political elites in 1993 in Russia

Occupation in 1988	Occupation in 1993		
	New economic	New political	Other
Economic elite	55.22	12.23	9.62
Political elite	26.74	69.96	22.07
Other	18.04	17.81	68.31
All (*n*)	100% (920)	100% (466)	100% (426)

Table 4.11 Effects of parameters for a model of the determinants of elite membership, 1993

Variables	Economic elite 1993		Political elite 1993	
	Logits (*b*)	Odds multiplier (*e*^*b*)	Logits (*b*)	Odds multiplier (*e*^*b*)
Economic elite 1988	2.841	17.133	0.457	1.579
	(0.143)		(0.229)	
	0.000		*0.046*	
Political elite 1988	0.839	2.314	1.475	4.371
	(0.158)		(0.170)	
	0.000		*0.000*	
Female	–0.473	0.623	–0.968	0.380
	(0.126)		(0.170)	
	0.000		*0.000*	
Age	0.087	1.091	0.072	1.075
	(0.003)		(0.004)	
	0.000		*0.000*	
University degree	0.705	2.024	0.439	1.551
	(0.140)		(0.173)	
	0.000		*0.011*	

Table 4.11 (Continued)

Variables	Economic elite 1993		Political elite 1993	
	Logits (*b*)	**Odds multiplier (*e*^*b*)**	**Logits (*b*)**	**Odds multiplier (*e*^*b*)**
Communist Party membership	0.563 (0.096) *0.000*	1.756	1.191 (0.116) *0.000*	3.290
Father's Communist Party membership	0.254 (0.064) *0.000*	1.289	0.284 (0.078) *0.000*	1.328
Bulgaria	0.202 (0.142) *0.155*	1.224	0.371 (0.184) *0.044*	1.449
Czech Republic	0.902 (0.098) *0.000*	2.465	0.601 (0.133) *0.000*	1.824
Poland	–0.005 (0.090) *0.952*	0.995	0.235 (0.117) *0.046*	1.265
Russia	0.971 (0.098) *0.000*	2.641	1.359 (0.119) *0.000*	3.892
1988 Political elite status and Communist Party membership	–0.530 (0.274) *0.053*	0.589	–0.589 (0.242) *0.015*	0.555
1988 Economic elite status and Communist Party membership	0.063 (0.167) *0.705*	1.065	0.642 (0.222) *0.004*	1.900
1988 Political elite status and sex	–0.435 (0.264) *0.100*	0.647	0.898 (0.251) *0.000*	2.455
1988 Economic elite status and sex	–0.146 (0.199) *0.464*	0.864	–0.362 (0.396) *0.361*	0.696
1988 Political elite status and education	–0.042 (0.173) *0.806*	0.959	0.241 (0.178) *0.174*	1.273
1988 Economic elite status and education	–0.423 (0.149) *0.005*	0.655	–0.126 (0.232) *0.586*	0.882
Intercept	(0.221) *0.000*	–5.313	(0.271) *0.000*	–5.473

Notes: 'Other' is the control group; standard error in parentheses; *p*-values in italics. *n* = 9138. *Pseudo R^2* = 2246.

Findings

Tables 4.1–4.5 show the types of jobs held in 1993 by those who held elite positions in 1988. The first two lines in Table 4.11 offers further evidence from a multinomial logistic regression model concerning the likelihood of survival for the old nomenklatura. These data offer a good opportunity to test the theory of political capitalism and to contrast this theory's explanatory power against the theories of market transition and technocratic-managerial class.

First, did the old nomenklatura transform itself into a grand bourgeoisie as was predicted by the theory of political capitalism? The data indicate that Staniszkis and Hankiss spotted a genuine trend. Despite the dramatic events of 1989 in all post-communist countries, those individuals who held nomenklatura positions in 1988 were more likely to remain in elite positions in 1993 than to exit the elite altogether. In Table 4.11, the four coefficients in the first two lines are all positive, three are significant, and one shows very substantial evidence of reproduction. The descriptive statistics in Tables 4.1–4.5 are consistent with these results as well. Overall, ignoring cross-country differences and differences among various factions of the elite, those individuals who were in the elite in 1988 did not fare poorly at all as a result of the collapse of communism. This, however, is not sufficient to claim support for the overall theory of political capitalism. The political capitalism thesis predicted that communist apparatchiks would be the big winners of reform (see H1). Furthermore, the theory predicted that the mechanism with which the former elite would achieve this post-communist victory would be their ability to use political power to accumulate private wealth and their ability to convert political capital into economic capital (see H2).

Constrained by these specifications, the theory of political capitalism faces considerable trouble against the data. First, in Bulgaria, Hungary and Poland there is evidence of substantial turbulence at the top of the social hierarchy – especially among members of the political elite – an outcome that actually contradicts H1. In fact, when weighed against the data, the political capitalism theory fares quite poorly. Contrary to the expectation of political capitalism theory, there is evidence of a massive outflow from the 1988 political elite in every country with the exception of Russia (Higley and Pakulski, 1995). About half of those who were in top political, Party or state jobs in 1988 were out of elite positions in 1993 (Baylis, 1998: 276–80). Many of these individuals retired, others moved into minor jobs and those who did manage to maintain their elite positions are, for the most part, equally split between elite positions in economics and politics. Indeed, if you were a high communist cadre in former-socialist Central and Southern Europe, survival was not a simple game. In fact, the degree of outflow from the political elite is more consistent with market transition theory and H3 than with the political capitalism thesis and H1.

In addition, the data cast doubt upon the accuracy of H2. As Table 4.11 indicates, party membership in 1988 helps to explain elite membership in 1993 (see line 6 in Table 4.11). However, the effect of party membership is not particularly strong in predicting survival among the economic elite and the effect of membership is actually weaker than the effect of education. Thus political capital mattered, but for selection into the new economic elite it was less important than other factors, such as cultural capital. This finding is all the more formidable considering that there was and is little variance in the level of education among elite members either in 1988 and 1993 – the overwhelming majority had or have university degrees. As indicated in Table 4.11, the interaction between membership in the 1988 political elite and membership is, in fact, negative. Though the coefficient is not significant, this outcome suggests that among those few individuals who were in the political elite in 1988 but who were *not* party members may have actually had a better chance to attain a position in the 1993 economic elite.

If, on the other hand, the current transition does not completely bring down the house-of-cards of state socialism, the predictions of the political capitalism theory may yet prove to be accurate. Indeed, in those countries where the shift from communism to capitalism has been relatively slow, such as in Russia, the political capitalism thesis has greater explanatory power. In fact, the political capitalism theory works quite well for Russia. Only 14 per cent of the 1988 political elite are no longer in elite positions by 1993 (Lane, 1997; 1999: 143–66). While the economy is not the main destination for former members of the Russian political elite, there is a substantial inflow from the 1988 political elite into 1993 economic elite positions. In fact, in Russia, 37 per cent of those who were in high-ranking political jobs in 1988 were in high-ranking economic positions in 1993.

While the political capitalism theory offers some insights, its predictions concerning the destination of the former communist nomenklatura were overdrawn in three key areas. First, there was substantial variation among various factions of the elite. For example, there was much more reproduction among the economic than the political faction of the elite. This outcome was not predicted by the theory of political capitalism and, to some extent, actually contradicts the tenets of the theory. After all, if political office had been manipulated for the accumulation of individual private wealth, one would expect that political office-holders would do better in transition than economic managers. Instead, our descriptive statistics and our multinominal logit model show that reproduction was higher among managers than among political office holders. This finding supports H6 of the technocratic managerial class theory rather than H1 of the political capitalism theory.

Second, Tables 4.1–4.5 show substantial downward mobility, particularly among high-ranking communist political cadres – a finding that is not at all consistent with the political capitalism theory. The substantial downward mobility for those who were in the 1988 political elite offers limited support for market transition theory because this finding is more consistent with H3 than with H1.

Finally, there is substantial cross-country variation in terms of the occupational destination of the 1988 political elite. Russia shows the highest rate of reproduction; the Russian political elite had a better chance to survive the transition and switch over into economic elite positions than in any other country. In other words, H1 works well for Russia, but a combination of H3 and H6 best applies to the rest of the countries in our survey. Thus, at least in terms of the destination of the former communist elite, market transition and technocratic-managerial class theories seem to offer a better fit to this data than the political capitalism theory.

What are the relative strengths and weaknesses of market transition and the technocratic-managerial class theses? Market transition theory was vigorously attacked for a number of reasons. Among many critics of this theory, both Rona-Tas (1994) and Walder (1995, 1996) suggested that market transition theory underestimated the continuity in personnel at the top of the social hierarchy between communism and post-communism. As Rona-Tas argued: it is not the last that becomes the first, but the first that remains the first. Walder, in his ground-breaking article published in 1996, further suggested that the nomenklatura could not be treated as a unitary phenomenon. He argued that there were two career trajectories for former nomenklatura: while those in bureaucratic positions might suffer, those who were 'experts' rather than 'reds' were likely to do well.

While the criticisms of Rona-Tas and Walder seem appropriate, our data offer some support for market transition theory. First, among the three theories, only the market transition thesis offered a theory of downward mobility of political cadres (see H3), which is well-supported by the data in Tables 4.1–4.5. Second, both political capitalism and technocratic-managerial class theories emphasized the convertibility of political capital and the crucial importance of social capital and social networks in the process of capital accumulation. Only market transition theory predicted that cultural capital would become more important than social or political capital in the transition period (see H5). Our data do not support the hypothesis that former political capital became a handicap in the transition period because, in fact, party membership was positively and significantly associated with 1993 elite membership. However, the results presented in Table 4.11 support the claim that cultural capital was more important than political capital at least in terms of recruitment into economic elite positions (compare lines 5 and 6 in Table 4.11). Other analyses also support these findings (Hanley and Szelenyi, 2001). Overall, education 'steals the show' when the task is to explain who is likely to avoid unemployment and/or early retirement and who is likely to end up in the top income bracket during market transition.[9]

Finally, previous analyses have provided H4 with empirical support (Hanley, 1997). For example, there is evidence that a family history of entrepreneurship and participation in the second economy during communism are important predictors of entrepreneurial activity in the post-communist period. Such evidence may not be sufficient to pave the road to a new grand bourgeoisie, but such factors are certainly major mechanisms that facilitate petty embourgeoisement.[10] It is also important to add that there is also evidence that former cadres benefited disproportionately from privatization (Kryshtanovskaya and White, 1996: 716–21). Once privatization is complete, however, it remains to be seen whether the new bourgeoisie will do well in genuinely competitive markets (Eyal *et al.*, 1998: 177–86).

We do not dismiss the criticism of market transition theory offered by Rona-Tas and Walder, however. Indeed, market transition theory did not predict the fact that former elite members were clearly privileged in terms of recruitment into the new economic elite. Tables 4.6–4.10 and line 1 in Table 4.11 offer strong support for the technocratic-managerial class theory, and in particular for H6. Arguably, the single most powerful finding presented here is that members of the 1988 economic elite were approximately *17 times* more likely than others to be members of the 1993 economic elite. Furthermore, this theory is also supported by two interaction terms in Table 4.11. First, support for technocratic-managerial class theory is provided by the interaction between 1988 economic elite membership and party membership (which was positively associated with 1993 economic elite membership just as H7 predicted it would be). Second, the interaction between 1988 economic elite membership and cultural capital was negatively associated with 1993 economic elite membership – a finding that is also consistent with H7.

The technocratic-managerial class theory accurately predicted that middle-aged members of the technocratic intelligentsia would be, beyond doubt, the biggest winners of transition (Steen, 1997: 107–11). There is little doubt that the thesis on market transition overemphasized the circulation of elites, underestimated the enduring importance of political capital, and did not account for the exceptionally strong tendency for members of the managerial elite to retain economic command positions. The technocratic-managerial class theory accurately pointed out these weaknesses of the market transition theory.

There are shortcomings in the technocratic-managerial class theory as well, however. For example, there is evidence of a substantial drop-out from the political elite. In fact, with the exception of Russia, about half of the 1988 political elite was out of power by 1993. The drop-out rate was not trivial from economic elite positions either: in Bulgaria and Hungary the drop-out rate is approximately 20 per cent, in Poland it is approximately 15 per cent, and in the Czech Republic and Russia it is under 10 per cent.[11] The technocratic-managerial class theory does not explain these findings.

Furthermore, there was substantial inflow into new elite positions and, in particular, into new political elite positions. About half of the incumbents of the 1993 political elite did not hold elite positions in 1988; we interpret this finding as a massive changing of the guards. The same is not true for Russia, however, where only 18 per cent of the members of the 1993 political elite had not held elite positions five years earlier. The differences among the four other countries in this respect were not substantial. The data basically allow us to dismiss the argument that rank-and-file professionals were not upwardly mobile during the post-communist transition. In 1993, about half of the highest-ranking government positions were filled by individuals who had held rank-and-file positions in 1988 (with the exception of Russia). Thus, we can conclude that there was a rapid ascent of intellectuals to political power during the transition (especially if we take into consideration that in 1988 many top political figures were intellectuals) (Baylis, 1994: 318).

The story of inflow into the economic elite is quite different, though not as strikingly so as in the case of outflow. On the whole, about a quarter of the new members of the economic elite were recruited from those not in elite positions in 1988. The new economic elite included many young people who, due to their age at the time, could not have held elite positions in 1988 (Baylis, 1994: 319). New economic elites also included a substantial number of rank-and-file professionals who moved into the business sector after 1989, as well as some people from the second economy or the private business sector who rose up the ranks during transition. In particular, the massive outflow from the 1988 elite, and to some extent the rather substantial inflow into the 1993 political elite, suggests that the technocratic-managerial class theory substantially overstated the reproduction of social structure. Therefore, the correction to this theory offered by the post-communist managerialism thesis – specifically by H9 – seems to be warranted.

Furthermore, while the data make clear that market transition theory misread the potential effects of former political capital on elite survival, it is also evident that the technocratic-managerial class theory overstated the significance of political and social capital. At a minimum, cultural capital played as much of a role as former political or current social capital in terms of elite reproduction and circulation. Once again, the correction offered by post-communist managerialism theory's H8 appears to be closer to the target.

Finally, both market transition and technocratic-managerial class theories assume a single destination for former elites and even a single path leading to this destination. The most important correction offered to these theories – consistent with the theory of recombinant property – is that no single destination has emerged and post-communist countries seem to be travelling on divergent paths. For example, the emergent Russian style of capitalism is, beyond doubt, very different from the types of capitalism emerging in Central Europe. Perhaps what we need, therefore, is not a single theory of capitalist transition, but a theory of comparative capitalisms.

Conclusion

The data presented thus far strongly refute the political capitalism theory for Central and Southern Europe, though the data do not completely eliminate the usefulness of this theory for Russia. As far as market transition theory is concerned, the record is mixed. Undoubtedly, there was substantial circulation of elites in all countries, including Russia, and there is little doubt that those possessing higher levels of human capital did better than those possessing only political capital. There was some upward mobility even from the 'lower' ranks of the political and economic elite, whether this mobility was higher than it would have been under state socialism, however, is difficult to estimate. Undoubtedly, a change of guards took place, in particular in Central and Southern Europe, and this change was consistent with the predictions of market transition theory.

In terms of the economic elite, the technocratic-managerial class theory gained the most support. This theory, however, overstated the reproduction of social structure during the post-communist transition and did not account for either the substantial outflow from the 1988 political and economic elite or the significant inflow into the 1993 political elite from non-elite positions. The theory also erred in assuming that political and social capital would be better predictors of 1993 elite destination than cultural capital. Therefore, the synthesis offered by the theory of post-communist managerialism must be considered as a viable alternative.

Most importantly, all three theories reviewed above assumed that capitalism was a single destination and that all former socialist societies would travel on a single path towards this destination. Such assumptions are not supported by our data. What is needed, therefore, is not a single theory of transition from socialism to capitalism, but rather a theory of comparative capitalisms.

Appendix

Data

The data analysed in this paper come from Szelényi and Treiman's 1993/1994 large-scale comparative survey project, titled 'Social Stratification in Eastern Europe after 1989' (available at http://archiv.soc.cas.cz/SSEE). The data collected include a general population sample, as well as samples of past and current elites in the following five countries: Bulgaria, the Czech Republic, Hungary, Poland and Russia. Because the current analysis is primarily concerned with elite circulation and reproduction, our analysis relied exclusively on the elite samples.

In each country, three random samples of elites were collected. First, the *nomenklatura sample* is a random sample of 1000 individuals who held nomenklatura positions as of 1 January 1988. Second, the *new political and cultural elite sample* is a random sample of 400 individuals who were incumbents of political and cultural decision-making positions, analogous to those defied by the nomenklatura lists, as of 1 January 1993. Finally, the *new economic elite sample* is comprised of interviews with CEOs of 600 firms, randomly selected from the 3000 largest business organization (industrial firms, commercial and financial institutions) in each country.

Defining elites

Nomenklatura

For the purposes of our sample, we defined members of the nomenklatura as the incumbents of those positions for which the approval of some organ of the Central Committee of the Communist Party was required. This could include the plenum of the Central Committee, the Politburo, secretaries of the Central Committee apparatus, or other officials of the apparatus. Our random samples were drawn from the lists of such positions now available in the party archives.

In addition, the nomenklatura included two types of positions. First, most nomenklatura positions were full-time jobs or occupations. Other nomenklatura positions, by contrast, were positions to which the incumbents were elected, and which were generally not full-time jobs. Examples of the second kind of position include some Members of Parliament, and Members of the National Academy of Sciences. These differences between these two types of positions had two consequences for our sample. First, in terms of their occupation, many members of our nomenklatura were not elite at all, and, in fact, might include manual workers. A second consequence was that some people were incumbents of several nomenklatura positions simultaneously. In this case, we decided that we would enter a person's data as many times as they were selected for our sample. In fact, interview teams in each country reported dozens of such multiple selections.

In October 1992, *a team of experts from all the countries in our sample reviewed nomenklatura lists*. From this review, we discovered substantial variation over time and between countries. For this reason, in order to ensure comparability across countries, our team of experts developed a broad 'ideal-typical' nomenklatura list. This final list included all positions ever monitored by the Central Committee of Communist Parties in any of the countries in our sample, with a few exceptions. First, we decided to omit officers of the armed forces from the population due to the difficulties in identifying, locating and interviewing such individuals. Second, we decided to define economic elite positions by the three to four leading executives of 50 of the largest firms in each country. To this list, we added the next 200 most important national firms, which were linked to the special phone system in communist countries. We defined CEOs of these firms listed in the phone directory of this system as members of our nomenklatura population. Finally, our populations were defined as national, not federal, nomenklatura, to avoid definitional problems in those countries (Czechoslovakia and Russia), which broke up after the fall of communism.

Current political and cultural elites

Unlike the nomenklatura positions under communism, we could not rely on a list of positions to define post-communist political and cultural elites. Therefore, we decided to *simulate* such a list for post-communist conditions. Using the nomenklatura lists as our point of departure, we eliminated positions, which no longer existed, added new organizations, which appeared to be of similar importance to the previous ones.

Such a definition of current elites is not without problems. First, some positions that gained in importance during the transition were not included, such as clergy. Similarly, some positions that had declined in importance during transition, such as Members of the National Academy of Sciences, were left in our population for purposes of comparability. As a result of such decisions, there was a major reduction of the number of slots between the 1988 nomenklatura sample and the 1993 elite sample, with the nomenklatura population being about twice as large as the population of the new political and cultural elite.

New economic elites

We defined current economic elites as the CEOs of the 3000 largest firms (defined by size of turnover) in each country. We avoided using number of employees as a measure of firm size in order to avoid overrepresentation of moribund large state-owned, or formerly state-owned, firms, and to ensure that we selected enough of the more profitable businesses, which operated with relatively small numbers of employees.

Sampling procedures

Preparation for sampling began after all the elite populations were defined. As a first step, each national team identified the name of the incumbents (or former incumbents) of each position. After the naming procedure, a random sample was drawn from each population. All elite samples were then divided into strata. National teams were instructed to treat each sample as a stratified sample. Thus, in the case of missing addresses, refusal and so on, one had to replace addresses within the same stratum.

Fieldwork

Once addresses for all incumbents in our sample were determined, interviewers in each country contacted incumbents, set up appointments and interviewed respondents. The reported response rate was approximately 50 per cent. Non-response is largely attributable to incorrect addresses, changes in addresses, and the inability of survey firms to locate current addresses. While the stratification of our sample should ensure that differences in response rates between strata would not affect the representativeness of our sample, it is likely that our results are biased toward the higher levels of the nomenklatura due to the difficulty in finding addresses for lower-level nomenklatura, such as party secretaries of very large firms. The actual refusal rate was approximately 10 per cent, and there is no evidence of disproportionate refusal among any particular group.

Cross-country deviations

The most serious deviations from our sampling procedure occurred in the case of defining economic elites. First, in terms of identifying the former economic elite, our partners in the Czech Republic did not follow our instructions. Instead, they selected a sample of currently existing enterprises, and defined as 'old economic elite' those managers who were managers in the same firm in 1988. As a result, it is not possible to estimate the outflow from the 1988 Czech economic elite.

Second, a very small sample of old economic elites was produced in Russia and it is unclear why this happened. It is possible that this is due the size of the Russian nomenklatura population. Because the number of firms sampled was the same in all countries, and because the size of the nomenklatura was much larger in Russia than in all other countries, there might have been a lower probability of selecting a member of the old economic elite in Russia. However, there is no reason to believe that the Russian sample is not representative of high economic nomenklatura.

Third, in terms of identifying new economic elite, Poland deviated most from the proposed procedure. The Poles selected 200 enterprises from a list of only 600 large firms, and interviewed the three top officials at each firm. As a result, the Polish new economic elite sample represents managers of much larger enterprises than in the other countries.

Finally, the definition of size of firm varied across countries due to reliance on available statistics and information. Only Hungary defined the 3000 largest firms in terms of annual turnover, in the Czech Republic the measure was the number of employees, and in Poland and Russia size was defined by a combination of annual turnover, profit, and number of employees.

In terms of nomenklatura and current political and cultural elites, the samples are sufficiently similar in all countries. The only major difference is the absence of Foreign Service officials, and the underrepresentation of the nomenklatura in the state bureaucracy in the Czech sample. While the Hungarian, Polish and Russian data seem to be the most comparable, little is known about exact sampling procedures used to collect the Bulgarian data.

Notes

1 See also Lengyel and Róbert (Chapter 5) for an interesting discussion on the social origins of the emerging entrepreneurial class in CEE. These authors argue that this new class is primarily recruited from two distinct groups: First, from among the self-employed skilled workers and artisans and, second, from among a small group of professionals with economic influence.

2 As far as we can judge, Elemer Hankiss first presented this thesis in 1988 at a conference in Bonn sponsored by the Adenauer Foundation. Hankiss then published an outline of his theory in English in 1990. Independently of Hankiss, Staniszkis was working on a similar thesis in 1988. Her first publication outlining the new theory first appeared in English in 1991 (Staniszkis, 1991a, 1991b).

3 According to Mihályi, the value of total national wealth in 1990 was approximately 14 billion Hungarian forint. Only one-third of this was 'productive capital'. Value accumulated in housing properties constituted a substantial proportion of the remaining two-thirds and members of the nomenklatura were more likely to own real estate that could be mobilized such as second or third properties. Also see Windolf's article (1988b) for a discussion of capital accumulation among members of the nomenklatura in the pre-transition and transition periods.

4 It should also be noted that, during this same period, some children of the communist cadres began to use early private business opportunities in the so-called 'second economy'.

5 It was such a process of privatization from within that Frydman *et al.* (1996) termed 'capitalism with a comrade's face'.

6 See Szelényi and Kostello (1996) for a more thorough discussion of Victor Nee's market transition theory.

7 We have previously published results from this survey. *Theory and Society* (24, 5) published a special issue of our findings in 1995 and we published an article in the *New Left Review* in 1997 titled, 'Capitalism Without Capitalists'. In addition, Gil Eyal, Iván Szelényi and Eleanor Townsley co-authored a book titled, *Making Capitalism Without Capitalists* (1998). The data we present in this chapter are not identical to any of the previous publications, however. First, for the first time we present data from all five countries in our survey so that we now have a broader comparison than before. Second, we have re-coded our data. In all of the previous publications we defined our respondents by their nomenklatura position – determined by one's occupation or by non-occupational positions, including membership in Parliament, the Academy of Sciences, or the Central Committee of the Communist Youth League. Incumbents of such non-occupational positions did not necessarily have 'elite' jobs. In fact, some of these individuals were ordinary workers, rank-and-file professionals, or pensioners. In the data we present in this chapter we classify an individual's elite position by occupation only. Thus, in Tables 4.1 through 4.5 when an individual is classified as a member of the 'political elite', this classification indicates that this individual held a high-ranking job either in the party or in the government. The story that emerges from these figures is not drastically different from those previously published, but the figures are of course not exactly the same as in our earlier publications.

8 For a discussion of change and continuity during transition among elected incumbents of elite positions, see two articles by Baylis (1994, 1998).

9 For a discussion of the effects of education on unemployment patterns in transition, see Gimpelson (Chapter 3). In terms of education, Gimpelson argues that a universal pattern is emerging in CEE and Russia in which the 'structure of labour

market withdrawal is...evidence of shifting patterns of return to education and skills'. Specifically, he presents data that a university diploma is an asset for maintaining employment status in transition and that managers and professionals have the lowest rate of outflow into unemployment. Gimpelson's findings are certainly consistent with the findings presented here.

See also Baylis (1998: 287–92); Kryshtanovskaya and White (1996: 726–27); and Lengyel (1998: 203–4) for further discussions of the importance of education in elite reproduction and circulation during transition.

10 In Chapter 2, Timo Piirainen argues that a new class of 'grand capitalists' is indeed being formed by members of the nomenklatura who have maintained positions in the new economic elite, as well as by an emerging entrepreneurial elite.

11 See Lane's analysis (1999: 167–82) for a more complete discussion of elite reproduction and circulation among the Russian economic elite.

References

Baylis, T. A. (1994) 'Plus ça Change? Transformation and Continuity Among East European Elites', *Communist and Post-communist Studies*, 27(3): 315–28.

—— (1998) 'Elite Change After Communism – Eastern Germany, the Czech Republic and Slovakia', *East European Politics and Societies*, 12(2): 265–99.

Böröcz, J. and A. Rona-Tas (1995) 'Small Leap Forward – Emergence of New Economic Elites', *Theory and Society*, 24(5): 751–81.

Eyal, G., I. Szelényi and E. Townsley (1998) *Making Capitalism Without Capitalists. The New Ruling Elites in Eastern Europe*. London and New York: Verso.

Frydman, R., A. Rapaczynski and J. S. Earle (1993) *The Privatization Process in Central Europe*. Budapest: CEU Press.

——, K. Murphy and A. Rapaczynski (1996) 'Capitalism with a Comrade's Face', *Transitions*, 2(2): 5–11.

Hankiss, E. ([1982] 1986) 'Kinek az érdeke? (In whose interests?) in E. Hankiss, *Diagnozisok 2*, Budapest: Magvetö Kiadó, pp. 383–97.

Hanley, E. (1997) *Privatization and Marketization in Eastern Europe*, PhD dissertation, UCLA.

—— and I. Szelényi (2001) 'Changing Social Structure During Market Transition – the Case of Central Europe', in F. Tarifa (ed.), *The Breakdown of State Socialism and the Emerging Post-Socialist Order*. The Hague: CESTRAD/ISS.

Higley, J. and J. Pakulski (1995) 'Elite Transformation in Central and Eastern Europe', vol. 30: 415–35.

Kryshtanovskaya, O. and S. White (1996) 'From Soviet Nomenklatura to Russian Elite', *Europe–Asia Studies*, 48(5): 711–33.

Lane, D. (1997) 'Transition under Eltsin – the Nomenklatura and Political Elite Circulation', *Political Studies*, 45: 855–74.

—— (1999) *The Transition from Communism to Capitalism: Ruling Elites from Gorbachev to Yeltsin*. New York: St Martin's Press.

Lengyel, G. (1998) 'The Hungarian Economic Elite in the First Half of the 1990s', in J. Higley, J. Pakulski and W. Wesolowski (eds), *Postcommunist Elites and Democracy in Eastern Europe*. New York: St Martin's Press, pp. 203–12.

Manchin, R. and I. Szelényi (1987) 'Social Policy under state Socialism', in G. Esping Anderson, L. Rainwater and M. Rein (eds), *Stagnation and Renewal in Social Policy*. White Plains: M.E. Sharpe, pp. 102–39.

Nee, V. (1989) 'A Theory of Market Transition – From Redistribution to Markets in State Socialism', *American Sociological Review*, 54(5): 663–81.

Offe, C. (1991) 'Capitalism by Design? Democratic Theory Facing the Triple Transition in East Central Europe', *Social Research*, 58(4): 865–92.

Rona-Tas, A. (1994) 'The First Shall be the Last? Entrepreneurship and Communist Cadres in the Transition from Socialism', *American Journal of Sociology*, 100(1): 40–69.

—— (1998) 'Path Dependence and Capital Theory – Sociology of the Post-Communist Economic Transformation', *East European Politics and Societies*, 12(1): 107–31.

Staniszkis, J. (1991a) *The Dynamics of the Breakthrough*. Berkeley: University of California Press.

—— (1991b) 'Political Capitalism in Poland', *East European Politics and Societies*, 5(1): 127–41.

Stark, D. (1992) 'Path Dependence and Privatization Strategies in East Central Europe', *East European Politics and Societies*, 6(1): 17–51.

—— (1996) 'Recombinant Property in East European Capitalism', *American Journal of Sociology*, 101(4): 993–1027.

Steen, A. (1997) 'The New Elites in the Baltic States – Re-circulation and Change', *Scandinavian Political Studies*, 20(1): 91–112.

Szalai, E. (1981) *Kiemelt vállalat – beruházás – érdek* (Privileged firms, investments, interests). Budapest: Akademiai Kiado.

—— (1989a) *Gazdasági mechanizmus, reformtörekvések s nagyvallalati érdekek* (Economic mechanism, reform scenarios and interests of large firms). Budapest: Közgazdasági és Jogi Kiadó.

—— (1989b) 'The New Elite', *Across Frontiers*, 5(Fall–Winter): 25–31.

—— (1991) 'Integration of Special Interests in the Hungarian Economy – the Struggle Between Large Companies, the Party and State Bureaucracy', *Journal of Comparative Economics*, 15 (June): 304–24.

Szegö, A. (1983) 'Gazdaság és politika – érdek és struktura' (Economic and politics – interests and structure), *Medvetánc*, 2–3: 49–92.

—— (1985) 'Vita a reform alternativákrol' (Debate about reform scenarios), *Kritika*, 6: 3–5.

Szelényi, I., G. Eyal and E. Townsley (1997) 'The Theory of Post-Communist Managerialism', *New Left Review*, I (222): 60–92.

—— and E. Kostello (1996) 'The Market Transition Debate – Toward a Synthesis', *American Journal of Sociology*, 101(4): 1082–96.

Walder, A. (1995) 'Career Mobility and the Post-Communist Political Order', *American Sociological Review*, 60(3): 309–28.

—— (1996) 'Market and Inequality in Transitional Economies: Toward Testable Hypotheses', *American Journal of Sociology*, 101(4): 1060–73.

Windolf, P. (1998a) 'The Integration of East German Firms into Western Market Economy', in S. Immerfall (ed.), *Territoriality in the Globalizing Society: One Place or None?* Heidelberg: Springer, pp. 65–90.

—— (1998b) 'Privatization and Elite Reproduction in Eastern Europe', *Archive Europeenne de Sociologie*, 39(2): 335–76.

5

Middle Classes in the Maki in Central and Eastern Eu

*György Lengyel and Péter Róbert**

Introduction: the concept and relevance of middle classes

A widely prevalent metatheoretical view assumes that broad middle classes are the social precondition for democracy. 'Teargas loses against the middle classes', Huntington (1991) says quoting *The Economist* when he is discussing the transformation of the business community, the mainstay of authoritarian regimes, into the main support of the late twentieth-century wave of democratization. A volume of the proceedings of an East European conference – 'The Middle Class as a Precondition of Sustainable Society' – takes the middle class as a precondition of sustainable society (Tilkidjiev, 1998). Although these statements appear plausible, since after all what is in the middle is normally associated with a lack of political or social extremities, it is not certain they are applicable without reservations. One may ask, for example, whether the intellectuals playing a key role in both revolutions, and the emergence of authoritarian regimes, do not belong to the middle classes by their structural position?

Classical class theories failed to make significant reflections upon the problems of the middle classes. The Marxian concept, especially its most widespread ideological version, lays stress on the conflict between two major classes, emphasizing the values of the working class. That the original approach was more complex could be reconstructed among others from a conceptual analysis of the Marxist theory (Burris, 1995). Weber derives the class situation not only from property but also from the market relations in

* We acknowledge the comments of Jarosław Górniak, Tamas Kolosi, Vladimir Mikhalev and Iván Szelényi.

esmen and customers are confronted, thus he also underlines the nce of the economy. On the basis of the criteria of market performance, an differentiate upper classes with positive privileges and lower classes hout privileges. Weber's theory is better suited to represent the upper classes with positive privileges than the lower classes without privileges. Although entrepreneurs and freelancers are mentioned in the positively privileged classes by profit and earnings, while office clerks and the petty bourgeoisie are touched on in the negatively privileged groups, this multidimensional analysis ignores the middle classes. The bureaucracy typology is a suitable frame to describe the recruitment of administrators and inner labour markets. It is also true that Weber's class concept used to describe the mobility regimes includes the groups of petty bourgeoisie, office workers and intellectuals, hence in theory it may be used for the representation of a middle-class theory.

Evoking the *Neuer Mitterstand* of Lederer and Marschak (1995 [1926]), Dahrendorf introduces the concept of the New Middle Class in his work on class conflicts, and immediately discards it on the basis of the theory of conflict. In his interpretation, the post-Marxian period witnessed not only the decomposition of the working classes and of capital but also the emergence of middle classes doomed to disintegration (Dahrendorf, 1959: 51 ff). Officials tend to be ranged with the bourgeoisie, while the lower strata of white-collar workers tend towards the working classes in the basic conflict of industrial society. Thus, in Dahrendorf's view, conflict and middle classes preclude one another, in that 'from the point of view of a theory of conflict, there can be no such entity as a middle class' (Dahrendorf, 1959: 52). He adds, however, that in view of earnings and prestige, there are sizeable groups in the middle of society.

Wright (1985) puts exploitation in the focus, differentiating three dimensions related, in turn, to property relations, power relations and stock of knowledge. In his view, those are precisely the members of the middle class who are in contradictory positions. Thus, by the concept of contradictory class locations Wright and Martin (1987) realized a variant of the decomposition model of conflict theory. With that, however, they did not solve but merely reduced the importance of the problem of the middle class.

Giddens (1973) went back to the concept of market competence, also stressing three criteria: ownership of the means of production, control over labour power in the process of production, and possession of educational and technical qualifications. In this theory, the possession of productive goods places entrepreneurs with the middle classes, the control over the work of others places managers there, and market capability based on knowledge and professional training places the professional intellectual there.

Agreeing with Goldthorpe (1982), one may stress that managers, professional groups and clerks are united by the common characteristic of enjoying the distinguished trust of their employers, entailing higher labour market status and most often greater autonomy. Keeping to Goldthorpe's terminology, these common features combine these strata in a service class.

We accept as a starting point Goldthorpe's approach. In the first half of the century, the exponents of newly-arising professional occupations and managerial roles were the members of the new middle class as against the traditional petty bourgeoisie (Vidich, 1995). This is quite the other way round in the late-century CEE transformation: the newly-arising entrepreneurial class is viewed as the new middle class (Wallace and Haerpfer, 1998). We are trying to adduce arguments that the distinction of old and new middle classes is not convenient, not only because the 'new' was once already the 'old'. We do not apply this chronological classification because in our days the groups regarded as elements of the traditional middle class seem to appear as new qualities as well. In other words in CEE, next to the entrepreneurial class, a service class is emerging. Every social class has their precedents, and the groups constituting the service class – similarly to the entrepreneurs – existed in the late phase of planned economies. In the 1990s, however, the service class has appeared significantly as the service sector has gained predominance among the branches of the economy and, obviously, this sector employs a significant part of the service class members. Not only the extension of trade but also, among other things, the strengthening of the banking sector, the radical growth in demand for financial specialists, resulted in the immense increase in the significance of skills and market positions defining the service class. The same structural trends – demotion of heavy industry and agriculture, the legitimization and spread of private property, the expansion of tertiary education – which pointed towards the emergence of an entrepreneurial class, also contribute to the growth in the relative weight of the service class, as will be discussed.

When critically reviewing the theories of the middle class, Savage and his colleagues picked six different meanings of the service class in research literature (Savage *et al.*, 1992). Among others, in accordance with Goldthorpe's tenet, the specificity of the service class relationship is based on trust, autonomy and discretion. Savage and his collaborators also acknowledge the importance of trust, but suggest that the difference between high-trust vs low-trust occupations should not be taken as differences in quality but in degree, thus the conditions of creating trust can be more fluid. This critique is realistic and may be accepted, but it does not question the fact that high-trust occupations are widely spread in the service class as compared to most low-trust jobs in the lower class.

There must be more precise definitions at this point, however, for both Goldthorpe and Savage seem to disregard the fact that trust and autonomy are important operative criteria for both main components of the middle classes, that is, for the service class and for entrepreneurs as well. Is there need to quote the authors who have argued that the entrepreneurial spirit, that trade itself curbs passions, abolishes double morals since it must rely on trust in the business partner? (Weber, 1961 [1923]; Hirschman, 1977). Thus both components of the middle classes are characterized by the distinguished importance of trust and autonomy, and if there is difference between them, it must be searched for in the institutional relations laying the foundations for trust and in the possessed assets as the basis for autonomy.

At this point, the improved Hayekian concepts suggested by Coleman could be of assistance: they differentiate between spontaneous and constructed organizations (Coleman, 1991). Spontaneous organizations are voluntary relations between two parties to sustain which there is enough inner motivation available. Business relations created upon the partners' free will are typical of this, since both parties feel it is in their interest to sustain the relationship. By contrast, constructed organizations are hierarchical relations in which there may be at least one party whose interest is not to maintain the relation. Therefore its sustenance requires a third party or external motivations.

Thus, the main difference between the entrepreneurial class and the service class lies in the former being attached primarily to spontaneous organizations, the latter to constructed organizations. It needs stressing, of course, that primary relations are meant here, since entrepreneurs also have relations with constructed organizations and, conversely, members of the service class are involved in spontaneous relations as well. Yet, when it comes to subsistence and life-chances, the main difference is the former being attached to spontaneous, the latter to constructed organizations. One places his trust in his partner, hoping that his partner will observe the contract and act correctly; his autonomy is founded on economic, as well as social and cultural assets. The other receives trust from his employer and gives his loyalty in return; his autonomy is delegated, and is founded mainly on cultural and social resources. According to certain arguments, even the managerial and professional groups are endangered by the devaluation of local knowledge and profession-specific competence (cf. Crompton and Jones, 1984).

Trust, autonomy, a distinguished labour market position and non-manual nature of the work are strongly connected characteristics of the middle classes. Greater autonomy makes higher discretion, greater probability of managerial, marketing and organizing skills, as well as creative imagination more probable; though they are at a certain point in inverse connection. Members of the service class typically do non-manual work and have delegated autonomy from their employers. Self-employed members of the entrepreneurial class on the other hand frequently combine manual and non-manual activities, but they do not have employers at all.

In Bill Martin's (1998) view, the characteristics of the new middle class lie in the bricolage. He argues that the significance of organizing skills, local knowledge and attached loyalty is decreasing. Gallie (1996) emphasizes the importance of three main factors: qualification, training required for performing specific jobs, and (local) experience. One can observe rapprochement between certain jobs in the service class and others in the lower class; this may underlie the grouping together of skilled workers in the services and the administrative labour by Erikson and Goldthorpe (1992). In this argumentation, both 'downgrading' (for example, decreasing job security among some intellectual occupations) and 'upgrading' (for example, increasing work autonomy among some workers, the inclusion of physical employees by the management's decision-making) are discussed. Nevertheless, what truly determines the trust relations in all three groups of the service class (managers, professionals, clerks) apart from the delegated licences is the signal importance of loyalty, a specific relation of trust. In a typical case the members of the service class are loyal to their employer and the organization – as their main lineament.

Naturally enough, the service class has a salient role in the literature devoted to post-industrial societies (cf. Esping-Andersen, 1993). The main precondition for the emergence of the service class, in Esping-Andersen's view, is that in modern welfare states the public sphere gains predominance, the traditional labour market is transformed, and employment conditions and individual life-chances become dependent on the government's financial possibilities and on collective political decisions. In a 'post-Fordist' society, a considerable part of job-takers pursue economic activities related to social reproduction, to leisure-time activities. These mainly include business services (counselling, financial assistance), social services (education, healthcare) and personal services.

Middle-class research carried out in the 1990s is embedded in the broader context of class research. Lockwood (1995) stresses that an investigation of the middle class and its inner stratification can never be removed from the class structure of the entire society and from the long-term historical processes of class formation. In this regard, one must consider economic aspects (for example, working conditions, work security, career chances), personal relations (for example, relations of service and, more broadly, the interpersonal relations of the class members including friendships, marriages and so forth) and normative aspects (such as values, norms, preferences). In his overview, Butler (1995) states that the salient question of the discussion is the growth of the service class, its characteristics pointing beyond the traditional factors, its market competence and assets, or disposition.

The study of the middle classes is always placed in a distinct political context (Savage, 1995) – even if no class policy as such can be talked about. Broader thematic issues include, accordingly, the interrelation of classes and genders (effemination), the closed or open character of a class (social mobility and migration), class-specific consumption, lifestyle, and the political mobilization potential or value order of the members of a class. The present authors wish to embark on some of these issues. Summing up the different elements of the previous approaches we define middle classes as major social groups which might be characterized with great autonomy, distinguished labour market positions, typically non-manual work and high-trust relations. The middle classes consist of the entrepreneurial class and the service class that has three major components: managers, professionals and clerical workers.

In what follows, first, we review some long-term social trends that have fundamentally influenced the formation of middle classes in CEE. Then, relying on the findings of comparative surveys, we describe the main social characteristics of the middle classes in the late phase of state socialism and in the period of transformation. Finally, we analyse the earning chances of middle-class groups, their social determinants, followed by some conclusions.

The central and the middle: social trends influencing the formation of middle classes in CEE

Two groups of factors are to be stressed among the social trends influencing the emergence of middle classes: one is the long-term change in the social structure of the economy, the other is the transformation of higher education. At the turn of the nineteenth–twentieth centuries, most CEE countries had predominantly agrarian or agrarian-industrial economies. The agricultural sphere employed over half to four-fifths of the population in Hungary, Poland, Bulgaria and Russia. The only exception was the Bohemian province of the Austrian-Hungarian monarchy with the two-fifth share of agriculture. In the course of interwar industrialization, the contribution of the industry to the GDP grew but the transformation of the sectoral structure of employees lagged behind. As compared to the one-third to two-fifths of the population employed by industry and about one-third employed in the tertiary sector in the German, Austrian and Bohemian areas, in most CEE countries employment in the industrial and the tertiary sector did not exceed one-quarter. Still, one concomitant of this protractedly starting industrialization (Berend and Ránki, 1974) was the rallying of a considerable segment of labour in large organizations. In addition, the managerial, professional and administrative roles spread on a mass scale. Since private property was not delimited except for the Soviet Union, the rate of entrepreneurs was still high in trade and services.

A decisive feature of socialist modernization carried out in the 1950s–1960s was the radical restriction of private property, reducing the class of entrepreneurs to an insignificant social group. Its other typical feature was the radical sectoral restructuring of the economy, adjusting the employment structure to the sectors' share of the GDP. This means that in most countries significant agrarian masses were channelled into industry, which was practically carried out in the Soviet, Hungarian, Bulgarian and Slovakian economies. The known exceptions were the Czech and East German cases where the given sectoral shares had been developed earlier, and the case of Poland where the land was not collectivized, and thus agriculture could preserve its employment-retaining power. It was a common feature of socialist modernization that the rate of industrial labour increased (amounting to one-third or half of the earners). Parallel with that, the employment in the tertiary sector also grew at a slower pace, to about one-quarter or one-third (Historical Statistics, 1997).

Owing to state ownership and the growing rate of public services, the presence of constructed large organizations was further buttressed and became predominant in all areas of economy and society. All this inevitably entailed the further expansion of managerial and professional roles, and a related increase in demand for relevant tertiary education. However, the modification of the inner proportions and structure of tertiary education cannot be simply interpreted as responses to the political and economic trends; this transformation had some independence as well.

At the beginning of the twentieth century, it was commonly typical of higher education in European countries that university and high-school students amounted to about one-thousandth of the entire population. In Italy, Hungary and Bulgaria, the corresponding figures were even smaller, while in Poland and Switzerland, for example, it exceeded triple. In the early 1970s, the difference between higher education in West and East European countries was attributable to the substantially greater share of technical students in the latter countries, among other factors. By that time, the rate of higher education enrolment increased to about one-hundredth of the population, without significant differences between East and West (UNESCO Statistical Yearbook, 1987).

There was a significant modification in these rates in the 1970s. While in Western countries the higher education attendance increased one and half to two and a half times, in the CEE countries this rise was only 20–40 per cent. The next great change only came in the 1990s with a significant increase in students' rates (with the exception of the Soviet Union where their share was saliently high back in the 1970s and practically stagnant ever since) (UNESCO Statistical Yearbook, 1998). Thus, in the mid-1990s, the rate of tertiary education attendance amounted to some 3–4 per cent of the total population, with about 2 per cent in most East European countries. Now the main structural difference is in the rate of social and behavioural science studies: their rate is one-tenth to one-quarter in Western countries and only 2–4 per cent in East European countries. In the 1980s, the share of women in higher education was generally higher among East European students than in the West. This was caused partly by the effemination of the teaching profession, but two-thirds to three-fourths of business administration students were also female. There was no tendentious change in these proportions over the 1990s in the East European countries (in Hungary and Poland they decreased slightly and in Bulgaria increased) (Genov and Krastev, 1999). As a result, the gender composition of business administration students significantly differs in Western and Eastern countries, the latter being far more feminized. As for the whole of the student population, however, the rate of women increased in Western countries as well in the 1990s, thus the two halves of Europe came closer in this regard.

There was a similar tendency for levelling out in the sectoral composition of employment in the 1990s. In the previous decades, the employment in the tertiary sector significantly increased, amounting to some 60–70 per cent in the 1990s in Western countries. This rise took on impetus in the 1990s in the East European countries, with 40–60 per cent of earners becoming employed in the services sector (Countries in Transition, 1996). The rise in the share of the tertiary sector in employment and the increase of university and high-school students as a percentage of the total population – two marked tendencies of the 1990s – occurred as characteristic features of post-socialist countries. One may additionally remark that with the legal recognition of private property, the self-employed rate has also increased considerably. Thus, employers and self-employed workers amounted to some 6–10 per cent of the labour force in the first half of the 1990s. Small ventures, however, have little labour-absorbing capacities, thus the overwhelming majority of earners are still employed by large organizations.

Data and variables

Two data-files are used in the empirical part of the chapter:

1 Social Stratification in Eastern Europe after 1989 (SSEE) (principal investigators: Iván Szelényi and Donald J. Treiman), was fielded in 1993 in six countries: Bulgaria, the Czech Republic, Hungary, Poland, Russia and Slovakia. In all countries, the surveys were based on nationwide probability samples being representative for the adult population aged over 18. Only respondents in the labour force were included in the analysis. For all tables and estimates in the chapter, we have used weighted data in accordance with the documentation of the data.
2 International Social Survey Programme (ISSP), 1996 Module, contains data from more than 20 countries, including Bulgaria, the Czech Republic, Hungary, Latvia, Poland, Russia and Slovakia, which we considered for our analysis. Nationwide probability samples representing the adult population over 18 were interviewed in all countries. We selected respondents only in the labour force and applied weights in accordance with the documentation of the data.

The main variable in this chapter measures class. In line with the theoretical consideration, our class variable distinguishes: (a) the lower class from the middle classes (a few cases who belong to the elite have been left out); (b) the service class and entrepreneurs within the middle classes; and (c) managers, professionals and clerical workers (administrators) within the service class.

Additional variables used in the analysis are gender, age, social origin, education and economic branch. The special advantage of the SSEE data is that these variables are available for 1988 and 1993. Both data-files contain measures of personal income and family income (with numbers of people in the household), so personal income and per capita family income (both on a monthly base) were used in the analysis. We made corrections for the income data; and outlier cases were deleted from the file.

The middle classes in the making, 1988–93

Micro data indicate the same trends as expected on the ground of long-term changes in the social structure of the economy, described in the previous section. A general increase of educational level as well as movement of the workforce into the tertiary sector have resulted in an increase of middle classes in post-socialist societies (see Table 5.1). In consequence of the system transformation, this process speeded up between 1988 and 1993. During this small interval the proportion of those belonging to the middle classes increased by 4–5 per cent, and the middle–lower class distribution is roughly half-and-half among the earners.

The impact of rapid historical changes in addition to the long-term processes is clearly demonstrated by the emergence of an entrepreneurial class. Even in those countries like Hungary and Poland where the 1990s cannot be considered as a sharp caesura in terms of social restructuring, the proportion of entrepreneurs doubled between 1988 and 1993. The largest increase of the self-employed occurred in the Czech Republic. In the Czech Republic, Hungary and Poland about one-fifth of the middle classes belong to the entrepreneur class in 1993.

In consequence of the huge emergence of an entrepreneurial class, the service class seems to shrink. In fact, both entrepreneurial and service classes increased in size but the increase was much more significant for the entrepreneurs (see Table 5.2). The service class extended in Hungary, Poland and Russia to a larger degree, while in Bulgaria, Slovakia and especially in the Czech Republic to a lesser degree.

Modifications inside the service class are quite moderate. Data do not indicate significant changes in the proportion of managers, professionals and clerks within the service class, and the distribution of the inner structure of the service class did not change much either.

The social distance between middle and lower classes

The middle–lower class division embodies a major cleavage in most societies. Although inconsistent features of the class structure in the former socialist countries, especially in respect of cultural and financial attributes, diminish

Table 5.1 Class distribution in six post-socialist countries, 1988 and 1993

Social class	Bulgaria		Czech Republic		Hungary		Poland		Russia		Slovakia	
	1988	1993	1988	1993	1988	1993	1988	1993	1988	1993	1988	1993
Middle vs lower class												
Middle classes	36.6	40.0	44.9	50.2	44.8	49.7	55.3	59.7	47.1	48.6	46.0	50.1
Lower classes	63.4	60.0	55.1	49.8	55.2	50.3	44.7	40.3	52.9	51.4	54.0	49.9
Within middle classes												
Entrepreneurs	7.6	15.9	2.6	20.4	10.8	19.8	9.8	22.2	3.2	7.0	2.3	14.6
Service class	92.4	84.1	97.4	79.6	89.2	80.2	90.2	77.8	96.8	93.0	97.7	85.4
Within service class												
Managers	12.9	13.9	24.8	22.2	21.6	19.5	24.0	19.7	20.3	20.6	23.2	22.8
Professionals (+technicians)	54.0	52.2	41.0	40.3	42.0	42.6	33.7	36.1	55.8	55.3	42.4	40.2
Clerical workers	33.1	33.9	34.2	37.5	36.4	37.9	42.3	44.2	23.9	24.1	34.4	37.0
Total	100.0	100.0	100.0	100.0	100.0	100.0	100.0	100.0	100.0	100.0	100.0	100.0
n	2447	2753	3262	3706	1999	2306	1916	2245	3125	3688	2859	3264

Source: SSEE (see text, p. 106).

Table 5.2 Increase of the entrepreneurial and service classes in six post-socialist countries between 1988 and 1993

Social class	**Bulgaria**		**Czech Republic**		**Hungary**		**Poland**		**Russia**		**Slovakia**	
	1988	**1993**	**1988**	**1993**	**1988**	**1993**	**1988**	**1993**	**1988**	**1993**	**1988**	**1993**
Entrepreneurial class	100	248	100	1016	100	232	100	294	100	262	100	790
Service class	100	108	100	103	100	113	100	112	100	115	100	108

Source: SSEE.

the barriers between these classes, this distinction represents a definite split in the post-socialist societies as well. As possible factors of class division, we consider the composition by gender, age, social origin, education, economic branch and earnings. We also investigate changes in time between 1988 and 1993.

The proportion of women is higher in the middle than in the lower class, and the effemination of the middle classes was especially massive in Bulgaria and Russia. The lowest proportion of women is apparent in the Czech Republic. In the course of the political and economic transformation, between 1988 and 1993, the proportion of women decreased in the middle classes, which is naturally connected to the fact that employment levels decreased in the post-socialist countries, especially among women. The degree of decrease was about the same in all of the studied countries.

As regards the age composition of the middle and lower classes, the proportion of those below 45 varied somewhat in the studied countries. A particularly high level of the young could be found in Slovakia in 1988, and a relatively low rate in the Czech Republic. In 1993, the Polish middle class was the youngest, the Czech the oldest. In the rest of the countries, no significant change could be found in the age composition of the middle and lower classes.

Working-class origin was some 20 per cent smaller in the middle classes than in the lower class. Hardly any change could be demonstrated in this regard between 1988 and 1993, apart from a slight decrease by 1–2 per cent in the rate of middle-class members with working-class backgrounds.

The rate of those with tertiary qualifications in 1993 ranged between 14–17 per cent (see Table 5.3). In the middle classes, however, this rate doubled and varied between 26–34 per cent. The coexistence of middle-class position and tertiary education was similar in 1988. The rate of diploma holders increased only by about 1 per cent in the middle classes from 1988 to 1993. Consequently, the post-socialist middle classes do not appear more qualified than the middle classes before the system transformation. In Bulgaria and Slovakia, tertiary education seems to be a stronger requirement for middle-class position. The percentage of diploma holders within the middle class is the lowest in Hungary.

According to the survey, employment in the tertiary sector varied between 34–43 per cent in 1988 (see Table 5.4). Roughly every fourth member of the lower class was employed in the services; this rate was one-third in Poland. The percentage of those working in the tertiary sector was, however, over 50 per cent in the middle class already in 1988. In the course of the transformation, employment in the service sector grew by some 6–7 per cent. A more powerful, 10 per cent rise was demonstrated in Hungary where in 1993 52 per cent was employed in the tertiary sector. The 1993 figures reveal that more than two-thirds of the middle classes in Hungary are employed in the service sector.

Table 5.3 Proportion of tertiary-educated in the middle class and lower class in six post-socialist countries, 1988 and 1993

Social class	**Bulgaria**		**Czech Republic**		**Hungary**		**Poland**		**Russia**		**Slovakia**	
	1988	**1993**	**1988**	**1993**	**1988**	**1993**	**1988**	**1993**	**1988**	**1993**	**1988**	**1993**
Middle class	33.1	34.5	26.9	26.1	25.2	25.9	27.7	28.0	28.8	29.4	31.1	31.9
Lower class	2.9	3.9	1.2	1.5	1.8	2.3	2.8	2.9	2.3	2.7	2.0	2.1
Total	13.4	16.4	12.5	13.8	11.7	14.0	16.4	17.9	14.8	15.6	15.1	17.0
n	3156	2629	4083	3695	2915	2295	2439	2238	3478	3597	3569	3240

Source: SSEE.

Table 5.4 Proportion of those working in the service sector in the middle class and lower class in six post-socialist countries, 1988 and 1993

Social class	Bulgaria		Czech Republic		Hungary		Poland		Russia		Slovakia	
	1988	1993	1988	1993	1988	1993	1988	1993	1988	1993	1988	1993
Middle class	55.0	62.7	55.2	60.7	60.1	68.7	52.0	57.4	57.3	61.7	55.6	60.7
Lower class	22.4	26.8	25.8	31.0	28.2	35.9	32.3	34.2	27.3	29.8	27.2	30.5
Total	34.0	41.1	38.6	45.9	41.6	52.2	43.0	48.0	41.5	45.3	39.9	45.7
n	3227	2677	4049	3658	2901	2280	2430	2224	3513	3632	3520	3193

Source: SSEE.

Middle-lower class differences in earning inequalities and determination will be discussed in more detail later. In descriptive terms, data on net taxed earnings (in US$) per month taken from a person's full-time job show that Russia stands at the lower end of the income scale, while Hungary can be found at the upper end. At the same time, the standard deviation is more than double the average in Russia. In general, the standard deviation of middle-class earnings is higher than that of lower-class earnings in the post-socialist societies.

Characteristic features of the entrepreneurial and service classes

The gender distributions of the two components of the middle classes, entrepreneurs and the service class, are sharply different (see Table 5.5). This was so in 1988 when the proportion of women among entrepreneurs was lower (about one-third), becoming slightly more pronounced in 1993, whilst for the service class the proportion was much higher, about two-thirds, for both years. Some difference can be found among countries in this respect, too: in the Czech and Slovak service class the proportion of women was below 60 per cent and in Russia and Bulgaria near 70 per cent.

As regards composition by age, in the late phase of state socialism, some three-quarters of the service class were below 45 in the investigated countries. A similar rate could be demonstrated, with larger standard deviation, in the entrepreneurial class. In 1988 there was no substantial difference between the two segments of the middle classes (except for Bulgaria). In 1993, however, two-thirds to four-fifths of the entrepreneurs and an average of two-thirds of the service class were below 45. The proportion of young people was some 5–10 per cent higher among entrepreneurs than among service class people in each country.

In late state socialism, more than half the middle classes came from lower-class backgrounds, equally in both components of the middle classes and in every studied country. Intergenerational mobility into the middle classes was the lowest in the Czech Republic and the highest in Bulgaria. The recruitment rate of the service class does not reveal significant modifications for 1993, but a social closure was found in most countries for the entrepreneurs. With the rise of the entrepreneurial class, the rate of those with already middle-class backgrounds increased. Nevertheless, it holds true that in 1993 more than half of entrepreneurs came from the lower class, as their fathers were manual workers or peasants. More than half – in Poland and Russia nearly two-thirds – of the service class also came from the lower class. A salient exception is the Russian entrepreneurial class which became far more closed than earlier, and is more closed than the rest of the CEE entrepreneurial classes. In 1993, more than half the Russian entrepreneurs came from middle or upper-class families, most typically from intellectual backgrounds.

Table 5.5 Proportion of women in the entrepreneurial and service classes in six post-socialist countries, 1988 and 1993

Social class	**Bulgaria**		**Czech Republic**		**Hungary**		**Poland**		**Russia**		**Slovakia**	
	1988	**1993**	**1988**	**1993**	**1988**	**1993**	**1988**	**1993**	**1988**	**1993**	**1988**	**1993**
Entrepreneurs	39.8	34.3	41.0	34.9	35.0	35.9	21.0	27.4	47.8	37.0	47.4	28.5
Service class	67.4	69.2	56.7	57.0	63.1	64.2	63.4	64.0	70.0	69.0	58.3	58.9
Total	64.1	61.5	56.3	52.2	59.5	54.9	59.4	55.9	58.1	54.2	58.1	57.7
n	1069	1010	1793	1841	1201	1099	1070	1081	1655	1758	1613	1621

Changes over time indicate no major differences in composition of the entrepreneurial and the service classes by qualification. Less than one-fifth of the entrepreneurs and, on average, less than a third of the service class had tertiary education in 1988. In 1993, about one-fifth of the entrepreneurs and a third of the service class had diplomas. Thus, the level of education of the entrepreneurs increased in most studied countries. It is easier to understand the implications of the change for entrepreneurs. A formerly narrow social stratum mostly having the competence and qualification of skilled works extended into a sizeable class, one of the typical career patterns contributing to this enlargement being that of the professionals. For professional groups with marketable knowledge, the freedom of enterprise opened up new alternatives.

On the other hand, the expansion of the service sector is a symptom of the class coalescence of the white-collar worker groups. Consequently, the rate of tertiary-educated graduates and the significance of the diploma did not decrease after the late phase of state socialism. While a great part of positions in the public sector were tied to formal criteria of qualification, in privately-owned firms no such requirements exist for the great majority of posts. In spite of this, the level of education did not sink and this is attributable to the fact that the mass emergence of new structural positions posed a challenge to young graduates in the first place.

The rate of those with tertiary education did not change in the service class because this qualification is the admission criteria in the professional groups to public service. Though some incongruency can be found among managers, it is not enough to lower the level of education in the service class. The third component of the service class includes office workers and technicians for whom selection criteria do not necessarily include tertiary education. Compared to the population in the labour force, the rate of diploma-holders among entrepreneurs is high. In the Czech and Hungarian cases, highly-qualified entrepreneurs made up only one-sixth of their class, while their rate is one-quarter or more in Russia and Slovakia. All this tends to bear out the assumption that the new CEE entrepreneurial class was typically recruited along two career patterns: one based on a large group of self-employed, the other based on a numerically smaller group of professionals with greater economic influence.

In the late phase of state socialism, less than 60 per cent of entrepreneurs and of the service class worked in the tertiary sector in CEE. This rate has been modified in every country concerned, rising by some 5–15 per cent. Two-thirds of both entrepreneurs and the service class worked in the tertiary sector in 1993 (see Table 5.6). For entrepreneurs the great motivation came from prospects in trade and catering, a particularly marked phenomenon in Russia and Bulgaria, (as well as Romania and Albania not investigated in this chapter). As for the service class, the expansion of the service sector is not surprising; what needs explanation is the deviation

Table 5.6 Proportion of those working in the service sector in the entrepreneurial and service classes in six post-socialist countries, 1988 and 1993

Social class	Bulgaria		Czech Republic		Hungary		Poland		Russia		Slovakia	
	1988	1993	1988	1993	1988	1993	1988	1993	1988	1993	1988	1993
Entrepreneurs	47.8	64.8	44.3	60.8	58.3	71.5	57.7	71.4	55.0	72.3	54.2	54.9
Service class	59.9	65.9	55.5	61.5	61.7	70.7	65.1	70.8	57.6	61.2	55.6	62.0
Total	55.0	62.7	55.2	60.7	60.1	70.8	64.4	70.9	57.3	61.7	55.6	60.7
n	1044	984	1778	1817	1191	1091	1063	1074	1653	1755	1651	1590

Source: SSEE.

between those employed in the tertiary sector and the size of the service class.

By definition, all belong to the service class who are employees but not workers, peasants, top managers or entrepreneurs. Although most of these are indeed in the tertiary sector, and hence the service sector is the crystallizing point of the service class, there are still considerable deviations between the two categories. On the one hand, there are maintenance and other workers in the tertiary sector who themselves belong to the lower class, and there are top managers in this sector who are members of the small but highly influential elite, not discussed here. On the other hand – and more importantly – there are special intellectuals, white-collar workers, lower and middle-ranking managers in industry and agriculture who are members of the service class. The real challenge to the service sector as regards jobs may only come from large-enterprise administration but, as has been seen, employment in the service sector has increased, with the overlapping of service-sector and service-class groups becoming greater than at the end of state socialism.

Entrepreneurial earnings surpass service-class earnings by an average of one and a half times. The greatest difference – more than three and a half-fold – can be observed between Russian entrepreneurs and service-class members, whilst the smallest deviation is in Hungary. It must be added, however, that the relatively high income of Russian entrepreneurs falls to the lower zone of entrepreneurial earnings in Central and Eastern Europe. What does stand out is the saliently low income of the Russian service class. As for earnings, the standard deviation is greater among countries than between entrepreneurs and the service class in general. The earnings of the Hungarian service class are double that in Bulgaria and are sevenfold compared to Russia.

Earning determination

In order to examine the determination of earnings in the middle classes, three regression models were fitted to the data (Table 5.7). In each case the dependent variable was the logarithm of the full-time net earning per month (in US$). For each model there is a base version involving only the direct class effects, and an extended version including gender, age, education, economic branch as well as countries and interaction terms between class and country.

The first model examined what earning advantages the middle class has over the lower class, and what kind of social structural components can determine those advantages. The second model refers to earning differences between entrepreneurs and the service class within the middle classes. The third model investigates the earning determination of managers and professionals as compared to clerical workers.

Table 5.7 Earnings determination: effects of class on the logarithm of personal earnings, 1993. Regression analysis, standardized beta estimates

Explanatory variables	Model 1 Middle class vs lower class		Model 2 Service class vs entrepreneurs		Model 3 Managers and professionals vs clerical workers	
	Direct effects	Controlled effects	Direct effects	Controlled effects	Direct effects	Controlled effects
Class						
Middle = 1	0.105***	0.066***	–	–	–	–
Lower = 0	–	–	–	–	–	–
Service = 1	–	–	–0.204***	–0.159***	–	–
Entrepreneurs = 0	–	–	–	–	–	–
Managers = 1	–	–	–	–	0.115***	0.112***
Professionals = 1	–	–	–	–	–0.010	0.055***
Clerical workers = 0	–	–	–	–	–	–
Education						
tertiary = 1	–	0.128***	–	0.172***	–	0.168***
secondary = 1	–	0.081***	–	0.098***	–	0.102***
primary = 0	–	–	–	–	–	–
Economic branch						
industry = 1	–	0.075***	–	0.057***	–	0.046***
business service = 1	–	0.058***	–	0.053***	–	0.050***
personal service = 1	–	0.033***	–	0.040***	–	0.040***
agriculture = 0	–	–	–	–	–	–

Gender						
male = 1	–	0.202***	–	0.170***	–	0.138***
female = 0	–	–	–	–	–	–
Age						
age	–	0.017***	–	0.042***	–	0.038***
age-squared	–	–0.051****	–	–0.055***	–	–0.054***
Country						
Bulgaria = 1	–	0.577***	–	0.399***	–	0.519***
Czech Republic = 1	–	0.835***	–	0.714***	–	0.818***
Hungary = 1	–	0.814***	–	0.707***	–	0.794***
Poland = 1	–	0.678***	–	0.569***	–	0.637***
Slovakia = 1	–	0.786***	–	0.679***	–	0.799***
Russia = 0	–	–	–	–	–	–
Interactions						
Bulgaria by middle class	–	–0.002	–	–	–	–
Czech R. by middle class	–	0.005	–	–	–	–
Hungary by middle class	–	0.017*	–	–	–	–
Poland by middle class	–	0.003	–	–	–	–
Slovakia by middle class	–	–0.002	–	–	–	–
Bulgaria by service class	–	–	–	0.094***	–	–
Czech R. by service class	–	–	–	0.095***	–	–
Hungary by service class	–	–	–	0.091***	–	–
Poland by service class	–	–	–	0.088***	–	–
Slovakia by service class	–	–	–	0.086***	–	–
Bulgaria by managers	–	–	–	–	–	–0.014
Czech R. by managers	–	–	–	–	–	–0.014
Hungary by managers	–	–	–	–	–	–0.011
Poland by managers	–	–	–	–	–	0.007
Slovakia by managers	–	–	–	–	–	–0.030**

Table 5.7 (Continued)

Explanatory variables	Model 1 Middle class vs lower class		Model 2 Service class vs entrepreneurs		Model 3 Managers and professionals vs clerical workers	
	Direct effects	Controlled effects	Direct effects	Controlled effects	Direct effects	Controlled effects
Bulgaria by professionals	–	–	–	–	–	–0.014
Czech R. by professionals	–	–	–	–	–	–0.009
Hungary by professionals	–	–	–	–	–	–0.005
Poland by professionals	–	–	–	–	–	0.010
Slovakia by professionals	–	–	–	–	–	–0.022*
R-Square	0.011	0.774	0.041	0.784	0.014	0.805
n	16326	16326	7700	7700	6571	6571

Notes: significance *** = 0.001; ** = 0.01; * = 0.05.

According to the significant class effect in the first model, middle classes have an earning advantage over the lower class – though the explanatory power of the model is small. It is noteworthy that the class effect remains significant when the control variables are added to the model in the second step. Of course, the class effect drops indicating that gender, educational or sectoral characteristics are constituent elements of class position. In fact, the second most powerful explanatory factor is gender after country in regard to earning. Country effects, however, are huge: the greatest difference is between Russia and the rest of the East-Central European countries in terms of earnings of the population in the labour force. Qualification takes only third place but its direct effect is stronger than the class effect. Age displays the usual reversed U-curve pattern. Economic branch (whether the respondent works in the agriculture, industry, personal or business service) proved to be significant too. Industrial earnings seem to be better not only in comparison to agricultural earnings (reference category), but employment in industry is an advantage as compared to the service branches as well. Interaction terms between class and country are not remarkable. In Hungary, the advantage of the middle class is larger as compared to the lower class than in Russia. The extended model explains 77 per cent of the variance of the logarithm of earnings.

According to the significant negative class effect in the second model, the margin of entrepreneurs' earnings over service-class earnings is considerable. But the comparison of the base and the extended models reveals that this income difference can basically be attributed to the different gender composition and qualification structures of the entrepreneurs and the service class. Being male and having tertiary education have the largest impact on earning capabilities. Still, the extended model shows a substantial and significant class effect as well. The economic branch is a significant but not a strong predictor of earnings. The age effect forms a reversed U-curve again. The country effects display the strong cleavage between Russia versus the other countries in the model. Moreover, the significant interaction terms indicate that the advantage of entrepreneurs over the service class is much smaller in the other five post-socialist countries than in Russia where the earning gap between entrepreneurs and the service class is much higher. The extended version of the second model explains 78 per cent of the variance of the logarithm of earnings in the middle class.

The third model explaining the earning inequalities among managers, professionals and clerical workers also shows significant class effects. Accordingly, managers earn considerably more than clerks (the reference category), while professionals' earnings are somewhere between that of the managers and of the clerical workers – but closer to the latter. The reason for this result could be that this fraction of the service class includes technicians, too. Managers' earning advantages are related partly to their schooling, and to the different gender and age composition of the group. The extended version of the third model reveals the large impact of tertiary education and gender, that is, being male. At the same time, the effect of managerial position on earnings did not diminish after the inclusion of the control variables. The economic branch has significant but small impact in this case, too. Advantage of working in industry is not present. The age effects are the same as in the previous models. The pattern of country differences is also the same: the Russia versus other countries cleavage is characteristic. Interaction terms are not significant in this case. The complete model explains 80 per cent of the variance of the logarithm of earnings in the service class.

Country effects as well as interactions between countries and class showed large variations among the six nations. Therefore the extended models were also run separately for each country examining the impact of predictor variables. The estimates are omitted here for lack of space but the findings are summarized.

To illumine the deviations in the earnings of the entire population in the labour force, gender and schooling proved to be the most powerful factors in every studied country, followed by the effect of the difference between the middle and lower classes. In this relation, however, qualification was not significant in Russia, and the explanatory power of the model itself was slight.

The models investigating the deviations between the entrepreneurial and the service class outline a similar picture. The Russian model had slight explanatory power again. The most important factors were gender, followed by qualification and the dichotomy of the entrepreneurial class versus the service class. In the Slovakian and Russian models the fact of being an entrepreneur contributed much more to income inequalities than gender or schooling, while in the Hungarian model qualification proved to be more important than gender, and even age (seniority) had greater impact than being a member of the entrepreneurial class.

As regards information on models describing the earning inequalities of managers, professionals and clerical workers, it is noteworthy that qualification was a more important factor in explaining the differences in earnings than gender in the Hungarian and Czech cases. This may be connected with the proportion of women in the group of clerks in the two countries. In the Polish case, the negative effect of the tertiary sector proved to be significant. The Russian model of managers and clerical workers is much better than the model describing the earning chances of the Russian middle class and Russian entrepreneurs. Qualification was not significant; gender and managerial position had positive influence; while age had a negative impact. This outlines the dichotomy of a young managerial apparatus, mainly of middle-class background, versus an older administrative personnel consisting mainly of women, not differentiated by higher education. This is hardly a surprise in view of the high rate of Russian tertiary educational enrolment, so it is presumed that the deviations could rather be explained by type of qualification and prestige differences among diploma-issuing institutions.

As for the earning chances of professional (and semi-professional) groups versus clerical workers, we found qualification to be the most significant – similarly to the Hungarian case – in Bulgaria and Slovakia. In the rest of the cases gender played the greatest differentiating role. Beside these factors, age had a positive effect in most cases, and middle-class origin was also positive in Hungary, Bulgaria and Poland. In the Bulgarian, Hungarian and Slovakian cases these factors offset the effect of the professional versus clerical worker distinction. Belonging to the professional groups was, anyhow, not more significant by itself than higher education or male–female difference in explaining earning inequalities.

Income inequalities: individual earnings and family income per capita

For investigating the inner stratification of the post-socialist middle class and its place in the social structure, income is decisive. Income inequalities are examined from the perspective of personal earnings and family income (the latter being controlled by the number of persons in the household). For both measures of income, deciles have been computed and then the ratio of the average in the top decile and the average in the bottom decile has been computed. Table 5.8 displays the highest/lowest decile ratios for individual earnings and income per capita, for all earners in the labour force, for the middle class, for the service class fraction of the middle class, and for the entrepreneurs.

The most important feature of income inequalities in the examined post-socialist countries is that the difference between top and bottom within the middle class is somewhat larger than, or as large as the difference among, all earners in the labour force. This holds for personal income and family income as well. This finding about earning differences in the middle classes being not smaller than those in the labour force probably means that there are widely diverging life-chances and interests within the emerging middle classes as well.

The middle classes as defined for this analysis include managers, professionals, clerical workers and entrepreneurs, and these are very heterogeneous groups as to income inequalities in these countries. As data reveal, the strongest cleavage within the middle classes appears between the service class and entrepreneurs. Income inequalities within the service class are somewhat smaller than the differences observed for all earners in the labour force. At the same time, in this segment of society smaller inequalities were found than in the middle class on the whole. In these countries, there is a widespread view that the earnings of professionals do not reflect their greater educational investments, and that the earnings of managers fail to

Table 5.8 Ratio of the highest/lowest deciles in personal income and family income per capita, 1993

	Personal income *H/L* (*n*)				Family income/capita *H/L* (*n*)			
	All labour force	Middle class	Service class	Entrepreneurs	All labour force	Middle class	Service class	Entrepreneurs
Bulgaria	4.4	4.5	3.9	5.2	8.8	9.2	8.3	15.0
	(2787)	(1018)	(815)	(137)	(2971)	(1078)	(835)	(159)
Czech Republic	3.8	4.0	3.7	4.6	5.5	5.6	4.8	7.9
	(3579)	(1747)	(1419)	(314)	(3699)	(1844)	(1455)	(372)
Hungary	3.6	3.6	3.6	3.3	6.9	6.7	6.7	7.3
	(2213)	(1071)	(827)	(205)	(2336)	(1131)	(875)	(214)
Poland	5.0	5.6	4.1	6.6	8.9	8.8	8.5	10.4
	(1970)	(1173)	(749)	(198)	(2239)	(1318)	(830)	(198)
Russia	6.8	7.5	6.6	8.6	6.8	7.5	6.2	20.6
	(3312)	(1643)	(1540)	(93)	(3008)	(1528)	(1407)	(110)
Slovakia	3.4	3.4	3.2	4.1	6.1	6.2	5.6	10.2
	(3159)	(1564)	(1339)	(210)	(3272)	(1614)	(1366)	(233)

Source: SSEE.

reflect their larger responsibility. On the other hand there are great differences between the earnings of professionals and entrepreneurs.

In general, inequalities by family income per capita are larger than differences of individual earnings. This reveals that – in addition to earning capabilities – family composition, life-cycle and differences in fertility contribute to social inequalities strongly in the post-socialist countries. In respect of earnings, the largest differences can be observed for Russia. However, inequalities are largest for Bulgaria and Poland if family income per capita is considered.

Entrepreneurs constitute a very heterogeneous group in post-socialist societies; part of the group has low income while another part is able to earn large amounts. The ratio between the top and bottom deciles reveals the largest differences for this group, and this holds especially for Russia.

An important finding of a recent study dealing with Russian income chances (Gerber and Hout, 1998) is that in this case professionals may not be counted among the winners of the transformation, which clearly does oppose the predictions of enhanced returns of education. According to these calculations, Russian professionals' income is a quarter of that of proprietors, and is just slightly above that of routine non-manuals. In this case of the market transformation – among the conditions of the emerging merchant capitalism as Burawoy and Krotov (1993) put it – presence on the capital market proves to be a more brutal explanatory factor of income chances than in the rest of the investigated countries. No wonder, therefore, that Russian intellectuals are opposing most vividly the validity of the concept of the middle classes. Occupational class position and lifestyle-status indicators, as well as objective and subjective class identities, are contradictory in their case. They cannot afford the way of life they need or even what they are accustomed to, which is associated to their occupational prestige. But in our view this is clearly a sign of the middle classes being in the process of formation. Newly emerging capital and labour market positions are inevitably associated with asynchronies between objective and subjective indicators. In the longer run, however, presence on the capital market and on the internal labour markets, and the stronger interest-representation capacities of professional associations and chambers make the relative income chance of the middle classes more promising.

The differences of entrepreneurial income are, on the other hand, conspicuously low in Hungary. It is possible that the Hungarian entrepreneurial class is less heterogeneous than that in the other post-socialist countries. But, one may not preclude the assumption either that the Hungarian figures indicating consistently lower income inequalities than the rest of the post-socialist countries are underestimated.

Table 5.9 shows a similar calculation from an alternate data-file from 1996. Here we focus on earners in the labour force and middle classes only, and do not go into the details of income inequalities of various fractions of

Table 5.9 Ratio of highest/lowest deciles in personal income and family income per capita, 1996

	Personal income *H/L* (*n*)			Family income/capita *H/L* (*n*)		
	All work force	Middle class	Service class	All work force	Middle class	Service class
Bulgaria	9.0	9.5	6.5	11.3	14.5	13.0
	(371)	(190)	(150)	(369)	(189)	(148)
Czech Rep.	4.5	4.6	4.5	5.4	5.5	5.4
	(494)	(289)	(243)	(446)	(259)	(214)
Hungary	5.2	5.9	4.9	5.7	6.6	6.4
	(559)	(246)	(208)	(719)	(230)	(195)
Latvia	8.2	8.6	8.7	9.4	11.7	10.1
	(574)	(312)	(270)	(583)	(310)	(267)
Poland	7.6	7.9	4.8	10.3	8.7	7.3
	(527)	(310)	(199)	(515)	(298)	(190)
Russia	15.2	13.6	12.3	12.8	14.8	12.1
	(572)	(246)	(231)	(537)	(236)	(219)
Slovakia	5.8	5.3	5.2	7.0	5.9	5.6
	(419)	(228)	(156)	(375)	(199)	(136)

Source: ISSP (see, p. 106).

the middle classes. Both individual earnings and family income per capita are considered.

Basically, the ratios of the highest and lowest deciles are larger by these data, indicating more inequality as compared to the figures calculated from the other data-file. However, there are three years of time difference between the two data collections in 1993 and 1996 which can explain the dissimilarity. In the course of the 1990s, income inequalities increased in post-socialist societies, which is a common lesson from various national studies. We want to emphasize three features of changes in income inequalities. First, ratios of top and bottom deciles have increased for personal earnings to a larger extent than for family income per capita. Second, in most cases the former finding persists, that is, income inequalities are larger for the middle classes than the differences observed for all earners in the labour force. Country differences display the same pattern as well, the strongest income inequalities are present in Russia and Bulgaria. Third, in most of the countries, income differences observed for the service class are smaller than those for the middle classes, and this holds for both personal earnings and family income. We have no doubts that the large income inequalities within the middle classes are due to the large differentiation for entrepreneurs. We cannot demonstrate this on the ISSP data, as we did on the SSEE data, because the number of cases of entrepreneurs is too small in that data-file.

Conclusion

We defined middle classes as possessing autonomy, distinguished labour market position, typically non-manual work and high trust relations. There are two major components of the middle classes: the entrepreneurial class and the service class. It was found that macro-structural trends – the enlargement of the tertiary sector, the spread of private property and the expansion of higher education – largely contributed to the considerable spread of entrepreneurial and service positions in CEE though with variations by country. Both fractions of the middle classes – entrepreneurs and service class – have extended, but the pace of increase was larger for the entrepreneurs embedded in spontaneous organizations, especially in the Czech Republic and Slovakia. This trend resulted in a relative decrease in the proportion of the service class within the middle classes, despite its moderate increase in absolute terms.

Apart from being mostly male, entrepreneurs are mostly younger and socially constitute a closing group. Although the rate of employment decreased after the great turn, there was a relative growth in the middle class as against the entire population in the labour force. This is mainly attributable to the rising entrepreneurial class and to the fact that especially those in the lower class get squeezed out of the labour market. Further features of the upcoming new entrepreneurial class in CEE countries are that the proportions of women and those coming from lower class backgrounds are decreasing, and the proportion of those with higher education is increasing. There is considerable cleavage in post-socialist earnings: although earnings in general are far lower in Russia than elsewhere, the ratio of the uppermost and lowest earning deciles is highest in Russia. In terms of service-class earnings Russia differs greatly from the rest of the other CEE countries investigated. The earning inequalities within the middle classes are best explained by earnings of the entrepreneurs and managers, apart from differences by country and gender. The earning chances of entrepreneurs acting mostly in spontaneous organizations are systematically more favourable than those of the service-class members working mainly in constructed organizations. Within constructed organizations, the earning chances of managers remained more favourable compared to the groups of both professionals and clerks after being controlled for schooling and gender.

The more expansive fraction of the middle classes, the entrepreneurs, played a larger role in the economy of the 'reform-countries', Hungary and Poland, before the system transformation. The Czech Republic has caught up very fast in this respect as demonstrated by our data (or cf. Večerník's 1995 comparative study and Chapter 9). Much more contradictional structural changes have happened in Russia and in other new democracies of the FSU. The entrepreneurial class in these societies is highly segmented and differs very much from the service class in terms of average earnings.

The counter-argument against middle classes in the ex-Soviet countries usually refers to the situation of their service class, that contains the still 'proletarianized' and extremely low-paid occupational groups of teachers or physicians (cf. Mikhalev's Chapter 1) However, even in Russia there are competent occupational groups that can form the seed of an emerging middle class (Borivikova and Evdokimova, 1999; Khakulina, 1999). Of course, the circumstances of such large groups as teachers or physicians might improve more slowly.

Measured by the ratio of top and bottom deciles, distances within the middle classes were not found to be smaller than within the entire population in the labour force of the respective countries. This is related to the fact that the average earnings of clerical workers did not significantly exceed that of the lower class.

As we have seen, besides the factors of non-manual work and market positions, common preconditions for the functioning of both the entrepreneurial and the service classes are trust and autonomy. The trust of entrepreneurs is placed primarily in spontaneous organizations, while that of the emerging service class is laid in constructed organizations. Individual groups of the middle classes are not characterized by individual assets but by various combinations of assets. Entrepreneurs are mostly characterized by economic assets, apart from cultural and social capital (Rona-Tas and Lengyel, 1997). Professional groups, on the other hand, might invariably be described by their combination of cultural and social assets, besides their respective skills and symbols. As regards trust in the service class, in all groups – those of managers, professionals and clerks – loyalty has a salient role.

In the typical case, the entrepreneur behaves loyally with business partners and expects correct relations, while service-class members are loyal to their employers and the organization that identifies them. However, it must be realized that the transition in CEE has produced side effects that may undermine the identity of the middle classes. Hardly ten years have passed and the press is full of criminal cases involving entrepreneurs – both as victims and culprits – and research findings and interviews register a chronic lack of trust in entrepreneurs.

As for the service class, the main problem is not adaptation to the functioning of the democratic institutional setting. The point is that the emergence of this setting entails frequent changes of hierarchies which result in constant uncertainty. Closing down, merger or inner restructuring of ministries, welfare and productive hierarchies, frequent appointment and dismissal of bosses, the threat of losing one's job – all this has become the daily experience of the CEE service classes. All this eventually leads to the erosion of organizational and personal loyalty, or to its excessiveness. In the late phase of the planned economy, professionals were characterized by job security and clear career perspectives. Criticism, if any, was aimed at 'counter-selection' (non-meritocratic selection) and gerontocracy, the petrifaction of old cadres blocking the careers of younger generations. Today, job security is not granted but career perspectives are present. Little criticism is levelled at the lack of meritocratic selection or gerontocratization, but there are critical voices of excessive political involvement of special professional bureaucracies, warning of the revival of excessive political loyalty. Some extreme populist critics question the competence of professional specialists. This segments the service class by behavioural patterns, not by type of assets. Some are self-assured, orientating well in the labour market, bothering less about organizational loyalty, while others try to recompense their fears caused by uncertainty with excessive loyalty. One finds that in every single country, the better off someone is the more he tends to undervalue his relative position. All this points towards problems of identity and latent dissatisfaction.

Democratization – and hence, a model of sustainable society – has several fundamental preconditions. Huntington himself lists economic growth and the compromise of elites, apart from the size of the middle class. With regard to the developments in CEE, we are inclined to argue similarly, although with more caution. As for the middle classes, it is not merely their size and social proportions that count, but their inner structure and consistency. In our view, a social situation may easily arise in which social distances within the middle classes widen so much in life-chances or value systems that the middle classes will eventually become the hotbed of social conflicts. There is every reason to presume that the extended variant of the conflict model of Dahrendorf may also work. What happens when in a specific historical situation the middle classes are not neutral but incorporate conflicts? Or, what happens if conflicts do not arise between social groups but – as frequently experienced – politicians become the targets of dissatisfaction? The latter phenomenon is not independent of the problems of the middle classes. For, even if in most cases dissatisfaction is aimed at the political elite, the concomitant jealousy and negative stereotypes are levelled at entrepreneurs, the rank and file of managers, professionals and administrators.

The number of entrepreneurial and service positions has significantly increased: there are clearly middle classes in the making in CEE. They are in the making in a rather negative sense of the word as well: they do not meet all of the criteria for proper functioning. So that the middle classes may indeed act as a moderating force, relations of trust must be functional. The chronic lack of confidence keeps gnawing at the operative conditions of the middle classes, undermining their moderating function.

The pace of middle-class formation is not the same in the various countries in CEE, and the middle classes had been unequally developed already before 1989. The contours of a service class, a term used by Goldthorpe, have been and are much more visible in the Czech Republic, Poland or Hungary (cf. Gimpelson's study on labour-market segmentation, Chapter 3). The post-socialist service class is coloured by specific features that are partly consequences of the transformation processes in the last decade, and also partly rooted deeply in the history of CEE. As an example, the phenomenon of emerging managerialism was described by Szelényi (1995). According to this, post-socialist societies can be characterized by the lack of Western-type capitalists. Instead, managers who don't own the means of production but control the economic processes play a significant role in the class structure. This specific feature is more present in such countries in CEE where transformation is less rapid. A long-term historical attribute of social structure under post-socialism is represented by the special role of professionals that is clearly seen in the phrase traditionally used in these societies: *intelligentsia*. A somewhat shorter-term historical feature is the narrow gap between the middle and lower classes as expressed by income relations, lifestyle and living conditions. This is a consequence of the egalitarian socialist politics after 1949 producing a special form of status inconsistency under socialism where higher education and middle-class position go together with low income (Machonin, 1970; Kolosi, 1988). This policy also has an impact on the present circumstances; material and cultural living conditions are highly inconsistent in CEE as another analysis on the six countries of the SSEE data reveals (Róbert, 1997). These facts can explain that several scholars doubt the existence of middle classes in post-socialist societies, even in such countries as Poland (cf. Górniak's argument in Chapter 8, or Domanski, 1994). Other scholars, however, do not search for the ideal-typical Western middle class in the post-socialist societies. They do not conclude that middle classes already exist, but find signs for their emergence. Mateju (1998) speaks about the 'revival of the middle class', although he does not deny that this process will take a long time.

We have argued that the inner structure of the middle classes within each society is crucial, it is perhaps more important than their size. In conclusion, we can add that consistency of reforms at the international level is also essential. Structural changes in post-socialist societies occur at a different pace; developments are more radical in some of them while others show more gradual or even slower changes. From a more global, supranational viewpoint, the future and stability of CEE depends on how these processes may tend to become more consistent, and how the differences among the European societies may tend to decrease.

References

Berend, T. I. and G. Ránki (1974) *Economic Development in East-Central Europe in the 19th and 20th Centuries*. New York: Columbia University Press.

Borivikova, S. and E. Evdokimova (1999) *From Soviet Intelligentsia to Russian Middle Class. Competent specialists on the labour market of St Petersburg*. Paper presented at the 4th Conference of European Sociological Association, Amsterdam.

Burawoy, M. and P. Krotov (1993) 'The Soviet Transition from Socialism to Capitalism: Worker Control and Economic Bargaining in the Wood Industry', in S. Clarke *et al.* (eds), *What about the Workers? Workers and Transition to Capitalism in Russia*. London and New York: Verso.

Burris, V. (1995) 'The Discovery of the New Middle Classes', in A. J. Vidich (ed.), *The New Middle Classes*. London: Macmillan – Palgrave.
Butler, T. (1995) 'The Debate Over the Middle Classes', in T. Butler and M. Savage (eds), *Social Change and the Middle Classes*. London: UCL Press.
Coleman, J. S. (1991) 'Prologue: Constructed Social Organizations', in J. S. Coleman and P. Bourdieu (eds), *Social Theory for a Changing Society*. Boulder: Westview Press, and New York: Russell Sage Foundation.
Countries in Transition (1996) *WIIW Handbook of Statistics*.
Crompton, R. and G. Jones (1984) *White Collar Proletariat*. London: Macmillan – Palgrave.
Dahrendorf, R. (1959) *Class and Class Conflict in Industrial Society*. London: Routledge & Kegan Paul.
Domanski, H. (1994) 'Non-conventional View on Social Stratification in Poland', *Polish Sociological Review*, 1.
Erikson, R. and J. Goldthorpe (1992) *The Constant Flux*. Oxford: Clarendon Press.
Esping-Andersen, G. (1993) 'Post-Industrial Class Structures: An Analytical Framework', in G. Esping-Andersen (ed.), *Changing Classes. Stratification and Mobility in Post-industrial Societies*. London: Sage.
Gallie, D. (1996) 'New Technology and the Class Structure: The Blue Collar/White Collar Divide Revisited', *British Journal of Sociology*, 47(3): 447–73.
Genov, N. and A. Krastev (eds) (1999) *Bulgaria, 1960–1995*, Trends of Social Development – National and Global Development, Sofia.
Gerber, T. and M. Hout (1998) 'More Shock than Therapy: Market Transition, Employment and Income in Russia, 1991–1995', *American Journal of Sociology*, 104(1) (July): 1–50.
Giddens, A. (1973) *The Class Structure of the Advanced Societies*. London: Hutchinson.
Goldthorpe, J. (1982) 'On the Service Class, its Formation, and the Future', in A. Giddens and G. MacKenzie (eds), *Social Class and the Division of Labour*. Cambridge: Cambridge University Press.
Hirschman, A. O. (1977) *The Passions and the Interests: Political Arguments for Capitalism before its Triumph*. Princeton: Princeton University Press.
Historical Statistics 1961–1995 (1997) Paris: OECD.
Huntington, S. (1991) *The Third Wave: Democratization in the Late Twentieth Century*. Norman: University of Oklohama Press.
Khakulina, L. (1999) *The Middle Class in Russia: Fiction or Reality*. Paper presented at the 4th Conference of the European Sociological Association, Amsterdam.
Kolosi, T. (1988) 'Stratification and Social Structure in Hungary', in W. R. Scott and J. Blake (eds), *Annual Review of Sociology* (Palo Alto: Annual Review, Inc.) pp. 405–19.
Lederer, E. and J. Marschak (1995 [1926]) 'The New Middle Class', in A. J. Vidich (ed.), (1995) *The New Middle Classes*. London: Macmillan – Palgrave.
Lockwood, D. (1995) 'Marking Out the Middle Class(es)', in T. Butler and M. Savage (eds), *Social Change and the Middle Classes*. London: UCL Press.
Machonin, P. (1970) 'Social Stratification in Contemporary Czechoslovakia', *American Journal of Sociology*, 75: 725–41.
Martin, B. (1998) 'Transforming the Contemporary "New Middle Class": From Professionals and Managers to Bricoleurs' in *Ivan 60. Essays in honour of Iván Szelényi* (manuscript).
Mateju, P. (1998) 'The Middle Class Formation in the Czech Republic', Working Papers of project Social Trends No. 6.
Róbert, P. (1997) 'Social Determination of Living Conditions in Post-Communist Societies', *Czech Sociological Review*, 5(2): 197–216.

Rona-Tas, A. and G. Lengyel (1997) 'Entrepreneurs and Entrepreneurial Inclination in Post-Communist East-Central Europe', *International Journal of Sociology*, 27(3) (Fall).

Savage, M. (1995) 'Class Analysis and Social Research', in T. Butler and M. Savage (eds), *Social Change and the Middle Classes*. London: UCL Press.

——, J. Barlow, P. Dickens and T. Fielding (1992) *Property, Buerocracy and Culture. Middle Class Formation in Contemporary Britain*. London and New York: Routledge.

Szelényi, I. (1995) 'The Rise of Managerialism: The "New Class" after the Fall of Communism', Discussion Papers No. 16, Collegium Budapest.

Tilkidjiev, N. (ed.) (1998) *The Middle Class as a Precondition of Sustainable Society*. Sofia: AMCD.

UNESCO Statistical Yearbook (1987, 1998). Paris, London: UNESCO-Bernan Press.

Večerník, J. (1995) 'Incomes in Central Europe: Distributions, Patterns and Perceptions' (manuscript).

Vidich, A. J. (ed.) (1995) *The New Middle Classes. Life Styles, Status Claims and Political Orientations*. Basingstoke: Macmillan – Palgrave.

Wallace, C. and C. Haerpfer (1998) 'Some Characteristics of the New Middle Class in Central and Eastern Europe: A 10 Nation Study', in N. Tilkidjev (ed.), *The Middle Class as a Precondition of a Sustainable Society*. Sofia: AMCD, pp. 158–70.

Wright, E. O. (1985) *Classes*. London: New Left Books.

—— and B. Martin (1987) 'The Transformation of the American Class Structure', *American Journal of Sociology*, 1: 1–29.

6
Lower Classes, Poverty and the Poor

Alastair McAuley

Introduction

Transition to a market economy has been accompanied by considerable redistribution of economic power and consequently life chances for many social groups. The importance of wages has fallen while the role of property income and the rewards from entrepreneurship have risen. The market has opened new opportunities and intensified upwards and downwards social mobility benefiting the winners but also creating many losers whose ranks may be adjoined by part of those who initially did well in the new market economy. A major factor here are the changes in the labour market which (as in the advanced industrial economies of Western Europe) result in a reduction in job security. The most important outcome has been an unprecedented rise in inequality and social polarization. Increases in inequality have been associated with the expansion of poverty with all its negative consequences for human development.

While transitional processes have a deep influence on social structure, this impact will be mediated for a considerable period of time by status hierarchies inherited from the socialist – and, indeed, the pre-socialist – past. The social structure of socialist states was determined in part by that of their antecedents: this helps to explain why social structure in Soviet Russia differed from that in Soviet Uzbekistan on the one hand, and from that in postwar Czechoslovakia or Hungary on the other. Long-term trends going back to pre-socialist times lie behind the rural–urban divide and the subordinate role assigned to the peasantry in many societies.

Transitional social changes will also be induced to a greater extent than in the past by influences derived from the global economy, mediated by institutional structures into which states may have been incorporated. The states of CEE were not only socialist before 1989–91, they were also remarkably insulated from economic, cultural and social changes taking place in the rest of the world. Collapse of Soviet power has led to an opening of the region to the global economy, to modern cultural influences, which will also affect social stratification. One apparent result of the impact of globalization can be that the traditional working class, employed for life in large manufacturing establishments, is likely to decline in significance. The traditional peasantry is likely to disappear. (Consider what has happened in Italy over the last 40 years.) The decline in economic factors may create room for other influences to determine social cleavages; this may already have happened with the enhancement of centrifugal forces of political nationalism.

It is less clear, however, what will be the characteristics of the stratum that will make up the base of the new social pyramid. Some economists have argued that if a country is to cope with the demands of the new global marketplace, it will require a flexible and educated labour force willing (and able) to respond to market stimuli, to change jobs and even professions on several occasions in the course of their working lives (Marris, 1996). Equipped with such a workforce, the economy will generate continuing growth. Rising living standards for all would contribute to social stability. If the bulk of the (male) population continues to be educated as in the past – equipped with limited skills that cannot be adapted to new production opportunities – and if the labour market is structured in such a way as to preserve the forms of job-security that were achieved in the post-second world war period, the economy is likely to be characterized by persistent and high levels of unemployment. Stagnant or even falling living standards may result in social instability. Even worse, society may produce an ill-educated and largely unemployed underclass displaying significant features of social *anomie* (Wilson, 1997).

How might the existence of substantial numbers of poor people affect the evolving social structure? That will depend on who the poor are, why they have become poor and how their poverty affects their values and behaviour. As I argue below, if poverty is caused by a catastrophe (environmental or social) and thus strikes families in a random way and, further, if the experience of poverty is not too prolonged, then poverty is unlikely to have a significant impact on social stratification. At most, it is likely to make those who experience it more risk-averse, more conservative and less entrepreneurial. On the other hand, if poverty is prolonged, if it is the result of structural characteristics in economy or society it is likely to lead to adaptations in both values and behaviour among the poor. Such poverty is likely to be self-reproducing. It will almost certainly have an impact on social stratification. This impact will be reinforced if other factors – for example ethnic or religious discrimination – as well as poverty result in the social exclusion of particular groups.

The evidence that I have seen so far is ambiguous, but I believe that the following conclusions can be supported. Much of the poverty that exists in Russia (and elsewhere in former socialist states) is the result of economic processes associated with the collapse of the social system. It is random – and often intermittent or short-lived. It poses a significant burden on inadequate social safety nets, but is unlikely to exert a significant long-term effect on social stratification. On the other hand, there are structural weaknesses in many of these economies. Some of these existed before the collapse of communism; others have emerged (or have become more apparent) since the breakdown of economic planning. These have led – or are likely to lead – to the emergence of a culture of poverty, to the persistence of social exclusion and, possibly, to the growth of an underclass (Lokshin and Popkin, 1999).

This chapter is organized as follows. In the following section we look into the evolution of major social groups constituting lower classes in transition societies, such as the working class, peasants and pensioners. This provides the context in which the character and extent of poverty is discussed. Key features of different concepts of poverty are then described, indicating how they relate to social stratification and introducing the idea of social exclusion. This is followed by an examination of some of the evidence about the nature and extent of poverty in transition economies – primarily Russia – in an attempt to explore the possible impact of poverty on social structure. This theme is then continued by considering how far there is a separate culture of poverty emerging in transition economies. The various elements of this argument are drawn together in the conclusions of the final section.

The diversity of lower classes

Unlike Western industrial societies where the majority is represented by the urban middle class, in transitional economies where the elite is very small and the middle class is not so numerous two-thirds of the population rather belongs to a lower class. Russian sociologist Zaslavskaya (1997) has suggested regarding the majority of the Russian population as a 'base stratum'. These are most of the workers engaged in wage labour, mainly in the state sector and privatized industrial enterprises. By occupational status they are quite diverse comprising lower-level medical staff (nurses), supporting staff in research and education, low-ranking employees in administration, the bulk of the blue-collar workers, peasants, and the majority of pensioners. Their income level is not much different, and is just about the level of moderate sufficiency. It is mostly equal or only slightly above official subsistence minima. In many cases, however, it may be lower than the official level of subsistence. Thus a considerable part of the base stratum of the population in countries with higher poverty levels (especially in the FSU and SEE) falls into poverty.

A substantial majority of these groups have experienced deterioration in their social status, so may be considered as losers of the reform. The loss of social status occurred because these people have been deprived of their former social guarantees, once the egalitarian redistributive system ceased to exist, while they had no social capital to be converted or marketed under the new conditions. This is particularly true of the unskilled and semi-skilled proletariat which has been dispossessed of 'its "hegemonic status", however false and illusory it may have been' (Starikov, 1996).

The bulk of the working class has suffered a substantial decline in real incomes and faced the threat of mass unemployment due to industrial decline and impending reorganization of the economy, with ensuing closures of many unprofitable enterprises. The frustration and disillusionment of the working class has been made worse by the perversion of insider privatization which failed to give workers more control over production and make the administration more accountable to employees. Once managements amassed controlling power over privatized firms, workers became even more powerless than before.

The majority of the base stratum has limited strategies available for coping with the hardships of transition. Since they rarely possess valuable social networks and/or marketable skills, they typically resort to more passive non-competitive forms of behaviour. The most widespread strategy is to keep employment at the enterprise, even facing short-time working, forced leave and wage arrears, while seeking activities in the informal economy. This includes in some cases unofficial commercial activity (shuttle and street trading) but more often traditional forms of self-subsistence such as household food production on individual country plots.

Peasantry represents another big disadvantaged social group in all countries in transition. The cuts in subsidies to the agricultural sector combined with the strongly negative effect of price liberalization on inefficient farming led most farmers to particularly difficult financial straits. Price increases for energy, agricultural machinery and industrial inputs considerably raised the cost of agricultural products and undermined their competitiveness. The terms of trade changed dramatically in favour of urban residents. Agricultural producers faced demand constraints and intense competition from imports on the product markets, and the incomes of farmers and farm employees fell more sharply in comparison with industrial workers. Economic hardships do not allow outdated machinery and farm equipment to be replaced. For all these reasons many regions experienced a profound decline in farm production. Some regions have considerable hidden unemployment in agriculture, resulting in a loss of wage income for the affected farm workers. Rural areas are also disadvantaged in possibilities for alternative employment and hence sources for additional incomes. Thus opportunities for the rural population to improve their well-being are extremely limited. In addition, there is a widespread collapse of infrastructure and social services in rural areas, which have always been far inferior to those of the cities. Rural poverty, however, is less acute in fertile regions, which are used for intensive farming, allowing household food production to provide adequate food products for rural families. Such self-subsistence produces virtually no cash income, so the livelihood of households in such regions may consist entirely of consumption of the harvest collected from private plots.

The agricultural sector has been more prepared for market reforms in CE countries, Slovenia and the Baltics than in much of the FSU and SEE. Where rural residents have managed to establish themselves as individual farmers oriented to the market, they have secured better material well-being and higher social status. Agricultural reform in Russia and the CIS, however, proved much more difficult. The large-scale grain production there is still dominated by the collective sector, which, although having been reformed into joint-stock companies, remains quasi-market and centralized. It is still based on fixed prices and depends on massive subsidies. The economic interests of the collective farmers are concentrated rather in their small private plots, which they use mainly for subsistence of their families and urban relatives. Purely private farms that have been allowed and emerged in limited numbers are not competitive to large collective farms. They prove unviable under existing circumstances due to underdevelopment of markets for commodities, land, services and labour. Moreover, the severe 'class competition' with collective farms unfolds not in favour of individual farmers. In Russia the latter are faced with hostility by rural communities due to deep-rooted collectivist traditions of communal land ownership of many past centuries (Starikov, 1996). Psychological unreadiness of the rural population for market-oriented entrepreneurship combined with the dilapidated state of the rural infrastructure does not present favourable prospects for rapid reforms and development in the farming sector and thus improvement in the social status of the peasantry in quite a number of countries in transition.

Pensioners form a very important and numerous part of the local populace falling mainly into the base stratum of the social structure. They constitute about 40 per cent of the electorate and are thus a politically vocal and influential group. In Russia they number 36 million or 19 per cent of the population. Retirement pensions – which took the largest share of expenditure on social transfers – were in general better adjusted to inflation compared to other social benefits. This has meant that any expansion of poverty among pensioners has not been move than for the population at large. Nevertheless, the value of pensions in real terms has decreased resulting in a substantial fall in living standards. In general, pensioners clearly consider themselves as losers, although they are at no higher risk of poverty than the working age population. In some cases (for example Poland, Hungary and the Czech Republic) pensioners seem to have done relatively well (Kramer, 1997). The elderly have also been actively involved in housing privatization.

There are, however, wide variations in the positions of different groups of pensioners. Pensioners who are still employed (about 20 per cent of their total number in Russia) run virtually no risk of poverty. This risk is also significantly lower for the elderly who live in larger households together with their children. The situation is more difficult for households composed purely of pensioners; however, two pensioners living together are less likely to be poor. Pensioners living alone are at the highest risk, and this increases further with age. There is also a gender difference among the elderly. For elderly females the poverty rate is nearly twice as high as that of males (44 per cent against 22.5 per cent by Russian Longitudinal Monitoring Survey [RLMS] data on Russia) (World Bank, 1995: 21), the latter representing less than a third of all the pensioners due to the considerably lower male life expectancy in Russia.

The diverse group of lower classes embraces socio-professional groups that have experienced a decline in social status in the course of transition. In extreme but not infrequent cases this downward mobility has taken the form of poverty and social exclusion. The rest of this chapter is addressed to the following question: what implications does the experience of poverty over the past decade (or even longer) have for social stratification in post-communist society? Further, it is clear from the argument so far that if poverty is to result in or contribute to social stratification, the poor must constitute a distinct group in society – membership of which should be relatively permanent. Second, poverty – and the poor – should lead to forms of social behaviour or social attitudes and values that are self-reinforcing or self reproducing. If these features are not present, poverty, although a social problem, does not contribute significantly to the underlying social structure of post-transition societies.

Poverty and social exclusion

There are various concepts of poverty that have been put forward by economists and sociologists in the last thirty or forty years and they have somewhat different implications for social stratification. These are spelled out, briefly, in this section. I also discuss the concept of social exclusion. This has been quite widely used in the last decade or so. It is somewhat broader than poverty but has a direct relevance to the process of social stratification – and thus to the subject of this chapter.

Most conventional studies of poverty in transition economies define the poor as those living in households whose per capita or equivalent income falls below a poverty line. This poverty line may be defined in absolute terms or relatively. In either case, however, poverty is conceived as need. The poor are those whose resources are insufficient to allow them to attain an officially specified standard of consumption. This concept of poverty pays little attention to the social context in which the poor live or how they adapt to their status. Often, measurement of poverty in this sense pays little attention to how far the consumption of individual households falls below the officially sanctioned standard; it may also ignore the issue of how long the family has been in poverty (Ravallion, 1992).

If the poor are to receive social assistance, however, it is desirable if not essential for the authorities to have a simple, objective and relatively cheap set of rules which will allow them to distinguish between those entitled to social support and the rest of the population. This is provided by an officially defined poverty line – and by a procedure for checking the incomes of claimants to see whether they are above or below the threshold. The concept of poverty as need satisfies these criteria. Furthermore, a statistical estimate of the extent of poverty can be derived from a conventional family-budget survey. As Amartya Sen (1976) showed over twenty years ago, this approach can be developed to measure the intensity as well as the extent of poverty by means of the so-called poverty-gap and head-count indexes. Sen's initial insight has been extended by Foster *et al.* (1984) to incorporate various degrees of poverty-aversion.

Decomposition routines allow the analyst to explore the relative importance of various factors in producing a given level of poverty and this is of some interest. But the concept of poverty as need and the empirical estimates of the extent and intensity of poverty based on it fail to capture essential features of poverty as a factor determining social structure. In the late 1960s or early 1970s, Peter Townsend developed the concept of relative deprivation. According to this,

> families and groups in the population can be said to be in poverty when they lack the resources to obtain the type of diet, participate in the activities and have the living conditions and amenities which are customary, or at least widely encouraged or approved, in the societies to which they belong. Their resources are so seriously below those commanded by the average individual that they are...excluded from ordinary living patterns, customs and activities.
>
> (Townsend, 1979)

Poverty here is socially constructed: it is the society and its accepted norms which determine whether a family is deprived – and hence poor. Further, the deprived are distinguished from the remainder of society not only (or not necessarily) in terms of either what they consume or how much they can afford to purchase. Families can be deprived if they do not or cannot participate in accepted social rituals – from organizing children's birthday parties to holding a wake for the deceased. In practice, most of the 'living patterns, customs and activities' that have been the focus of discussion in this context have been elements of current consumption. But there is no reason in principle why they should not include investment in human capital – and thus affect the effectiveness of future generations brought up in deprived households (Townsend, 1979).

Attempts have been made to identify the elements which are considered 'expendable' and thus which make up the deprivation index in various West European countries (but not, so far as I am aware, in the USA). These studies have also sought to measure the extent of relative deprivation. Recently we published a study of relative deprivation in St Petersburg and

Vyazniki – a small town in Vladimir *oblast'* (*Bednost*, 1998) – but, to the best of my knowledge the Townsend approach has not been used in other transition economies.

Relative deprivation provides a framework in which the behaviour and attitudes of the poor can in principle be distinguished from those of the rest of society. It thus allows the analyst to pose questions about the existence of what may be referred to as a culture of poverty and about the ways in which this might affect social stratification. But it also suffers from certain shortcomings: primarily, it fails to incorporate an explicit time dimension. Intermittent experience of deprivation and persistent deprivation will have different consequences for stratification, but this is not reflected in conventionally defined deprivation indexes.

In the 1970s, as well as emphasizing the need to determine the intensity as well as the extent of poverty in particular societies, Amartya Sen (1992, 1993) introduced the idea of capability and suggested that the poor could be characterized as those who enjoyed restricted capabilities. The idea of capability has proved suggestive – even though, to the best of my knowledge, it has never formed the basis of an empirical study of poverty. Sen suggested that a capability should be thought of as a capacity to act and gave the example of a bicycle conferring on its owner a 'capability for mobility'. He suggested that all families are faced with a number of needs or potentials for action. How far they can be realized depends upon the resources – or capabilities – at their disposal. The poor lack capabilities and are thus forced to lead restricted lives; or, they may be dependent on the capabilities of others – landlords, *kulaks*, or more powerful relatives.

This idea of capability emphasizes a feature of poverty ignored or underemphasized by other concepts of poverty: the poor are constrained to lead limited lives; they are restricted in the measures that they can take to escape from their situation. This feature of Sen's approach to poverty has important implications for the impact of poverty on social stratification.

In the last decade or so, both analysts and policy-makers have begun to use the concept of social exclusion. To the best of my knowledge, this was developed in a EU context by French analysts. It can be thought of as an extension or generalization of the concept of relative deprivation. As Townsend developed his concept, lack of resources can prevent particular families from participating in activities and enjoying the amenities that are regarded as customary for their society or environment. As a result they are socially excluded. But lack of resources is not the only reason why families or individuals might be excluded from participating in social life. They could suffer from racial discrimination or religious persecution; they could be disabled – blind, deaf or suffering from disease; they could be the victims of prejudice; or they could suffer from socially imposed sanctions – as is often the case with those recently released from prison. The concept of social exclusion covers all of these groups (Wilson, 1987).

Social exclusion in this sense is relevant to the process of social stratification since many of the causes of exclusion imply the existence of permanent (or at least relatively long-lived) groups with their own internal structures. Such groups may be self-reproducing and will, therefore contribute to the emerging social structure. In the next section I will examine the nature and extent of poverty in transition economies as it has been revealed by recent empirical studies and ask, in the light of this discussion, how poverty might affect social stratification in post-communist societies.

The nature and extent of poverty in transition economies

It is not my intention to provide a great deal of statistical information in this section; this can be found later in the country case studies (also UNDP, 1998; World Bank, 2000). Rather, I intend to consider some of the social characteristics displayed by those adjudged to be poor and to ask whether such features might affect social stratification.

The feature of poverty in any society that is most commonly mentioned is its extent – usually measured by the headcount or headcount ratio – either the number of persons (households) or the proportion of the population in poverty. This may determine the challenge facing those responsible for social assistance, but, for our purposes, the prevalence of poverty is not particularly important. It does not necessarily mean that the poor constitute an identifiable social group; nor does it imply that poverty is self-reproducing.

The second feature of poverty upon which economists have focused – its depth (usually measured by the so-called poverty gap) – is only somewhat more important. The poverty gap measures how far the average incomes of the poor fall short of the poverty line set in any particular society. The larger the poverty gap, for any given headcount ratio, the more the incomes (and, possibly, the lifestyles) of the poor differ from those of the rest of society. The more the lifestyles differ, the more plausible it is to talk of a separate culture – and to suggest that poverty may be self-perpetuating.

More important, perhaps than the extent or depth of poverty is its duration. This is something that is not usually captured in the sorts of household income and expenditure surveys upon which statistical assessments of poverty are usually based, but it is a feature that can be derived from panel surveys (Lokshin and Popkin, 1999; Braithwaite, 1999).

There is clearly a difference between the experience of those who suffer occasional interludes of poverty and that of those who are in poverty for much or all of their lives. Households or individuals who spend considerable periods of time in poverty are likely to have accumulated fewer consumer durables. They are likely to have smaller savings and, possibly, less access to credit. This means that the constraints they face in any intertemporal optimization are likely to be more severe. Insofar as our preferences are determined by our experiences (an assumption that poses problems for the neo-classical synthesis but, surely, the only one which is consistent with materialism), such individuals are also likely to have higher rates of time-preference. Further, one may speculate that hardship is likely to make such individuals more than usually risk-averse. These three features of their experience imply that the long-term poor are less likely than others to invest (even in human capital), they are more likely to favour immediate gratification. They are also unlikely to be entrepreneurial. In this sense, if in no others, it may be possible to talk of a difference in 'culture' and to suggest that poverty may be self-reproducing (Ravallion and Lokshin, 1998).

This is not to suggest that those who are plunged into poverty occasionally will be unaffected by that experience. But what the effects will be will, in part, depend upon the cause of their loss of income and on the duration of their experience of poverty. If poverty is the result of factors beyond the individual's control – say the non-payment of wages in a single month – and if the household's resources are not reduced significantly below the poverty line, then the experience is likely to have only a transitory effect on attitudes and behaviour. This is particularly so if the household has reserves or savings which it can use to make good the shortfall in income. At most, one might expect such households to become more conservative, more willing to take out 'insurance' against the future recurrence of such risks. (On the other hand, the sudden experience of poverty may have a devastating effect on the psychological equilibrium of individuals – even if its material consequences are minor.)

A factor which may affect the social consequences of poverty is the nature of what may be called its precipitating cause. This is not something that is always clearly revealed in conventional surveys of income and expenditure, but it can be brought out in panel studies. Transition between poverty and non-poverty is often the result of demographic factors: the birth of an additional child, the death of a spouse or divorce is often associated with a descent into poverty. Equivalently, marriage or remarriage may be associated with the transition out of poverty. These economic consequences of social or demographic changes can be alleviated to a certain extent by social policies. (For example, an appropriate child allowance system may reduce the likelihood that the birth of a child will be associated with a descent into poverty.) They will also be affected by social attitudes: in traditional societies there is likely to be less divorce and hence fewer incomplete families.

Another set of factors affecting transitions into and out of poverty is to be found in the labour market: the loss of a job – through redundancy, disability or retirement – is also frequently associated with a descent into poverty, while finding a job or being promoted can lead to the reverse move out of poverty. Thus the nature of the experience of poverty and the frequency with which poverty is experienced will depend upon the character of the labour market and, in addition, upon the effectiveness of labour-market policies. After all, unemployment insurance is intended to ensure that the loss of a job does not result in an immediate plunge into poverty.

According to the second version of the Russian Longitudinal Monitoring Survey (which was one of the few panel surveys in transitional economies) of those families which appeared in all three waves, some 13 per cent were always poor – and 42.4 per cent were never poor. In terms of individuals the proportions were 17 and 37 per cent respectively. (It should be pointed out, however, that levels of poverty obtained in the RLMS were somewhat or substantially higher than official estimates. RLMS suggested a level of poverty in the period 1994–96 of between a third and two-fifths of households; Goskomstat estimates for the same period were between a fifth and a quarter [Braithwaite, 1999: 11].) There is a reason to believe that the prevalence of long-term poverty in other CIS countries is not smaller than in Russia, while in CEE it is in all probability less (Milanovic, 1998).

Whether or not poverty is long-term, however, is only one feature that is relevant for an assessment of its relevance for social stratification. As I have suggested in several places above, the socioeconomic characteristics of the poor will determine to a considerable extent whether they constitute a distinct social group or whether their poverty is as socially irrelevant as the colour of their hair or eyes.

It has become something of a convention among analysts of poverty in Russia to write about old and new poverty, and a similar distinction is sometimes encountered in discussions of poverty in other transition economies (see Braithwaite, 1997, for the first use of this distinction). The distinction underlines the claim that there was poverty even under socialism. It was often claimed that, before 1989, poverty was a result of the failure of social policy and that the poor mainly consisted of single parents, those with large families, the elderly or the disabled. The new poor consisted of families where both parents worked and was thus the result of low pay – or other failures of the labour market. However, both of these claims are, strictly speaking, false, although they convey a useful generalization. Although there was some low pay in socialist planned economies and this did result in poverty – particularly among workers with large families – most poverty was the result of inadequacies or rigidity in programmes of social insurance or the absence of social assistance (see McAuley, 1979, or Atkinson and Micklewright, 1992, for a more detailed discussion of poverty under state socialism). Equally, in post-transition economies the failure of social insurance benefits to be uprated in line with inflation, their failure to adequately take account of new risks and, in Russia at least, the failure of the state to honour the commitments it has made have all contributed to poverty – that would have been classified as 'old' according to the distinction introduced above.

On the other hand, it is true that, certainly in the so-called newly independent states, a substantial amount of poverty has been caused by failures in the labour market. There has been a sharp increase in wage dispersion. For those earning the lowest wages, real earnings have fallen – sometimes far enough to push wage-earners into poverty. This is particularly true for the low-skilled or for those working in sectors of industry that cannot compete with imports from the more advanced firms in Western Europe or North America. The effects of increased wage inequality have been reinforced by layoffs (the so-called *administrativnye otpuska*), and by unemployment. Of course, the situation has been made considerably worse by wage arrears. In a certain sense, all of this poverty could be categorized as 'new'.

Insofar as this new poverty is more likely to affect those with children, than (at least some of) the so-called old poverty, it is more likely to have an impact on the attitudes and preferences of the next generation. It will, therefore contribute more to the creation of a culture of poverty – the acquisition of a style of life that tends to perpetuate the poverty of those who possess it. Braithwaite (1999) also showed that, according to RLMS data, relatively long-term poverty was almost three times as likely in rural areas as in large cities. Even in small and medium-sized cities it was more than twice as likely as in Moscow or St Petersburg. (But, in part, this result depends on the way in which the poverty lines for children and the elderly were set and the fact that the populations of the two capitals are relatively elderly. [Braithwaite 1999, Annex 2].)

There are two further points to be made about the structure of poverty in Russia and, perhaps to a lesser extent, in other transition economies. First, almost all current estimates of the scale of poverty omit what may be called the sub-marginal strata of the population: the homeless, the institutionalized and/or those recently released from institutions. They also often omit refugees and forced migrants. This is because such groups are not captured by the sampling frames used in the design of population surveys. It is true that not all of these strata are poor; but it is plausible to assume that the incidence of poverty among these groups will be higher than in the rest of the population. Hence most estimates of the extent of poverty are likely to be too low. On the other hand, it is not clear how far such groups will contribute to the development of a self-perpetuating social stratum – rather than reflecting a more or less permanent residue of social failure.

Finally, I would like to move on to the more general concept of social exclusion. In certain circumstances, poverty is associated with groups that suffer from economic or social discrimination. An example of this in CEE are the Roma or, as they are often known, the Gypsies. In Western Europe or North America the black population finds itself in a similar position. The interaction of the culture of the discriminated against group and the prejudices of the majority combine to create a vicious circle of poverty and social exclusion. Because of their colour and/or their culture, such groups are excluded from many mainstream employment opportunities; they live in poverty; the children of such households acquire limited aspirations. Their poverty is perpetuated. (Wilson, 1987, provides an analysis of the link between discrimination and social exclusion.)

In summary, then, although much of the increase in poverty that has occurred in transition economies in the last decade or so will probably not leave a permanent trace in the emerging social structure, there is reason to believe that some forms of poverty are likely to be self-perpetuating. Those who, because of changes in social attitudes or because of failures in the labour market, have been forced into long-term poverty are likely to acquire attitudes which may make them (or their families) less likely to escape from poverty in the future. These include the low-skilled or unskilled; they may also include children living in incomplete families, and possibly those living in small towns and rural areas. They will also include those who are socially excluded because of racial or social prejudice.

Is there a culture of poverty in transition economies?

In the previous section it was suggested that among the poor in transition economies there were groups who might have acquired a distinctive set of attitudes towards savings and investment, towards education and employment, that might lead them to perpetuate their poverty. In some Western economies, this culture of poverty has interacted with the forms in which social assistance has been provided to create so-called poverty and unemployment traps (Lewis, 1968). In this section I ask whether there is evidence that such a culture, such a set of attitudes, is developing in transition economies.

As might be expected since we are dealing with a social phenomenon that has emerged relatively recently, the evidence is mixed. There is some evidence to suggest that certain groups have failed to adapt to the imperatives of a market economy; rather, they have withdrawn into an attempt to recreate a subsistence way of life. This was first observed and commented on extensively in many works by Richard Rose, but the idea of the urban peasant who grows the food his family consumes has become something of a commonplace – particularly among journalists writing about those Russians who have not been paid for months if not years. Given the productivity of labour that could be attained on the plots of land at the disposal of these urban households and their rejection of much of the division of labour, such groups are likely to be poor – and to remain so as long as they persist in rejecting the market.

At the same time, the existence of such groups has been challenged. Simon Clarke and his associates (Clarke *et al.*, 1998) have challenged the so-called myth of the urban peasant and have argued that there is no evidence of a withdrawal from the market in their samples (drawn from such towns as Syktivkar, Samara and Kemerovo). They, in turn, have been criticized on the grounds that the surveys upon which they base their conclusions are inappropriate; that such 'withdrawal' is widespread in smaller Russian towns but that these are not included in the sampling frame from which Clarke's survey is drawn.

There is little evidence, either, that the reemergence of an urban peasantry is a common phenomenon in CE – with the possible exception of Romania. But there is a great deal of anecdotal support for the phenomenon in other parts of the FSU.

There has been a significant expansion in informal activity in transition economies – particularly in the FSU and among the apparently poor. This is badly reflected in family budget surveys, due to concealment or, at least, to underreporting. It is said to be a response to layoffs and wage arrears. In many respects it is similar to what is found in market economies like Britain among the long-term unemployed. Despite the myths, jobs in the informal economy are likely to be undercapitalized and hence have low productivity. As such, most of them are presumably low-paid. Earnings (and indeed work itself) are also likely to be irregular. Finally, such work is likely to be associated with tax-evasion and other forms of illegal or fraudulent behaviour. In Western market economies such informal economic activity is often associated with the culture of poverty – or with the emerging underclass, if such a thing exists. It is plausible to assume that this is also true in transition economies. In many respects this is even true of shuttle-traders (*chelnoki*) even though such activity calls for a certain amount of capital and involves a certain amount of entrepreneurship.

In their attitudes towards work, the acquisition of skills and the exercise of initiative, Russians exhibit similar attitudes to those of the so-called urban poor in market economies. The same is true of many of the poor and unemployed in other transition economies. Groups in both Russia and the rest of Eastern Europe continue to look to the state to supply them with economic necessities and social services, they are still trapped by the dependency culture that was so typical of state socialism. In this, too, there are similarities with the welfare states of the West.

All of these observations suggest that, in Russia at least, a separate culture of poverty may have begun to emerge. But there are other observations which suggest that this process has not proceeded very far, that in terms of their attitudes and in much of their 'material culture' the poor are not distinguished from the rest of society. As part of the study of relative deprivation, for example, respondents were asked which of some 36 or so indicators they associated with poverty. Some 90 per cent or more of the sample identified around 16 of them and these formed the basis for the subsequent construction of deprivation indices. In this context there was no significant difference in the answers given by the poor and the rest of the sample. In this respect, then, the values of the poor did not differ from those of the rest of society. It should be pointed out, however that the study only covered St Petersburg and Vyazniki and, as Braithwaite (1997) has shown, long-term poverty is not particularly widespread in the first of these. On the other hand, in this respect at least there was little difference between Vyazniki and the second capital. (More generally, incomes were lower and poverty more extensive in the small town of Vyazniki.)

Further, a number of surveys have shown that households with per capita incomes below the official poverty line did not differ substantially from the rest of the population in terms of the range and number of consumer durables they possess. These results relate to the middle 1990s and it is to be expected that, where poverty has persisted, households will have become more 'asset-poor'. Thus one may expect that a certain bifurcation will have occurred: some households will have been able to replace worn-out consumer durables and even to acquire a wider range. Some will not; they will have been impoverished by comparison with the position they enjoyed at the beginning of the decade. For Russia, this dichotomy is reinforced by information on savings: only 40 per cent of the population is reported as making savings in 1996–97 (*Sberezhenia,* 1997: 101). The situation in much of the rest of the region is not very different.

Finally, in a number of transition economies there is evidence that secondary school enrolments are falling. At least a part of this fall reflects a reduction in enrolments in trade and technical schools (for Russia see *Doklad,* 1998: chapter 4). This is understandable: for many, there can be little point in acquiring professional training when there are few if any prospects of a job. But the result will be the emergence of larger numbers of semi- and unskilled young people, which, in the long run, may result in higher levels of unemployment among young people – and longer durations of unemployment as well. It may contribute to the emergence of an underclass in the sense used by Robin Marris (1996; Wilson 1997). Further, in some countries, it is not clear that even those who do enrol in technical schools receive the skills or training required for success in a market economy. In Russia, again, there is little evidence of substantial revision of curricula or the retraining of teachers.

Conclusion: poverty and social stratification

It is now widely accepted that, almost everywhere, transition has been accompanied by a substantial increase in inequality. In conjunction with the so-called transition recession, this has led to a substantial increase in poverty – almost however defined and measured. This poverty has been made worse by policy failures in many countries. But in and of itself poverty need not have a lasting impact on social structure. In part, poverty may be a reflection of deeper-seated social processes; in part it may be one of the epiphenomena of social change.

From the point of view of social stratification, what is important are those forms of poverty which are self-perpetuating. Such poverty is likely to be long-term, and it is likely to affect families with children – who are socialized into particular attitudes towards work, savings and investment (particularly investment in human capital). These attitudes may be reinforced by inappropriately formulated social policies – creating poverty and unemployment traps, as we know in Britain.

The concept of poverty that is more relevant in this connection is relative deprivation rather than simple need, although the latter is necessary to measure the scale of the problem faced by social insurance and social assistance programmes. Concepts of social exclusion, the result for example of social prejudice and discrimination, complement relative deprivation as a motor for social stratification.

There was long-term poverty in most state-socialist economies, and the scale of this poverty has increased almost everywhere since 1989. In Russia, for example, surveys suggest that between a third and two-fifths of households are poor and that almost a fifth of these live in permanent poverty. That is, the long-term poor constitute approximately 10 per cent of the population.

If the poor are to constitute a separate and self-replicating group (and thus contribute to a new social structure in transition societies), it should be possible to talk about a culture of poverty and to indicate how such a culture induces behaviour that 'keeps people poor'. Some of the processes involved have been studies in other developed market economies, and there is evidence that such a culture is emerging in some transitional societies – particularly Russia. There is also evidence which points to the possibility that the poor still do not constitute a culturally distinct stratum. This is perhaps to be expected, since the so-called transition process is relatively recent and social change is not normally very rapid. At present, therefore, most transition societies do not contain a clearly defined stratum of the poor. Nor, for the most part, can one talk of an unambiguous underclass. But there are no grounds for complacency; there are sufficient signs to suggest that deprivation and social exclusion may become as characteristic a feature of transition economies as it is of mature industrial democracies.

References

Atkinson, A. and J. Micklewright (1992) *Economic Transformation in Eastern Europe and the Distribution of Income*. Cambridge: Cambridge University Press.

Bednost (1998) *al'ternativnye podkhody k opredeleniu I izmereniu*, Nauchnye doklady Vypusk no. 24, Moscow: Carnegie Endowment for International Peace.

Braithwaite, J. (1997) 'The Old and New Poor in Russia', in J. Klugman (ed.), *Poverty in Russia: Public Policy and Private Responses*. Washington DC: World Bank.

—— (1999) *Adresnost ' I otnositel'no dlitel'naia bednost' v Rossii*, mimeo, World Bank, February.

Clarke, S., M. Karelina, L. Varshavskaia and S. Yaroshenko (1998) *The Russian Dacha and the Myth of the Urban Peasant*, mimeo, Department of Sociology University of Warwick.

Doklad (1998) *Doklad o razvitii chelovecheskogo potentsiala v Rossiiskoi Federatsii*. Moscow: UNDP.

Foster, J., J. Greer and E. Thorbecke (1984) 'A Class of Decomposable Poverty Measures', *Econometrica*, 52: 761–5.

Giddens, A. (1984) *The Constitution of Society*. Cambridge: Polity Press.

Kramer, M. (1997) 'Social Protection Policies and Safety Nets in East-Central Europe: Dilemmas of the Post-Communist Transformation', in E. B. Kapstein and

M. Mandelbaum (eds), *The Social Safety Net in Post-Communist Europe.* New York: Council on Foreign Relations.
Lewis, O. (1968) 'The Culture of Poverty', in D. Moynihan (ed.), *On Understanding Poverty: perspectives from the social sciences*. New York: Basic Books, pp. 187–220.
Lokshin, M. and B. H. Popkin (1999) 'The Emerging Underclass in the Russian Federation: Income Dynamics, 1992–1996', *Economic Development and Cultural Change*, 47(4) (July): 803–29.
Marris, R. (1996) *How to Save the Underclass*. Basingstoke: Macmillan – Palgrave.
McAuley, A. (1979) *Economic Welfare in the Soviet Union*. Madison: Wisconsin University Press.
Milanovic, B. (1998) *Income, Inequality and Poverty during the Transition from Planned to Market Economy*. Washington DC: World Bank.
Ravallion, M. (1992) *Poverty Comparisons: A Guide to Concepts and Methods*. Living Standards Measurement Study: Working Paper no. 88, mimeo. Washington DC: World Bank.
—— and M. Lokshin (1998) *On the Dynamics of Subjective Welfare: A Longitudinal Analysis for Russia*, mimeo, August. Washington DC: World Bank.
Sberezhenia (1997) *Sberezhenia naselenia Rossiiskoi Federatsii: analiticheskii doklad*, Moscow Infograf.
Sen, A. (1976) 'Poverty: An Ordinal Approach to Measurement', *Econometrica*, 46: 437–46.
—— (1992) *Inequality Re-examined*. Oxford: Clarendon Press.
—— (1993) 'Wellbeing and Capability', in M. Nussbaum and A. Sen (eds), *The Quality of Life*. Oxford: Oxford University Press.
Staniszkis, J. (1991) *The Dynamics of Breakthrough in Eastern Europe: The Polish Experience.* Berkeley: University of California Press.
—— (1992) *The Ontology of Socialism*. Oxford: Clarendon Press.
Starikov, E. N. (1996) 'The Social Structure of the Transitional Society (An Attempt to Take Inventory)', *Russian Social Science Review*, March.
Townsend, P. (1979) *Poverty in the United Kingdom*. Harmondsworth: Penguin.
United Nations Development Programme (UNDP) (1998) *Poverty in Transition.* New York: UNDP.
Weber, M. 1961 (1923) *General Economic History*. New York: Collier Books.
Wilson, W. J. (1987) *The Truly Disadvantaged: The Inner City, the Underclass and Public Policy*. Chicago: Chicago University Press.
—— (1997) *When Work Disappears: The World of the New Urban Poor*. New York: Alfred Knopf.
World Bank (1995) *Poverty in Russia: An Assessment*. Washington DC: World Bank.
—— (2000) *Making Transition Work for Everyone. Poverty and Inequality in Europe and Central Asia*. Washington DC: World Bank.
Zaslavskaya, T. (1997) 'Social Disequilibrium in the Transitional Society', *Russian Social Science Review*, 38(5).

Part II

Structural Comparison of Inequality and Social Structures among Archetypal Country Case Studies

7
Russia

Nodari Simonia

Introduction*

In the whole group of countries in transition, Russia in many aspects occupies a unique position. First of all, it is necessary to point out that Russia was the *epicentre* and *pioneer* of that blind-alley economic and social system, that thanks to Stalin received the name of 'socialism' in this specific understanding of the term. Hence there is the strongest possible opposition and resistance to change, and not just within the old ruling stratum as is often believed, and thus particular difficulty in attempts to reform Russian society. Therefore, although the first shock to this 'socialist' system originated from Moscow as its centre, a real breakthrough out of it had to take place (and indeed happened) in its 'periphery' (that is, in the countries of CEE).

The easier transition to a market economy and to a Western type democratic system that is taking place in a number of CEE states is to a large extent explained also by geographical and, most importantly, by civilizational closeness to Western Europe (contrary to *Eurasian* Russia). Besides, their participation in the 'socialist camp' began considerably later, and was much shorter. Due to all that and many other factors, East European societies had been more prepared for major changes, to the process of Westernization, and therefore the changes once started required a shorter time frame. In Russia, however, the significant mass of people yearning for Western welfare out of a 'demonstration effect', was absolutely not ready to perceive Western values and rules of the 'capitalist game'.

Second, Russia stands out for its size in territory, population and natural resources. Being in principle a positive factor, such magnitude makes systemic transformation more difficult. Together with an erroneously chosen reform strategy, Russia's greatness turned into a negative factor, creating additional complications on the way to the society's transformation.

This chapter is based on analysis of processes prior to 2000.

Third, Russia is known for the great diversity in economic and social development of its many regions, the heterogeneity of its national-ethnic composition, and its variety of cultural and historic traditions which have come to the surface during transition and have complicated it in many ways.

Finally, for Russia (as well as for Ukraine) incompleteness is typical not only regarding socioeconomic reforms, but also in such processes as state-building, the formation of the political system, and in the working out of development strategies. In the majority of CEE states the above problems have been largely overcome. In Russia throughout 1992–98 no social consensus was achieved. Political battles between the executive and the legislative branches of power, as well as those inside the executive itself, are still going on perpetuating political instability.

Social structure in the Soviet period

Mikhalev and Piirainen have already described general features of social structures of the so-called socialist societies in the opening chapters of this volume. Besides, a lot has been written on this matter before, which is why I shall discuss only some features specific to the particular Russian model.

Even from the Marxist point of view the system built by Stalin in Russia can by no means be called socialism. According to Marx, the decisive criterion of socialism as a formation superior to capitalism was its higher productivity of labour. However, Stalin created not merely a society more backward than a capitalist one, but a special type of a state – a *totalitarian* one – which does not fit into Marx's scheme of socioeconomic systems (I have examined these in Simonia 1975 and 1991).

It must be admitted that Weber's principles of social stratification, his general idea that pre-market societies were stratified into 'status groups' rather than into classes, are more useful for understanding the social nature of pre-transitional Russia. At the same time it must be kept in mind that the Soviet totalitarian model emerged in an epoch of highly developed capitalism, and was a model of 'catching-up development' within the framework of an industrial paradigm. This means that the model was quite dynamic, and that its development was determined not by natural evolution, but by centralized interference 'from above'. That is why borders between main 'status' social groups were quite mobile and constantly faded away. Thus, as a result of urbanization during the 70 years of Soviet rule, the rural population was drastically reduced (Table 7.1).

Incidentally here lies another very important difference between Soviet society and pre-bourgeois traditional societies. Under the Soviet system, education was an important channel through which distinctions between social 'status' groups was reduced or eliminated. The total number of students in the USSR increased from 47.6 million in 1940 to 110.1 million in 1986, and, naturally, a considerable part of those who received education,

Table 7.1 Urbanization dynamics of Russia – USSR

Year	Population	
	rural	urban
1913	82.0	18.0
1940	67.5	32.5
1970	43.7	56.3
1987	34.0	66.0
including USSR	26.5	73.5

Source: *Narodnoye Khozyaistvo SSSR* (1987): 5, 373.

especially at secondary and higher levels, changed their original social status (*Narodnoye Khozyaistvo SSSR*, 1987: 9–11).

Egalitarianism was another important peculiarity of the Russian totalitarian society. Of course it was not absolute, but in that totalitarian society all were equally subordinated to the will of the party and the state. It was the highest party-state *nomenklatura* who determined how many workers the country needed and in what industries, how many millions of peasants were allowed to leave the countryside and become workers or employees, how many workers, peasants, employees and professionals had to replenish lower and middle circles of the nomenklatura itself, and so on.

The country completely lacked civil society. All the social groups of society were integrated into a single bureaucratic socio-industrial entity where all interactions were determined by Gosplan, Gossnab, branch ministries, departments, and so forth. Notwithstanding the sphere of activity, everybody was in a position of a *state employee* (except for collective farmers whom we shall discuss later). Even 'creative unions' of writers, artists, architects or filmmakers, sport organizations and so on were no more than bureaucratic sprouts of the central party-state apparatus.

The totalitarian state not only forcefully shaped the social structure of the whole society, but by means of political and economic terror changed *the very nature* of status groups. Thus, regarding peasantry at large as a 'hostile class', Stalin physically destroyed or sent to their inevitable extinction in Siberia not only the kulaks, but the best part of the middle-class peasantry. Those left were driven into collective farms (*kolkhozy*) where a *kolkhoznik* (*kolkhoz* member) was no longer a peasant in economic, social or psychological meaning. Stalin's *kolkhoznik* is a truly unique social type, someone close to a semi-serf. With the introduction of a 'passport system' in 1932–33, a *kolkhoznik* was deprived of a passport, and along with it the right to move from his village without permission. More than that, all the product of his labour save for an absolute minimum was obligatorily taken away by the state. All the works (sowing, harvesting and so on) were strictly directed by commands from a regional party committee (*raikom's*). Peasants found themselves deprived of any incentive or initiative as well as their natural attachment to the soil. Hence, indifference, and often devil-may-care attitudes towards the means of production and labour itself, and a persistent thirst for egalitarianism, grew.

Blind-alley types of social systems, such as Soviet totalitarianism, inevitably enter a stage of decay. In the USSR this process began with the rebuttal of Stalinism under Khrushchev and dragged on for almost 40 years. In the economic sphere an important sign of the society's decay was the expansion of the 'shadow economy', understood not only in a narrow sense of underground business (*tsekhoviks* – underground workshops producing consumer goods and so an), but in a wider sense as widespread lobbying in Gosplan, Gossnab and ministries ('pushers') for allocation of resources above planned limits, barter transactions between enterprises, inflated reports on achievements of planned production targets, and so forth. Thus a peculiar dual economy evolved in the former USSR: the upper tier of a virtual official economy existing in Gosplan plans and reports of CPSU General Secretaries, and the lower tier of the real economy, which could not function other than in defiance of official law.

What kind of capitalism is formed in Russia?

From the vantage point of modern Western capitalism, systemic changes in Russia appear paradoxical and even incomprehensible. Confronted with this paradox, the majority of Western observers and Russian liberal economists have attempted to explain the failure to establish a Western type of capitalism in Russia by mistakes and inconsistencies of *liberal* reforms. From their viewpoint, the alternatives for Russia were either a classical Western variant of capitalism, or a return to the old administrative-command economic model. However, no such alternative option exists in Russian reality: neither preservation of the old economic system, that began stagnating in the course of Gorbachev's *perestroika*, nor, unfortunately, direct adoption of a modern Western model are possible.

Any alternatives for Russia exist within the evolving bureaucratic capitalist model as a choice between two of its versions, as we shall discuss. Such a type of capitalism is not a product of natural historic evolution (as happened in the West), but emerged as a result of active intervention of state bureaucracy into the country's economic life (Simonia, 1996: 5–9). In this respect Russia is hardly unique. The model of bureaucratic capitalism is typical of a large group of countries in the process of 'catching-up development'. It came to life in such countries as Kuomintang China, Turkey of Atatürk times, post-war Egypt, Thailand, Indonesia, South Korea, and a number of other states.

Out of the variety of forms of bureaucratic capitalism, I would like to single out two distinct versions (differing in the means of bureaucratic involvement in economics). The *first* version comes into existence when bureaucracy at large as a ruling class initiates revolutionary reforms, or 'revolution from above' (Trimberger, 1978). In accordance with its chosen strategy, it 'cultivates' capitalists and regulates economic development in national interests (prewar Japan, South Korea from the 1960s, New Economic Policy [NEP] in Russia in the 1920s). This is a peculiar bureaucratic capitalism where the state acts as a system-forming factor. With all its shortcomings, this version of capitalism by and large corresponds to the goals of national development, as is proved by success in industrialization and economic growth in respective countries. This version is usually realized under a *strong* state.

Where the state is *weak* the *second* version of bureaucratic capitalism is more likely to emerge. With weakening of government control over bureaucracy, the latter quickly 'gains its freedom' and ceases to be law-abiding. It abandons adhesion to national strategy (if any) and any concern for national interests. Its individual representatives or groups avail of their 'state' status, powers and privileges in order to set up private businesses (individual, family or collective). It is not merely a matter of corruption that is endemic to the formation bureaucratic capitalism, bureaucracy itself makes use of its control over state property to appropriate financial and productive assets (essentially by outright illegal means) to establish own private businesses. This variant of bureaucratic capitalism (Indonesia from the end of the 1950s, Russia from 1992) is of a particularly rapacious and parasitic nature, that proves utterly destructive for national economic development.

Bureaucratic capital in Russia already became apparent in the years of Gorbachev's *perestroika* (Simonia, 1990: 10). Adoption of laws 'On Enterprise', 'On Lease', 'On Cooperation', while creating certain opportunities for small and medium-sized businesses, also gave much freedom to *economic nomenklatura*. New conditions allowed enterprises' directors to concentrate their control over state property; and, simultaneously, industrial ministries, committees and other governmental institutions controlling large assets (offices, equipment, transport and communication, and so on) began to transform into commercial firms, associations, concerns and banks. This is how 'Gazprom', 'Lukoil' and many other large corporations and commercial banks came to life.

With the break-up of the USSR, bureaucracy received unlimited freedom. *Ideological nomenklatura* ceased to exist while *economic nomenklatura* got a free hand on the verge of anarchy. The governmental apparatus continued to grow alongside a general decline in bureaucrats' professional level but expansion of their 'prehensile reflexes'. The situation of legislative chaos, rivalry between executive and legislative powers, disruption of links between the former Soviet republics and the subjects of the Russian Federation itself, economic collapse and absence of control and regulation (as a result of which energy and raw materials exports became sources of enrichment of the bureaucratic bourgeoisie) – all this constitute a favourable environment where all possible varieties of bureaucratic capital began to thrive.

Privatization was one of main, but not the only, channels of capital accumulation by the bureaucracy. During 1992–97, 129,500 enterprises were privatized (see Table 7.2). Simultaneous trade and price liberalization also speeded up this process. In 1991–94 fortunes were made on the margin between domestic and international prices of export commodities, and on exchange-rate differentials. Over 2500 'commercial banks' appeared at that time. By hook or by crook they tried to obtain from appropriate state officials access to cheap credits, to the 'oil pipeline' (that is, oil export quotas), and altogether to the most lucrative spheres of economic activity. It was particularly profitable to control state budgetary funds. Senior government officials chose favoured commercial banks – 'authorized banks' – which were granted the right to deposit and handle budgetary funds (including those in foreign currencies) or finance 'the richest' state corporations. The banks regularly delayed financial transactions, held funds for weeks, sometimes for months, and lent money at higher interest rates to smaller banks and companies.

In sum, corruption in Russia became a pervasive systemic feature rather than an exception or an anomaly. It may even be called a way of life, as even honest people who are not directly involved with the bureaucracy have to live according to these unwritten illegal rules.

Economic restructuring in Russia developed in full conformity with the interests of that variant of bureaucratic capitalism which was established in Russia in 1992–97. The interests of bureaucratic capital are naturally concentrated in the most profitable spheres that bring large and quick returns, that is exports of raw materials, and the financial and commercial sectors. On the contrary, the abandoned unprofitable sector of real production, especially manufacturing, was doomed to stagnation, decline and eventual extinction in a number of industries.

Table 7.2 Number of privatized enterprises by original forms of property

	1993	1994	1995	1996	1997	1998
All privatized enterprises including:	42,924	21,905	10,152	4997	2743	2129
Municipal	26,340	11,108	6960	3354	1821	1544
Regional	9521	5112	1317	715	548	321
Federal	7063	5685	1875	928	374	264
Among them (%) in:						
Industry	28.1	26.9	20.6	17.3	13.3	10.8
Agriculture	1.7	3.0	1.9	2.2	1.6	2.3
Construction	9.2	11.0	9.3	10.2	6.8	4.9
Trade	34.6	28.8	32.1	29.1	27.3	22.6

Source: *Russia in Figures* (1999): 160–3.

Exporters of raw materials and the financial-commercial group therefore represent the two main factions of bureaucratic capital in Russia. They *de facto* ruled the country from 1992 to the summer of 1998. Struggling with each other over their influence on the President and positions in the government, they sometimes acted as allies in the face of attacks by the industrial lobby and the left-wing opposition. This rivalry constituted the essence of political struggle, at least from late 1993.

Social reranking and new social stratification

Consolidation of this predatory version of bureaucratic capitalism in 1992–97 had a deep impact on the formation of new classes and social groups.

The new 'elite'

For purposes of analysis of the social structure I shall use a narrower definition of the elite proposed by Olga Kryshtanovskaya and Stephen White (1996: 712): 'By "élite" we understand the ruling group in a society consisting of the people who take decisions of national significance'. In their interesting article the authors present data on the proportion of representatives of the old nomenklatura in new elite groups in 1995: in the Presidential Council their share amounted to 75 per cent; in the Government, 74.3 per cent; in the regional elite, 82.3 per cent; in the business elite, 61 per cent; and among leaders of political parties, 57.1 per cent (*ibid.*: 729). However, focusing on succession of individuals, the authors ignore the *specific nature* of Russian capitalism and thus come to an idea of virtual *reproduction* (with some new fragments) of the old elite.

Such an approach may lead to erroneous political conclusions about restoration of the administrative-command system itself (which, by the way, is frequently heard in the course of internal political struggle in Russia). In reality this is a much more complex process of a synthesis of certain elements of the collapsed old system with new forms and structural elements borrowed from the West. Concentrating their attention on the succession of individual personalities (which, generally speaking, is natural since otherwise where could different human material appear from?), Kryshtanovskaya and White overlook the new nature of forming a Russian elite, which lies in the *synthesis* of bureaucracy and capital.

Formally, in a physical sense the two components of the new elite could exist (and in a majority of cases do exist) separately. Every morning an official goes to a public office, while a business executive goes to an office of his corporation; but economically they are partners in the same business. The official is involved in this private business at all stages – starting it up, securing licences and privileges, and sharing profits. Often closest relatives or other accomplices are drawn into this business (as is widely seen in Asia too).

The 'synthesized' nature of the new forming elite reveals itself in the lifestyles of its members. On the one hand, having become impetuously rich they enjoy a lifestyle of millionaires: buying jewellery, purchasing properties abroad, spending holidays in exotic countries, sending their offspring to prestigious colleges and universities, visiting the most expensive restaurants, paying for the services of world-known couturiers, possessing the most prestigious car models ('Mercedes-600', 'Cherokee', often not just one, but a whole fleet of 3–5 cars for one family), participating in endless public events such as presentations and celebrations, with demonstrations on TV, and so on. On the other hand, they behave like new nomenklatura. All the old privileges remain practically intact – especially polyclinics and special hospitals, subsidized restaurants and cafeteria, state dachas, office cars with government license plates and special signalling systems, servants and escorts, special aeroplanes, sanatoria and resorts. However, all the above 'inheritance' of the old nomenklatura has been considerably modernized and enriched. One such new feature is seen in elite schools for children where bodyguards protect them.

The merger of the economic elite with top government officials brought to life bureaucratic financial-industrial groups (B/FIGs) which emerged in Russia after 1995. This development changed boundaries between factions within the bureaucratic bourgeoisie. Before that they were mainly grouped by industries, whereas nowadays factions have become more clan-based. Uneximbank formed the 'Interros' group that controls 'Norilsky nikel', 'Leningrad optical-mechanical union', SIDANKO oil company, and others. Bank 'Menatep' created B/FIG 'Rosprom', that, in particular, controls UKOS oil company. Boris Berezovsky invented an original system of 'cross participation' which ensured him control over AvtoVAZ, AVVA, 'Sibneft', Aeroflot, first TV channel ORT, and several other big companies. In 1995 alone, eight B/FIGs came into being (Blasi *et al.*, 1997: 155). As of June 1997, 63 groups were listed on Russia's B/FIG register, 26 of them based only in Moscow, seven registered in regions, but their banks based in Moscow. Nine regional B/FIGs had significant participation by Moscow financial institutions; two though being essentially regional were registered in Moscow; and only 18 B/FIGs were purely regional.

Top managers form an essential component of the Russian elite class, and their power has become greatly enhanced in the course of privatization (on the scope and speed of Russian privatization see Blasi *et al.*, 1997). According to an assessment of the World Bank, Russia turned out to be the only transitional country where privatization was completed with such an impressive predominance of insiders (see Astapovich *et al.*, 1998: 54). Having amassed considerable blocks of shares in their enterprises managers used many means to increase their economic power and wealth: leasing of space, workshops, selling equipment, raw materials, and so forth. Widely practised was the illegal investment of subsidies allotted for payment of salaries to personnel, the use of 'companies-mediators' in marketing products and allowing proceeds to be hidden in secret bank accounts or off-shore companies. Such practices are not unknown to directors of state-owned enterprises as well.

Such all-mighty bureaucratic capital is stifling *free* private business, and this is exacerbated by the weakness of the state, a lack of necessary legislation and law enforcement. One of the most effective means of bureaucratic control over private business has been the permissive system of licensing rather than registration. Under such conditions businessmen are left to the mercy of complete arbitrariness and are defenceless against extortion by bureaucrats. To perpetuate the flow of rents, bureaucrats constantly change the rules of the game. Here we should add the persistent reluctance of ruling circles to carry out tax reform; the principal burden of high taxation has fallen on middle and small businesses, forcing them into the informal sector. Poor tax regulation and the inability of the government to introduce tax reforms also plays to the interests of the bureaucratic bourgeoisie. While oligarchs have many ways of tax evasion available to them, the main burden of high taxation falls on medium and small-sized businesses.

All the above conditions impede the formation of a bourgeois class in Russia in its classical meaning. To be engaged in free private business in today's Russia means to face extreme danger. A private businessman is pressured from 'above' (bureaucracy and bureaucratic capitalism) and from 'below' (mafia structures). That is why cases of physical elimination of private businessmen are so frequent in Russia. Forty-five business people were assassinated from 1993 to 1996 (Blasi, 1997: 119). Since then, however, this list has been considerably revised, and practically all the cases of assassinations remain unsolved.

'Middle class'

Regarding the existence of a middle class in today's Russia, there are various points of view. Liberal and radical-democratic politicians and economists unambiguously contend that it does exist, although after the August 1998 crisis many of them as unambiguously announced the beginning of its death. These persons have used only income-level criteria to determine this class. Other scholars have as flatly repudiated and still repudiate the existence of such a class. Tatiana Zaslavskaya (1997: 10–13) uses the term 'embryo' in relation to the Russian middle class, and divides Russian society not into classes, but into strata: upper, middle, basic and lower.

How did Russia use that human capital that she inherited from Soviet times, and that could form a basis for the formation of a middle class? Much of this capital is being wasted and skills lost due to the *massive deprofessionalization* taking place. Many researchers, professionals, teachers and medical staff, and highly skilled workers have left for small businesses or into the informal sector. According to estimates by the Institute of Labour under the Ministry of Labour up to 20 million people are employed in the informal sector (Maslova, 1997: 38, 40). Other estimates, however, give lower figures for informal-sector employment; that is, no more than 12 million, or up to 15 per cent of the economically active population (Astapovich *et al.*, 1998: 135). Those highly educated professionals who stayed in their pre-reform occupations have the lowest income levels; their once prestigious status has greatly declined as for many in the society wealth and prosperity have become dominating criteria of social rank. Part of the professionals, however, joined the ranks of the middle class, which is in the process of formation.

Small business in modern Russia is the most significant means of involvement of people in commercial activities. In 1996 there were estimated to be 900,000 small enterprises with about 9 million employed. This includes all enterprises with up to 200 employees, but in reality most of them are very small with only a few employees, operating in the trade and service sector (Blasi *et al.*, 1997: 26). A mid-1997 survey by the Russian Chamber of Trade and Commerce and the East European Consultative Centre (Germany) concluded that the growth of new businesses over the years was largely due to small enterprises numbering about one million; 30 per cent of them were in the trade and service sector and 14 per cent, in agriculture.

All 'shuttle-trade' businesses fall into the informal-sector 'grey economy'. They employ about 10 million people, or up to 30 million if family members are included (Maslova, 1997: 44). In 1996 'shuttlers' imported US$14.3 billion worth of consumer goods, amounting to 24 per cent of the total volume of Russian imports (*Russian Economy in 1996*, 1997: 106). Shuttle-trade business forms part of a large sector of retail trade ranging from small-lot wholesaler to tiny markets spreading in cities around any busy metro station. This commercial activity is largely illegal and criminalized. Here are sold not only goods imported by shuttlers, but also those by large foreign firms. These goods pass through the following chain: large wholesaler to small wholesaler-merchant, who controls several stalls at markets; and finally to merchants who directly sell goods at small stalls (usually a hired worker or family members of a merchant of higher rank). Markets and prices there are strictly controlled by members of the Azerbaijan, Tajik or Georgian-Abkhazian diaspora in Moscow and other large Russian cities. The main distinctive feature of this business, however, is interaction with local law-enforcement authorities and municipal officials who regulate and control the local trade system.

Another stratum of the middle class in the making consists of people engaged in mainly intellectual work and professionals – medium-level managers, brokers, traders, bank employees, employees of large firms and corporations, accountants, designers, consultants, those who work in the advertising business and tourist agencies, lawyers, doctors, engineers, and so on. One hundred of the largest Russian banks employed about 280,000 people as of 1 January 1999 (*Finansovye Izvestia*, 1999). On the eve of the crisis the number of these banks amounted to 1700; and earlier more than 2500.

Over the years of the reforms the total number of people working in the banking and insurance business more than doubled, making 1.3 per cent of all the employed in 1996 (Beliaeva, 1998: 34).

The main public function of this rather numerous stratum so far has been catering to the needs of the two dominant factions or various clans of bureaucratic capital. However, all these banks, corporations and trade firms appeared to be 'colossi on feet of clay'; severely hit by the 1998 crisis, this sector shed white-collar workers in great numbers.

Social reranking of the rural population

The December 1991 Presidential Decree on reorganization of *kolkhozy* and *sovkhozy* was expected to push *kolkhozniki* out of *kolkhozy* and *sovkhozy*. The reality, however, proved very different. The absolute majority of *kolkhozy* and *sovkhozy* were 'transformed' into joint-stock companies or open types of associations. As for the set of individual private farms, although it received a certain initial impetus, it failed to acquire a sufficiently large scale without consistent state support (Table 7.3).

At the same time, much of the rural economy moved into a vast informal sector. It consisted of rural household plots belonging to members of *kolkhozy* and *sovkhozy*, pensioners, employees and so on. Two decrees of the President: 'On Regulation of Land Relations and Development of Agrarian Reform in Russia' (1993) and 'On Realization of Constitutional Rights of Citizens to Land' (1996) encouraged this development. According to those decrees, any rural resident had the right to his share of collective farm land (approximately 1.5–1.6 hectares per household) to be used as a household plot. The overwhelming majority of rural households remained members of *kolkhozy*, which in the absence of support from the government remained the essential source of subsidized forage, gasoline and fertilizers. As in the Soviet times, it was not uncommon to plunder these resources from the *kolkhoz* for personal needs, and for that reason an estimated one-third of total incomes raised from household plots cannot be regarded as of perfectly legal origin (*Moskovskie Novosti*, 1999).

Table 7.3 Farmers' households

	1993	1994	1996	1999
Number of registered households (000s)	182.8	270.0	280.1	270.2
Total lands (thousands of hectares)	7804	11342	12011	13845
Average size of household plots (hectares)	43	42	43	51

Source: *Russia in Figures* (1999): 160.

Table 7.4 Agricultural production by the type of produce, 1997

	Agricultural enterprise	Farmers	Personal households
Total area under cultivation (million hectares)	165.8	11.7	10.2
Share in production (%)	47	2	51
Including:			
Potatoes	7.7	1.0	91.3
Vegetables	22.2	1.5	76.3
Milk	51.3	1.5	47.2
Wool	44.3	4.4	51.3
Meat	42.5	1.6	55.9
Grain	93.0	6.2	0.8
Sunflower seeds	87.8	10.8	1.4
Sugar beat	95.7	3.5	0.8

Source: *Russia in Figures* (1999): 202–4.

Production from household plots, unlike those registered by farmers, largely falls into a mass informal sector, as is the case with other individual agricultural activities (including those by urban residents at their dachas, orchards or vegetable gardens). As is shown in Table 7.4 the informal household sector contributes a very significant share to annual agricultural production.

The 'base stratum'

Unlike developed Western societies, where the majority of the population can be attributed to a middle class, in Russia two-thirds of the whole population belongs rather to a poorer 'base stratum' (Zaslavskaya, 1997: 15). Due to hard social and economic conditions, this stratum includes blue-collar workers and the majority of employees of state and private enterprises, doctors and medical personnel, cultural workers, rank-and-file employees and supporting staff in research and science, teachers in secondary and higher education, and workers of agricultural enterprises.

During the years of the reforms there was a considerable reduction in the number employed in the economy. In 1986 the total number of workers, apprentices and junior attending personnel amounted to 31.4 million people (*Narodnoye Khozyaistvo SSSR*, 1998: 64). In 1992 the total industrial labour force numbered only about 20 million people. In the subsequent years, 1992–97, the number of enterprises considerably increased from 61.7 thousand in 1992 to 157,000 in 1997. At the same time the number of those employed in industry fell to just over 13.8 million people (*Russia in Figures*, 1998: 160). This is evidence of the fact that new enterprises were created mainly in the small and medium-sized enterprise (SME) sector, and that there was a considerable reduction of the number of workers in already existing enterprises.

Workers in industrial enterprises are frequently subject to short-time working, forced leaves, wage arrears, and the threat of mass dismissals. In many enterprises workers lose their professional skills as they spend much of their time on activities in the informal sector (either directly at their workplace at the enterprises or outside) to earn a living.

Workers in healthcare, culture, arts and social care, numbering about 12 million in 1997, found themselves in particularly dire situations. Low salaries and delays of payment for many months, acute shortages of medicines, medical equipment, educational and training materials and so on provoked these categories of workers to go on strike.

The situation in science is equally hard. There is a narrow layer of new research institutes and universities established at the initiative of top government officials (and partially headed by them) that attend to interests of bureaucratic capital and to the needs of respective state bodies. These privileged institutions have no financial difficulties, whilst the remaining sector of science (both fundamental and applied) is virtually abandoned. No wonder that the number of scientists and supporting workers in science decreased by half – from 2.8 million in 1990 to 1.4 million people in 1997 (Astapovich *et al.*, 1998: 890). Science has considerably lost its former prestige. A poll carried out in six elite higher educational institutions (such as Moscow State University, Moscow Bauman State Technical University, and Moscow Aviation Institute) revealed that in all of them over half of new graduates did not intend to work in the profession they had trained for (*Informatsionny Vypusk RAN*, 1999).

The socially deprived

Poverty existed in the USSR among certain social categories such as single mothers, families with many children, pensioners living alone, and so on. However, as a result of ultra-liberal reforms the groups and numbers of people affected by poverty have greatly expanded. Most importantly, 'new poor' have emerged; that is, people who lost the sufficient and stable incomes they had enjoyed before the reforms. According to UNDP data, at the end of the 1980s people considered to be poor numbered 2 per cent of the population, but by 1993–94 their proportion had reached a dramatic 45 per cent. Although it is less than the average for Central Asia (59.5 per cent), it is strikingly higher than in the Czech Republic, Slovakia (1 per cent), Hungary (3 per cent) and even Poland (19 per cent) (UNDP, 1998: 212).

Who are the people forming the ranks of the 'new poor'?

First of all, this a considerable part of the unemployed, and an entirely new category for Russia. Chapter 3 by Gimpelson in this volume provides important data on the scope and structure of unemployment. What should be highlighted is a particularly disturbing trend of an increasingly chronic nature of unemployment for a certain group of people who lose their jobs. Thus the share of those unemployed for more than a year increased from 15.1 per cent in March 1996 to 23 per cent in December 1997. Moreover, contrary to a typical case in developed market economies, the growth of unemployment took place against the background of remaining latent unemployment: the number of those who worked short-time increased from 1.6 million people in 1993 to 3.4 million in 1996, while the number of people on forced administrative leave grew from 1.7 to 2.4 million (Astapovich *et al.*, 1998: 132–3, 391, 393).

Another considerable social group joining the ranks of the 'poor' are *pensioners*, especially those 80 per cent of them who do not have an official job, that is approximately 28.8 million people. Although the average pension/average wage ratio has slightly improved from 33.8 in 1991 to 38.1 in 1995, it is much lower than in the Czech Republic (46.3) or Hungary (59.1), where it worsened, and only about half of that Poland (72.8) where it considerably improved (UNDP, 1998: 99). This improvement in Russia has little meaning in practical terms. Salaries in Russia are considerably lower than in CE, and, accordingly, pensions in absolute terms are miserable. That is why many of the elderly who depend upon extremely low minimum pensions as their sole source of income have fallen into extreme poverty.

Poverty in Russia has widely affected *children* of various social groups. In 1994 the poverty rate among children under 15 stood at 46 per cent, and a phenomenal 73 per cent of families with three or more children were impoverished (UNDP, 1998: 16–17). Out of 37 million children in 1996, around two million found themselves without shelter, more than 596,850 were registered as orphans, or 'social orphans', that is abandoned children (*Russian Statistical Yearbook*, 1998: 267; *Obschaya Gazeta*, 1998). Pre-school education enrolment rates (as a percentage of the 1–6-year-old population) decreased from 69.3 in 1989 to 55.0 in 1996 (UNDP, 1998: 71).

In 1998, according to official data, 367,000 pupils were sent down from schools and did not restart their studies; 424,000 minors and over 202,000 parents who do not attend to their parental duties are on the books of the Home Ministry (*Segodnya*, 1999). The number of robberies, plunders, thefts and group crimes committed by minors is threateningly increasing (Table 7.5).

Simultaneously, specific categories of the poor have appeared in Russia: homeless and vagrants, beggars, refugees and displaced people, and prostitutes. An important characteristic feature of the majority of the above categories of people is that many of them are involved in real 'black' business, which is of large scale and efficiently organized. Hundreds of millions and even billions of 'dirty' dollars are made in this business that involves certain representatives of the lower and medium-level bureaucracy, and a considerable part of law-enforcement agencies.

Table 7.5 Youth crime indicators (000s)

	1990	1993	1996	1997
Number of crimes committed by minors or with their participation	164.7	223.7	202.9	182.8
Number of convicted young (up to 30) criminals	311.5	431.2	560.6	553.5
Including crime against property	102.4	178.9	357.3	364.7

Source: *Russian Statistical Yearbook* (1998): 336.

Begging is a typical example. With very rare exceptions all the beggars in Moscow city are institutionalized, that is divided among various mafia groupings and allotted to certain regions. The number of such beggars, only by information from the municipal militia (police) administration, amounts to about 70,000 (*Nezavisimaya Gazeta-Krug Zhizni*, 1998: 3).

Dumps in large cities represent a specific social phenomenon, and peculiar hierarchical social structures have evolved around such dumps. According to estimates, the Moscow city dump helps more than half a million people to survive, including those residents of small towns and villages who live near the dumps (Maslova, 1997: 45).

The army of the poor is also enlarged by forced migrants – refugees from other republics of the FSU and also displaced persons inside Russia itself. In the year 1995 alone there were about 272,000 new migrants, in 1997 a little over 131,000. All in all from the beginning of registration up to 1 January 1998, the Federal Migration Service registered about 1,192,000 people (these are only those who received the official status, including 235,000 refugees) (*Russia in Figures*, 1998: 38).

All of this evidence leads to the conclusion that a new phenomenon – pockets of an underclass of the poor – is springing up in large Russian cities.

Social differentiation and inequality

Social differentiation deepens in Russia against the background of a sharp reduction of GNP per capita. According to UNDP calculations (on a PPP basis), this indicator decreased from US$4070 in 1987 to US$2240 in 1995, and accordingly the index of real net wages (1989 = 100) in 1995 fell to 45.1 (UNDP, 1998: 212). The public revenue/GDP ratio declined from 1992 to 1995 by over 37 per cent, with direct adverse effects for social welfare. For comparison, in Poland and the Czech Republic in approximately the same period (1991–94) this index decreased by about 17 per cent, in Hungary (1991–95) by less than 16 per cent (UNDP, 1998: 96).

The differentiation of the Russian population according to the distribution of incomes between various groups is shown in Table 7.6. The income

Table 7.6 Distribution of household income by quintile groups

	1992	1993	1994	1995	1996	1997	1998
First group (lowest income)	6.0	5.8	5.3	5.5	6.2	6.0	6.2
Second	11.6	11.1	10.2	10.2	10.7	10.2	10.5
Third	17.6	16.7	15.2	15.0	15.2	14.8	14.9
Fourth	26.5	24.8	23.0	22.4	21.5	21.6	21.0
Fifth group (highest income)	38.3	41.6	46.3	46.9	46.4	47.4	47.4
Gini coefficient	0.289	0.398	0.409	0.381	0.375	0.381	0.379

Source: *Russia in Figures* (1999): 110.

disparity between the 10 per cent richest people and the 10 per cent poorest has changed for the worse in the years of the reforms. In the difficult year 1992, the richest 10 per cent received eight times more income than the 10 per cent poorest. In 1997 this gap widened to 13.2 times, and in 1998 (before the crisis) to 13.3 times (*Federalny Spravochnik*, 1998: 237). Soon after the 1998 crisis the Goskomstat announced that this same ratio reached 16 times (*Moskovskie Novosti*, 1998). According to the data of the Institute of Population of the Russian Academy of Sciences, 2.5 million Russians can be considered rich (up to 7 million with family members), and this 1.5 per cent of the population possess 65 per cent of the national wealth (*Moskovskie Novosti*, 1998). The above data are close to estimates by UNDP experts, who believe that in 1996 the richest 5 per cent of the population controlled a share of income equal to that of the bottom 60 per cent (UNDP, 1998: 20).

The situation was aggravated by endless delays in adoption of the law 'On the Subsistence Minimum'. As a result the unnatural situation persisted when the minimum wage was much lower than the subsistence level. In 1993 it ranged between 39 to 21 per cent of the subsistence level, in 1995 between 17 to 8 per cent, and in 1996 between 20 to 15 per cent (Maslova, 1997: 105–6). The government's policy actually contributed to polarization in society by keeping the minimum wage at an unacceptably low level, by manipulating wage tariff rates, and by delayed and incomplete indexing of incomes (Table 7.7). As a result the proportion of the population with incomes lower than the subsistence level steadily grew.

It should be noted that *average* indicators in Russia's conditions have relative and rather limited meaning. In the mid-1990s, Mikhalev and Björksten (1995: 22–3) pointed out serious differences in wage levels depending on region or industry. Since then the situation has only got worse. Taking the August 1998 average wage (1047 roubles) as 100 per cent, the average percentage figures in industry equalled 118.5; in electric energy 187.9; in non-ferrous metallurgy 192.9; in the fuel industry 228.4; in oil extraction 248.7; and in

Table 7.7 Subsistence-level indicators

	1992	1993	1997	1998*
Minimal subsistence level (average, per capita/per month)	1.9	20.6	411.2	493.3
Including:				
Economically active population	2.1	23.1	462.4	554.7
Pensioners	1.3	14.4	289.9	347.9
Children	1.8	20.7	415.1	498.2
Minimal wages	0.7	6.1	83.5	83.5
Minimal pensions due	1.1	11.3	222.0	234.2
Number of population with income below minimal subsistence level:				
millions	50.2	46.9	30.7	35.0
% of total population	33.5	31.5	20.8	23.8

Note: In thousands of roubles; * 1998 – in roubles after depreciation of currency.
Source: *Russia in Figures* (1999): 102–3.

the gas industry 458.5 per cent. On the contrary, in science wages were 90.1 per cent of the average; in engineering 85.8; in education 54.3; in light industry 52; and in agriculture 44 per cent (*Federalny Spravochnik*, 1998: 238–9).

In Russian regions, wages and pensions differ not only in their amounts, but also in their relation to local subsistence levels as shown in Table 7.8.

Decline of the welfare system

In the FSU the state traditionally provided a range of social services and offered comprehensive benefits. Full employment was guaranteed, so there was no unemployment insurance. Social protection focused on the old and the disabled. In-kind subsidies (housing, energy and so forth) played an important role. After Russia's transition to the market this system of universal coverage became no longer affordable, but till now has not been replaced by more targeted programmes. Adapting the welfare system to the new conditions has proved politically difficult. Due to the Russian type of bureaucratic capitalism, the transition towards a market economy has proved incompatible with the development of a social security system capable of providing effective protection to low-income and vulnerable groups, and mitigating inequality via social transfers.

There is one more important aspect of the problem. Until 1991 social infrastructure managed by *state enterprises* provided a range of social services to more than half of the working population. In addition, industries and enterprises offered 'patronage' of municipal social assets (schools, recreation centres and so on) and regional and federal assets (theatres, institutes of higher education). But after privatization enterprises have no economic incentives for maintaining these social assets, and the first act of many

Table 7.8 Minimal subsistence level by regions, 1997 (in roubles, average per month)

Russian Federation	411,236		
Northern Region		*Central Region*	
Vologod *oblast*	402,708	Bryansk *oblast*	289,292
Nenets autonomous area	701,284	Moscow Municipality	529,254
Volga-Vyatka Region		*Central-Chernozem Region*	
Nizhny Novgorod *oblast*	313,644	Belgorod *oblast*	316,033
Kirovsk *oblast*	405,800	Tambov *oblast*	268,754
Volga Region		*North-Caucasus Region*	
Penzensk *oblast*	368,583	Ingush Republic	378,170
Ul'yanovsk *oblast*	271,175	Dagestan Republic	282,325
Ural Region		*West-Siberian Region*	
Sverdlovsk *oblast*	432,514	Yamalo-Nenets auton. area	779,237
Bashkir Republic	305,583	Omsk *oblast*	348,383
East-Siberian Region		*Far-Eastern Region*	
Taymyr auton. area	747,143	Koryak auton. area	1,541,525
Ust'ordinsky Buryat auton. area	367,000	Jewish auton. *oblast*	471,018

Note: We selected two areas from each of ten large socioeconomic regions of the Russian Federation, with the lowest and highest minimal subsistence levels.
Source: *Russian Statistical Yearbook* (1998): 226–7.

privatized enterprises was, therefore, to dispose of the old social assets. During 1993–97, enterprises divested 80 per cent of their assists in housing, 76 per cent in kindergartens, 75 per cent in children's recreation camps, 82 per cent in polyclinics and hospitals, and 84 per cent in cultural and in sports facilities (Healey *et al.*, 1998: 19, 25).

As for the state social security system, it works exceptionally ineffectively, even in those cases where social transfers have been quite considerable, for example pensions. In spite of many years of long talks about the necessity to make social transfers more targeted, in reality nothing has been accomplished as yet (to a considerable degree also due to vested interests of the many deputies of the Duma). Large sums of pension transfers are 'blurred' across a wide spectrum of the population without taking into consideration the differences in average per capita family incomes and other factors. As a result, really deprived people remain in a dire situation, while working pensioners in well-off families receive even more. The situation of poor pensioners has been made worse by the inability or unwillingness of the government to index pensions adequately.

The introduction of new transfers, such as unemployment compensation, also appeared to be ineffective. Unemployment benefits are given, naturally, only to officially registered persons, but the majority of the unemployed

Table 7.9 Life expectancy at birth and mortality indicators

	1989	**1995**
Life expectancy at birth		
Total	69.2	64.8
Men	64.2	59.6
Women	74.8	72.2
Infant mortality (per 1000 live births)	17.8	17.6
Birth rate, crude (per 1000 people)	14.6	9.3
Death rate, crude (per 1000 people)	10.7	14.7

Source: UNDP (1998): 213–16.

(due to various reasons, including psychological ones) avoid registration. Unemployment benefits amounted to only 10 per cent of the total spending on all kinds of social benefits other than pensions in 1997 (as compared to 36 per cent on temporary disability allowances, and 45.9 on maternity benefits. The total share of all the payments on social assistance did not exceed 1.8 per cent of GDP and 3 per cent of the volume of the population's monetary incomes (*Russia in Figures*, 1998: 75). All social assistance benefits are poorly targeted according to family income situations and are often paid only after long delays.

Hard economic and social situations in the country negatively affect the population's health, birth rate, mortality rate and life expectancy. Russia experiences the most severe health and mortality crisis as is clear from Table 7.9.

Policy conclusions

Under current conditions, all the attempts to formulate relevant policy approaches conductive to sustainable social development and social cohesion in Russia are blocked by the continuing processes of 'primitive accumulation' and formation of bureaucratic capital. Consolidation of the top supreme power (the President and Prime Minister) is an absolutely necessary condition for any social and economic progress in Russia, as the peculiarity of the moment lies in the fact that both relative social consensus and relative political stability may be established only *by volitional effort from above.*

- Our first conclusion from the above is that Russia should first of all undergo a political shift, the result of which will be the establishment of a consolidated, stable and strong executive power (this is possible even within the framework of the existing constitution, although, unfortunately, exit out of its setting cannot be completely excluded).
- Second, Russia needs a gradualist approach in transition to a full-value market economy. In the course of the transitional period modernization

of society will progress on the basis of a dynamic synthesis of borrowed and locally-based structures. The need for such an approach has been proven by counterfactual experience: accelerated privatization did not give Russia normal capitalists and a middle class, but parasitic bureaucratic capitalists and a 'consumer' pseudo-middle class.

- Third, the government in Russia has to restructure completely the whole financial system, to reorient it to the needs of the real sector of the economy. Industries based on exports of raw materials should also be restructured. Rather than serving their own self-interests, they must be subordinate to the priorities of general economic development. In the industrial sector it is necessary to single out eight to ten priority areas and there concentrate the efforts of state and private capital.
- Fourth, the state has to assume a key role in creating favourable conditions for medium and small businesses, and for foreign investments (direct rather than portfolio). This requires a clear and solid legislative framework, a reasonable tax system, and a registrative rather than permissive approach in licensing, and so forth. In general the country needs a reasonably effective balance between the regulating role of the state and the free market to make the economy work.

Until now the destructive (revolutionary) aspect of the reforms has predominated in Russia. There were, of course, certain positive results, such as a build-up of skills, or a better understanding of the realities of modern economies. However, these positive elements, as they are outside the general constructive and creative economic development strategy, will be easily lost. In other words, positive aspects of the reforms in Russia are still to be realized. Only then will it be possible to normalize the labour market, to reach a more equitable distribution of incomes, to block and reverse differentiation and polarization in society. Under such circumstances civil society will then be able to form, thus laying the essential base on which real democracy can be achieved.

References

Astapovich, A. *et al.* (1998) *Russian Economic Policy Survey, 1997.* Moscow: Bureau of Economic Analysis Foundation (in Russian).

Beliaeva, L. (1998) '"New Middle" in Russia', *Svobodnaya mysl* 7 (July) (in Russian).

Blasi, J. R., M. Kroumova and D. Kruse (1997) *Kremlin Capitalism. The Privatization of the Russian Economy*. Ithaca and London: Cornell University Press.

Federalny Spravochnik (1998) (Federal Reference Book. Social-economic Situation in Russia. January–September 1998). Moscow: Goscomstat *et al.* 1998 (in Russian).

Finansovye Izvestia (1999) Financial News, 16 February, Moscow.

Healey, N., V. Leskin and A. Svetov (1998) 'Privatization and Enterprise-owned Social Assets', *Russian Economic Barometer*, no. 2.

Informatsionny Vypusk RAN (1999) (RAS Information Issue), no. 10, 23–29 March.

Kryshtanovskaya, O. and S. White (1996) 'From Soviet Nomenklatura to Russian Elite', *Europe-Asia Studies*, 48(5): 711–33.

Maslova, I. (ed.) (1997) *Russia's Social Development Regulation*. Moscow: Institute of Economy, RAS (in Russian).

Mikhalev, V. and N. Björksten (1995) *Wage Formation during the Period of Economic Restructuring in the Russian Federation*. Paris: OECD.

Moskovskie Novosti (1998) Moscow News, 6–13 September.

—— (1999) Moscow News, 14–21 February.

Narodnoye Khozyaistvo SSSR (1987) (USSR People's Economy). The USSR Central Statistical Department.

Nezavisimaya Gazeta-Krug Zhizni (1998) October, no. 12.

Obschaya Gazeta (1998) 23–29 July.

Russia and CIS (1998) Moscow: Goscomstat (in Russian).

Russia in Figures (1998, 1999) *Russia in Figures. A Short Statistical Reference Book*. Moscow: Goscomstat (in Russian).

Russian Economy in 1996 (1997) *Trends and Outlooks*. Issue 16. Moscow: Institute for Economy in Transition.

Russian Statistical Yearbook (1998) Statistical Reference Book. Moscow: Goscomstat (in Russian).

Segodyna (1999) (Today), daily newspaper, 24 February.

Simonia, N. (1975) *Countries of Orient: Paths of Development*. Moscow: Nauka (in Russian).

—— (1990) 'State, Cooperatives and Bureaucratic Capital', *Moscow News*, no. 9, 4 March 1990 (in Russian).

—— (1991) *What Have We Built*. Moscow: Progress Publishers (in Russian).

—— (1996) 'About Bureaucratic Capitalism in Russia', *World Economy and International Relations*, no. 7 (in Russian).

Trimberger, E. K. (1978) *Revolution from Above: Military Bureaucrats and Development in Japan, Turkey, Egypt and Peru*. New Brunswick: Transaction Books.

United Nations Development Programme (UNDP) (1998) *Poverty in Transition?* New York: UNDP.

Zaslavskaya, T. (1997) 'Social Structure of Russian Society Today', *Social Sciences Quarterly Review*, XXVIII(3).

8
Poland

*Jarosław Górniak**

Social stratification prior to the transformation

In socialist systems, income differences were not a good measure of differences in access to socially desirable goods. Access to many goods was regulated by a system of rationing and group-specific rights, and thus by a non-market and non-pecuniary system of distribution. This system was not based on an individual's ability to compete in the market, but on his or her usefulness in maintaining the political order. In this case, we may argue that differences in access to goods resulted from varying levels of political capital, as was pertinently pointed out by Szelényi and Szelényi (1995). The political mechanism determining the distribution of goods likewise resulted in society being divided into the privileged (especially *nomenklatura*) and the non-privileged.

I propose, however, to expand this concept of political capital one stage further. Another form of political capital under socialism concerned the role of different interest groups (branch corporations) in maintaining social order (Górniak, 1989). The possession of political capital of the first kind (defined above) involved a greater sense of status based on individual achievement (although in political rather than economical terms). The possession of political capital of the second kind, resulting from affiliation to a branch corporation, involved a stronger sense of status gained through ascription, while maintaining to a large extent open access to corporations.

*I wish to thank the CSO, especially Mr W. Lagodzinski, for the data and kind assistance; J. Wasilewski for providing me with the newest data on Polish elites; S. Hanson, J. Wasilewski, V. Mikhalev and the authors of this volume who read the first draft of the paper for comments and suggestions.

The stratifying impact of political capital blurred the influence of traditional class positions on distributions of income. In the situation of permanent shortages in the market, the non-income-related privileges in access to goods made relationships between income and wealth measured by possession of goods and living standards quite complex. Pre-transformation Polish society may be divided into the following classes:

- the elite in politics, the economy and the media, the essential core of which was governed by the nomenklatura principle;
- the intelligentsia, which included directors, professionals and non-manual workers;
- private entrepreneurs – under socialism these were small-scale businessmen and craftsmen (the importance of this category gradually increased in the 1970s, and even more so in the second half of the 1980s);
- the working class, which was further divided into the following professional groups: intermediary categories (employees working in trade and services, skilled craftsmen), and skilled and unskilled workers; we may also include in this class a number of categories specific to socialism: agricultural labourers working in state farms and cooperatives, and peasant workers;
- peasants (individual farmers).

The governing elite in the communist system emerged on the basis of the nomenklatura system. Besides authority, this elite possessed a number of privileges, often officially reflected in the size and location of one's residence, the possession of an official car, personal bodyguards and so forth. The basic criterion adopted when assessing members of the nomenklatura was their political loyalty to the group exercising power at the time (Wasilewski, 1995).

It is difficult to describe the privileges of the communist elite in Poland in numerical terms. The official statistics are, not surprisingly, silent on this matter. But the bestowing of privileges on the nomenklatura was universally regarded as unjust and based upon exploitation of society. This feeling of unfairness and exploitation was one (but not the only one) of the stimuli for social protests in Poland, especially since 1980 (the *Solidarnosc* movement); it united the intelligentsia with workers and peasants.

Those members of the intelligentsia who did not belong to the nomenklatura before 1990 did not constitute a privileged class. Indeed, the complete opposite was the case, for in actual fact the intelligentsia was socially degraded during communism (Mokrzycki, 1997). One characteristic feature of this period was the status inconsistency; that is, a situation in which higher education and higher prestige of the occupation did not necessarily mean a high salary. In Poland, the correlation between education and income remained weak until the 1960s. It then grew stronger towards the mid-1970s, before weakening once more as the incomes of individuals with higher education steadily fell. While in 1968 more than 80 per cent of employees with higher education earned salaries above the national average, by 1981 60 per cent earned salaries below the national average. At the same time, wage differentials increased within particular categories of education (Domanski, 1990; Wesolowski and Mach, 1986), which was linked to a mechanism which I have called socialist corporatism. This trend was reversed with the onset of the transformation.

Private businessmen constituted an insignificant element in the class structure prior to the transformation, although their importance grew in the course of the 1970s and 1980s. Some small craftsmen could not cope with the new challenges brought by the transformation, especially with the appearance of competition, but there were also others who transformed their small firms into prosperous enterprises. They, together with the managerial elite, supplied a considerable part of Poland's present class of enterprise owners. Possession of economic capital at the beginning of the transformation presented individuals with unique opportunities. In the 1980s, small-time foreign trading constituted a good crash course in business as well as being a source of capital accumulation. There was a large black market for attractive goods and foreign currency, which meant work for a host of private businessmen.

Workers were not very numerous in Poland just after the Second World War. The vast majority of this class emerged in the process of the extensive socialist industrialization. In 1972, approximately one in every two workers in Poland came from a peasant background, which to a very large extent resulted in powerful cultural links between Polish workers and the countryside, also reflected in deep-rooted, popular religiosity. The migration from the countryside to the towns was related to sociocultural and material progress. The incomes of workers and, more generally, their access to goods and facilities depended on the branch in which they were employed. However, the extensive planned economy worked for the benefit of this class as a whole; the system generated a permanent demand for manual labour. The competition between industrial enterprises for workers led to the latter being privileged in terms of wages in relation to non-manual workers and members of the intelligentsia employed in the public services and the administration. The Polish working class was able to undertake collective actions, in 1956, 1970, 1976, 1980–81 and 1988–89, but unfortunately there is insufficient space to analyse here the working-class movements and the social movement of *Solidarnosc*.

In Poland there existed a strong private sector – in agriculture. The collectivization of farms was stopped in 1956, and the majority of agriculture production remained in the hands of private farmers. We have to consider the increasing differences which began to appear among households living from agriculture under socialism, and which became especially evident from the 1970s onwards. Income inequality in this group, measured by the Gini coefficient, equalled 0.359 in 1985 and 0.351 in 1989, and was clearly higher than in workers' households (0.269 and 0.259, respectively). Farmers' household incomes clearly improved in the 1980s, which was a decade of great hardship for the urban population as a result of continuing economic stagnation and acute shortages in the supply of consumer goods and food (Zienkowski, 1998: 9). The relatively good situation of farmers at the end of communism could not be maintained in the years that followed, as a consequence of which they have been one of the main losers in the reform process.

An important group in villages were so called peasant workers, having a small farm but at the same time working in factories in nearby towns. This class shared most characteristics with peasants, especially poor education, and emerged because of excessive demand for a simple workforce in the socialist economy. Another category living in rural areas constituted workers of the big state-owned farms (PGR). They usually lived in the villages around these farms, in the flats owned by farms, and had some support from them and used the public property for their own needs. These two categories were quite well off under socialism, but after the state-owned farms collapsed and factories were reduced to simple jobs, they became permanently unemployed and formed (especially PGR-workers) the base for the emerging underclass.

As regards income distribution, alongside the class structure of the socialist system described above there were important divisions resulting from the branch structure of the economy. The role of branch corporations in a socialist economy was so important that the level of investment, wages and subsidies depended on whether an enterprise did or did not belong to a given branch. Specific corporatist bargaining based on political power of branch corporations rather than a command system was essential for the regulation of the economy.

Great social mobility took place in Poland after the war and lasted until the mid-1950s. In the 1960s, when the expansive industrialization and migration from villages began to slow down, mobility compared across generations decreased. Then, in the 1970s, it stabilized (Domanski, 1990). Same-generation mobility also experienced a downwards trend, but the social structure has now stabilized.

The relative closing of the social structure in the area of professional mobility was accompanied by another phenomenon: the gradual closing of this structure in terms of educational mobility. In the immediate postwar period, the proportion of people with secondary or higher education increased. Even then, however, educational opportunities came to depend more and more on social origin, and in particular on the educational level of one's parents (Adamski *et al.*, 1990). *The closing of educational structures and the tendency of the intelligentsia to become a self-reproducing group has itself had long-term consequences.* Because the transformation brought a sharp increase in the importance of cultural capital, the intelligentsia managed to forge a privileged position for itself in the 1990s, having previously begun to restrict entry to its ranks.

Income inequality before transition was low. Indeed, we may say that the extent of this inequality points to an egalitarian society. The nomenklatura above all had power, and it was this political capital that opened the door to various other kinds of goods. However, aside from the nomenklatura and private business, the distance between social classes was small, and income inequality in society was low. As Milanovic (1998) shows, in 1987–88 the Gini coefficient stood at 0.26, which suggests that Poland was a quite egalitarian society. During this period there was no unemployment. Of course, there did exist a marginal group of non-working people, who usually abused alcohol and lived in very poor conditions. However, anyone who wanted to work could do so and earn a modest income. The share of working people in the total adult population was very high, so that in 1988, for example, work was the main source of livelihood for 78 per cent of the population while only 22 per cent of the population supported itself from sources of income other than work remuneration (Zienkowski, 1998).

At the eve of the transformation period, Polish society was in a very specific situation:

- higher education provided no advantage in terms of income;
- farmers enjoyed higher average wages than workers' families and were at the same time a highly differentiated group in terms of income;
- qualified workers earned similar wages to the intelligentsia;
- small entrepreneurs and craftsmen constituted a privileged group in terms of wealth; and
- average real pensions fell during the 1980s by around 4–5 per cent and the situation of pensioners' households worsened.

During the socialist period, living conditions were hard for a large proportion of society, but the distances between classes were small. The system provided few incentives and led to waste and crisis, but it gave social groups with no cultural, political or economic capital at their disposal the opportunity to survive at a basic level fairly easily. Aside from a few islands of wealth and privileged branch corporations, there functioned a system of 'rounding down' – a relatively equal division of poverty. Whilst analysing social and economic aspects, it should not be forgotten that this was an authoritarian system based on limiting individual freedom.

The transformation process

Political revolution and the demise of the nomenklatura

In 1989, a bloodless political revolution took place in Poland. The radical political changes can be briefly summarised thus: communism collapsed, the Communist Party was dissolved, and democratic government was introduced. A direct structural consequence of the political changes was the disappearance of the nomenklatura as a class, or rather its transformation. The rules of recruitment to the elite changed, but a large portion of the old nomenklatura found its place in the new elite. We have to admit that those members of the socialist political, managerial and administrative elite, who were really successful during the transition, were usually quite well-equipped with *cultural capital*: they were educated and had the necessary experience to find a position in the new situation. For more about the fate of the old nomenklatura see Chapter 4.

Radical reform, economic policy and economic performance in the 1990s

After the semi-democratic elections of June 1989, the Mazowiecki government, in which Leszek Balcerowicz was Finance Minister, prepared and introduced with the support of parliament a radical programme whose aim was significantly to reduce inflation and to liberalize the economy. As Balcerowicz (1992: 39) himself writes, the idea was to introduce a system, 'characterised by the following fundamental features:

1 the dominance of various forms of private ownership;
2 a competitive environment;
3 an open economy;
4 a strong and convertible currency;
5 a state that did not restrict enterprises with a mass of bureaucratic regulations, but instead provided them with a stable framework for activity. At the same time, the state had to be resistant to the pressure of various interest groups, including trade unions.'

From today's perspective, it may be said that item 5 has been the most difficult to realize.

To solve the problem of macroeconomic imbalance, Balcerowicz adopted a radical policy – 'shock therapy' – based on sudden increases of interest rates, the radical devaluation of the Polish zloty, and on the introduction of high tax penalties for state enterprises which raised wages without concomitant improvements in performance. These stabilizing measures were accompanied by radical liberalization, which consisted in completing the process of price deregulation, opening the economy to foreign competition, and removing the barriers to business activity. The initial effect of this 'shock therapy' was economic crisis (Table 8.1). Since 1992, there has been steady economic growth in Poland. In 1994 it stood at 5–7 per cent per annum; in 1998 it was about 4 per cent, largely due to the economic crisis in Russia, but also to the government's more restrictive financial and monetary policy. In 1997, Poland was the only post-communist country in which the GNP exceeded its 1989 level. At the same time, the consumption expenditure of households

Table 8.1 Changes in basic economic indicators in Poland

	1991	1992	1993	1994	1995	1996	1997	1991 = 100	1995 = 100
Gross domestic product	93.0	102.6	103.8	105.2	107.0	106.0	106.8	126.1	113.2
Prices of consumer goods and services	171.1	142.8	135.2	132.3	128.0	119.9	115.1	772.0	138.0
Unemployment rate	12.2	14.3	16.4	16.0	14.9	13.2	10.3	–	–
Average monthly real net wage and salary	99.7	97.3	97.1	100.5	103.0	105.7	107.3	110.5	113.4
Individual consumption expenditures of household sector	106.0	102.0	104.9	104.1	103.2	108.2	106.8	140.8	115.6

Note: In the columns concerning the years 1991–97 the changes are calculated year by year: the previous year is 100. The last two columns show the situation in the last year in the series (1997) compared with the base from 1991 and 1995 respectively.
Source: GUS, *Statistical Yearbook* (1998).

was rising, and inflation and unemployment was falling (until 1998). The budget deficit has been kept under control. The economic transformation lifted Poland out of the stagnation of the 1980s and lodged her firmly on the path of growth.

The development of the private sector in the economy

In Poland, the private sector had already begun to develop with increasing speed in the second part of the 1980s. However, very rapid development did not begin until the breakthrough year of 1990. Initially, this development took the form of a huge number of firms being set up in the small-enterprise sector. In time, however, the privatization of state enterprises also got underway. According to research on the economic activities of the Polish population, it is estimated that in 1998 more than 61 per cent of all employed people were working in the private sector (Table 8.2), a figure which included agriculture.

The development of the private sector in Poland was based to some extent on the privatization of state-owned companies, but the main stream of this process was the rapid growth of new private businesses. In 1996 the total number of active enterprises in Poland was estimated at 1,343,623 (in 1999 well above two million). Out of them 1,337,243 were private, and 6,380 public. More than 99 per cent of the private enterprises were small (up to 50 employees), many of them in commerce and services; there were only 1575 private enterprises with more than 250 employees (0.1 per cent). Out of 6380 active enterprises in the public sector 1779 (28 per cent) had more than 250 employees (GEMINI, 1998). The big private enterprises are usually privatized, formerly state-owned, companies. The numerous small enterprises are usually new establishments – the result of entrepreneurial activity.

Polish privatization was different from the Czech or Russian cases. In Poland there was a mass privatization of 512 companies via 15 National Investment Funds in 1997 (similar to the Czech case), but the majority of enterprises, which were privatized, were sold after liquidation, leased to employees, sold directly to strategic investors or privatized via the stock

Table 8.2 Employment in Poland by sector (private and public)

	2nd Quarter		
	1996	1997	1998
Public sector (%)	42.5	40.5	38.6
Private sector (%)	57.5	59.5	61.4
Including: employers and self-employed (%)	23.5	23.3	22.8

Source: GUS.

exchange. This kind of privatization, other than mass privatization, had a real impact on the management and corporate culture of the privatized companies and appeared to be a good way to form a real private and competitive sector. It is a slower but economically more effective way of privatization. Privatization of the public sector is still going on.

The expansion of the private sector has two structural consequences:

1 The number of self-employed people and owners of enterprises – the nucleus of the middle class – has increased (this has also opened a hitherto restricted channel of structural mobility).
2 Hired employees in industry have joined one of two sectors: private and public, and this has become an additional factor affecting income differentials.

The category of self-employed people is highly differentiated. The first line of division is between those who employ others and those who work individually, while the second concerns the size of enterprises. There are various types of owners in the self-employed category: owners of vast fortunes based on rapidly developing new firms, of fortunes made through financial speculation, and of enterprises bought as a result of privatization. But the vast majority are small businessmen.

The labour market

One effect of the transformation was the emergence of a real labour market. Central wage regulation was abandoned in favour of work contracts between employers and employees. However, differences still persist between the public and private sector, between branches, and between enterprises of various size.

During the transformation period, Poland has been characterized by rapidly increasing wage differentials accompanied by relatively low average wages. The Gini coefficient rose from 21–23 at the end of the 1980s, to 29 in 1995. Wage inequality in Poland is due more to the higher earnings at the top of the scale than to the lower earnings at the bottom. Wage disparities between the upper and lower decile groups are constantly increasing, as shown in Table 8.3, although this growth above all relates to men.

Table 8.3 Relation of average monthly wages in the upper and lower decile shares

	1991	March 1996	September 1996	September 1997
Total	4.6	5.8	6.3	6.4
Male	–	6.3	6.9	7.1
Female	–	4.9	5.1	5.3

Source: GUS: Borkowska (1998).

On average, better-qualified people receive higher levels of pay. Higher education is particularly beneficial where it leads to a management position, but apart from management positions higher education brings benefits above all in the private sector. This is affected, among other things, by the low benefits that education brings in the budgetary sector, particularly in education and healthcare (see Table A8.13 in the Appendix). While in 1996 in the private sector people with higher education usually received pay about double the average, in the public sector their pay was only 29 per cent higher than the average, although a secondary-school teacher with higher education earned only half as much as a miner.

A new phenomenon that appeared in Poland in the 1990s was unemployment. The unemployment rate rose rapidly until 1994, and then began to fall gradually, before stabilizing at a level of 10–11 per cent in recent years. In the first quarter of 1999 the unemployment rate increased and reached 12.5 per cent. Unemployment did not affect all groups in the same way, and in this case, too, education was one of the main factors giving protection against unemployment. Unemployment in Poland is accompanied by vacancies for highly qualified workers in upper and middle management positions.

The cultural capital accumulated by the intelligentsia during the communist period has borne fruit in the form of higher wages and greater job security. Workers, characterized by lower levels of education, have in most cases lost their relatively privileged positions, but farmers have been the biggest losers.

Changes in social security regimes

In the 1990s, the importance of social transfers within the budgets of domestic households grew significantly. During the 1988–95 period, the proportion of the population supporting itself mainly from work decreased from 78 per cent to 64 per cent. Thus, the number of people relying on forms of income other than remuneration for work, mainly social transfers, increased over this period by 58 per cent (Zienkowski, 1998). On average, transfers in Poland accounted for 34 per cent of the total income of households, while in other European countries this figure amounted to 20–25 per cent (Rutkowski, 1998). This was caused by the emergence of unemployment, and in particular by the rapid growth in the number of pensioners and the fairly high average level of pensions in relation to pay. The rapid growth in the number of pensioners was to some extent due to legislation that made it easier to begin retirement. For some elderly people, retirement was an alternative to unemployment, but for others (albeit a smaller group) it was an opportunity to increase their income. The latter group did not stop doing paid work, but rather switched to freelancing – signing short-term work contracts and thus avoiding social insurance contributions – or to part-time work.

In 1997, average per capita income in pensioner households was 22 per cent higher than the general average, which is largely explained by the fact that pensioners usually do not have children to support. At the same time, income differentiation per capita in this group of households was the lowest. In terms of the Gini coefficient, it stood at 0.25 (compared to 0.31 on average), while in terms of decile ratio (D_9/D_1), it stood at 3.20 (compared to 4.08 on average and 5.63 among people supporting themselves from income other than remuneration for work) (GUS: Zróznicowanie, 1998). However, a higher average income per capita does not mean that retirement is financially beneficial. The Polish pension system is a stable source (no arrears) of income for households, relatively high in comparison with other countries under transition. It carries out transfers from higher income groups to lower income groups and helps to level out income differences within the group of pensioners (Zienkowski, 1998: 19), even if on a general social level it causes the *income per capita* differences between households to increase (Rutkowski, 1998).

The growth of income disparities between households

These phenomena in the economy, on the labour market and in social policy have led to growing income disparities between households. In terms of income per capita and the OECD's equivalent adult classification, the transformation has led to higher income inequality, which appeared above all during the period of rapid growth (1994–97) (Table 8.4).

The growth in income disparities per equivalent adult – from approximately 0.25 before the transformation to around 0.30 at present, as represented by the Gini coefficients – is a moderate growth, although it is concentrated in time and therefore subjectively perceived as quite radical. In Poland, income inequality is similar to that of OECD countries with higher levels of income inequality, and lower than that of developing countries from the middle income group, where the Gini coefficient stands at around 0.45–0.50 (Rutkowski, 1998; Milanovic, 1998). The modest increase in general

Table 8.4 Income differentiation of households: Gini coefficients, 1987–97

Categories of household income	1987	1988	1989	1990	1991	1992	1995	1997*
Total household income	0.30	0.32	0.34	0.31	0.29	0.30	0.35	(0.31)
Income per person	0.26	0.26	0.27	0.27	0.26	0.28	0.34	(0.31)
Income per equivalent adult	0.24	0.24	0.26	0.25	0.24	0.25	0.31	(0.29)

Note: * Denotes data collected and income measured using methods different to those for 1987–95.
Sources: For 1987–95, Górecki and Wisniewski (1998): 140; for 1997, author's calculation based on GUS: Zróznicowanie (1998)

inequality at the beginning of the transformation can be explained by the economic crisis and by changes in the relative positions of large groups of households, especially the falling incomes of rural households and the rising incomes of pensioner households (Górecki and Wisniewski, 1998). The increase in inequality during the mid-1990s was linked to rapid economic growth and above all to the rising income of higher-income households.

What we observed in the case of wages can also be seen with regard to households: the levels of education of heads of households has a stronger influence than in the past on the household's income situation. Members of households whose head is self-employed, is a hired employee doing a non-manual job, or a pensioner (explained above) are more likely to have better material situations. Generally speaking, people with a higher level of human capital have benefited from the transformation.

The emerging social structure

Determinants of social stratification

Towards the end of the first decade of the new economic system in Poland, the operation of market forces – side by side with remnants of the old system – is clearly visible. Correlation between various status indicators – status consistency – has increased: better education means a better chance of professional advancement, which in turn opens the way to higher earnings. Appointments to high-ranking posts in the economy, culture and the media are predominantly based on the criteria of competence and merit. Cultural capital (education) has likewise grown in importance. A substantial private sector has appeared in the economy, where success is based on human and financial capital, and in many cases this capital had already been accumulated before the transformation began.

Although the nomenklatura are gone, having largely converted their political capital into economic assets, the importance of political capital has hardly diminished. It now has to be gained under a democratic party system, and is still convertible into economic capital, especially in the public sector and in those areas which remain dependent on the arbitrary decisions of state officials. Seats on the boards of directors and managerial posts in companies owned by the state Treasury are seen as part of the spoils to be distributed by the ruling parties among their supporters in the aftermath of a victory at the polls.

There is a growing tendency for the intelligentsia to become a self-reproducing group, and the data in Table 8.5 show that its reproduction rate is approaching the level observed among the generation whose adult life (and university education) began before the Second World War. In the youngest generation of university graduates, still more than a third come from families where the father's education finished at the vocational level at

Table 8.5 Level of education of fathers of university graduates, by age group (%)

Year of birth	Primary or less	Basic vocational	Primary + basic vocational	Secondary	Tertiary (academic)	Persons with tertiary education (%)
Before 1921	11	11	22	40	37	4.2
1921–30	48	3	51	41	8	5.7
1931–40	44	9	54	29	17	8.7
1941–50	53	8	62	25	13	10.8
1951–60	26	22	48	35	17	11.8
1961–70	11	25	36	32	32	13.4
1971–80	11	26	37	31	31	4.6*

Note: * A part of this cohort was too young to complete education.
Sources: Author's calculation based on GUS: Zróznicowanie (1998), $n = 11{,}730$ ('don't know' answers excluded).

best (most of them were workers or farmers), but this is markedly less than in previous generations.

Research carried out by Domanski (1997, 1998) shows that in the course of the transformation of the 1990s, the mobility of particular socio-professional categories increased, but it is still lower than in 1948–52 when changes in the social structure were most profound. Transformation-related mobility in Poland remained on a similar level as in the Czech Republic (where it was highest), Hungary and Slovakia, and was greater than in Russia and Bulgaria (Table 8.6).

Such levels of mobility were mainly connected with the emergence of new types of jobs following the market transformation, and the disappearance of others; the dynamic growth of the private sector has also played a major role here. On the other hand, barriers between social strata have not become more permeable (Domanski, 1997). The social structure is beginning to stabilize and one now hardly observes such massive shifts and general openness to change as occurred in the postwar period when many vacant slots in the social structure simply waited to be filled.

The differences between various social classes as regards access to goods and general market opportunities have been deepening. This, in my opinion, constitutes a fundamental structural feature of the transformation. The ongoing changes are far from complete: corporatist mechanisms in the economy have hardly disappeared, with all their consequences for the income structure; and in the public sector the distinction between the 'productive' and 'non-productive' sector persists. Nevertheless, the situation of entire social classes has changed, which is leading to increasing interdependencies between various determinants of status: education and professional position correlate ever-more strongly with earnings, and access to goods is increasingly governed by market mechanisms. As a result, the situation of farmers has, relatively speaking, deteriorated; and the same is also true, though to a lesser extent, of the working class. The state intervenes in these processes by means of a system of transfers, but with the sole exception of

Table 8.6 Percentage of males who changed their socioeconomic status in the years 1948–52, 1952–63, 1983–88 and 1988–93

	1948–52	1952–63	1983–88	1988–93
Bulgaria	21.1	12.3	12.2	17.2
Czech Republic	38.4	20.9	8.1	23.6
Poland	27.1	12.2	9.7	20.0
Russia	n.d.	n.d.	11.2	15.1
Slovakia	38.8	25.5	8.8	19.7
Hungary	38.1	22.4	13.4	19.5

Note: n.d. indicates no data.
Source: Domanski (1998): 40.

old-age pensioners, described above, this does not make much qualitative difference.

The principal social classes and groups

The highest positions in the social hierarchy are occupied by the administrative-managerial elite, whose members come from different circles, including the old elites, as well as the former anti-communist and trade-union opposition. Candidates for such positions (that is, prospective members of the upper class) are not as yet associated with any stable segment of society defined on the basis of class criteria. The boundaries and distances between classes are still blurred; class membership is mostly determined by one's professional position, education and capital in the economic sense of the term.

Poland's class structure can be construed in the following categories:

1 high-level managerial circles in administration, politics and the economy, culture and the media, managers and owners of larger-scale private enterprises (with more than five employees working on the basis of employment contracts); of special importance is a subset of this group which deserves separate analysis but has rarely been taken into account even in large-scale studies – the elite group of holders of the highest posts in the state and in the economy;
2 the middle class, construed as a cluster of categories which occupy the position between non-manual workers and the managerial elite; the following subcategories should be distinguished within this class:

   (a) hired employees (middle management, professionals),
   (b) the self-employed;

3 non-manual workers (lower middle class);
4 manual workers;
5 farmers (peasants).

I believe that pensioners should be treated as a separate, internally differentiated category within the social structure. It is a category of individuals who have retired from the market, no longer affected by structural transformations. Their income is relatively less differentiated than in other groups, and they are also the collective addressee of regulatory efforts by the state that puts them in the position of a separate interest group. This group is further divided by previously practised profession and level of education. Yet another demarcation line is between pensioners who come at least from the middle class, and others (including farmers as a separate subgroup). We can thus add to our list:

6 pensioners:

   (a) originating from the middle class;

(b) farmers;
(c) others.

I have also decided to distinguish a category of people who rely on sources of income other than remuneration from work (mainly unemployment benefits). Persons in such circumstances hold a weaker position in the market than others, although this is also an internally differentiated group; for example, from the point of view of education – people from middle-class occupational groups constitute a minority in this category. We have thus reached the final category:

7 the lower class – operationally defined as those who rely on other sources of income, not related to gainful employment, mainly unemployment and social benefits. Such operationalization is determined by data collected by the Polish GUS.

In the following discussion of these classes, I leave out pensioners whose situation has been presented in the section on social insurance.

Managerial and political elites

In 1993, members of the old, nomenklatura elites accounted for approximately 30 per cent of the new top elite in Poland. A similar situation occurred in Hungary, while in Russia the old nomenklatura dominated the scene (see Chapter 4). Research by Wasilewski conducted in 1998 shows that one half of the leaders in each area of life (the highest-level elites) already held high-ranking posts in politics and the economy in 1988 (Table 8.7). Many of these posts were not directly linked to the principle of nomenklatura, so this category must not be unquestioningly equated with the old power elite. One in every three members of the highest-ranking elites used to be a specialist, teacher or university lecturer – in other words, a member of the intelligentsia outside management circles. Currently, only 7 per cent of the elites come from professional groups of a lower status. This demonstrates the ability of people who possessed human or political capital in the past to convert this capital into new market and political assets (see also Table A8.12 in the Appendix). It is striking that two-thirds of business leaders were directors, deputy directors and managers in large state-owned enterprises.

Nine per cent of members of the business elite are former general managers of enterprises, while deputy general managers represent a larger group (19 per cent) and 38 per cent were departmental managers in 1988. This is a classic case of the 'second in command' taking the lead.

In Wasilewski's study, the sample was chosen at random from the political elite construed as 'a group of persons whose official position allows them to exert a lasting and significant influence on decisions of national

Table 8.7 Occupation in 1988 as a source of elite segments in Poland in 1998 (%)

Occupation in 1988 (% of total)	**Segment of the elite**				
	MPs and party leaders	**Administration**	**Media, culture**	**NGOs and social associations**	**Business**
Politicians, public officials (14)	17	23	7	13	6
Managers in large companies (35)	24	15	39	17	64
Managers in other companies (2)	3	3	0	0	2
Academic teachers (14)	12	20	22	13	9
Other professionals and teachers (20)	23	25	26	30	10
Other, lower professions (7)	13	5	0	13	4
Not applicable (didn't work) (7)	7	8	7	13	5

Source: Author's own calculations based on data from a survey of the elites conducted by Wasilewski *et al.* (1998); $n = 637$.

importance' (Wasilewski *et al.*, 1998). Included in this group were persons who occupied a key position in the areas mentioned in Table 8.10 (for instance, in the case of business – directors of key enterprises in Poland, as identified experts). Of these, 90 per cent were university graduates, 96 per cent had studied at institutions of higher education, 11 per cent held doctorates, and 5 per cent held post-doctoral degrees.

These data can be compared with information on the education level of respondents' parents. A third of the fathers of the elite members under study had a university education, but a quarter had at most elementary education, an additional 13 per cent had vocational education, and the remaining 30 per cent had only secondary education. Among the mothers, elementary and secondary education predominated; just 16 per cent had university education. As many as 61 per cent of the respondents declared that their fathers had held posts involving leadership, although only 30 per cent were managers in the sense of an international standard (Group 1 in the ISCO88 classification). All in all, two-thirds of the fathers represented professions involving mental work of varying degrees of complexity, and one-third did manual work (14 per cent were farmers).

The comparison indicates that a large proportion of today's elites have definitely reached a higher position than their parents. It may not be concluded that the present-day top elite simply reproduces the former generation's pattern of elites. What does emerge from the picture is the tendency to inherit the educational status of one's parents, but this is not to say that members of the elite come from some stable, class-related sector of society.

The middle class

The middle class as a segment of the social structure does not duplicate the characteristic ways of the upper class, which forms a closed exclusive circle in possession of authority, wealth and prestige passed down from generation to generation (such a class has not yet reestablished itself in Poland). It does, on the other hand, possess significant assets: capital in the economic sense, human resources, managerial positions and leadership – achieved step by step through persistent effort. It is usually assumed that a well-developed middle class should have a distinctive lifestyle, system of values and attitudes, including a preference for economic liberalism and a democratic state based on the rule of law. No such fully developed and consolidated middle class exists in Poland.[1] Nevertheless, some people have at their disposal more economic, cultural or social capital than others. This is a heterogeneous group, for it is usually taken to include, on the one hand, people of good education, such as teachers, and on the other, managers and owners of large or medium-sized companies or enterprises who typically represent a financial elite. One cannot say unequivocally either that such a 'middle class' consists in all its segments of the 'winners' of the transformation process, or that a considerable proportion of its members count among the 'losers'. The fortunes of sizeable groups from this category are still being decided by the policy of the state: teachers, qualified social workers, and a large proportion of doctors and academics are indeed underpaid. In this sense, these groups have so far been losers. But even so, their opportunities for a better quality of life connected with the cultural capital at their disposal are greater than in the case of workers, farmers and low-level employees in the service sector.

What all members of this class have in common is better-than-average education. Data from the GUS show that the education of the head of the family is one of the most significant single factors determining the level of household income (Table 8.8).

Of course, the best-educated group is characterized not only by the highest average income, but also by the highest dispersion of earnings. This is connected, among other things, with the communist legacy of disproportion between wages in the public services and administration sector (formerly called 'non-productive') and the enterprise (or 'productive') sector.[2] Thus, there is no consolidated middle class in Poland as yet, although a trend towards such consolidation has emerged.

In my comparative analysis, I have divided the broadly-construed middle class into categories distinguished by the essential features of their members' social position. On this interpretation, the upper tiers of the middle class comprise the management and owners of larger enterprises,[3] while the remaining part is divided into the self-employed and hired employees. Such a division serves to bring out with greater precision the differences between particular segments of this differentiated 'class' and its position *vis-à-vis* other social classes.

Non-manual workers – the lower middle class

This group, which comprises professions involving simpler types of mental work, has not benefited from the transformation in a way comparable to the middle class. A strong competitive pressure on the labour market is felt by this category, while wages are way below those of professionals or managers, although they may be comparable with the earnings of teachers or doctors who do not have a private practice. Characteristically, persons belonging to this class earn on average less in the private sector than in the public sector (GUS: Earnings, 1997).

From the point of view of market opportunities and access to goods, this class shows a greater similarity to workers than to the middle class, that is to say, the intelligentsia. One can expect that with steady differentiation of incomes, the relative position of this class will worsen. This class is also to some extent a transitional phenomenon; its internal differentiation is going to increase, and some professions will require ever-higher qualifications and will bring higher rewards typical for the middle class, while others will be assimilated into the working class.

Table 8.8 Household income by education of the head of the household

	Monthly household income		**Monthly household income per capita**		**Monthly household income per equivalent adult**	
	Mean*	**Median***	**Mean***	**Median***	**Mean***	**Median***
Higher (academic)	1.61	1.60	1.71	1.62	1.70	1.63
Post-secondary	1.14	1.20	1.11	1.13	1.14	1.16
Technical secondary	1.13	1.20	1.10	1.10	1.12	1.15
General secondary	0.95	1.00	1.13	1.17	1.08	1,14
Basic vocational	0.96	1.00	0.80	0.78	0.84	0.87
Primary	0.80	0.83	0.86	0.91	0.84	0.89
Non-finished primary	0.67	0.68	0.92	0.99	0.85	0.88

* Total sample = 1

Source: Author's calculation based on GUS: Zróznicowanie (1998).

Workers

Workers are the class who (apart from farmers) have suffered the greatest loss during the transformation. They are exposed to a serious risk of structural unemployment resulting from the inadequacy of their qualifications to the requirements of the changing economy. Under Polish conditions, these qualifications are usually limited to basic vocational training, or rather full technical secondary education. This is the consequence of a system oriented towards preparing young people to work in socialist-era enterprises. It severely restricted general education, and this situation often prevented workers from participating in higher forms of culture and limited their opportunities to adapt to the changing technological and economic environment. Now that workers have lost the income position they held in the socialist economy, this deficiency of cultural capital is a serious barrier not only to improvement, but even to maintaining their position in the market.

Workers in state-owned companies, which are the post-socialist big companies with strong trade unions, preserved their bargaining power and their (at least official) income situation better than that of workers in the private sector. They are able to force state authorities to grant financial support or special privileges to their particular company or branch of industry. The interest articulation of workers is more and more linked to a particular branch, section or even profession. In comparison, trade unions in private sectors are very weak or non-existent. All this is reflected in wage differentials between the private and public sectors: in 1996 industrial workers and craftsmen in the public sector earned 106 per cent of the average, while those in the private sector earned only 86 per cent of the average (GUS: Earnings, 1997).

Workers in various sectors do not share enough common interest to undertake massive collective actions comparable with the *Solidarnosc* movement at the beginning and the end of the 1980s. However, growing polarization of incomes can stimulate massive protests in case of economic crisis. Since 1990–91 such crises did not in fact endanger the Polish economy.

Farmers

Farmers have been the great losers in the transformation, but even this class has become reoriented, at least partly, towards the market. The size of farms is becoming differentiated: in the years 1988–97 the number of the smallest farms, of 1–2 hectares, increased (owners of such farms are still eligible for unemployment benefit); the number of medium-sized farms (up to 15 ha.) dropped; while the number of large farms (in excess of 15 ha.) increased and their share in the ownership of arable land doubled. Very large farms also appeared, exceeding 100 ha, and there are about 6700 of these in Poland.

They account for a mere 0.3 per cent of the overall number of farms, but between themselves they hold 7.5 per cent of Poland's arable land (Wilkin, 1999).

The profitability of farms depends on their size. In view of the drop in profitability of farming production, the differentiation of the farmer class has not yet been fully reflected in the differentiation of per capita income in farmers' households, which stood at 0.33 in 1997 (GUS: Zróznicowanie, 1998: 83). The main problem of the farming class is poor education, and they form the worst educated social category in Poland. The low level of education is replicated over generations as a result of parents' low aspirations concerning their children's education, the poor educational infrastructure in rural areas, and the growing costs of obtaining education. The poor education of farmers and their families is becoming a major barrier to the modernization of rural areas in Poland.

The difficult situation of Polish agriculture, aggravated by competition from imported products, further deteriorated towards the end of the 1990s, leading to vehement protest during which farmers set up road blockades all over the country. Farmers as a class have become better organized and are prone to undertake collective actions to protect their interests.

The lowest class and the poverty issue

The bottom of the social ladder is occupied by persons who have dropped out of the labour market (persons who rely on other sources of income, not related to gainful employment). Unemployment, the dynamics of which has been shown above, is the main factor responsible for living below the poverty line. The classification presented in this study aims to create a measurement of social position in terms of types of professional activity and associated income. Members of the group in question do not undertake *any* professional activities, and in most cases this lack of involvement is involuntary.

Poverty is not restricted to the lowest class in the social structure, but this class is worst hit by it. Estimates of the extent of poverty depend on the method of calculation. Table 8.9 shows the range and depth of poverty estimated according to four different criteria used to draw the boundary line for the class.

An unequivocal assessment of the range of poverty in the light of this evidence is difficult. A large percentage of the population lives below the welfare standards minimum, which indicates in most cases a threat of poverty but is not tantamount to living below the poverty line. The proportion of people living below the subsistence level amounts to 5.4 per cent, and the expenditure gap indicator amounts to approximately 17 per cent. This means that one person in 20 faces serious poverty (lack of sufficient funds for subsistence), although the extent of their poverty is not yet dramatic. It should be added that of the group in question, one-third were children

Table 8.9 The threat of poverty in Poland, 1997

Poverty lines	Poverty rate (% of persons below poverty line)	Poverty depth (expenditure gap)[d](%)
Social minimum	50.4	Ca. 31
Subsistence minimum	5.4	Ca. 17
Relative poverty line: 50% of mean (equivalent) household expenditures	15.3	Ca. 20
Subjective (Leyden) poverty line[a]	30.8[b]	Ca. 26[c]

Notes: [a] IV quarter; [b] percentage of households; [c] measure of income gap; [d] the difference between the average expenditure of households from the sphere of poverty and the poverty line used.
Source: Szukieloc-Bienkuska (1998): 16.

below 14, and nearly a half had not yet reached 19 years of age. This is a consequence of the fact that poor families tend to have numerous children (Szukieloc-Bienkuska, 1998). Panel studies conducted by the GUS allow the number of persons facing long-term relative poverty (expenditure below one-half of the average expenditure of comparable households) to be estimated at approximately 1.4 million (3.6 per cent of the population). The average expenditure gap in this group amounted to 28 per cent of the relative poverty line and was thus markedly higher than average.

A vital question is whether the poor benefit at all from the economic growth. In the late 1980s and early 1990s, the extent of poverty increased, and by 1990 the number of the poor had doubled compared to 1988. This number increased again noticeably in 1994 (Beskid, 1998). In 1995–96, the growth of poverty was checked and the percentage of people living below the subsistence level subsequently dropped from 6.4 per cent in 1994 to 4.3 per cent in 1996. In 1997, this indicator rose again and exceeded 5 per cent, even though on average there was an improvement in households' situation as regards real income and expenditure. However, this latter tendency was especially marked in the case of higher-income groups (Szukieloc-Bienkuska, 1998). No data are available for 1998, but it may be assumed that poverty increased, especially in rural areas.

Although it appeared in 1996 that the poor benefitted from economic growth, too, the data for 1997 did not confirm expectations that the extent of poverty was diminishing. Aside from the mentioned components of the poverty syndrome, which include unemployment, numerous offspring and a low level of education, we should not forget alcoholism, which tends to concur with the other factors.

McAuley (Chapter 6) indicates that the culture of poverty is distinctive for the class of poor (we may use the word 'underclass'). There are two categories of people who can possibly become a nucleus of the emerging underclass:

the former workers of the state farms, *panstwowe gospodarstwa rolne* (PGR), which collapsed at the beginning of transition, and the permanently unemployed, particularly those from small industrial towns in areas with high structural unemployment (Miś, 1998). The former PGR-workers are especially endangered by the possibility of permanent marginalization: they are poorly educated, dependent on social benefits, not involved in political and social life of the country and isolated in their post-PGR villages (Tarkowska, 1998). Homeless and permanent alcoholics are there as well, they are unemployed and usually poorly educated, but belonging to this category is not linked to other special structural factors. It is still too early to speak about an underclass, but there is a potential for its emergence. For now we can speak of a lower class, which is for many only a temporary abode, but for some might already be a permanent trap leading to an underclass.

Differentiation of social classes in Poland with respect to income and access to goods

Here I shall concentrate on households whose place within society's class structure is determined by the social class of the head of the family. The capacity of household members to buy goods is measured by per capita income in the family, or, better still, income per equivalent adult.[4] This measurement is commonly used in analyses of income distribution. Social classes in Poland differ perceptibly from one another with respect to their income status, and synthetically this is illustrated by the box-and-whiskers plot presented in Figure 8.1 and by Table 8.10.[5]

Apart from typical income per individual, social classes in Poland also differ from one another in terms of income differentiation. Average income drops in line with class position. The median of the overall income of households in the upper-middle class is four times the median in the lowest class, which consists mostly of households of the unemployed (Table 8.11). Differentiation of income per equivalent adult is a little lower, but still high. Income in the middle class is, on average, three times as high as that at the bottom of the hierarchy. The middle class also exhibits the greatest internal differentiation, which is to some extent a consequence of the adopted criterion of membership in this class: it depends on the accuracy of available data on the profession pursued by given individuals.

The low position of farmers' households is partly a result of their lower overall income (roughly similar to that of workers' households) and of the markedly greater number of persons in a household (an average of 4.4 persons as opposed to 3.9 in workers' households). The farmers' situation further deteriorated in 1998 due to the crisis on the agricultural goods market.

Pensioner households have overall incomes at a relatively low level, but because of the smaller number of household members the average income per individual is clearly better than in farmers' and workers' families. Pensioners form another category marked by considerable internal differentiation

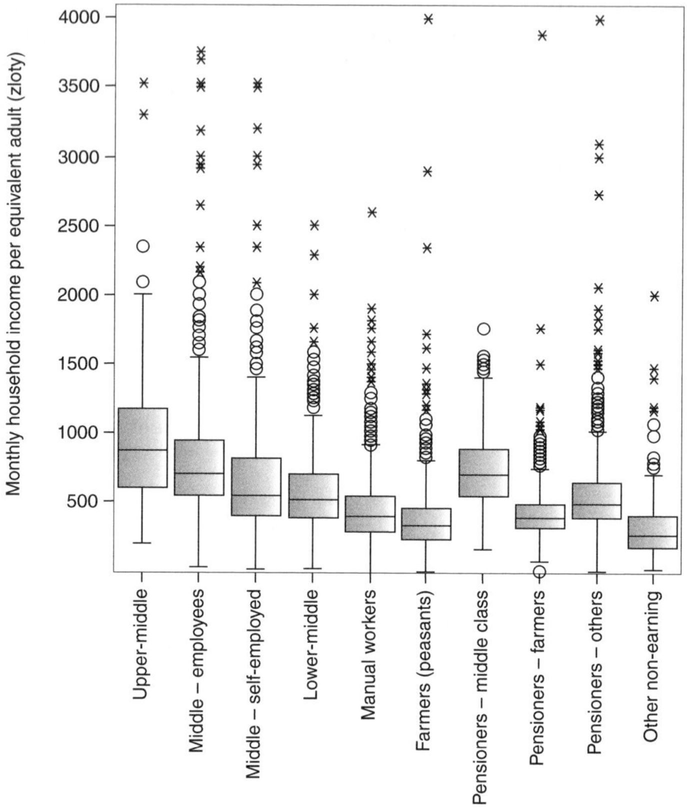

Figure 8.1 Income differences among social classes in Poland (household income per equivalent adult)

Notes: Extremes over 4000 zl not shown.
Explanation of a boxplot

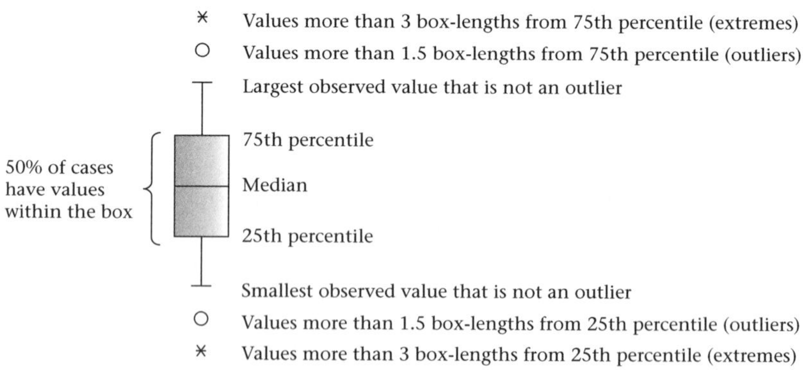

Source: Author's calculations based on GUS: Zróznicowanie (1998).

Table 8.10 Household income differences between social classes in Poland

Social class of household head	Monthly household income (class/total)		Monthly household income per capita (class/total)		Monthly household income per equivalent adult (class/total)		Average number of persons per household	Average number of equivalent adults per household	% of total number of house holds
	Mean*	Median*	Mean*	Median*	Mean*	Median*			
Upper-middle	1.89	2.00	1.81	1.86	1.85	1.88	3.2	2.4	1.1
Middle – employees	1.57	1.60	1.57	1.43	1.59	1.50	3.1	2.3	6.6
Middle – self-employed	1.46	1.50	1.23	1.04	1.31	1.18	3.7	2.7	6.2
Lower-middle (technicians, clerks, service workers)	1.15	1.20	1.06	1.04	1.10	1.10	3.3	2.5	9.8
Manual workers	1.01	1.10	0.77	0.78	0.83	0.87	3.9	2.8	23.1
Farmers (peasants)	0.99	1.00	0.65	0.65	0.71	0.71	4.4	3.2	6.5
Pensioners from middle class	1.19	1.20	1.56	1.56	1.47	1.51	2.2	1.8	3.3
Pensioners – farmers	0.73	0.77	0.85	0.91	0.81	0.85	2.6	2.1	8.8
Pensioners – others	0.81	0.90	1.06	1.14	0.99	1.06	2.3	1.9	30.9
Other non-earning	0.53	0.50	0.60	0.52	0.59	0.57	2.9	2.1	3.7
Average in Poland	1171.25 zl	1000.00 zl	437.02 zl	385.00 zl	533.50 zl	470.59 zl	3.1	2.4	
Eta	*0.41*		*0.39*		*0.41*				

* Total sample = 1.

Source: Author's calculation based on GUS: Zróznicowanie (1998).

Table 8.11 Income differences among basic social classes

Social class	**Monthly household income**		**Monthly household income per equivalent adult**		**% of total *n***
	Mean*	**Median***	**Mean***	**Median***	
Middle	1.48	1.50	1.48	1.42	17.2
Non-manual and manual workers	0.94	1.00	0.95	1.00	63.8
Peasants	0.84	0.82	0.76	0.81	15.3
Lower (unemployed)	0.53	0.50	0.59	0.57	3.7

* Total sample = 1
Source: Author's calculation based on GUS: Zróznicowanie (1998).

with respect to income. This differentiation has to do with the social class to which a given person belonged during his/her professional career. Middle-class pensioners generally have lower incomes than professionally-active members of the middle class, but when income per equivalent adult is taken into account it turns out to be on a similar level.

The profession-related classification of the population – including pensioners – into basic social classes blurs to some extent the differences between the groups with highest and lowest incomes. On the other hand, it does emphasize the distinction between the middle class and the rest of society with lower earnings. The observed trends in income change and the factors behind such change allow us to assume that the distance between the middle class and the rest of society will gradually widen. Its actual extent will depend, among other things, on public-sector wage policies and on the development of the private sector.

As we have noted above, education is an important factor that differentiates the income status of households, and that largely determines one's position in the social structure. Table A8.15 in the Appendix and Figure 8.2 illustrate the differences in the level of education (educational capital) between social classes. The middle class clearly occupies a privileged position compared to other classes, although this is less so in the case of small-business owners than hired employees. Small business often means retail trade and services, which is still capable of generating greater income than the work of a teacher or young doctor, even though this kind of activity is pursued by people with poorer education.[6] This can be called an 'entrepreneurship rent'. Even so, in this class higher education likewise facilitates obtaining higher incomes.

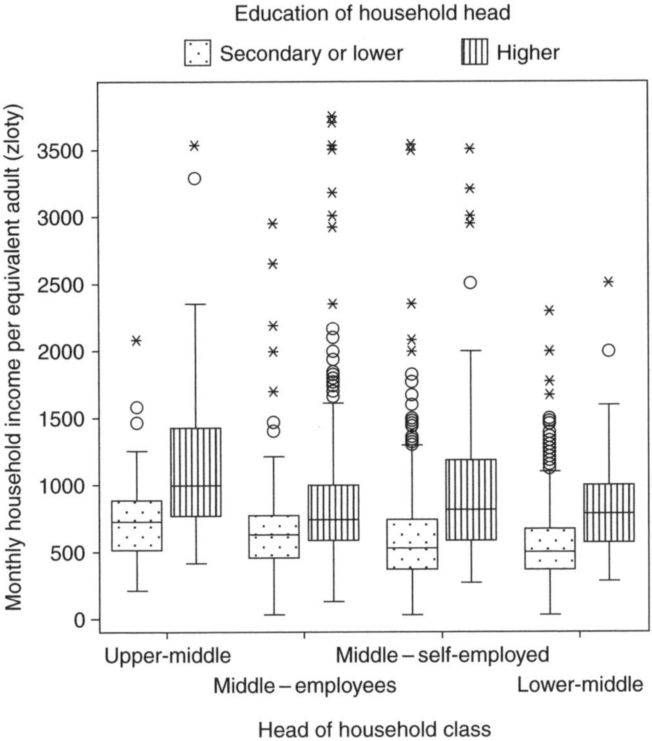

Figure 8.2 Income differences among social classes controlled by education (household income per equivalent adult)*
*Extremes over 4000 zl not shown.
Source: Author's calculation based on GUS: Zróżnicowanie (1998).

Differences in access to goods in a market economy are best expressed in terms of differences in income. Other types of property-related difference (for example, resulting from inheritance) are usually of secondary importance in Poland and boil down to income differences. This is one of the consequences of the socialist revolution of the 1940s (although there are exceptions and the reprivatization process is still on-hold). Additional data illustrating the differences between households from various social classes in respect of possession of certain commodities is presented in Table A8.14 in the Appendix. The overall picture is consistent with the results of the income distribution analysis, although there are some differences. The highest percentage of households with cars can be found in the upper-middle class and in the self-employed sector of the middle class (83 per cent and 85 per cent, respectively); in the middle-class sector comprising hired employees, two-thirds of households have cars, as compared with half in the lower-middle class. In the countryside, 61 per cent of farmers have cars (usually the cheapest models), but it should be borne in mind that in rural areas having a car is usually essential. Pronounced differences between classes can also be observed when it comes to the proportion of VCRs, CD-players and computer owners; the possession of a summer house is similarly becoming a middle-class determinant, although this is not widespread as yet.

Differences between social classes also exist in the subjective dimension, in the sphere of self-evaluation of one's living standards and expectations for the future. No comments are necessary about the distribution of responses to questions in this area included in the GUS questionnaire, save for one point: interclass differences in the subjective perception of one's material standing are smaller than the objectively observable contrasts, which nicely illustrates the old Polish adage that appetite comes with eating.

Conclusions

The transformation of Poland's economy and its political system has brought about a number of significant macrostructural social changes. These can be described as shifts in the profitability structure of capital assets. The importance of education for one's position on the job market has clearly increased, and so have returns on educational capital. This is particularly true of the private sector, where education, which opens the way to career advancement or better productivity, translates into greater differences in wages than in the public sector. The role of competence and merit in appointments to top jobs in economic institutions and public administration is also increasing. This is not to say that political capital has lost its importance. In the still-sizeable public sector, many managerial posts are still treated as electoral spoils by the leading political parties. Economic capital, in turn, allows one to become rich by fully legal means and to reach for posts of political significance. Political capital exhibits a strong tendency to pool with big economic capital, a phenomenon that the institutions of democratic control and rule of law are too weak to counteract.

There have occurred shifts in the social structure caused by the rapid development of private business outside agriculture: this sector is already the principal source of income for over 9 per cent of adult Poles. There has also emerged a sizeable category of unemployed people, who often live in desperate material conditions and make up 11 per cent of the labour force. The rapid increase in the number of pensioners is not so much the consequence of ageing or inability to work, but rather of a shortage of jobs and the resulting measures adopted in the field of social policy. The category of peasant workers, on the other hand, has largely disappeared. They have lost their jobs in industry and joined the ranks of the unemployed, smallholding farmers, pensioners and the rural poor. The intelligentsia, which was excluded under communism from access to power and wealth, is now in a position to pursue these goals. By converting its educational capital into economic and political assets, members of this group are gradually losing their intelligentsia ethos and becoming professionals.

The new elite resembles the intelligentsia as far as education and previous professional experience are concerned, but when it comes to social background a considerable proportion of them come from families of a lower social status. Some sections of the new elite and the middle class originate from the communist nomenklatura; in the latter category, about one-third of its members transformed their political capital into high-level positions within the new elite, and the remaining ones, with a few exceptions, have also established themselves profitably in other areas of social life. The success of this conversion has to some extent been due to the higher quality of available human capital.

Gradually diminishing educational mobility is attributable to factors of a structural type (the different economic potential and educational aspirations of various classes) and institutional type (the increasing costs of obtaining education, the greater importance of cultural competence acquired at home in overcoming successive educational barriers, the disadvantaged position of villages and small towns in terms of the school network and teacher qualifications). Such circumstances will favour the development of a better-educated and richer middle class, as well as the self-reproduction of elites and the gradual emergence of an upper class. The latter process, however, may take a long time, and may also depend on the functioning of the political system as well as the forms of social inequality.

An important dimension of the transformation is connected with the changing positions of various social classes with respect to access to material goods (income) and quality of life. The transformation has brought about a growth in average living standards, but the distribution of this growth has been unequal. This is due to the changing functions of very large social groups in the new economic system, and also to the elimination (outside a few isolated enclaves, such as coal-mining) of the political capital related to socialist corporatism and the economic advantages that resulted from the lack of competition and market shortages. The beneficiaries of the new order include a large proportion of the intelligentsia, or rather professionals and managers; on the other hand, the great losers are farmers (except for those engaged in large-scale commercial production, whose current problems are merely the result of a temporary fall in demand) and the working class, which – ironically – used to be a great champion of change. Workers still maintain a relatively advantageous position in the public sector, but this sector is gradually shrinking due to privatization and the financial crisis of many state-owned enterprises. Farmers will have no chance to reclaim the high rank on the scale of income (though not of prestige) which they enjoyed during the final days of communism. The two classes will further differentiate. Farmers will be ultimately divided into affluent farmers and the rural poor, and unless new jobs are created in the countryside the latter category will live in truly abject poverty. Workers, in their turn, will divide into a 'working-class aristocracy' – a class of highly-skilled workmen nearly always capable of finding employment and becoming progressively assimilated with the middle class – and the 'proletariat', living in hardship and under constant threat of redundancy.

There is a serious danger of a further polarization between the elite and the middle class (to be joined in due time by the richest farmers) on the one hand, and the working class, farmers and the poorest segments of society on the other. At the moment, poverty in Poland may be widespread, but it is still relatively shallow. But even in this form it can be dangerous, particularly if it blocks all chance of social advancement; for instance, if the children of workers, farmers or non-manual workers are denied access to education. This would mean a gross injustice to children who had the misfortune of being born into a poor family, in a poor region of the country or simply in the countryside; such a situation would violate the fundamental principle of equality of opportunity. It would also have an economic, social and political impact. In the economic dimension, it would lead to a waste of human resources. The social dimension would have to do with expanding poverty, which might soon degenerate into a self-perpetuating subculture of destitution and crime. In the political dimension, a disadvantaged majority would pose the threat of rebellion. The farmers' protests of 1998 and 1999 indicate that the lower classes of Polish society possess a great potential for self-organization when it comes to airing their grievances.

It would hardly be possible to discuss in this necessarily brief text the social policies needed to address these problems. However, the present analysis indicates that any such policy would have to concentrate on equalizing the educational opportunities of children, and on programmes to facilitate the professional training and retraining of adults to allow them to adjust to the requirements of the market. Such measures should be supplemented with a policy oriented towards job-creation.

The political class pays lip-service to these issues, while education (to give but one example) is losing out in the competition for resources. Major educational reform was launched in September 1999; its fate will depend on whether the key interest groups understand that its success will be to everyone's advantage.

Appendix: statistical annex

Table A8.12 Outflow from the 1988 nomenklatura categories into the 1993 destination in Poland (% of elites; $n=888$)

1988 nomenklatura category	1993 destination								
	n	Business	Politics	Directors in state sector	Managers and professionals	Non-manual	'Lower' classes	Early retirees	Pensioners
Party	165	25.5	1.8	6.1	24.8	13.9	9.1	17.0	1.8
State	280	20.0	12.5	5.0	23.2	5.4	2.5	21.1	10.4
Mass organizations	57	35.1	26.3	5.3	8.8	3.5	1.8	10.5	8.8
Economy	263	30.8	0.4	34.2	10.6	1.9	0.4	17.5	4.2
Media, culture	123	18.7	– *	28.5	25.2	–	0.8	17.9	8.9
Average		25.0	6.1	17.1	19.1	5.1	2.8	18.1	6.6

* Due to its small size, the 'business and politics' category has been combined with 'business'.

Source: Wasilewski (1998).

Table A8.13 Earnings of the employees in the Polish economy in 1996, by sector and gender (in Polish zloty)

Education	**Total**	**Public sector**		**Private sector**	
		Male	**Female**	**Male**	**Female**
Total	849.74	1021.24	776.24	814.68	679.09
Higher	1224.89	1376.66	1007.62	1625.51	1336.13
Technical secondary or post-secondary	839.02	1039.60	752.61	873.48	720.18
General secondary	839.83	1045.55	824.39	909.92	743.01
Basic vocational	756.14	941.30	616.79	681.24	527.97
Primary or less	707.99	877.26	596.82	655.12	558.65

Source: GUS (1997).

Table A8.14 Households furnished with selected durable goods, 1997 (% of households in a social class)

Social class of household head	Automatic washing machine	Colour TV set	Satellite TV or cable TV	Video recorder	CD player	Personal computer	Car	Summerhouse
Upper-middle	93.9	98.5	67.7	79.6	52.5	34.6	82.6	11.3
Middle – employees	91.2	96.7	63.8	72.1	48.1	31.7	66.8	6.0
Middle – self-employed	89.9	96.4	60.6	79.7	41.3	28.9	84.8	6.4
Lower-middle (technicians, clerks, service workers)	82.5	95.5	57.5	73.1	30.7	17.8	51.3	2.6
Manual workers	64.1	94.2	42.7	67.9	19.9	9.6	49.3	1.1
Farmers (peasants)	39.1	83.5	11.8	40.6	10.2	3.9	61.0	0.4
Pensioners from middle class	77.1	93.1	45.8	46.7	17.2	11.1	50.4	8.1
Pensioners – farmers	21.2	61.5	8.8	16.3	4.6	2.0	24.7	0.3
Pensioners – others	51.0	84.9	30.2	28.7	7.6	3.4	25.0	1.4
Other non-earning	49.8	72.4	31.6	34.2	15.9	7.3	22.2	1.3
Total	*60.1*	*87.4*	*37.8*	*49.2*	*18.5*	*10.4*	*43.3*	*2.2*

Source: Author's calculations based on GUS: Zróznicowanie (1998).

Table A8.15 Social class of household head by education (row %)

Social class of household head	**Level of education of head of household**						
	Higher	**Post-secondary**	**Technical secondary**	**General secondary**	**Basic vocational**	**Primary**	**Non-finished primary**
Upper-middle	52.4	4.0	30.6	8.3	4.7	0	0
Middle – employees	77.7	4.7	13.6	2.8	0.9	0.2	0
Middle – self-employed	14.5	2.5	39.8	5.9	32.6	4.3	0.3
Lower-middle	10.4	7.0	48.7	14.1	15.3	4.2	0.3
Manual workers	0	0.5	16.2	1.7	61.5	18.7	1.4
Farmers (peasants)	0.8	0.4	12.3	1.5	38.8	42.7	3.5
Pensioners from middle class	57.5	3.5	20.5	8.8	6.5	3.1	
Pensioners – farmers	0.8	0.2	2.0	1.5	7.2	53.1	35.3
Pensioners – others	1.8	0.6	15.7	7.6	22.4	40.6	11.4
Other non-earning	3.7	1.4	19.1	9.9	34.4	27.3	4.2

Source: Author's calculations based on GUS: Zróznicowanie (1998).

Notes

1 According to Domanski, 'in no contemporary society does there exist a "middle class", and the positions within the social hierarchy typically associated with the notion of "middle class" do not form in any way a coherent whole; or if they do, this is not enough to warrant the use of the term "class"' (Domanski, 1994: 6).
2 I have no access to any variable that would make it possible to distinguish employees in these sectors for analytical purposes.
3 Members of the very top of the elite, as described above, are not likely to be included even in a sample as large as 12,500 respondents, such as that used by GUS in its survey of living standards.
4 In accordance with OECD standards, the first adult in the household is assigned a weight of 1, all other persons a weight of 0.7, and children below 14 a weight of 0.5.
5 In the CSO study under analysis, the data concerning income are based on statements made by respondents, who usually have a tendency to lower the actual figures. Unfortunately, we do not know to what extent.
6 This is one of the categories where one is likely to encounter lowered income figures.

References

Adamski, W., I. Bialecki and K. Staszynska (1990) 'Pokoleniowe aspekty konfliktu interesow', pp. 85–104, in W. Adamski (ed.), *Interesy i konflikt. Studia nad dynamika struktury spolecznej w Polsce.* Warsaw: Ossolineum.

Balcerowicz, L. (1992) *800 dni.* Warsaw: BGW.

Beskid, L. (1998) 'Ubostwo w Polsce', in RSSG przy radzie Ministrów. Raport 29: *Podzial dochodu i nierownosci dochodowe. Fakty, tendencje, porownania.* Warsaw: RSSG: 101–32.

Borkowska, S. (1998) 'Zroznicowanie wynagrodzen w Polsce w okresie transformacji', in RSSG przy radzie Ministrów. Raport 29: *Podzial dochodu i nierownosci dochodowe. Fakty, tendencje, porownania.* Warsaw: RSSG: 53–90.

Domanski, H. (1990) 'Przemiany struktury spolecznej a stabilnosc systemu', in W. Adamski (ed.), *Interesy i konflikt. Studia nad dynamika struktury spolecznej w Polsce.* Warsaw: Ossolineum: 63–84.

—— (1994) *Spoleczenstwa klasy sredniej.* Warszawa: IFiS PAN.

—— (1997) 'Constant Fluidity with Rise in Total Rates. Social Moblity in Six East-European Nations', *Polish Sociological Review*, 119(3): 267–83.

—— (1998) 'Dwie transformacje w krajach Europy Środkowo-Wschodniej a ruchliwośb społeczna', *Studia Socjologiczne*, 1(148): 27–59.

GEMINI (1998) Raport o stanie sektora małych i średnich przedsiębiorstw w Polsce w latach 1996–1997. Warsaw: USAID GEMINI.

Gorecki, B. and M. Wisniewski (1998) 'Zroznicowanie dochodow gospodarstw domowych w Polsce w latach 1987–1995', in RSSG przy radzie Ministrów. Raport 29: *Podzial dochodu i nierownosci dochodowe. Fakty, tendencje, porownania.* Warsaw: RSSG: 133–70.

Górniak, J. (1989) 'Economy and Education in the Socialist Corporate System', *Innovation*, 2(1–2).

Glówny Urzad Statystyczny (GUS) (1998) *The Republic of Poland Statistical Yearbook 1998.* Warsaw: GUS.

GUS: Budzety (1998) *The 1997 Household Budget Surveys.* Warsaw: GUS.

GUS: Earnings (1997) *Earnings of the Employees in the National Economy by Occupation as of March 1996*. Warsaw: GUS.

GUS: Warunki (1998) *Living Conditions of the Population in 1997*. Warsaw: GUS.

GUS: Zróznicowanie (1998) *Diversification of the Polish Population in 1997*. Warsaw: GUS.

Miś, L. (1998) 'Nowoczesna kwestia socjalna – bezrobotni w strukturze społeczej lat 90' in *Śląsk – Polska – Europa: Zmieniające się społeczeństwo w perspektywie lokalnej i globalnej. Xięga X Ogólnopolskiego Zjazdu Socjologicznego*. Katowice: Wydawnictwo Uniwersytetu Śląskiego.

Milanovic, B. (1998) *Income, Inequality, and Poverty during the Transition from Planned to Market Economy*. Washington DC: World Bank.

Mokrzycki, E. (1997) 'Od protokapitalizmu do posocjalizmu', in H. Domanski and A. Rychard (eds), *Elementy nowego ladu*. Warsaw: IFiS PAN: 33–46.

Rutkowski, J. (1998) *Welfare and Labor Market in Poland. Social Policy during Economic Transformation*, World Bank technical paper no. 417. Washington DC: World Bank.

Szelényi, I. and S. Szelényi (1995) 'Wstep – zalozenia teoretyczne i metodologia', in I. Szelényi, D. Treiman and E. Wnuk-Lipinski (eds), *Elity w Polsce, w Rosji i na Węgrzech. Wymiana czy reprodukcja*. Warsaw: Instytut Studiów Politycznych PAN: 7–34.

Szukieloc-Bienkuska, A. (1998) *Poverty in Poland (In View of Household Surveys in 1997)*. Warsaw: GUS.

Tarkowska, E. (1998) 'Ubóstwo w byłych PGR-ach: w poszukiwaniu dawnych źródeł nowej biedy', in *Śląsk – Polska – Europa: Zmieniajce się społeczeństwo w perspektywie lokalnej i globalnej. Xięga X Ogólnopolskiego Zjazdu Socjologicznego*. Katowice: Wydawnictwo Uniwersytetu Śląskiego.

Wasilewski, J. (1995) 'The Old Apparatus in a New System: The Case of the Communist Nomenklatura in Poland', in U. Van Beek (ed.), *South Africa and Poland in Transition. A Comparative Perspective*. Pretoria: HSRC Publishers: 257–83.

—— (1998) 'Hungary, Poland, and Russia: The Fate of Nomenklatura Elites', in M. Dogan and J. Higley (eds), *Elites, Crises, and the Origins of Regimes*. Lanham: Rowman & Littlefield: 147–67.

—— *et al.* (1998) *Liderzy w polityce, administracji, gospodarce i komunikacji spolecznej*. Codebook no. 1 (manuscript). Warsaw: Instytut Studiow Politycznych PAN.

Wesolowski, W. and B. Mach (1986) *Systemowe funkcje ruchliwosci spolecznej w Polsce*. Warsaw: IFiS PAN.

Wilkin, J. (1999) *EU Monitoring III – problematyka rolnictwa i obszarów wiejskich* (manuscript).

Zienkowski, L. (1998) *Dochody gospodarstw domowych w okresie transformacji 1989–1996 (proba syntezy)*. Warsaw: Zaklad Badan Statystyczno-Ekonomicznych GUS.

9
Czech Republic

Jiří Večerník

Economic inequalities play a key role in three areas. From an individual and narrowly economic point of view, they have an important motivational role, beginning with the choice of school and ending with an individual's work performance. From a larger social and societal perspective, they have both a differentiating and integrating function: they are a tool for distinguishing the social classes and, simultaneously, link them together. Finally, from the psychological and political perspective, the degree of perception of the legitimacy of existing disparities has an impact on political preferences and stability of the regime.

Data on economic inequalities are rather abundant, but analyses of their individual sections (personal earnings, household incomes, family wealth) are separated. Moreover, even though economic inequality is the very base of social stratification, both structures are only scarcely analysed in their close relationships. Using various sources we try to put together individual information. After a brief description of the pre-1989 situation, we show the basic changes in class composition and income distribution brought about by implosion of the communist regime. Further, we document changes of individual social strata in more detail. In the third and last section, we observe processes of social structuration involving individual and collective shifts, objective and subjective reranking of people.

Social structure prior to the transition

The communist putsch in 1948 triggered a complete transformation of the economic and social structures of the former Czechoslovakia. At the time, it was an economically advanced country with a democratic political system, although limited due to the postwar political pressure of the Communist Party, backed by the USSR and the Soviet army. Czech lands at that time were a relatively homogeneous middle-class society in which petty bourgeoisie and white-collar workers represented a large middle class, serving as reference groups for the rest of society.

Instead of supporting the middle class, the communist regime tried to equalize society around the working class. It proceeded by eliminating entrepreneurs and the self-employed, limiting services, collectivizing peasantry and degrading the 'intelligentsia' in rewards and prestige. Unlike East Germany, Hungary and Poland, small entrepreneurs and private farmers were eradicated completely in Czechoslovakia and wage disparities were attenuated to an extreme extent. Within the working class itself, its traditional sections of skilled workers in light manufacturing experienced degradation (accompanied by feminization and a corresponding wage decrease), while new sections of mining and heavy industry were promoted, following the plan to transform Czechoslovakia into a 'smithy of the socialist camp'.

Despite all the pressures of homogenization of society and equalizing the level of living, differences among people did not disappear completely. Many remain but most disappeared from the statistics. Postwar social statistics say virtually nothing about the main changes in the late 1940s and early 1950s. After a break, statistics reappeared again in the late 1950s in a completely new form, tailored according to Soviet classifications. The social categories observed by the new statistics were only the working class, 'other employees', cooperative peasants and pensioners (with private peasants and the self-employed as a negligible remainder).

After 1968, when efforts to reform the communist system were stopped by Soviet tanks, data display a frozen landscape of 'brotherhood classes'. As Table 9.1 shows, the 'working class' saw many changes in the 1970s but decreased somewhat in the 1980s, in favour of 'other employees'. The 'class of cooperative peasants' was kept stable over the entire period. Also, the share of pensioners did not change, and even decreased during last communist decades due to an advantageous age structure. The true differences among people returned back into the darkness of private life and political privileges. In fact, there were several additional sources of well-being and inequality:

- *In-kind incomes*. Due to very low real incomes, food expenditures were a substantial drain on household budgets (decreasing only from about 45 per cent to 30 per cent during the period 1948–88). Any opportunity to economize in this area constituted a special advantage and considerably increased a household's general welfare. After the 'class of cooperative peasants' was formed by the forceful collectivization of land and farming facilities, its members were privileged by being able to retain pieces of land where food could be produced.
- *The informal economy*. A huge reduction in the service sector directly provoked a demand for the work of craftsmen while a scarcity of consumer goods provided salesmen, who could then charge higher shadow prices, with an opportunity for greater profit. The black market encompassed a wide range of services, including those in the social sector, be it

Table 9.1 Households and household incomes by 'social group' (%)

Social group	1970	1976	1980	1988	1992	1996
Composition of households:						
Manual workers	40.7	40.9	41.1	34.5	30.0	30.3
Other employees	25.0	26.3	26.8	31.6	24.9	25.1
Cooperative farmers	5.4	4.7	5.1	5.6	3.0	0.6
Private farmers	0.3	0.1	0.0	0.0	0.5	0.6
Self-employed	0.1	0.1	0.1	0.2	5.8	8.7
Pensioners	28.1	27.5	26.2	27.7	34.2	32.3
Other	0.4	0.4	0.7	0.4	1.6	2.3
Total	100.0	100.0	100.0	100.0	100.0	100.0
Household income per capita:						
Manual workers	98.1	96.8	98.0	103.2	95.6	93.0
Other employees	113.8	112.9	111.7	112.3	117.7	124.2
Cooperative farmers	108.0	105.4	104.7	108.9	91.4	89.4
Private farmers	–	–	–	–	–	125.0
Self-employed	–	–	–	–	142.6	127.9
Pensioners	81.4	86.2	83.5	80.4	85.8	83.2
Total	100.0	100.0	100.0	100.0	100.0	100.0

Sources: See Data Sources at end of chapter, pp. 240–1: Microcensuses 1970–96.

in healthcare, access to education, the allocation of apartments, the provision of departure visas, and so on. With each successive 'triumph' of communism, the list of informal activities extended further.

- *Party privileges and hidden ownership rights*. On the one hand, party officials enjoyed privileges such as free or very cheap goods and services unavailable to the ordinary citizen (including special stores, health services and recreation areas). On the other hand, although private ownership of the means of production did not officially exist, in actual fact owners did. Managers, administrators, directors and party officials had extensive opportunities and incentives to transform the ownership status of many goods from state to quasi-private, as well as enjoying greater benefits from public services.

By ideological intention, the communist system tried to turn the pyramid of society upside down, encouraging especially manual workers (by position or origin) and directing them to higher education and, consequently, to managerial positions. While in the 1950s, 'new intelligentsia' was expressly trained in several-month courses (such as lawyers), class origin was systematically used for affirmative action in favour of working-class children. In education, it had in the end only little effect. Whereas the administratively-based redistribution failed to attenuate social inequality in educational attainment, it however succeeded in weakening transparent competition and devastated the educational system (Matějů, 1991).

Regarding wages, analysis showed that contrary to the rhetoric about the importance of rewards as work motivation ('each according to his capacity, to each according to his work'), disparities in both earnings and family income followed rather demographic characteristics of workers (sex and age) and of households (numbers of economically active members and dependent children). Because disparities in earnings were kept stable since the end of 1950, the distribution of household income changed mostly following the demographic composition of households (Večerník, 1976). But in the 1970s and 1980s, no important change was found either in the distribution of wages or household income (Table 9.2).

Nevertheless, behind the stability in the overall earnings distribution, important changes occurred in the relative positions of different groups. First, the peak of the age curve gradually shifted in favour of older employees, as a 'founding generation' of communism maintained their once-gained advantages. Second, the relative wages of those in the productive sector improved continuously, while the position of the service branches deteriorated. Third, the relative position of university-educated people declined and differences between various levels of education gradually narrowed. All of these changes can be considered in consonance with the 'logic' of the communist regime and the full control it exerted over the economy and the population (Večerník, 1991).

The overall system of distribution continued to be ruled by the 'need principle', which means the primary focus on the basic needs for the

Table 9.2 Earnings and household incomes (quantile characteristics in % of median)

Characteristic	1970	1975/76	1980/81	1988/89	1992/93	1996/97
Earnings:						
P10	62.7	64.2	63.9	62.1	56.9	58.7
P25	78.1	76.4	78.6	75.9	73.4	77.6
P75	124.2	124.1	127.7	126.1	136.5	128.2
P90	154.1	151.6	155.5	152.0	181.5	170.0
P90/P10	2.46	2.36	2.43	2.45	3.19	2.90
Gini coefficient	0.20	0.20	0.20	0.20	0.25	0.24
Household income per capita:						
P10	56.7	62.1	63.4	66.8	66.0	60.9
P25	75.8	78.3	79.5	81.1	82.7	78.6
P75	128.0	128.2	128.6	128.7	127.7	131.8
P90	161.4	161.5	162.9	162.4	167.5	177.1
P90/P10	2.85	2.60	186.8	2.43	2.51	2.91
Gini coefficient	0.22	0.21	0.21	0.20	0.23	0.26

Sources: Atkinson and Micklewright, 1992 (up to 1980); Wage surveys, 1988, 1993 and 1997; also see Data Sources: Microcensus 1988, 1992 and 1996.

reproduction of the labour force and understood mainly as individual and uniform persons ('soldiers of work').[1] Due to this, inequality of per capita income was compressed, following assumptions that people had about more or less equal needs. By contrast, inequality of total household income remained considerable, given the primary dependence of household income on the number of active earners. Both effects caused an extreme range of household income between single pensioners at the bottom and families with multiple earners at the top of the income distribution.

Officially, there was neither richness nor poverty under the communist system. Poverty was alleviated thanks to the system of social security that covered the whole population from the late 1960s. The very reason for the small incidence of relative poverty was, however, low income inequality. The narrow range of income distribution created a situation in which the bottom sector of the population was not too far from the average. By impoverishing the population as a whole in absolute terms, the communist regime succeeded in camouflaging individual poverty in relative terms.

In terms of starvation and lack of shelter, there was indeed little poverty in Czechoslovakia. This does not mean, however, that poverty in absolute terms was entirely eliminated. Extremely low pension benefits allotted to the members of the former bourgeoisie and expropriated peasants were used as weapons in the 'class war' of the 1950s and early 1960s. Due to the absence of any valorization or indexing, the purchasing power of older people's pensions dropped below the average pension and the average pension dropped behind the average wage.[2] The living conditions of single women with children were also very acute.

However, the communist world of stagnation also brought full employment and decent welfare. 'Social-class policies' in the distribution of scarce goods (better meat and fruit, imported textile and durable goods) were adopted to prefer working-class localities and regions. The regime maintained its support especially among workers of privileged branches and cooperative farmers. In spite of this, satisfaction with the regime decreased. According to confidential surveys at the time (the respondents of which could still not be sure that their answers would not be used against them in some way), in 1970 49 per cent of respondents saw their standards of living improve over the previous five years, followed by 44 per cent in 1985 and 38 per cent in 1989. The outlook for the next five years was also perceived optimistically with a decreasing tendency: 38 per cent in 1970, 34 per cent in 1985 and 32 per cent in 1989 (Opinions of Citizens, 1989).

Classes and incomes in the transition process

The transformation that started in former Czechoslovakia in 1990 after the implosion of the communist regime involved the introduction of a democratic political regime and the thorough reform of the economic and social system.

The starting point was depriving the Communist Party of its leading role in politics and the economy in order to make possible all processes of liberalization. The former political elite disappeared, its top members going mostly into retirement, the lower sections into business. Most members discarded their membership card which had ceased to be a 'work permit' for important functions. Loyal, mostly older communists remained organized with the Communist Party which still has the largest membership.[3]

The political system was established on a new, democratic base. The original anti-communist movement Civic Forum was transformed into political parties of which the Civic Democratic Party of Václav Klaus dominated the political scene during the period 1992–97. Both parties surviving from the past (the Communists and the Christian Democrats) and the new parties (among them especially Civic Democratic Alliance and the Social Democrats) started to shape political life and channel attitudes of the population. The transformation of the political system was accompanied by the Slovak drive for independence which finally led to the split of Czechoslovakia into two separate states since January 1993.

Economic reform launched price liberalization and the privatization of the land, houses and all means of production. Along with restitution and standard methods of privatization (auctions and purchase), coupon privatization was launched in which vouchers were given to six million adult Czechs. This method was supposed to be just (because the property was distributed to the whole population), fast (no search for investors was needed) and capitalist (a lesson in investment for all people). However, as unexpectedly numerous and energetic investment privatization funds entered the scene, the ownership of this property quickly became concentrated, along with transfer of capital, into unknown hands. Privatization is still in process, the biggest banks being on the agenda for 1999–2000.

Consequently, administration of labour was removed and the labour market has reappeared with its opportunities and risks. However, the expectations of the population in the early 1990s seemed gloomier than the subsequent reality. Due to the huge absorption capacity of the tertiary sector, expanding self-employment and the departure of pensioners from the labour force, unemployment remained low in the Czech economy up until the mid-1990s. In this, also, the reluctance of firms to restructure played an important role. Because of the cross-ownership of former state enterprises (owned by investment funds, in turn owned by the bank giants, which were themselves owned by the state), little or no pressure on increased productivity was exerted and labour was continuously hoarded for an unpredictable future.

In the former state sector, wage regulation was maintained for some time.[4] In contrast, new and foreign firms had considerably greater liberty in wage settings, with many of them seeking to attract highly qualified people by offering much better rewards. Labour mobility increased as individuals found better paid jobs, created private firms or sought work abroad. It introduced marked movements in the sources and extent of earnings inequality, created the conditions necessary for improving returns to education, providing better work incentives and gradually adjusting the reward system to that in the West. After the price shock and labour shrinkage of 1990–91, wages started to rise more rapidly than productivity of labour.

Provoked by the changes in the labour market, it was necessary to put in place certain social measures from the very beginning of the transformation: introduction of unemployment benefits, the valorization of pensions and other benefits, the fixing of the guaranteed minimum wage and the establishment of the minimum subsistence income (the Living Minimum). More consistent changes of the social system began after 1995. This move was proclaimed as a shift away from the paternalistic state towards an efficient and targeted welfare policy, strengthening the responsibility of individuals and families. On the whole, the social reform was in the end less radical than anticipated. The transformation of the social security system was developed in three fields:

- Within *social insurance*, the regulation of pension insurance had to take into account the deteriorating dependency ratio. This was the reason for a new scheme which accepted a gradual rise in the retirement age.[5] The government is obliged to valorize pensions against inflation (in each case of price increases of 5 per cent or more) and real wage rises (by at least one-third of this rise).
- Within *state social support*, several family benefits were combined and based on the Living Minimum as a testing basis.
- *Social assistance* was oriented towards households with incomes below the living minimum and is conceived at the maximum possible decentralization of decision-making on benefit entitlements. Since 1993, additional pension insurance has enabled citizens to insure themselves with commercial insurance companies, this with the help of a state contribution.

Privatization and creation of *de novo* private firms changed the composition of the labour force according to sector of ownership completely. Whereas in 1989, only 1 per cent of workers were employed in the private sector, this share increased to 31 per cent in 1992 and to 59 per cent in 1996; in 1996, another 14 per cent of workers were employed in the mixed sector. The statistical indicator of 'workers according to type of management' was replaced in 1997 by 'employees by sector', according to which 66 per cent of employees worked in the private and 34 per cent in the public sector (Statistical Yearbooks).

Despite the formal completion of the main privatization steps, the whole process may not be considered as finished. The withdrawal of the state from the economy was largely nominal. The interim result is a 'recombinant property' with the government's central role as a core investor indirectly controlling the most important banks and, through them, the most important enterprises (Stark, 1992). Confused corporate governance and lack of capital led to weak restructuring of companies and their stagnating efficiency. The Social-Democratic government in power since mid-1998 is searching for a way to revitalize the core firms of Czech manufacturing industry.

In the transformation period, the informal economy expands due to free private business, open borders and a temporarily weak legal and institutional framework. In the Czech Republic, the informal economy is not as large as in other transitory economies: its share in GDP is estimated at 10–15 per cent. A very frequent form is avoiding taxes and employment regulations by small entrepreneurs, which is paralleled by large firms not paying social contributions. Since 1989, Czech society has seen a lot of scandals concerning tax fraud. Freedom in business licences is largely used by employees with part-time self-employed status who sell the same skills outside their main job and often also share the same working time.

Despite a considerable share of the informal economy, coping strategies of households are based mainly on a monetary base – concretely speaking, labour mobility, secondary jobs and the use of savings. A slight decreasing trend is also observed in a 'do-it-yourself' strategy (EEA surveys). Together with the decreasing agricultural population and relatively favourable prices of food, fewer people produce food for their own households than under the communist regime. No significant demonetization of the Czech economy is then appearing.

Transformation of the economic and social system brought about considerable movements in previously static income disparities. Some of the measures adopted have had equalizing effects: the introduction of the minimum wage (which was, however, frozen for many years), legal establishment of the Living Minimum (previously existing only as a recommendation for social administration) and valorization criteria for pensions. But the main movements have led to greater variation in all individual sources of income except pension benefits. This process has resulted in rising inequality of household income.

In the observation of income inequality, indicators of income per household and per capita are to be distinguished. Statistical income surveys show that the rise has been slower in income per household and faster in per capita income (Table 9.3). The changing pattern of distribution is indicated by correlation coefficients; while the correlation between income per household and the number of active earners as well as between per capita income and dependent children is weakening, the correlation between the two indicators of income is strengthening. This indicates that disparities in market income are becoming wide enough to prevail over a family's participation in the labour market: even households with only one active earner have the chance to prosper.

Table 9.3 Characteristics of distribution of household income

Indicator	**Per household**			**Per capita**		
	1988	**1992**	**1996**	**1988**	**1992**	**1996**
Coefficients and decile ratio:						
Variation	0.53	0.69	0.73	0.40	0.56	0.65
Gini	0.29	0.32	0.33	0.20	0.23	0.26
Decile ratio (*D*90/*D*10)	5.12	4.95	5.21	2.43	2.51	2.91
Correlations (Pearson coefficients):						
Size of household	0.59	0.55	0.52	−0.64	−0.51	−0.15
Number of active earners	0.73	0.59	0.61	0.04	0.10	0.18
Number of children	0.29	0.28	0.28	−0.75	−0.59	−0.21

Notes: Income per capita is weighted by persons; correlations are computed on households as the observation unit; all coefficients are significant at the level <0.001.
Sources: See Data Sources: Microcensus 1988, 1992 and 1996.

Disparity between shifts in distribution of income per household and per capita is also explained by the changing composition of households. While the average size of households in the period 1988–96 remained the same (2.66 members) and the number of dependent children decreased slightly (from 0.76 to 0.69), the number of economically active members decreased considerably (from 1.48 to 1.24). Two opposite effects have contributed to this result: the pushing of working pensioners to leave the labour force (by heavily taxing earnings taken in parallel with pension benefits) and a pulling of women, who can be supported by their better-paid husbands, to stay at home and/or support them in the family business.[6]

Table 9.4 shows income distribution by decile groups. According to income per household, the bottom group increased slightly and the top group rose considerably. According to income per capita, the top group rose too but the other categories behaved differently in the two periods. Between 1988 and 1992, the relative position of the lower half of the income distribution was largely maintained while the upper half rather lost. This was the preprivatization period of the social-liberal government which maintained universal social benefits and kept wages under control. Between 1992 and 1996, relative stability or increase was rather registered in the upper half while the lower half has lost. This was the privatization period of the self-proclaimed liberal government which replaced universal benefits with targeted ones, removed wage regulation, froze the minimum wage and finally allowed a rapid rise in earnings not endorsed by the growth of productivity of labour. In both periods, the middle of the income distribution was squeezed.

Real income of the population collapsed in 1991 and reached its 1989 level only in 1996 (Figure 9.1). According to categories of household income,

Table 9.4 Distribution of household income by declile groups and real growth (%)

Decile group	Per household (HH)			Per capita (PC)			Real growth in 1988–96	
	1988	1992	1996	1988	1992	1996	HH	PC
1	2.5	2.9	2.8	5.3	4.9	4.3	105.6	74.6
2	4.1	4.1	3.9	6.6	6.4	5.9	88.5	82.8
3	5.9	5.8	5.6	7.4	7.3	6.8	88.7	85.9
4	7.6	6.9	6.7	8.1	7.9	7.6	81.7	87.7
5	9.3	8.1	7.9	8.8	8.6	8.3	79.7	88.5
6	10.7	9.6	9.4	9.6	9.2	9.1	81.4	88.6
7	12.0	11.1	10.9	10.6	10.1	10.1	84.5	89.2
8	13.2	12.8	12.7	11.8	11.3	11.5	88.9	90.8
9	15.1	15.2	15.4	13.6	13.2	13.7	95.0	93.7
10	19.6	23.5	24.7	18.2	21.1	22.6	117.3	116.1
Total	100.0	100.0	100.0	100.0	100.0	100.0	93.4	93.4

Notes: Income per capita is weighted by persons.
Sources: See Data Sources: Microcensus 1988, 1992 and 1996.

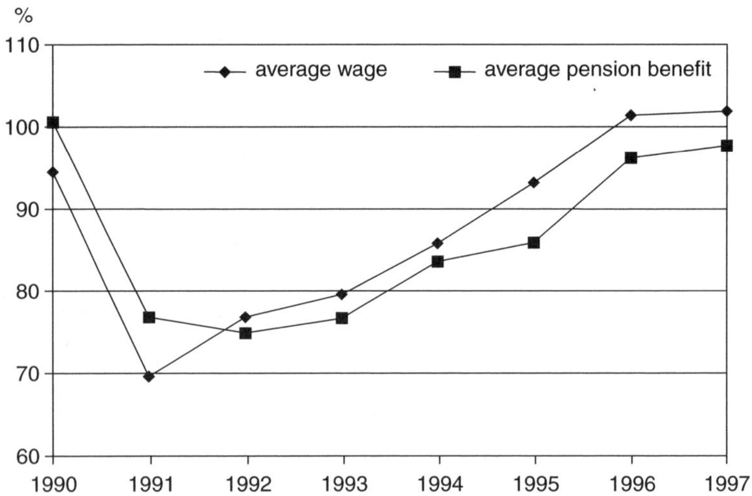

Figure 9.1 Real incomes, 1990–97 (1989 = 100)
Source: See Data Sources: Statistical Yearbooks.

it seems that while the lowest and highest income categories have increased their standards, middle incomes lost 10–20 per cent of their purchasing power.[7] However, the real rise of the bottom decile group is rather spurious because there was a considerable demographic mobility within it. In terms of income per capita, only the top decile group gained and the bottom

Table 9.5 Analysis of variance of (ln) household income (% of total variance)

Factor	No. of categories	Per household		Per capita	
		1988	1996	1988	1996
Main effects		62.82	43.73	59.26	48.22
No. of active earners	3	24.21	27.86	3.84	3.92
No. of children	5	5.42	2.40	31.84	19.43
Age of the household head	7	1.89	0.23	3.03	0.22
Non-manual	2	0.16	0.70	0.00	1.43
Education	4	3.29	3.45	1.19	3.59
Locality	3	0.08	0.18	0.07	0.64
2-way interactions		3.16	2.36	2.60	1.75
Explained		65.98	46.08	61.86	49.97

Notes: Only households with head in prime age (25–54) included; income per capita is weighted by persons; all coefficients are significant at the level < 0.001.
Sources: See Data Sources: Microcensus 1988 and 1996.

decile group lost the most. Results given by the two income indicators are disproportionate which informs us about the uneven change in various categories of the population, in particular the replacement of pensioners by children in the lower part of the income distribution. In other words, the lowest income ceased to be represented solely by transfer income (pensioners = non-working poor = old poverty) and is newly-represented by low market income (families with children = working poor = new poverty).

In considering the variance of income, we observe a considerable weakening of the lifecycle profile of household income in favour of its occupation profile (Table 9.5). According to income per household, the specific importance of age of the household's head approaches zero and the weight of the number of children tends to disappear, especially following the diminishing relation of family allowances to their earnings. According to income per capita, the specific weight of the number of children more than halved. From the other side, the importance of labour-market characteristics of individuals (household heads) has increased. The manual/non-manual distinction, not distinguishable in the communist period, reappeared in both income indicators. In packaging of income per capita, education tripled its importance.

After 1989, hitherto hidden income redistribution was also made more transparent in several steps. The first step was the abolition of price subsidies in the mid-1990s; the second step was unification of different kinds of income tax into one in 1993 when the (almost flat at the time) wage tax and other schemes for the self-employed were replaced by a new universal income tax for physical persons. Simultaneously, the former turnover tax was

Table 9.6 Relative taxes and social benefits according to decile groups (%)

Decile share	According to income per household				According to income per capita			
	Taxes		Social benefits		Taxes		Social benefits	
	1988	1996	1988	1996	1988	1996	1988	1996
1	16.1	16.6	17.0	17.9	10.3	11.9	30.1	30.5
2	14.1	16.0	23.4	22.0	11.9	14.8	24.0	22.0
3	13.6	16.3	24.2	21.8	13.0	16.4	20.4	17.6
4	14.4	17.2	21.2	18.3	13.7	17.4	18.0	15.5
5	14.9	18.0	18.5	15.4	14.1	18.3	16.6	14.1
6	15.2	18.2	16.6	13.6	14.8	18.8	15.3	13.8
7	15.3	19.7	15.6	11.2	15.4	19.8	14.4	11.7
8	15.7	20.2	14.7	9.9	16.0	20.4	14.2	10.1
9	16.0	21.4	13.8	7.8	17.2	21.6	14.1	7.8
10	16.1	24.1	12.4	4.8	17.4	24.6	15.4	4.4
Total	15.3	20.0	16.7	11.9	15.3	20.0	16.7	11.9

Notes: Only households of non-farm employees included; income per capita is weighted by persons. Relative tax is computed as a percentage of income tax and social contributions in gross household income. Relative social benefits are computed as a percentage of social benefits in net household income.
Sources: See Data Sources: Microcensus 1988 and 1996.

replaced by VAT, and a new system of employee and employers' pension and health contributions was introduced.

If we take the population as a whole, the rise in the financial burden of households appears: according to income surveys of 1988 and 1996, direct taxes and contributions of households rose from 13 to 17 per cent of their gross income while transfer income rose from only 25 to 26 per cent of their net income. Regarding change in distribution over time, we can compare only non-farm employee households (Table 9.6).[8] Both taxes and social benefits are distributed more steeply among households, following the reform design. The progressiveness of the new system appears despite the fact that the majority of the active population were still hit only by the first band of income tax (15 per cent) and only very few by the second (20 per cent). Regarding social benefits, their targeting was the main purpose framed by the new system of state social support introduced in 1996.

Shifts registered by income surveys document change of the system as a whole. Generally speaking, Czech society is moving from a distribution of income based on family lifecycle to distribution based on family labour-market participation regarding both its extent (the number of active earners) and intensity (relative earnings). The communist system of distribution was mostly shaped following the principle of basic needs and reproduction, indicated clearly by the number of children. The new system appears to be determined differently, addressing the economic (labour market) capacity of a household. However, the effects of lifecycle surface if we take into account the entire population including pensioners: redistribution by age cohorts is even more striking in 1996 than in 1988. This is shown by a slightly growing gap between average earnings and pension benefits which developed from 1992 onwards.

Emerging new social structure

The transformation started to reshape the social stratification in several ways. First, it allowed the appearance of the old differences, bringing them back into the external sphere of monetary income and conspicuous wealth. Second, it created new sources of disparities, especially through privatization and the functioning of market forces. The character of these sources is twofold: in the business sphere, besides honest entrepreneurship, black markets expanded and speculation flourished using the transformation intermezzo of lack of legislation and the insufficient performance of controlling mechanisms; in the labour market, besides involuntary unemployment and other sources of deserved poverty, also the lack of a work ethic, disinterest and crime increased when totalitarian repression disappeared.

During transformation, markets open and invite all people to redefine their social status. Simultaneously, channels of mobility enlarge and make various types of motion in the social space possible. Consequently, the hierarchy of prestige changes and the lifestyles of people develop in response to the Western example. The structure of stratification within the country changes according to the Weberian typology.[9] However, in transforming countries, stratification remains more obscure than in traditional capitalist countries. If we propose a more comprehensive delineation in the Weberian sense, we should observe not only changes in occupation, but also in material conditions of life, associative links and people's opinions.

Not only the market scene and corresponding labour effort are here in play. The lack of rules in a transitory situation led to the expansion of rent-seeking behaviour and its growing success. Instead of market forces, corporatist negotiations or settings prevailed in establishing important prices (such as meat or fuel), wages (of entire industries under control of unions) and access to some occupations. Here, state remained active in wage control (up until 1993), the control of rents of former state apartments (about a third of all housing) and other prices (energy and public transport). Not only the activity, but also the inactivity of the state matters: this is because in the actual system creditors are disadvantaged against debtors, and misuse of credit (bank or business) became a special field of rent-seeking.

In perception of the system regarding sources of life success, in the first place is individual effort and hard work, and in the second place 'social capital',

Table 9.7 Opinions about factors of life success (index)

Factor	1992	1997	1999	Difference		
				1997–92	1999–97	1999–92
Rich background	36.8	49.1	39.3	12.3	–9.8	2.5
Educated parents	30.4	41.8	36.1	11.4	–5.7	5.7
Higher education	48.5	63.9	54.5	15.4	–9.4	6.0
Ambitions	70.3	75.2	72.6	4.9	–2.6	2.3
Talent	68.6	71.4	68.3	2.8	–3.1	–0.3
Hard work	75.5	72.3	75.4	–3.2	3.1	–0.1
Good contacts	63.7	71.6	64.3	7.9	–7.3	0.6
Political connections	31.4	50.1	38.7	18.7	–11.4	7.3
Race or ethnicity	19.2	30.4	27.7	11.2	–2.7	8.5
Religion	12.0	13.2	12.7	1.2	–0.5	0.7
Locality of origin	23.5	20.3	28.7	–3.2	8.4	5.2
Gender	26.8	30.5	28.7	3.7	–1.8	1.9
Political opinions	34.3	31.3	29.5	–3.0	–1.8	–4.8

Note: Index is constructed from 5-point scale where 100 = substantial and 0 = not important at all.
Sources: See Data Sources: ISSP-1992, ISSP-1997, ISSP-1999.

especially useful acquaintances. In third place comes social background and in the last place ascriptive characteristics (Table 9.7). Whilst, up until 1997, the importance of all factors was increasing, they were decreasing after 1997. This might be connected with a smoother interface between liberalism and socialism after the 1997 elections. Despite the fact that the opinion on the market roots of individual success increased in the transformation period, it did not become dominant. In comparison with other reform countries, social background and political connections are considered as weaker in Czech society.

The most apparent and immediate change occurred within the political elite which was exchanged almost completely. However, expectations of a radical break were not fulfilled. The Czech 'Velvet Revolution' nominated a top communist bureaucrat as the first prime minister of the new democratic government (as an example to follow) and stifled any debate about the eventual banning of the Communist Party. None of leaders of the pre-1989 regime was ever punished, not even for inviting the Soviet occupation army to the country in 1968. The 1991 Lustration Law which prohibited members of the former nomenklatura and secret police from taking up public positions was passed against huge domestic opposition and criticism from international bodies. Upon its application, the people affected easily passed from public services into the economy using their unique social networks, enriching themselves considerably.

A different story concerns the economic elite – that is, the directors of big firms (Table 9.8). The prevailing recruitment mode was called a 'revolution of deputies', meaning that the majority of newcomers had occupied the position of deputy director or department manager under the previous

Table 9.8 Characteristics of the economic elite (directors) by sector of ownership

Characteristic	State	Privatized	Private	Total
Age:				
20–29	1.3	1.2	6.8	2.1
30–39	14.4	14.0	24.7	15.8
40–49	40.6	45.7	47.9	44.3
50–59	39.4	3.3	17.8	33.0
60 or above	4.4	5.8	2.7	4.8
Tertiary major education:				
No tertiary	21.9	14.0	13.7	16.6
Technical	34.4	48.6	35.6	41.8
Economics	31.9	28.8	38.4	31.3
Other	11.9	8.6	12.3	10.3
Ever member of the Communist Party:				
Yes	64.4	60.1	56.2	60.9
No	26.3	31.7	37.0	30.7
Missing	9.4	8.2	6.8	8.4
Own business in 1993	16.3	19.3	68.5	25.8
Father as party member	47.1	44.8	37.7	44.6
Family business	32.1	35.9	45.9	36.1

Sources: See Data Sources: SSEE; Hanley *et al.* (1998).

regime (Hanley *et al.*, 1998: 27). The managerial class has continued unhindered in the transition from central-planning to the market system (similarly as in Russia) and is climbing into (if not remaining within) the upper class. Their salaries followed Western patterns even in unprosperous firms in state ownership, and 'golden handshakes' are given even to the top managers of heavily failing state banks.[10] Managers took considerable power and privileges without shouldering the responsibilities for their firms.

Regarding the emerging middle classes, we distinguish the 'old' middle class, occupied in the production and distribution of material goods and services, and the 'new' middle class, occupied in the production and distribution of symbolic knowledge (Berger, 1986: 67). It turns out that whereas the old (entrepreneur) middle class was almost completely destroyed, sections of the new middle class remained 'physically', but not 'socially'. The reestablishment of the entrepreneurial middle class is much slower and more complicated than was expected, and the transformation of important sections of public employees into the intellectual middle class is marked by disintegrative disparities between the private and public sectors. Vain expectations and weakening middle-class support can threaten thorough reforms and stop the transforming process mid-way (Večerník, 1999).

The main mass movement launched by liberalization of the economy was the introduction of small-scale entrepreneurs to the scene. However, it can hardly be termed an explosion: 6.2 per cent of the labour force were self-employed and 2.5 per cent were entrepreneurs at the beginning of 1993, while 9.2 per cent were self-employed and 4.2 per cent were entrepreneurs in mid-1998 (LFS). According to the statistics, around 2.5 times more business licences have been issued than corresponds to the group of self-employed people in the labour force. This means that a great deal of self-employed work is still backed by dependent employment and formally constitutes a second job. Even much larger is the percentage of licenses that are used only occasionally. Survey data tell us that in 1998 still only 15 per cent of licence holders were exclusively engaged in private business, 37 per cent as primary employment, and 48 per cent as a supplementary source of income (EEA surveys).

In the Czech reform, there has not been much support for small private entrepreneurs. No tax holidays or allowances were accorded to these beginners in business and tax rates were established on a level comparable with the most redistributive Western countries. Credit access is distorted by the fact that the banking giants largely owned by the state have maintained a strong monopoly of power and have made credit expensive. As regards business policy, the liberal enthusiasm of the 'liberal' government led to an underestimation of the importance of establishing the legislative framework and building institutions to enforce it.

When compared with the rebirth of the 'old' (business) middle class, the transformation of employees in the state sector into the 'new' middle class is less visible but still in some sense easier. However, expectations concerning the return to its previous position have been left unfulfilled as wage statistics witnesses: the rise of financial sector and public administration contrast with the stagnation of education and health services (Table 9.9). Hence the new situation has affected the various categories to varying degrees and it is necessary to at least distinguish between state bureaucracy, banking and public services.

Against expectations, the bureaucracy expanded both in numbers and rewards: its number rose from 88,000 employees in 1989 to 172,000 in 1997, and the average salary improved in relation to the average wage from 102 to 110 per cent. The finance sector has seen a spectacular rise since 1989. Despite bankruptcies of new private banks and poor lending practices of old state banks, numbers rose from 25,000 employees in 1989 to 82,000 employees in 1997, and the average salary improved its position in relation to the average wage from 98 to 174 per cent. In contrast with finance, economy and law, public services lagged behind. This social category, represented most typically by teachers, physicians and researchers, was exposed to the expanding market with tight budgets. Despite a marked increase in the skill disparities of earnings, this process affects typical intellectuals to a lesser degree.

Table 9.9 Branch structure of earnings in two historical periods (% of average)

Branch	Czechoslovakia		Change	Czech Republic		Change
	1948	1953	1948–53	1989	1997	1989–97
Manufacturing	92.6	107.9	+15.3	104.4	100.3	–4.1
Construction	101.2	114.7	+13.5	111.2	104.9	–6.3
Agriculture	80.2	72.1	–8.1	108.2	79.5	–28.7
Transport	109.4	110.2	+0.8	106.4	105.8	–0.6
Trade	102.6	90.0	–12.6	83.8	98.3	+14.5
Health & welfare	120.9	92.1	–28.8	90.1	90.0	–0.1
Education	124.8	90.0	–34.8	89.8	88.1	–1.7
Banking and insurance	134.5	104.3	–30.2	98.3	174.4	+76.1
Administration & defence	–	–	–	101.3	110.2	+8.9
Average	100.0	100.0	0.0	100.0	100.0	0.0

Sources: See Data Sources: Statistical Yearbooks.

The transformation has destroyed all signs of working-class privileges. The break with the communist past is witnessed by changing branch composition, wage disparities and job securities. After a long period of stability of branch structure under the command economy, the agriculture and manufacturing industries are rapidly diminishing in favour of services. Despite the widespread hoarding of labour by privatized firms in the first years of transformation, manufacturing has finally reduced its personnel by one-fifth, mostly in favour of trade and services. The privileged sections of the working class (mining, metallurgy, heavy machinery) have lost their position and their wage levels have sunk to near the average. Wage disparities became wider to the disadvantage of manual labour, and unemployment started to affect workers with lower than secondary education (Table 9.10).

Where state-socialist manufacturing saw considerable decline after 1989, cooperative-socialist agriculture experienced a true fall. Under the communist regime, collectivized agriculture was subsidized, while peasants could combine decent (and not taxed) earnings from cooperatives with income in kind from private plots. As privatization of cooperatives remained mostly in their hands, many peasants never got their property back. Also due to large openness to EU market, farming turned into an unprofitable activity. No surprise that farmers were much less supportive of reforms than other citizens. Despite large differences in individual farmers' fates, agriculture usually offers little more than simple survival. This is reflected in frequent mass actions of agricultural associations.

Liberalization of prices and the opening of the labour market has enlarged sections of the population exposed to poverty. Whereas under the communist regime poverty was linked with the lifecycle (the 'old' poverty), the new sources of inequality start to link it to unemployment and low wages (the

Table 9.10 Economically active population and earnings by education (%)

Education	Total			Men			Women		
	1988	1992	1996	1988	1992	1996	1988	1992	1996
Composition of the population:									
Elementary	20.7	11.9	10.4	14.5	7.5	7.2	28.6	17.1	14.4
Vocational	41.6	46.5	47.1	48.8	53.8	55.2	32.4	38.0	37.3
Secondary	27.6	30.7	30.9	24.3	26.0	24.7	31.9	36.3	38.4
Tertiary	10.1	10.8	11.6	12.4	12.7	12.9	7.1	8.6	9.9
Total	100.0	100.0	100.0	100.0	100.0	100.0	100.0	100.0	100.0
Earnings:									
Elementary	90.5	75.7	69.6	90.5	81.0	73.0	93.1	80.3	74.6
Vocational	95.4	92.9	87.6	95.4	90.3	85.9	93.9	85.2	81.8
Secondary	101.4	103.7	106.9	102.2	104.5	110.3	104.3	112.6	112.7
Tertiary	134.0	144.0	164.7	124.6	140.0	161.3	133.1	145.4	160.7
Average	100.0	100.0	100.0	100.0	100.0	100.0	100.0	100.0	100.0

Sources: See Data Sources: Microcensus 1989, 1992 and 1996.

'new' poverty). However, the degree of social deprivation is still generally low in the Czech Republic. This is caused by the good performance of the economy (until 1997) and a quite generous social system. The exception is the Roma ethnic group which is extremely vulnerable to all the risks of the market economy, due to its very low skill level and weak labour commitment (its unemployment rate is near to 30 per cent). On the other hand, this category of usually large families is substantially much attracted to and trapped by the steep benefits allocated according to the Living Minimum.

In concrete terms we can speak of poverty as follows:

- *Legal poverty*. In 1991, the Living Minimum was established on a very steep equivalence scale (high dependence of amounts on the number of household members). It is increased each time when the living costs of low-income households increase by more than 10 per cent. According to the income surveys, the percentage of households declaring incomes below the legal poverty line is falling (Table 9.11). The first decrease after 1989 was caused by the new and stricter arrangement, and another small decrease occurred due to the fact that in 1993 an amendment introduced additional eligibility conditions, excluding people reluctant to work, who change their jobs on insufficient grounds, or who do not cooperate with the labour office. It seems that targeted benefits are quite efficient in alleviating poverty, in particular among couples with children.
- *EU poverty*. The standardized relative definition considers as poor households those whose income is below 50 per cent of the average income per

Table 9.11 Poor households and persons by family status

Family status	**Legal poverty line**			**EU poverty line**		
	1988	**1992**	**1996**	**1988**	**1992**	**1996**
Households:						
Family with children	1.1	3.2	2.7	0.7	2.0	6.3
Single parent family	8.1	10.2	8.3	5.0	7.5	16.4
One person household	13.5	1.4	1.0	19.9	2.6	3.9
Other	1.8	0.9	0.3	3.0	1.1	0.7
Average	4.5	2.7	2.1	6.1	2.3	5.0
Persons:						
Family with children	1.1	3.6	3.2	0.7	2.1	7.0
Single parent family	8.6	11.3	9.3	4.8	8.1	17.5
One person household	13.5	1.4	1.0	19.9	2.6	3.9
Other	1.6	0.9	0.3	2.6	1.1	0.7
Average	2.7	3.3	2.7	3.1	2.4	5.9

Sources: See Data Sources: Microcensus 1989, 1992 and 1996.

equivalent adult (computed as 1.0 for the first adult, 0.7 for other adults and 0.5 for each child). In comparison with the legal poverty line, the weight of children is here lower, the weight of adults higher and the burden of common household costs also slightly higher. In the late 1980s, the percentage of poor was low in the former Czechoslovakia, especially affecting pensioner households. After 1989, this proportion decreased due to intervention policy affecting low-income households. Larger income disparities in the mid-1990s brought about a higher proportion of poor households.

- *Feeling poor*. Perceived poverty is a relational feature dependent on the social environment and expectations. Low incomes could be purely transitional, without reflecting financial problems as an actual poverty status. Feeling poor seems to be rather more stable over time, amounting to about 8 per cent of households. The price liberalization in 1991 and the tax reform in 1993 caused a slight increase in the self-declaration of poverty. These indicators have risen again since 1997, reflecting the ongoing economic recession (Figure 9.2). Subjective poverty is especially striking in retirement age and among unskilled people.

Social reranking and status inconsistency

The transformation has revealed social ranking instead of an apparently equalized but hidden polarized society (between 'the people' and the ruling class). Economic inequalities have ceased to be derived from political positions and have started to be produced by the labour market to a considerable degree. Not only do people move within a given social space, but also various

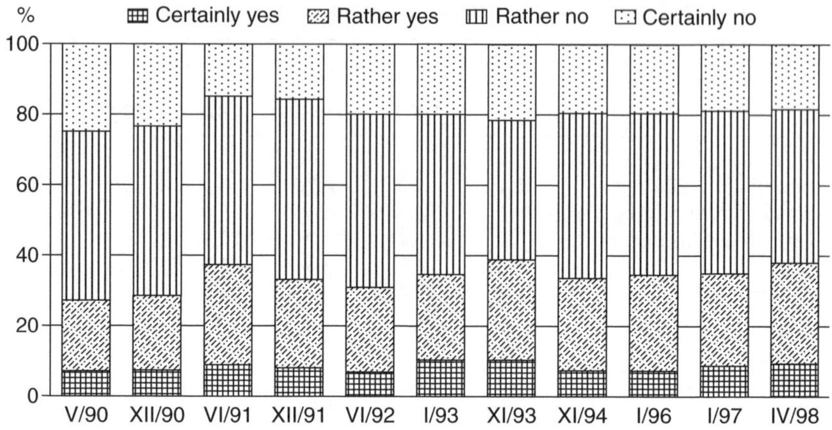

Figure 9.2 Those who consider themselves a poor family (%)
Sources: See Data Sources: EEA surveys.

dimensions of this space are changing considerably. Not only individual mobility between stable social categories develops, but also a 'collective' mobility which changes the relations of the rewards and prestige of occupations. Moreover, the perception of these motions by people themselves may differ and add an additional 'subjective' dimension of social mobility reflecting the other than occupational motions.

Changes in the socioeconomic structure of the economically active population are certainly significant but far from impressive. Most changes have evolved due to the opening markets and flows towards services, but not by the modernization of the economy and administration which should especially promote the group of professionals. Surprisingly, Hungary and Poland (where the category of self-employed existed even before 1989) scores higher in the change of population composition than the Czech Republic and Slovakia, in which the self-employed represented a negligible category and occupational mobility was also very weak.

The survey *Social Stratification in Eastern Europe after 1989* (which is the best available source of information) limits our comparative analysis of socioeconomic composition and mobility of the population only up to 1993.[11] Table 9.12 shows the greatest stability but also the smallest downward mobility and greatest inflow to self-employment in both countries of former Czechoslovakia. In contrast, Hungary and Poland show extensive inflows into unemployment and also early retirement (pushed by the labour market and pulled by legislation).

Along with vertical movements, important horizontal movements also occur (change in position within a firm or change of employer) which might lead to an improvement or worsening in rewards, work conditions

Table 9.12 Intragenerational class mobility of persons of working age (%)

Type of mobility	Czech Republic		Hungary		Poland		Slovakia	
	1983–88	1988–93	1983–88	1988–93	1983–88	1988–93	1983–88	1988–93
Significantly decreased	1.9	3.2	2.3	2.7	2.3	2.2	2.0	2.2
Decreased	2.4	3.8	3.5	3.4	3.0	4.2	2.3	3.8
No change	86.7	70.0	81.1	57.7	80.8	60.0	88.0	68.8
Increased	3.6	3.4	3.7	3.5	4.0	3.9	2.9	3.0
Signicantly increased	3.3	3.5	3.6	3.3	3.9	3.4	2.7	3.2
To self-employed	0.2	8.9	2.2	5.6	2.7	7.7	0.2	6.1
To unemployed	0.0	1.9	0.3	14.2	0.4	10.2	0.0	7.6
Early retirement	1.8	5.1	3.3	9.6	2.7	8.4	1.8	5.3
Total	100.0	100.0	100.0	100.0	100.0	100.0	100.0	100.0

Sources: See Data Sources: SSEE; Matějů (1999).

Table 9.13 Subjective mobility of economically active persons (%)

Type of mobility	Czech Republic	Hungary	Poland	Slovakia	Total
Significantly decreased	10.5	13.1	15.4	15.1	13.3
Decreased	23.5	43.6	29.0	31.0	30.8
No change	46.3	32.2	36.7	39.8	39.7
Increased	16.6	9.6	14.7	11.9	13.5
Significantly increased	3.1	1.5	4.2	2.1	2.7
Total	100.0	100.0	100.0	100.0	100.0

Sources: See Data Sources: SSEE; Matějů (1999).

and satisfaction. In addition, the position of social classes and occupational categories may change in ways that even a worker who stays in the same job might perceive a shift in his or her individual position. For all that, it is useful to ask about change in position, as it is perceived by people themselves. The percentage of subjectively stable people was much lower than the percentage of objectively stable (Table 9.13). In comparison with other CEE countries, the Czech population declared the most stable and upwards mobility.

Only about a half of objectively stable respondents in the Czech Republic, and even fewer in the other countries, declared stability in subjective terms. The two types of mobility are largely independent of the extensive collective mobility of nominally similar categories. The advancing social groups were especially professionals (the higher more than lower), the self-employed (entrepreneurs and freelance more than simple independent workers) and, consequently, people with higher education. An interesting point is the effect of political background: while simple membership in the Communist Party appeared to have no effect on subjective mobility, membership to party cadres has a positive effect, mostly due to providing the 'social capital' that helps when starting a business.

The relationship between objective and subjective mobility refers to status consistency vs inconsistency. In theoretical and normative terms, the ideal model of social stratification in a market economy is expressed by the 'meritocratic triad' of education, occupation and income (Kreckel, 1992: 97). Achievement ideology legitimates the income inequality which is supportive of economic efficiency and growth. Since the harmony of education, occupation and income can never be reached, we can only measure how the system is gradually adjusting to this standard. If the market mechanism replaces the centralized bureaucratic allocation of jobs and administration of wages, we can expect that all three dimensions of social status will stream towards more consistency.

Table 9.14 Objective status consistency: results of exploratory factor analysis methods – principal components analysis, oblimin rotation and pattern matrices

	1991		1995		1997	
	SES-CON	SES-INC	SES-CON	SES-INC	SES-CON	SES-INC
Explained variance (%)	57.2	31.7	63.0	27.8	65.1	26.1
Factor loadings before rotation						
Education	0.901	–0.136	0.899	–0.223	0.896	–0.249
Index of socioeconomic status	0.878	–0.262	0.884	–0.289	0.887	–0.289
Income	0.383	0.922	0.545	0.837	0.602	0.798
Factor loadings after oblique rotation						
Education	0.897	0.067	0.915	0.037	0.923	0.023
Index of socioeconomic status	0.925	–0.061	0.940	–0.034	0.941	–0.021
Income	0.001	0.998	0.008	0.999	0.000	0.999
Factor correlations (after rotation)	0.153		0.291		0.345	

Notes: Variables: education – The highest achieved education (8 categories); job – International Index of Socioeconomic Status (ISEI); income – Net personal income from all economic activities.
Sources: See Data Sources: Social Justice 1991 and 1995; ISSP 1997; Matějů and Kreidl (1998).

Table 9.14 shows a growing consistency of education, job and income in the 1990s (Matějů and Kreidl, 1998).[12] As the explained variance in the top part of the table witnesses, the percentage of consistent component of socioeconomic status had increased and the percentage of the inconsistent component had decreased. Simultaneously, income joined the consistent part in an increasing degree. In the bottom part of the table, the most relevant information is the correlation between both axes of socioeconomic status which strengthened from 0.15 in 1991 to 0.34 in 1997.

The surveys tell us also about growing links between the objective situation and subjective location in the social hierarchy. In early 1999, we asked people to locate themselves on ladders representing social position, income and standard of living, both now and in retrospect, as they were 10 years ago. When using such a long retrospective horizon, it is necessary to be very cautious. Usually, people are much more critical towards the present than towards the past. Similarly, the reference levels change too: what might be taken as a decent standard under communism, is considered as a near poverty situation today.

Table 9.15 summarizes self-ranking on social and income ladders in 1989 and 1999, and the corresponding change over time. We may conclude the following: (1) a decrease of individuals occurred in both types of ranking, but on average not by more than one point on the 10-item scale; (2) in

Table 9.15 Self-ranking by social position and income (%)

Decile scale	Social position		Income		Change in 1989–99	
	1989	1999	1989	1999	Social position	Income
1	2.0	4.2	4.6	5.7	2.0	2.3
2	3.4	7.9	6.3	11.9	1.5	1.9
3	8.5	15.5	15.2	17.4	1.1	1.0
4	13.4	17.7	18.3	18.5	0.3	0.3
5	17.5	17.4	26.1	20.8	–0.4	–0.5
6	30.2	26.0	12.2	12.9	–1.1	–1.3
7	13.6	7.6	10.2	7.6	–2.2	–2.2
8	7.8	3.2	5.3	3.8	–2.7	–3.7
9	2.9	0.3	1.4	1.0	–3.7	–4.4
10	0.8	0.1	0.5	0.3	–5.8	–5.6
Total	100.0	100.0	100.0	100.0	–0.8	–0.4

Sources: See Data Sources: ISSP (1999).

1999, the population is generally more dispersed, especially lower on the scale; (3) the overwhelming trend is rather an exchange of position and not polarization, as weak correlation coefficients between positions in 1989 and 1999 document (0.24 for social position and 0.15 for income); while from the perspective of 1989 the lower positions increase and the higher ones decrease, from the perspective of 1999 the opposite is true.

Who are the 'winners' and 'losers' of transformation, according to people themselves? This is approximated by correlation coefficients of social positions and mobility with various characteristics of people (Table 9.16). Regarding the position in 1999, the most important factors of perceived deprivation are retirement, unemployment and low education level. By contrast, those people who feel significantly better-off tend to be the self-employed or entrepreneurs, and people with higher education. Within the labour force, age, the size of locality and the number of children seem to have no effect. Regarding the change of position in 1989–99, labour-force participation, self-employment and education all appear important in various degrees. In addition, younger people declare more intensive advancement on the social and income hierarchy than older ones.

Conclusion

The implosion of the communist regime in 1989 engendered substantial changes in all dimensions and areas of socioeconomic inequality. Not only was the falseness of the ideological facade of large 'brotherhood classes' and homogeneous society unveiled, but also actual social stratification, combining equalized conditions for the great majority of people with privileges for

Table 9.16 Correlation of self-ranking by social position and income in 1999 and their change in 1989–99 with characteristics of respondents (Spearman coefficients)

Characteristic	Social position	Income	Change in 1989–99	
			Social position	Income
Sex	–0.10	–0.07	–0.04	–0.02
Age	–0.06	–0.02	–0.13*	–0.17*
Education	0.34*	0.24*	0.17*	0.16*
Size locality	0.02	0.08	–0.01	0.06
Self-employed	0.20*	0.13*	0.23*	0.12*
No. of children	–0.02	–0.04	0.02	0.01
Unemployment	–0.23*	–0.27*	–0.24*	–0.18*
Retirement	–0.25*	–0.20*	–0.20*	–0.18*

Notes: All indicators are only for respondents in the labour force, except variable 'retirement' which is valid for all the population. All coefficients marked * are significant at the level < 0.001.
Sources: See Data Sources: ISSP (1999).

the ruling class, was set in radical motion. Many former inequalities have become more transparent and, simultaneously, new sources of disparities have appeared, be them from market sources or balancing between the formal and informal spheres of the economy. Inequalities have started to widen and cumulate, and due to their more manifest character it has become easier to observe them, but unfortunately still not easy enough to be able to provide an exhaustive picture.

When surveying all the various changes in economic inequalities, it is difficult accurately to distinguish between the 'market-conforming' functional inequalities replacing the former equalization needed to ensure economic efficiency on the one hand, and the excessive 'social costs' of the economic transformation involving the futile impoverishment of the population and thus distortion of social integration on the other. Indeed, market adjustment requires getting rid of excessive or unproductive labour for social or – even – political reasons. Hence, it is necessary to dismantle the old system of social guarantees based on compulsory work and replace it with a new system, based on social insurance for all citizens and state assistance for the poor.

Privatization and liberalization of the economy created a huge concentration of income and wealth, the transparency of which is rather problematic. If inequalities become extreme, especially if produced by illegitimate means (based on rent-seeking), the web of societal integration will be faced with collapse. This might have serious adverse consequences in the economic, social and political spheres. Economically, disincentives could start to outweigh commitments to work in the majority of the population and in such a case overall productivity of labour therefore would fall. Socially, relative poverty (if not starvation) would become more widespread and produce considerable dissatisfaction amongst families. And politically, dissatisfied people tend to blame the regime, eventually giving up on democratic procedures and turning to extremist parties.

In the Czech Republic, the data indicate an extensive adaptation of the economic system to a standard market economy. While the income distribution range is widening, demographic factors (as an expression of the 'need principle' and state control over the reproduction of the workforce) are gradually being replaced by economic factors in the determination of income (which indicate the growing strength of market forces). New social groups have emerged, such as the self-employed and entrepreneurs, and an important shift towards the tertiary sector in the branch structure of the labour force has occurred. Simultaneously, powerful forces of the past have supported a great deal of continuity in management and the bureaucracy, and this has been paralleled by weak restructuring of the economy and a slow adaptation of state institutions to serve the democratic society.

In fact, few social categories fit a simplistic picture of 'winners' and 'losers' of transformation: those who are clearly winning are entrepreneurs and the self-employed (despite the sometimes illegal ways of attaining their success), and those who are clearly losing are formerly privileged sections of the working class and cooperative farmers (despite the welcomed restitution of agricultural property). However, the overwhelming majority of the population need to be described using more subtle measurements, due to the complexity of transition which involves many discrepancies and compensations. A discrepancy can be observed between objective mobility and its subjective reflection which includes all possible 'horizontal' motions, 'collective' mobility and other personal gains and losses not accessible by statistical tools. Compensation can be seen between the difficult starting conditions and the attractive perspectives for educated people.

Although income inequality has grown, the degree of poverty has been kept rather low, due to the still good performance of the economy (up until 1997) and efficient social protection, transformed on the principle of targeting. However, as radical changes in the economy and institutions were postponed, the Czech Republic of the late 1990s is faced with a rather gloomy perspective, indicated by falling GDP, rising unemployment and growing discontent among the population. Increasing inequalities in income and wealth, perceived mostly as illegitimate, feed nostalgia for the past and undermine political support for successful completion of the economic and societal transformation. Despite a strengthening of redistribution through taxes and subsidies, social and regional disparities have tended to deepening, fuelling support for the communists and their radical solutions to bring the state back into the economic process and restore equality.

In view of this, the main failure of the development after 1989 appears – limited expansion of the middle class. It is contended here that the middle class is not only the result, but the foremost important condition of a successful transformation and the guarantee of its durability, because it has a fundamental and integrative role in the key areas of social and economic life. Its value system fully corresponds to an open democratic society and its central location between capital and labour ensures the integration of society. The economic activities of its various sections supports the main structures of an efficient economy – dynamic markets, rich information flows and functioning institutions. In political life it avoids extremes and displays enough patience to not outrun the slow pace of elections.

It can be seen that the Czech economic reforms have not been as beneficial to the emergent middle class as expected. The government was much more interested in the transformation of existing enterprises than in the creation of favourable conditions for the new entrepreneurs. It allowed the expansion of the financial and administrative sectors, but it neglected the public services of health, education and research. The core middle-class groups – such as teachers, doctors and researchers – have been frustrated by their inferior status, a situation many qualified people have solved by downgrading their skills and moving to private firms. The quality of public services has been deteriorating, thus endangering the development of human capital.

Despite all the recent gains in entrepreneurial freedom, in the use and development of skills, and in economic rewards and prestige, the middle class has been rather constrained in its expansion. This may have important consequences for future social stratification: whereas the upper classes will advance without limits, the poor will always remain well-protected at the subsistence level and the middle strata can expand only unevenly and with difficulties. This could result in a social polarization even if the lowest income category remains small, even though some sections of middle class will move closer to it.

To sum up, it appears that social mobility has been less extensive than expected. This can be framed by the use of the concept of a hidden 'social contract' between the regime and the population. The contract asserted by the communist regime was concluded with the lower strata, and it secured basic work and income for them and income equalization of the rest for the population. Because this contract was not accepted by a typical middle-class society, like the pre-communist Czech lands, it had to be supplemented by totalitarian rule. However, in a democratic system such a contract represents the sole base of social integration. The expectation here is that the new partner for the post-1989 regime would be above all the middle class and that the contract would, above all, guarantee to it equal opportunities in exchange for its support for full economic liberalization.

However, it seems that the government favoured much more the higher rather than the middle class, through the preferential treatment of the managers of former large state-owned companies, the permissive attitude towards the abuse of the system by former nomenklatura members, and huge redistributional flows from the middle-income categories to the top, through the toleration of fraud by small consumers, people with savings and small shareholders. The slow transformation of institutions and their weak performance has obviously damaged ordinary people much more than the upper few; a 'more equal chance' was given to the banking sector, top state administration and large companies than to education, health services and new entrepreneurs – a policy which cherished the former but squeezed the latter.

It has turned out that, in fact, the new political elite has concluded an imaginary contract with the upper strata – financial capital, top management and bureaucracy, many of whose members belonged to the former nomenklatura – rather than with the middle class. The widespread continuity of positions at the top has been paralleled by maintaining the attitudes of the majority of the population. This was manifested by a shifting of opinions to the left and by increasing expectations of state protection. It has resulted in a growing discontent with the 'liberal' (but in fact near to anarcho-liberal) tax and business policy, and in a decreasing support for the 'residual' social policy. This could undermine the legitimacy of the existing redistributive system as a whole.

Notes

1 The 'need principle' was explicitly formulated by Marx as the prominent mechanism of rewarding (and exploiting) hired labour by capitalists: they do not pay for the labour itself but for the reproduction of the labour force. Wrongly ascribed to capitalism, this principle was tacitly accomplished by 'real socialism'. Conversely, the 'market principle' is understood as the assertion of links between labour performance and results, with rewards and incomes (Večerník, 1999).

2 Pension and other benefits were increased from time to time according to government decisions. The increase was presented as a 'gift' from the party/state. The retirement pension dropped from 51 per cent of the average gross wage in 1960 to 41 per cent in 1975, then started to increase slowly again.

3 Although the Communist Party kept only about one-tenth of its previous members, with 160,000 members it is still by far the largest political party in comparison with the largest new parties – the Civic Democratic Party with 22,000 members and the Social Democrats with 14,000.

4 After no wage control whatsoever at the beginning of 1993, a tax-based wage regulation – to be removed upon completion of the large-scale vouchers privatization – was reintroduced. Wage regulation was definitively abolished in mid-1995.

5 The pension age was to be gradually increased from the current 60 years for men and 53–57 for women (according to the number of children), up to 62 for men and 57–61 for women by 2006.

6 The share of households with heads in the prime age range (25–54) with only a sole active earner has increased from 29.7 to 36.7 per cent, and the average of economically active members in those households has decreased from 1.86 to 1.82 between 1988 and 1996.

7 As Microcensus 1996 failed to cover all income sources of the population, the figure in Table 11.4 regarding real income growth 1988–96 is slightly lower than the aggregate figure of National Accounts.

8 Under the communist regime, taxes paid by self-employed households (almost absent anyway) were not registered in income surveys. Cooperative peasants were exempted from direct taxes.

9 Max Weber distinguishes the earnings class (*Erwerbsklasse*) by its market power, the 'social class' (*Soziale Klasse*) by an easy intra- and intergenerational mobility, and 'status group' (*Stand*) by lifestyle and prestige which is anyway very close to social class (Weber, 1956: 223–7).

10 According to the Trexima survey on managerial earnings, the average yearly salary of a managing director was between US$30,000 and US$40,000 in 1997. Apparently, managers of top banks and big firms were not included in the survey.

11 In the analysis of the survey *Social Stratification in Eastern Europe*, we largely refer to interpretations and tables made by Petr Matějů (1999).

12 Job position is measured on the ISEI scale. The International Socio-Economic Index of Occupations ranges between 0 and 96 and according to its authors (Ganzeboom *et al.*, 1992) is not a prestige scale but indicates how much human capital converts into income.

References

Atkinson, A. and J. Micklewright (1992) *Economic Transformation in Eastern Europe and the Distribution of Income*. Cambridge: Cambridge University Press.

Berger, P. L. (1986) *The Capitalist Revolution. Fifty Propositions about Prosperity, Equality, and Liberty*. New York: Basic Books.

Ganzeboom, H., P. De Graaf and D. Treiman (1992) 'A Standard International Socio-Economic Index of Occupational Status', *Social Science Research*, 21: 1–56.

Hanley E., P. Matějů, K. Vlachova and J. Krejci (1998) 'The Making of Post-Communist Elites in Eastern Europe', Working Papers of project Social Trends no. 4.

Kreckel, T. (1992) *Politische Soziologie der sozialen Ungleichheit*. Frankfurt/M: Campus Verlag.

Matějů, P. (1991) 'Who Gains and Who Losses in a Socialist Redistribution' (in Czech) *Sociologicky casopis*, 27(3): 39–56.

—— (1999) 'Social Mobility and Changes on Life Chances', in J. Večerník and P. Matějů (eds) (1999).

—— and M. Kreidl (1998) 'The Crystallization of Social Status in the Post-Communist Society. The Czech Republic 1991–1997', Working Papers of project Social Trends no. 7.

Opinions of Citizens (1989) On Selected Questions of Standard of Living (in Czech). Prague: Institute for Public Opinion.

Stark, D. (1992) 'Path Dependence and Privatization Strategies in East Central Europe', *East European Politics and Societies*, 6(1): 17–51.

Večerník, J. (1976) 'Change in Income Distribution in Czechoslovakia' (in Czech), *Sociologicky casopis*, 8(5): 472–85.

—— (1991) 'The System of Distribution in Socialist Czechoslovakia: Empirical Data and Explanatory Hypotheses' (in Czech), *Sociologicky casopis*, 26(1): 168–86.

—— (1999) 'The Middle Class in the Czech Reforms. The Interplay between Policies and Social Stratification', *Communist and Post-communist Studies*, 32: 397–416.

—— and P. Matějů (eds) (1999) *Ten Years of Rebuilding Capitalism. Czech Society after 1989*. Prague: Academia.

Weber, M. (1956) *Wirtschaft und Gesellschaft. Grundriss der verstehenden Soziologie I*. Köln-Berlin: Kiepenheuer & Witsch.

Data sources

Statistical surveys

Microcensus surveys started in 1958 as income surveys based on 1–2 per cent samples of households with wages confirmed by employers, and pension benefits confirmed by post-offices. They were regularly repeated every 3–5 years. Here, we use especially three of the last surveys:

- *Microcensus 1988* was conducted by the Federal Statistical Office on a 2 per cent random sample (n=69,912) in March 1989, including yearly incomes in 1988.
- *Microcensus 1992* was conducted by the Czech Statistical Office on a 0.5 per cent random sample (n=16,234) in March 1993, including yearly incomes in 1992.
- *Microcensus 1996* was conducted by the Czech Statistical Office on a 1 per cent random sample (n=28,148) in March 1997, including yearly incomes in 1996.

National sociological surveys

- *Economic Expectations and Attitudes* (EEA surveys) is a semi-annual (1990–92) or annual (1993 onwards) survey organized by the socioeconomic team of the Institute of Sociology of the Academy of Sciences headed by Jiří Večerník. The samples involve between 1000 and 1500 adults selected by a two-step quota sampling procedure, whereby the region and size of the locality were defined in the first step and gender, age and education in the second. Collected by the Centre for Empirical Surveys STEM.

Comparative sociological surveys

- *Social Stratification in Eastern Europe after 1989* was an international comparative research project conducted in 1993 under Donald J. Treiman and Iván Szelényi, University of California in Los Angeles. National samples of the Czech Republic, Slovakia, Hungary, Poland, Russia and Bulgaria involved about 5000 adult respondents from each country. Czech data were collected by the Czech Statistical Office. In order to produce household-specific characteristics, the person-level data were reweighted using the variable of the size of households. Income indicators refer to 1992.
- *ISSP* (International Social Survey Programme). Here we use the following modules: Social Inequality (1992), Work Orientations (1997) and Social Inequality (1999). Czech data were collected by the Centre for Empirical Surveys STEM.

- *Perception of Social Justice*. This survey was conducted in 1991 by the International Social Justice Project. The survey includes 13 countries, among them Czechoslovakia, East Germany, Poland, Hungary, Russia and Slovenia. It was repeated in the Czech Republic in 1995 and in 1999 (together with the ISSP module Social Inequality).

10
Uzbekistan

Richard Pomfret

Uzbekistan has been distinguished among the economies in transition from central planning by its gradual economic reform strategy and authoritarian political system. By most measures it ranks as one of the least reformed economies and least liberal states in Eastern Europe or the Former Soviet Union (FSU). Uzbekistan's economic performance has, however, been relatively strong with a modest drop in output by transition economy standards, and the increase in poverty has been moderated by an innovative social protection system. This chapter analyses changes in its social and economic structure during the transition era.

The first section summarizes the economic and social structure of the Uzbek Soviet Socialist Republic. The next two sections review the transition process since independence, and analyse the impact of transition on the income distribution and poverty in Uzbekistan. The fourth section describes the innovative social security delivery system based on local organizations which target assistance to poor households. This institution has also played a role in exerting social control, and the broader picture of the political and social structure in independent Uzbekistan is addressed in the fifth section. The final section draws some conclusions.

Economic and social structure in the Soviet era

The Uzbek Soviet Republic was created out of feudalistic societies which were economically and socially backward relative to the European parts of the Soviet Union. During the Tsarist era large parts of what would become Uzbekistan had remained under the direct rule of autocratic vassals, such as the Emir of Bukhara, while the city of Tashkent became the administrative and military centre of Tsarist power in Central Asia. The region was overwhelmingly rural despite the presence of the historic cities of Bukhara, Samarkand and Khiva, with a mixture of low-density herding and farming over much of the Republic and high-density mixed farming in the Fergana

Valley. Among the major goals of the Soviet leadership were transformation of the feudal society to destroy the power of landowners and religious leaders, and to create a more egalitarian society through improved access to education, health and other social services and removal of obstacles to equality such as gender discrimination. Between the 1920s and the 1980s the Soviet Union had considerable success in achieving these goals, although gaps remained between targets, official images and reality (Rumer, 1989; Pomfret, 1995).

Uzbekistan's main role in the Soviet division of labour was to supply primary products, especially cotton. Specialization in cotton became particularly pronounced in the decades following 1960 when the area devoted to cotton and mechanization of cotton farming both increased. Other primary products, such as minerals or energy products of which Uzbekistan had proven reserves, were neglected and a particular sore spot for Uzbek nationalists was the decline in self-sufficiency in food. During the 1941–45 war the Uzbek economy received a boost as many industrial plants were moved intact from western areas of the USSR threatened by German invasion. In the postwar period Soviet planners, who favoured building upon existing strengths, tended to locate new industrial projects for Central Asia in Tashkent. At the time of the Soviet Union's dissolution at the end of 1991, Tashkent with just over two million people was the fourth largest city in the USSR and the only real metropolis in Central Asia.

Despite the growth of Tashkent, the Uzbek Republic was primarily a rural economy. It was often described as a labour-surplus economy, in contrast to the perceived labour scarcity in the European republics, although the picture was more complex as some oblasts (for example, Dzijak) had labour shortages while others, notably the Fergana Valley oblasts, had labour surpluses. This picture clearly reflects the inflexibility of Soviet, and especially Soviet Central Asian, labour markets in which mobility was limited. For the Republic as a whole, Marnie (1992) has estimated that 14 per cent of the working-age population was not employed in the final years of the USSR, compared to 5.5 per cent in the Russian Republic, and that nine-tenths of the non-employed were rural women.

In rural areas the collective farm (*kolkhoz*) managers wielded considerable power, allocating jobs, garden plots and access to other in-kind benefits. They were intended to encourage loyalty to the state and foster Soviet values, while undermining preexisting attachments based on lineage and religion. To some extent this was achieved as the identity of ethnic groups such as the Kipchaks was merged into that of the Uzbek majority, and as open discrimination against women in the workplace was ended, but the relationship between the *kolkhoz* managers and their superiors was still often based on kinship and clan loyalties.

During the 1980s the Uzbek Republic became singled out as the Soviet Republic most riddled with clan loyalties, right up to the top of the political hierarchy. The First Secretary, Sharaf Rashidov (1959–83), became the first target of Mikhail Gorbachev's anti-corruption campaign. Although a timely death in 1986 allowed Rashidov to escape punishment for channelling into the Uzbek economy billions of roubles in payments for cotton which was not produced, some 2600 officials from the Uzbek Republic were imprisoned in 1987 for their part in the scam (Pomfret, 1995: 66). In an attempt to cleanse the Uzbek Republic's governance, Gorbachev tried to reestablish central (Moscow) control but, after Rashidov's replacement was dismissed and accused of similar corruption charges and another First Secretary came and went, he eventually had to admit defeat and appointed a local leader without strong ties to Moscow, Islam Karimov, as First Secretary of the Uzbek Republic in 1989. Karimov had a record of being relatively untainted by corruption, which he has retained since independence, but he was closely identified with the Samarkand region and his closest allies since independence have come from this region. Meanwhile, Rashidov has posthumously become something of a national hero for having diverted money from Moscow into the local economy.

As in all of the USSR, the *nomenklatura* enjoyed favoured treatment and superior social status, although in the Uzbek Republic the nomenklatura itself was based on older loyalties. The leadership in Ţashkent devolved considerable powers to local leaders, who often imposed their rule with a coarse brutality (Rumer, 1989: 144–57). The power of the state was reinforced by the economic structure in which most of the rural population was connected to the cotton economy which was dependent on centrally-administered irrigation systems and on the provision of fertilizers and pesticides.

The Slavic minority tended to occupy technical positions in the urban areas and thus enjoyed higher economic status, but this does not appear to be as a result of discrimination against Central Asian ethnic groups.[1] Lubin (1984) found that local nationalities had greater opportunities to pursue education and training, but they often chose to work in lower paid and lower prestige service and agricultural sectors because of their preferences for a traditional lifestyle and consumption patterns and because of greater opportunities to supplement income by home production and informal activities.

The economic and social structure had strong elements of continuity, but was not static during the final decades of the Soviet era. From the 1920s to the 1960s the dichotomy between traditional and modern was widely accepted, and ethnic Central Asians would often disown their heritage in the name of being 'modern'.[2] During the 1960s, however, with the satisfaction of basic needs and rise of consumerism, Central Asians began to reassert traditional consumption patterns, notably in arrangements surrounding major life-event ceremonies such as circumcision or marriage or death (Koroteyeva and Makarova, 1998). This coincided with the Rashidov era and was, as Gorbachev discovered, impossible to reverse in the political arena. With *perestroika* the communal assistance aspect of reciprocal relationships began to be eroded by money transactions.

With the dissolution of the Soviet Union in late 1991, Uzbekistan became a sovereign state and embarked on independent economic and social policies. Even if the government had wished to maintain the status quo, it was clear that the preindependence economic strategy was unsustainable. The rapid expansion of the cotton sector was running into diminishing returns in terms of output per hectare and creating huge environmental problems, highlighted by salinization of large areas and the shrinking of the Aral Sea. Transfers within the USSR, which had been running in the region of 14 per cent (Pomfret, 1995: 72) or 19 per cent (Griffin, 1996: 19) of GDP in the years before independence, declined rapidly in 1991 and 1992 and practically disappeared with the demise of the rouble zone in November 1993.

The transition process in Uzbekistan

Uzbekistan has followed an explicitly gradual approach to economic transition. Price and enterprise reform proceeded slowly, although practically all retail prices had been liberalized by 1996 and housing and small enterprises have been privatized. Trade policy is liberal as export taxes imposed in the early 1990s have been removed, but its impact is negated by stringent foreign exchange controls which were reintroduced in the second half of 1996. The government exerts more overt control than in neighbouring Kazakhstan or the Kyrgyz Republic, which creates a more stable environment but not one which has favoured the emergence of new private enterprises or entrepreneurial behaviour in general. The various synthetic measures of the speed and extent of liberalization in transition economies typically divide the Central Asian countries into two groups, with the Kyrgyz Republic and Kazakhstan somewhere in the middle and Uzbekistan, Turkmenistan and Tajikistan at the bottom of the list (Pomfret and Anderson, 1997: table 1). Despite a general positive relationship between the extent of liberalization and economic performance, Uzbekistan has been an outlier with the best output performance among former Soviet republics. The Uzbek model of gradual economic reform combined with political authoritarianism has thus offered support to many opponents of 'shock therapy' and of democracy, while creating a 'puzzle' for advocates of rapid economic transition.

Gradual transition in Uzbekistan is not easy to synthesize or define. It is not a euphemism for resisting change, as in Belarus or Turkmenistan. On the other hand, it would be too positive a gloss to refer to it as steady progress; Uzbekistan has had sharp U-turns, most notably on currency convertibility in October 1996, and oscillates between nationalism, regionalism and globalism as the guide to policy. While Uzbekistan has moved slowly in most areas of privatization, housing privatization was essentially completed by the end of 1994 (Pomfret and Anderson, 1997: 15). Privatization of larger enterprises was initiated in mid-1996 with the introduction of the Privatization Investment Fund, but it stalled in mid-1997. Price liberalization was also extensive by the mid-1990s, although the two key sets of prices in a market economy, interest rates and exchange rates, remain subject to intervention. Exchange-rate controls were drastically tightened in late 1996, and since mid-1997 sale of some important consumer goods (for example, flour and sugar) has been restricted to licensed outlets in which prices have been kept constant. Crude oil is also priced below the world price. Indeed, the hallmark of the Uzbek model appears to be a commitment to government intervention, within a market-based economy.

Symbolic of the guided market economy is the renovation of Tashkent city centre during the 1990s. Following immediate measures to replace the statues of Lenin and Marx with a globe and a statue of the Emir Timur (Tamerlaine), the government has pursued a long-term plan to create a substantial traffic-free and parkland area in the city centre. The main pedestrian thoroughfare came alive in the second half of the 1990s, when it became colloquially known as Broadway, lined with food and drink establishments, petty traders' counters and the occasional karaoke stall, representing market-driven activity. Other prominent public works in Tashkent include new city hall, central bank and parliament buildings, which created work and give some evidence of economic dynamism, without being so obviously extravagant as the presidential palace and new airport in Ashgabat or the construction of a new capital city in Kazakhstan.

Government intervention is especially apparent in the agriculture sector, where the increase in acreage sown under wheat after independence was determined by command in order to achieve greater national self-sufficiency. Despite frequent announcements of their reduction or even elimination, state orders continue to dominate the markets for the two main crops, cotton and wheat. Even though the percentage of the crops that must be sold to the state had dropped by 1998 to 30 per cent for cotton and 25 per cent for grain, these numbers are misleading. If a farm produces less than its target output, then the entire crop must be sold through the state order system; in a decade of long-term decline in cotton yields, this is not an uncommon outcome (Ilkhamov, 1998: 541–2). Because targets are defined in terms of the former *kolkhoz* land, the system puts pressure on and grants influence to the *kolkhoz* managers and has effectively inhibited the successive agricultural privatization schemes (Pomfret, 1998). Even if crop output were not subject to state orders, farmers face monopsonistic state-controlled buyers (for example, the state-owned cotton ginneries and flour mills).[3] Thus, although the land reforms of the mid-1990s have been compared to China's household responsibility system, Uzbekistan's farmers have responded neither with increased output nor market-driven changes in output mix.[4]

Financial reform remains limited. In rural areas, banks do not serve depositors, but serve the state in checking that funds are used appropriately. True entrepreneurial banking has not been established, but the government has created institutions to provide credit to new private ventures, such as the Business Fund established in 1995 (Klugman, 1998a; World Bank, 1996). Although the government remains the major source of finance, this has not been underwritten by loose monetary policy. Uzbekistan was one of the most successful former Soviet republics in controlling the budget deficit, which at 18.8 per cent of GDP was above the Soviet successor state average in 1992, but at 3.4 per cent was below the average in 1995 (Cheasty and Davis, 1996). Moreover, the reduced deficit was achieved while maintaining substantial expenditure on social policies such as health, education and social security (Pomfret and Anderson, 1997).

Uzbekistan suffered from a decline in output during the first half of the 1990s and from the hyperinflation common to all members of the rouble zone in 1991–93. The output decline was, however, the smallest of any successor state to the USSR and growth turned positive in 1996/97. The inflation rate declined after the collapse of the rouble zone in November 1993 and Uzbekistan's establishment of a national currency the following summer, although it took longer to bring inflation below 50 per cent per year (achieved in 1997 in Uzbekistan) than it did in the Kyrgyz Republic (1995) or Kazakhstan (1996).

The Uzbek puzzle has been addressed in a series of interconnected and overlapping papers by staff of the IMF (Taube and Zettelmeyer, 1998; Zettelmeyer, 1998; IMF, 1998: 7–34). They find that Uzbekistan's favourable output record can only be partially explained by measurement error, and that standard panel models of growth in transition economies systematically underpredict Uzbekistan's 1992–96 economic growth. The puzzle is not resolved by the public investment policy, which the Uzbek government argues is a component of its success. The puzzle is explained by a favourable initial production structure and by self-sufficiency in energy.[5] The IMF authors go on to argue that performance would be better with more liberal policies and without acceleration of reforms future growth prospects are mediocre.

Uzbekistan's relatively good economic performance also applies to unemployment, which has not increased substantially during the 1990s despite predictions of Soviet underemployment turning into open unemployment. Total employment, according to official figures, increased by about 4 per cent between 1990 and 1995. This is in contrast to declines in employment elsewhere in the CIS (for example, 7 per cent in Russia and 15 per cent in Kazakhstan), although these data are problematic due to widespread hidden unemployment (Klugman, 1998b: 99–109).[6] The sectoral shares of employment have changed, with the most dramatic change being the increase in agriculture's share from 25 per cent in 1990 to 30 per cent in 1995 (Klugman, 1998b: 103), which suggests that, as elsewhere in Central Asia and in Mongolia, transition has been accompanied by ruralization.

Income distribution and poverty

Assessment of changes in income distribution during the transition in Uzbekistan is hampered by the quality and availability of microdata. Knowledge of the distribution of income and of poverty in the Soviet era is based on the Household Budget Survey (HBS), which had well-known shortcomings but was reasonably consistent across the USSR.[7] Since 1991 the HBS has been continued in Soviet successor states, but in most cases has been supplemented by better-designed household surveys based on the World Bank's Living Standards Measurement Study (LSMS) project. In Uzbekistan, however, an LSMS survey initiated in 1997 broke down in acrimony over funding and was never completed. A European University Institute and University of Essex Survey of Uzbekistan (EESU) conducted in June 1995 covered about 500 households in each of three oblasts (Tashkent, Fergana and Karakalpakstan).[8] There have also been small-scale surveys, such as that of 130 respondents conducted in Tashkent in late 1994 and reported in Smith (1995). The HBS is probably taken more seriously in Uzbekistan than elsewhere, but the state statistical office is reluctant to share data other than in processed form. In sum, there is quantitative information to draw upon, but the publicly available data are of mixed quality and limited comparability to other transition economies.

At the end of the Soviet era the Uzbek Republic had the second lowest per capita income among the 15 republics (World Bank, 1992), and a Gini coefficient above the USSR average (Atkinson and Micklewright, 1992: table U13). Although poverty did not technically exist in the USSR, a 1974 decree had defined underprovisioned families as those with less than 50 roubles per month per person and provided a monthly supplement to them. Atkinson and Micklewright updated the poverty line to 75 roubles in 1989, and under this definition of poverty 44 per cent of the Uzbek Republic's population was poor, second only to the Tajik Republic. The 1989 estimates of Gini coefficients and poverty rates are based on HBS data. Marnie and Micklewright (1994) argue that the picture of relatively high poverty rates in Uzbekistan is a plausible one, whose magnitude is not seriously biased by the large household sizes in Uzbekistan, but is exaggerated somewhat due to undervaluation of agricultural output in the HBS data.[9]

The situation since independence is more difficult to measure. Milanovic (1998: 41) cites a Gini coefficient of 0.28 in 1987–88, the highest among the 18 countries in his study, and of 0.33 in 1993–95; the latter figure is higher than for most of the European transition economies, but lower than for any former Soviet republic except Latvia. These figures point to an increase in inequality in Uzbekistan during the first half of the 1990s which was much lower than in neighbouring countries (for example, the Kyrgyz Republic's Gini increased from 0.26 to 0.55 over the same period).

Milanovic's (1998: 68–9) poverty measures indicate an increase in the headcount measure from 24 per cent in 1987–88 to 63 per cent in 1993–95, which is severe, but smaller than the increase in the other Central Asian countries – from 5 per cent to 65 per cent in Kazakhstan; from 12 per cent to 88 per cent in the Kyrgyz Republic; and from 12 per cent to 61 per cent in Turkmenistan. Although Milanovic uses a common poverty line, these numbers are difficult to reconcile as they draw on underlying data of varying quality.[10] The Kyrgyz Republic, for example, has a bank of fairly high quality household surveys conducted under the aegis of the World Bank's LSMS project in 1993, 1996 (twice), 1997 and 1998 (Anderson and Pomfret, 1999).

Alternative poverty measures for Uzbekistan have been estimated by the Centre on Economic Research (CER) in Tashkent using HBS data. With a nutrition-based poverty line, CER (1997) reports a crude headcount measure of 58 per cent in December 1996. Home production is, however, negatively correlated with money income, and inclusion of home production in household resources, reduces the poverty rate to 46 per cent.[11] Adjustment for household size and composition, because larger families have lower per capita consumption but benefit from scale economies and because children consume less than adults, reduces the poverty count to 22 per cent.[12] The CER numbers are lower than those of Milanovic, which reflects primarily a lower poverty line, but the adjustments are difficult to assess. Marnie and Micklewright (1994) discounted the importance of scale economies before transition, but since housing privatization their argument holds to a lesser degree and it also seems plausible that home production has become relatively more important since independence, but how much to allow for these two factors is unclear.[13]

Despite these reservations about the quantitative results, it seems incontrovertible that there have been shifts in the income distribution and increases in poverty during Uzbekistan's transition. Although economic change has been limited by gradual policies and a small decline in output, the forces for increased income disparities inherent in a market economy are present in Uzbekistan, as in all transition economies. In sum, the direction if not the extent of distributional changes is predictable. The relatively stable output mix and heavy government hand on the economy suggest that the emergence of *nouveaux riches* in the private sector may be a lesser phenomenon in Uzbekistan than in other transition economies. The new poor may also be less numerous and less suddenly impoverished than elsewhere. Pomfret and Anderson (1997) review the mechanisms by which the government has restricted the extent of welfare changes and in particular how prudent government policies have softened the decline in key social services and provided an effective social safety net. The major novelty in this area, the *mahalla* system, will be analysed in greater depth in the next section.

Who have been the winners and losers? Coudouel's analysis of data from the EESU 1995 survey of three oblasts reveals patterns common to many transition economies (Coudouel, 1998; summarized in CER, 1997: 21–5). Large families have lower per capita incomes and expenditures; households with seven members or more account for 30 per cent of poor households and half of the individuals in poverty.[14] As elsewhere in the FSU, gender and age are not strong determinants of poverty in the early transition years. There is an ethnic dimension to poverty, at least based on simple cross-tabulations; Central Asians make up 79 per cent of the population and 92 per cent of those in poverty, while Slavs make up 16 per cent of the population and only 4 per cent of the poor. Regional differences between the three oblasts are large, ranging from a 10 per cent poverty rate in Tashkent to 60 per cent in Karakalpakstan. Rural–urban differences are large, but not robust when output measures are used; other measures suggest large rural–urban differences in living standards; for example, washing machine ownership is highest in Tashkent and higher in other urban locations than in rural households.[15]

Poverty among the elderly was limited in the USSR by a generous pension scheme giving universal entitlements to men over 60 and to women over 55, or over 50 for women with a large number of children. The entitlements were maintained after independence, and imposed a severe budgetary burden which was exacerbated by an unsustainable indexation policy in 1993 when pension payments amounted to 11.4 per cent of GDP (Griffin, 1996: 155–7). After a change of indexation rules, however, expenditures halved in 1994. The subsequent picture appears to be one in which old people still receive some protection and, especially when they are living in an extended family household, are not a major group in poverty, although single pensioners in urban areas are emerging as a group in poverty.

Education has played a role in Uzbekistan as in other transition economies, with tertiary education being a significant determinant of individual economic performance. While the returns to education have declined during the 1990s, individuals with tertiary qualifications have moved up the income distribution; Klugman (1998b) describes this as a cohort effect, and it is similar to the sorting effect identified from more extensive data in the Kyrgyz Republic (Anderson and Pomfret, 1999). Klugman (1998b: 298, 203–33) estimates that the returns to education are higher for women than for men, although women's subsequent returns to experience in the labour force are significantly reduced by breaks in employment.

Ethnic effects continue to exist. Smith (1995) on the basis of a small survey in Tashkent reported that Uzbeks had lower educational qualifications than Russians, and had lower average incomes. Holding sex, age, education and occupation constant, Smith found that being Russian had a significant positive effect on income. This is consistent with the results of Lubin's work conducted 15 years earlier. Klugman (1998b: 281) found similar results on the basis of her larger sample covering three oblasts in 1995. Klugman explains the persistence of ethnic effects in the face of independence and large Slavic emigration by self-selection as less well-paid Slavs would leave first, by the earnings premium capturing skills not measured in the formal modelling, and by the emigration being based on expectations rather than on current discrimination or falling relative incomes for Slavs.

The *mahalla* system

One of the admired elements of the Uzbek transition model is the decentralization of social security payments through local organizations known as *mahallas* (Coudouel and Marnie, 1998; Coudouel *et al.*, 1999) The precise composition and behaviour of *mahallas* varies from one locality to another, but their leadership tends to consist of the old local elite. Their legitimacy derives from a traditional social system, but also from a continuing sense that these leaders will look after their constituents. Whether this picture of reciprocal relationships matches reality or is simply the picture which the elite wishes to present is difficult to establish.

The innovative approach to social assistance was introduced in late 1994, coinciding with the removal of general food subsidies. About 12,000 local community groups, or *mahallas*, were set up which targeted assistance to needy families; each *mahalla* included 150–1500 households with an average of around 400. The new institution was legitimized by relating it to a traditional Uzbek, and Tajik, institution, although many *mahallas* were recent creations; in urban areas, for example, they often replaced the Soviet era *domkom* or housing committee which existed in large apartment blocks.[16]

The *mahallas* receive their funding almost entirely from the central government budget, although other levels of government can top up the funding and voluntary contributions are encouraged.[17] The amount was not huge, around 0.4 per cent of GDP in 1995 and 1996 (Coudouel and Marnie, 1998). The distribution across *mahallas* appears to be fairly equal. Thus, the government is using the scheme to correct intra-*mahalla* differences in economic well-being, but not to correct variations between *mahallas*. It is correcting relative poverty at a local level, but not aiming at a uniform national safety net.

The chairman and the committee running each *mahalla* are in principle elected by the local population. In practice, however, it appeared that traditionally and from the start of the revived institution the majority of committee members were appointed by the elders of the *mahalla*. The rules established for the *mahallas* include guidelines and a considerable degree of formality about what must be taken into account and what procedures must be followed in awarding assistance, and yet there is also considerable discretionary power insofar as there is no obligation for the *mahalla* to make or not make an award in any particular case.

Based on 1995 EESU data, Coudouel *et al.* (1999) find that the *mahalla* scheme delivers benefits more frequently to less well-off households than to better-off households, and this is robust to various indicators of household welfare. They also find some less desirable outcomes. The amounts of benefits paid are not related to observed measures of household well-being or even to some fairly obvious target indicators (for example, family income or children's nutritional status). Although the assistance given by *mahallas* favours children, female-headed households and the unemployed, it also (even when other variables are controlled for) favours ethnic Central Asian households. Coudouel *et al.* (1999) conclude that the *mahalla* scheme as it operated in 1995 was not transparent and failed to achieve horizontal equity, that is, equal treatment for households in equal circumstances.

The relationship between the *mahallas* and the state has evolved. By 1997 the chairman and secretary of the *mahalla* were both paid salaries by the state, and candidates for *mahalla* chairman had to be approved by local government offices. There is some evidence, reported by Coudouel *et al.* (1999), that ethnic Central Asians are more aware of *mahalla* matters and more likely to be involved, and that women very rarely participate in *mahalla* committees.

The official position is clearly that the *mahallas* have been a success. In 1997, 11 per cent of all households in Uzbekistan were receiving assistance through them.[18] Since 1997, their functions have been extended as child benefits, previously universal for all children under 16, are now also targeted through the *mahallas*. Child benefits involved more substantial amounts than the social assistance programme, with 2.6 per cent of GDP spent on child benefits during the first half of 1997 (Coudouel and Marnie, 1998). Eligibility for child benefits is more narrowly set out than for social assistance, focusing on family per capita income. Thus, the *mahallas* are more specifically involved in means testing of their member households. This may be intended to reduce the discretionary element in order to improve horizontal equity, but it has also enhanced the incorporation of *mahallas* into the state apparatus. A staff member of the local labour office has been attached to each *mahalla* in order to help with the paperwork involved in the more formal process of claiming child benefits.[19]

In addition to the *mahallas*, other traditional networks survived the Soviet era and revived in the 1990s. In fieldwork in Andijan oblast, Kandiyoti (1998) found that the *gap* (or *gashtak* in Tajik), a grouping traditionally of men, had evolved into women's self-help groups which were interpreted by Kandiyoti as a positive coping mechanism. Koroteyeva and Makarova (1998: 586) in a study based on 30 Samarkand life-stories found a remarkable revival of the *gap* since the 1970s, but are less sanguine about the benefits, as the *gaps* encouraged display and were often seen as vehicles for social pressure; in any case they were doomed to decay after cash transactions became more significant in the late 1980s. Koroteyeva and Makarova (1998: 593) conclude that the only network which has survived unchanged since the Soviet era and remains strong in Uzbekistan is kinship.

Kinship ties are known to be strong in Uzbekistan, but their economic significance is difficult to quantify. Coudouel *et al.* (1997) shed some light from EESU survey data from three oblasts in 1995. Almost half of the sampled households had been involved in private transfers during the 30 days prior to being interviewed. Over 70 per cent of in-kind transfers and provision of services came from relatives, as did over half of cash transfers; employers and neighbours were also important sources of interest-free loans. The amounts were substantial, for example cash transfers represented about one-tenth of total household cash income in the month preceding interviews, but the distribution was skewed, with transfers being both more common and of larger value among higher income groups than in lower income groups. Although based on a limited number of regions (and regional variation is large) and a single month, the EESU data suggest that private transfers are fairly common in Uzbekistan and linked to familial ties, although not necessarily being a redistributive mechanism from rich to poor relatives.[20]

Political and social structure

The political structure in Uzbekistan is tightly controlled from the centre (Klugman, 1998a: 79), and opposition to the regime was stifled early in the independence era. The decision-making structure runs through the governors of the 12 oblasts, who are presidential appointees and who have little autonomy. Below them, the administration is also tightly controlled, and, as indicated in the previous section, the *mahallas* have been incorporated into this system of top-down administration. There are also strong regional ties within the political structure; for example, the President is closely associated with his home base of Samarkand, although such ties do not appear to have been reflected in distribution of government expenditures or in mobilization of regional pride and animosities.

The local economic leadership is often intertwined with the political leadership. Within the rural sector, despite a land reform programme, the old state farm and *kolkhoz* managers have retained a dominant position (Pomfret, 1998; Ilkhamov, 1998). In the urban sector, too, there has been very little privatization, which might have allowed a new class to emerge with independent economic means. The private sector is limited to the petty traders and a few large transnational corporations which participate little in the domestic political scene. Without such disruptive economic forces, which have been far more significant in Kazakhstan or in Russia, Uzbekistan's political and social structure have remained remarkably unchanged during the 1990s. Apparently innovative economic policies, notably legitimization of *mahallas* as an instrument for targeted social assistance, have quickly been incorporated into the hierarchical and tightly controlled political system.

The growth of monetary transactions has affected this stability, and is likely to do so to a greater extent in the coming years. The reciprocal measures that are a traditional feature of the society have increasingly involved cash transactions. Entry into a prestigious school or university became more expensive in the 1990s as bribe-taking became endemic, but connections made within the *mahalla* or a *gap* or through kinship were still necessary preconditions to the exchange of cash; the original connections to be in a position to make a bribe were normally made through traditional networks, rather than bribes being the impersonal transactions of a market system. During the 1990s cash transactions have increased in relative importance and the market mechanism is probably displacing the reciprocity of traditional relations, but the latter and especially kinship ties remain important.

Conclusions

Of all economies in transition, Uzbekistan appears to have undergone the most limited change in economic and social structure. This is related to the economic strategy based on gradualism, but it also reflects some specifically Uzbekistani elements. Gradualism in Uzbekistan has not been a euphemism for no change (as in, for example, Belarus), and economic performance has been relatively good among transition economies. The government appears to recognize that political and social stability requires delivering economic success.

The government is authoritarian and brooks no opposition, but it has not promoted the kind of personality cult and allowed the inequitable distribution of economic benefits that is conspicuous in, for example, neighbouring Turkmenistan. President Karimov has presented himself as a more benevolent autocrat, and this appears to resonate at least to some extent with the population. Appealing to the historic heritage of Uzbeks and legitimizing social control mechanisms such as the *mahallas* by harking back to a pre-Communist tradition has been an important element in this strategy. The community-basis and paternalism of the *mahallas* is real, even if they are tightly meshed into the centralized political structure. Popular acceptance of the system and its ability to deliver social assistance are elements in the stability of the regime, although without democratic or legitimate means of expression it is difficult to assess how firmly based such stability is.

Is the Karimov strategy of limiting social and political change through gradual economic reform and a functioning safety net sustainable? On the economic front, Uzbekistan often evokes the Chinese model, but it is failing to create the dynamic farm sector that followed initial Chinese reforms or the small and medium-sized enterprises that have been the dynamic source of Chinese growth in manufacturing. On the social and political front, the biggest threat to sustainability is the fragility of the legitimization of traditional institutions such as the *mahallas* when the economy is becoming ever-more market-based. If the *mahallas* were to become more independent, there would be prospects of corruption increasing at the local level, allowing local power bases to be strengthened, but as they are absorbed into the centralized state apparatus the *mahallas* lose the legitimacy conferred by tradition and are likely to be challenged as an effective instrument of targeting social assistance. Kinship ties remain strong, but under the pressures of a modern economy, the extended family too must be under long-term threat. Gradual reform has delayed social and political change, but as long as it is reform towards a market-oriented economy it will eventually place pressure on existing social and political relationships.

Notes

1 There was also a substantial Russified Uzbek elite which played a key role in post-1991 nation-building, and whose existence left Uzbekistan less exposed to emigration of key administrators than, say, Kazakhstan or the Kyrgyz Republic.

2 The heritage was, however, never fully disowned; the bazaar and farmers' markets remained an overt feature of the economic landscape, unlike in European regions of the USSR where such institutions operated more circumspectly.

3 Klugman (1998a: 70–1) points out that product-specific differences in market access have emerged, with livestock, fruit and vegetables less subject to state control or influence than the main crops.

4 The sources of the former *kolkhoz* managers' power are multifaceted, but the role of irrigation in determining land value is often critical. Farmers allocated poorly irrigated land will not prosper, and with water grossly underpriced its provision is not market-driven but administratively allocated.

5 Pomfret and Anderson (1997) draw a similar conclusion based on buoyant cotton and gold prices during the early and mid-1990s and Uzbekistan's ability to substitute domestic production of energy and grain for imports. Thus, the predicted negative terms of trade impact on Uzbekistan of the dissolution of the USSR, based on pre-1992 trade composition (Tarr, 1994), was not harmful. Pomfret and Anderson also give some credit to gradual reform and relatively competent economic management in explaining Uzbekistan's superior economic performance amongst transition economies.

6 On the basis of the 1995 EESU survey, Klugman estimates that as many as a quarter of the labour force might be included in 'hidden unemployment', in the sense of not having been paid over the previous month. Before and after transition comparisons are, however, fraught, because before 1991 many people were on enterprises' or farms' books as employed, but were not working. Allowing for all the measurement problems, Klugman (1998b: 115) concludes that Uzbekistan's employment record during transition has been less adverse than in other former Soviet republics.

7 The methodology of the HBS is reviewed in Atkinson and Micklewright (1992) and in Falkingham *et al.* (1997: 48–52). HBS samples concentrated on households with earners in state factories and, to a lesser extent, on pensioners. Both tails of the distribution were underrepresented as households whose main employee was not working were absent and certain occupations were excluded (for example, party officials, high-level bureaucrats, KGB and military officers). Rural households were also undersampled, which is especially important for Uzbekistan.

Furthermore the samples were not rotated; once the sample was established in the early 1950s, households were only removed by attrition. The HBS is characterized by Falkingham and Micklewright as 'a survey with a long history and a terrible reputation' (Falkingham *et al.*, 1997: 48).

8 The EESU data are described in Coudouel (1998: 78–115) and have also been used in *inter alia* CER (1997), Coudouel (1998), Klugman (1998b), and Coudouel *et al.* (1999).

9 Low housing costs reduced scale economy effects for Soviet households. The agricultural bias arose from the importance of home production of food in Uzbekistan compared to western republics of the USSR.

10 The poverty line is set at 120 international dollars per month. For the late 1980s this works out to below the 75 roubles used by Atkinson and Micklewright, hence the lower poverty rate for Uzbekistan in the late 1980s reported in Milanovic's book.

11 According to the HBS data from 1996, home production accounted for 5.6 per cent of food consumed in urban areas and 18.9 per cent in rural areas (CER, 1997: 13).

12 The OECD equivalence scale (that is, a weight of 1 for the first adult, 0.7 for each additional adult and 0.5 for each child under 14) is used, but since the demographic composition of households is not available in the HBS data the adjustment is a crude downgrading of the poverty rate.

13 Housing privatization is especially difficult to assess in Uzbekistan because rural housing was privately owned before independence and utilities remain free or heavily subsidized, so that the change in costs actually born by households as a result of transition is unclear.

14 A high birth rate and large families were also a feature of the Uzbek republic before 1991, but the contrast with other transition economies has become starker in the 1990s as birth rates in Russia and elsewhere plummeted.

15 In Tashkent 71 per cent of households have washing machines. In Fergana oblast, 53 per cent of urban households and 22 per cent of rural households have washing machines. In Karakalpakstan, 29 per cent of urban households and 14 per cent of rural households have washing machines (CER, 1997: 24).

16 Among the Karakalpaks there was no tradition of *mahallas*, which is significant for fieldwork based on the EESU data covering three oblasts of which Karakalpakstan was one. Although the coverage of the *mahalla* system was nationwide, their operation clearly varied considerably.

17 Local supplementation appears to have occurred in the Navoi oblast, which is home to rich mining companies. In a scatter diagram of the relationship between average oblast income and the share of households receiving social assistance, based on a one-off Uzbekistan government survey of 20,000 households in 1995 (reported in Coudouel *et al.*, 1999), Navoi is the most striking outlier.

18 This is the first year for which the problem of double-counting of households making more than one application is addressed. Many *mahallas*, especially those with a traditional base, also played social roles such as trying to reconcile married couples considering divorce.

19 Koroteyeva and Makarova (1998: 592) describe a situation where *mahalla* practice contradicted the *sharia* (Islamic law); when the conflict was formally raised in mid-1995, the decision was an unenforceable compromise. Thus, as the *mahallas* are drawn under tighter government control they are diverging from the cultural and historical basis which is supposed to confer legitimacy on them.

20 Coudouel *et al.* (1997) suggest that important patterns are transfers from parents to adult offspring and among siblings, which may be seen as consumption smoothing over the life-cycle or as a form of mutual insurance.

References

Anderson, K. and R. Pomfret (1999) 'Poverty and Transition in the Kyrgyz Republic 1993–6', paper presented at the American Economics Association conference in New York, 3–5 January.

Atkinson, A. and J. Micklewright (1992) *Economic Transformation in Eastern Europe and the Distribution of Income*. Cambridge: Cambridge University Press.

CER (1997) 'Methods and Applications of Poverty Analysis: Case of Uzbekistan', *CER Report 1997/4*, Tashkent: CER, University of World Economy and Diplomacy.

Cheasty, A. and J. Davis (1996) 'Fiscal Transition in Countries of the Former Soviet Union: An interim assessment', *IMF Working Paper 96/61*, Washington DC: IMF (June).

Coudouel, A. (1998) *Living Standards in Transition: The case of Uzbekistan*, PhD thesis, Department of Economics, Firenze: European University Institute.

—— and S. Marnie (1998) 'The Mahalla System of Allocating Social Assistance in Uzbekistan', paper presented at the UNDP conference *Central Asia 2010* in Almaty, 20–22 July.

——, A. McAuley and J. Micklewright (1997) 'Transfers and Exchange between Households in Uzbekistan', in J. Falkingham, J. Klugman, S. Marnie and J. Micklewright (eds), *Household Welfare in Central Asia*. Basingstoke: Macmillan – Palgrave: 202–20.

——, S. Marnie and J. Micklewright (1999) 'Targeting Social Assistance in a Transition Economy: The Mahallas in Uzbekistan, *Centre for Economic Policy Research Discussion Paper 2064*, London (January).

Falkingham, J., J. Klugman, S. Marnie and J. Micklewright (eds) (1997) *Household Welfare in Central Asia*. Basingstoke: Macmillan – Palgrave.

Griffin, K. (ed.) (1996) *Social Policy and Economic Transformation in Uzbekistan*. Geneva: ILO.

Ilkhamov, A. (1998) '*Shirqats, Dekhqon* Farmers and Others: Farm Restructuring in Uzbekistan', *Central Asian Survey*, 17(4): 539–60.

IMF (1998) 'Republic of Uzbekistan: Recent Economic Developments', *IMF Staff Country Report 98/116*. Washington DC: IMF (October).

Kandiyoti, D. (1998) 'Rural Livelihoods and Social Networks in Uzbekistan: Perspectives from Andijan', *Central Asian Survey*, 17(4): 561–78.

Klugman, J. (1998a) 'Uzbekistan: Institutional Continuity Helps Performance', *MOCT-MOST, Economic Policy in Transitional Economies*, 8(1): 63–82.

—— (1998b) *Wages in Transition: The Case of Uzbekistan*, PhD thesis, The Australian National University, Canberra (December).

Koroteyeva, V. and E. Makarova (1998) 'Money and Social Connections in the Soviet and post-Soviet Uzbek city', *Central Asian Survey*, 17(4): 579–96.

Lubin, N. (1984) *Labour and Nationality in Soviet Central Asia; An Uneasy Compromise.* Princeton: Princeton University Press.

Marnie, S. (1992) *The Soviet Labour Market in Transition*, EUI Monographs in Economics. Firenze: European University Institute.

—— and J. Micklewright (1994) 'Poverty in Pre-reform Uzbekistan: What do Official Data Really Reveal?' *Review of Income and Wealth*, 40(4): 395–414.

Milanovic, B. (1998) *Income, Inequality, and Poverty during the Transition from Planned to Market Economy*. Washington DC: World Bank.

Pomfret, R. (1995) *The Economies of Central Asia*. Princeton: Princeton University Press.

—— (1998) 'Agrarian Reform in Uzbekistan: Why has the Chinese Model Failed?' *University of Adelaide School of Economics Working Paper 98–16* – also published in *Economic Development and Cultural Change*.

—— and K. H. Anderson (1997) 'Uzbekistan: Welfare Impact of Slow Transition', *UNU/WIDER Working Papers* 135. Helsinki: UNU/WIDER (June).

Rumer, B. (1989) *Soviet Central Asia: 'A Tragic Experiment'*. Boston: Unwin Hyman.

Smith, C. (1995) 'An Economic Analysis of Ethnicity in Uzbekistan', *Comparative Economic Studies*, 37(2): 97–110.

Tarr, D. (1994) 'How Moving to World Prices Affects the Terms of Trade of 15 Countries of the Former Soviet Union', *Journal of Comparative Economics*, 18: 1–24.

Taube, G. and J. Zettelmeyer (1998) 'Output Decline and Recovery in Uzbekistan: Past Performance and Future Prospects', *IMF Working Paper 98/132*. Washington DC: IMF (September).

World Bank (1992) 'Measuring the Incomes of Economies of the Former Soviet Union', *Policy Research Working Papers WPS 1057*, Washington DC.

—— (1996) *Uzbekistan, Creating Financial Markets; A Review of the Financial Sector*, Washington DC.

Zettelmeyer, J. (1998) 'The Uzbek Growth Puzzle', *IMF Working Paper 98/133*. Washington DC: IMF (September).

11
Kyrgyzstan

Vladimir Mikhalev and Georges Heinrich

Introduction

Since the start of the transition to the market, the Central Asian Republic (CAR) of Kyrgyzstan has cemented its reputation with the international community as a consistently liberal economic reformer and an upholder of democratic government in the southern part of the Former Soviet Union (FSU). Kyrgyzstan is a small country with a population of only 4.6 million people spread out over an area of 199,900 sq km. It borders China in the East, Tajikistan in the South, Kazakhstan in the North and Uzbekistan in the West. With a GDP per capita of US$2250 in 1997 – adjusted for purchasing power parity – Kyrgyzstan falls into the range of the least developed countries.

The evolution of the social structure in Kyrgyzstan under economic transition is determined on the one hand by the common heritage shared with the other Republics of the FSU and, on the other hand by the Asian dimension deeply rooted in the history and oriental culture of the Kyrgyz people. The legacy of over 70 years under Soviet socialism in this Central Asian country coexists with these specific Asian cultural, political, ethnic and demographic attributes. In this context, the transformation process differs substantially from developments in the European part of the FSU and, even more so, from those in Central Europe (CE). At the same time, Kyrgyzstan significantly diverges from South and East Asian societies due to its higher industrial potential and human capital than that initially found in China, Korea, India or Vietnam. Particularly significant were achievements in human development that are characteristic of the FSU. At the point of independence in 1991, most human development indicators in Kyrgyzstan were notably higher than those in countries with comparable levels of GDP per capita (Table 11.1).

Table 11.1 Kyrgyzstan: human development indicators

	Kyrgyzstan		Developing countries		Industrial countries	
	1990	1995	1990	1995	1990	1995
Life expectancy at birth (years)	68.8	67.9	62.8	62.2	74.5	74.2
Adult literacy rate (%)	93.0	97.0	65.0	70.4	–	98.6
Real per capita GDP (PPP $)	3114	1927	2170	3068	14,440	16,337
UNDP human development index	0.689	0.633		0.586		0.911
Annual population growth rate (%)	2.2	1.8	2.3	2.1	0.8	0.7
Crude birth rate	29.1	26.0	30.0	26.1	–	12.6

Sources: UNDP (1993; 1998).

Kyrgyzstan adopted many elements of the transition strategy pursued by Russia. The problems the country encountered in the process of transformation of its 'administrative command system' into a market economy are also in many respects similar. At the same time there are some fundamental differences seen both in economic performance and social development. In a small country like Kyrgyzstan some radical reform measures were easier and quicker to implement than in Russia, which is inherently more difficult to govern because of its sheer size and complex federal–regional relationships. The demographic structure of Kyrgyzstan is also significantly different from Russia and the East European countries: the local population is generally younger, the birth and population growth rates are higher and the average family size is larger.

Reforms in Kyrgyzstan are much facilitated by the assistance from international donors who are particularly active in this country considered as more committed to democratic market-oriented reforms than its Central Asian neighbours. At the same time, Kyrgyzstan is much poorer than Russia and does not possess the same natural riches as nearby Uzbekistan or Kazakhstan. Kyrgyzstan is a mountainous country with a rather small area of arable land. Even at the time of the Soviet Union, it had one of the lowest levels of income per capita of all the republics and was largely dependent on financial transfers from Moscow. The loss of subsidies from the all-union budget exacerbated the severe shock suffered by the local economy after independence in 1991 and consequently resumption and sustainability of economic growth, poverty alleviation and social development were more difficult than elsewhere.

The Kyrgyz Republic represents a particular archetype of economic reform characterized by a radical liberal approach implemented in a Central Asian context. The purpose of this chapter is to evaluate the social outcomes of this archetypal reform strategy and to assess its impact on social stratification.

In the next section we provide an overview of the social structure prior to transition. We then discuss key components of economic reform, such as privatization, changes in the labour market, agricultural reform and social-sector adjustment as major factors of social stratification, before analysing the main features of the evolving social structure that characterizes the social groups on the different levels of the social hierarchy – the upper classes, the middle class and the poor. The final section outlines policy priorities for social integration and social cohesion. The analysis is based on various statistics available from Kyrgyz government sources, the United Nations Development Programme (UNDP), the International Monetary Fund (IMF) and data from the 1993 Kyrgyzstan Multipurpose Poverty Study (KMPS) and the 1997 Living Standards Measurement Survey (LSMS).[1] To a large extent the observations made here are also based on the personal experience gained by the first author as a World Bank adviser on social policy reform to the Kyrgyz Government in 1997–98.

Pre-transitional social structure

Like the other Central Asian societies, Kyrgyzstan is predominantly rural with a majority of the local population working in agriculture. At the same time the country has a further specificity distinguishing it from areas of traditionally developed crop cultivation, in the first place Uzbekistan. The indigenous Kyrgyz population was historically occupied in nomadic animal husbandry. This predominant type of economic activity precluded transition to a settled life and impeded the formation of class divisions and government organization. Instead, clan and tribe associations formed the backbone of the social structure. Clan-based self-organization served as a means of collective survival under conditions of scarce economic resources – pasture lands and livestock, and the absence of settled communities and common statehood. The strength of tribe kinship was based on the need for collective labour and common use of land, as well as for joint defence against outside threats. Due to that, clan organization proved sustainable over centuries and helped to preserve the ethnic and cultural integrity of the Kyrgyz people (UNDP, 1997: 44). At the same time, distinctions by origin from different clans rather than social classes or status survived over generations and through seven decades of Soviet socialism.

Thus until the beginning of the twentieth century no apparent social stratification emerged in Kyrgyz society, and no substantial changes in the local social organization occurred with the advent of Russian imperial rule. Changes of a revolutionary nature began from the early years of the Soviet regime. In a uniquely short period of time Kyrgyz nomadic tribes were converted to a settled way of life and forcibly assembled into collective and state farms. Such enforced transformation suppressed their traditional economy and way of life (Zhukov, 1996: 125). The Soviet system introduced modern forms of production and increased the regulating role of the state. The country underwent industrialization and urbanization with the bulk of the industrial labour force, technicians and professionals coming from Russia and other Soviet republics. These processes of modernization involved part of the indigenous population, which moved to the cities and engaged in the urban economy. However, no noticeable working class emerged (UNDP, 1997: 12). The proliferation of education, however, led to the formation of a national intelligentsia.

Despite a very deep transformation under socialism, Kyrgyz society managed to preserve much more of its traditional features than in other parts of the FSU. As elsewhere in the socialist world it remained an egalitarian society with no clear class distinctions. The majority of the population remained rural and consisted mainly of the Kyrgyz *kolkhoz-sovkhoz* peasantry, which preserved a great deal of nomadic customs cultivated over generations. *Kolkhoz*-type collective property did not change the traditional nature of property relationships, because the *kolkhozy* and *sovkhozy* were in essence clan-based (UNDP, 1997: 46). The urban population was largely Russian-speaking working class. The composition of government bureaucrats and the intelligentsia was mixed, mainly Russian or other Slavic but also an increasing number of national cadres. As in other Soviet republics nationality policy provided for a balanced selection of ethnic Kyrgyz to managerial and governmental positions including the top ranks of the nomenklatura. This process affected the formation of the indigenous ethnic elite, which occupied upper levels of government and party structures. It also let traditional clan relationships and practices extend to the higher levels of social hierarchy and influence the local system of government.

Economic transition

A strategy to transform the Kyrgyz economy into a market system was adopted in full swing in 1992, immediately after the break-up of the Soviet Union. From the very start the newly-independent Republic followed a radical approach to economic restructuring. Kyrgyzstan is widely regarded as the most active and consistent reformer in Central Asia. During the initial stage of the transformation, the government liberalized prices for most goods and services, introduced a national currency (som), eliminated export duties, substantially reduced import tariffs, and removed most capital controls. Structural and institutional reforms included privatization, restructuring of the financial system and the development of market-friendly legislation. By 1998 over half of the industrial sector had been privatized, a two-tiered banking system had been created with new private banks operating in parallel to state banks. The land reform redistributed part of the *kolkhoz*-owned lands to private individual farmers. In addition, substantial progress had been made in the area of tax and budgetary reforms (IMF, 1998: 5, 6).

Economic and social-sector reforms carried out in Kyrgyzstan led to fundamental changes in peoples' lives. The system of centralized planning and subsidization of both producers and consumers was eliminated. Along with the removal of price controls, wages, other incomes and the majority of economic activities, including foreign investment, were deregulated. The social conditions of the Kyrgyz population changed dramatically: opportunities and incentives for independent economic activities, secondary employment and self-employment were created; the labour force was reallocated to the service, commercial and financial sectors; and private-sector educational and public health institutions and other social and cultural services began to emerge.

At the same time, the economic and social costs of the transition from plan to market were exacerbated by the disruption of economic links with the rest of the FSU. These difficulties revealed themselves in an unprecedented fall in output and living standards. Real GDP shrunk by 59 per cent between 1991 and 1995, industrial output by over 65 per cent, and agricultural production by over 30 per cent. Inflation initially surged to four digit levels (Table 11.2). The collapse in production and high inflation caused a considerable decline in real wages and the appearance of mass unemployment. Real incomes fell by 60 per cent in 1992, 8.2 per cent in 1993, 21.8 per cent in 1994, 11.3 per cent in 1995 and 18 per cent in 1996.

In order to shore up the flagging economy, the Kyrgyz government adopted a rigorous package of macroeconomic stabilization measures following recommendations by the international financial institutions. Starting in 1994, these measures yielded successful results in slowing down inflation and stabilizing the national currency. Real GDP started to increase in late 1995 and exhibited steady growth through 1996–97. The rate of inflation has fallen to a manageable 20 per cent per annum. Yet in 1998 the Kyrgyz economy was affected perniciously by the consequences of the Russian crisis. Economic growth slowed dramatically to only 1.8 per cent. The agricultural sector stagnated and industrial production increased by 4.5 per cent, due only to the output of the Kyrgyz–Canadian gold joint venture.

Table 11.2 Kyrgyzstan: economic indicators

	1991	**1992**	**1993**	**1994**	**1995**	**1996**	**1997**	**1990–97**
Real per capita GDP (annual % change)	–10.3	–16.6	–13.2	–20.2	–6.0	4.7	7.2	–29.7
Consumer price inflation	108.6	920.5	1211.5	278.0	38.9	28.3	–	185,261
Private consumption	–17.6	–42.6	–18.1	–13.2	–16.2	–2.3	–1.8	–63.1

Sources: World Bank (1999); *PlanEcon Review* (1997).

Stabilization and the resumption of economic growth could not noticeably offset the severe social consequences of the economic crisis of 1991–95. A 6.3 per cent increase in real incomes in 1997 was wiped out in 1998, and real wages amount to less than one-third of their pre-reform level (IMF, 1998: 98). The economic difficulties of the population in 1998 were exacerbated by the spread of massive wage and pension arrears which skyrocketed to 720 million som (about US$24 million).

The radical structural reforms had a profound impact on the social structure. Of the major components of the reform package, privatization, the emergence of a new labour market model, the restructuring of agriculture and changes in the social transfer system had a particularly profound influence on social stratification.

Privatization

Privatization in Kyrgyzstan essentially followed the Russian model, and proceeded in two distinct stages. The first phase (1992–93) consisted of the privatization of small enterprises in the consumer services, retail trade and construction sectors. The State Property Fund was established to manage this process. Several methods were used to transfer property to private owners: leasing, joint-stock company formation, competitive bidding, auction, sales to individuals, and sales to a worker collective (Roberts *et al.*, 1998). Vouchers were distributed to Kyrgyz citizens allowing them to exchange coupons for enterprise shares or housing. Almost one-half of public enterprises were privatized in the first stage (about 4500 in number). However, these were mainly small, easier to sell firms, of which 26 per cent were sold directly to the worker collective, 21 per cent to private individuals, 20 per cent through competitive bidding, and 18 per cent were transformed into joint-stock companies (Koichuev, 1996: 176). These results were nevertheless widely regarded as unsatisfactory as they were believed to reflect the outcome of a bureaucratic campaign to meet 'plan targets' without due care for real contents.

In 1994 the government extended the mass privatization programme (MPP) to 1300 medium and large-scale enterprises. The new programme aimed at a wider distribution of ownership, greater transparency and equity of privatization, stimulating outside ownership and more effective enterprise management. Shares were sold through voucher coupon auctions to the public. Thus individuals and investment funds could convert their coupons into share ownership. By mid-1997 approximately two-thirds of medium and large-scale firms employing about 70 per cent of the industrial workforce were sold. Furthermore in 1997, 4 to 15 per cent of the shares of large monopolies were offered for sale to the public (IMF, 1998: 33). The government retains control through majority ownership in large companies such as in the energy and utilities sectors and the national airline. The European Bank for Reconstruction and Development (EBRD) estimates that by mid-1997 the private sector generated about 60 per cent of GDP – the highest share among Central Asian countries (EBRD, 1997: table 2.1).

Privatization on such a large scale is likely to entail far-reaching distributional consequences since it implies a massive transfer of assets and capital incomes. The ideological thrust behind privatization, as in other transitional economies where it was undertaken on a large scale, was to make everybody a property owner. The real outcome, however, proved to be very different from how privatization was initially conceived and publicized.

In Kyrgyzstan employees have acquired the majority of privatized capital stock at a symbolically low price: 38 per cent of industry, 78 per cent of construction and 56 per cent of transportation (Rumer, 1996b: 59). However, the distribution of company shares among employee collectives did not turn them into owners of their enterprises. Despite the large number of individuals who became shareholders, the quantity of shares as well as their value is so small that none of the workers were real property-owners (Koichuev, 1996: 181). The actual owners are firm directors and managers who received substantial blocks of shares initially and later on bought out more shares from their employees at bargain prices. Collectivization through voucher sales in essence turned out to be privatization by firm managers. In some particularly profitable enterprises (for example, fur-processing factories) the personal share acquired by management is over 50 per cent while that of the employee collective is negligible (Koichuev, 1996: 185). Thus property distribution in such a way worked in favour of a tiny 3 to 7 per cent of the population producing an important, heretofore unknown, source of social inequality (Rumer, 1996a).

Further inequalities were exacerbated through the consolidation of the economic positions of government bureaucrats in charge of monopolies remaining under government control (a most well-known analogue being the Russian Gazprom). In the Kyrgyz case, the incorporation of Kyrgyzenergoholding (an electric energy company), Kyrgyzgasmunaizat (gas company), and Kyrgyz aba zholdoru (national airline) into state holdings served the interests of the upper levels of state bureaucracy – the technocratic, financial and administrative elites. It gave them enormous economic power and ways to amass considerable personal wealth. To a certain extent their monopoly positions benefited all enterprises and employees forming parts of the corporation. In general, however, the change of economic status of large companies under state control contributed to rapidly increasing inequalities.

The distribution of property income is highly skewed in favour of well-to-do households. Fewer than 10 per cent of Kyrgyz households receive positive property income. In 1993, over 70 per cent of the property income went to households in the top half of the expenditure distribution and the top two deciles appropriated over 25 per cent of all property incomes. In 1997, the share of households receiving property income has decreased relative to 1993. The concentration of property incomes among well-off households has increased: households in the top half of the expenditure distribution have received over 75 per cent of all property incomes. However, a larger share of these property incomes appear to be distributed to medium-wealthy households, the share of property income going to the top two deciles falling to just below 20 per cent. This may be interpreted as evidence for the emergence of an entrepreneurial middle-class.

Changes in the labour market

With the transition to the market, centralized controls over labour, which previously extended from decisions on employment and wage levels to permitted types of activities and their location, ceased to exist. Privatization drastically reduced the number of firms where labour was managed directly by the government. The decline in output led to major reductions in employment and considerable redistribution of labour by sector and type of economic activity. Simultaneously there has been a downward adjustment of real wages and a considerable increase in wage differentials by industry sector and occupation. All these processes have had a profound impact on social structure through changes in employment, occupational and income status of a vast number of people.

During 1991–95, total employment in the economy decreased by 6 per cent and only began to increase again slowly in 1996. Official unemployment statistics, arguably an unreliable gauge, show rapidly growing unemployment: from 4.1 per cent in 1994 to 7.8 per cent in 1996. Data from the 1997 Living Standards Measurement Survey (LSMS), obtained by interviewing respondents and defining as unemployed a person not currently working and seeking employment, yield an unemployment rate of 11.1 per cent, up from 7.1 per cent in the 1993 Kyrgyzstan Multipurpose Poverty Survey (KMPS). Unemployment in Kyrgyzstan is clearly associated with loss of social status and very often leads to extreme poverty. Since less than half of the unemployed register with the employment services, the majority of them are cut off from any kind of social support by the state. But for the registered unemployed who receive benefits, the assistance is insufficient to protect them from poverty as the benefit rate does not reach even half of the estimated poverty line.

In reality, job status has changed for a much larger proportion of workers than is reflected in unemployment statistics. Underemployment has become nearly as widespread as open unemployment, with many employers reluctant to resort to mass layoffs and workers unwilling to quit jobs voluntarily, preferring to keep their work record for future pension claims and access to work-related social benefits which were available to them prior to the reforms. As a result workers have to take involuntary unpaid leave or accept shorter working hours, with a corresponding drop in earnings. Hidden underemployment amounts to roughly 9 per cent of all workers in industry (MLSP, 1998: 76). Bearing this in mind, recent World Bank estimates put the unemployment rate (including underemployment) at 18 per cent in rural areas and 21 per cent in urban areas (IMF, 1998: 12).

Considerable social mobility, both upwards and downwards, is associated with the changes in employment structure by sector and type of economic activity. Privatization has led to a sizeable reduction in the share of the labour force employed in the public sector and growth in private-sector employment. In 1991–96 the share of public-sector employment declined from 74 to 27.5 per cent. Thus the majority of the Kyrgyz population is now employed outside the public sector. This does not, however, entail automatic change of type of employment, occupation or job status. In fact, privatized firms did not alter their behaviour very much. Like their counterparts in state firms, private-sector employees also suffer pay reductions. More importantly, the emergence of new private-sector firms has social implications: a new social class of entrepreneurs emerges and business activity becomes more widespread.

A large-scale reallocation of labour resources across economic sectors has occurred. The decline of industrial activity has led to a decrease in industrial employment while, at the same time, agricultural employment has increased. In 1990–96 the employment share in industry and construction fell from 27.9 to 14.6 per cent, while the share of agriculture increased from 32.6 to 46.8 per cent (Table 11.3). The expansion of rural-economy employment at the expense of the urban industrial sector is a trend characteristic of Central

Table 11.3 Kyrgyzstan: employment by sector (as % of total employment)

	1990	**1997**
Industry	19.1	10.2
Construction	8.7	3.4
Agriculture	32.6	48.0
Forestry	0.2	0.3
Transport	4.5	3.9
Communications	0.8	0.7
Retail trade & catering	5.0	10.2
Information & computational services	0.3	0.0
Housing & communal services	2.1	1.4
Health & physical welfare services	5.0	6.0
Education	11.0	5.6
Culture & art	5.3	5.0
Science & scientific services	2.0	0.8
Insurance services	0.4	0.4
General administration & defence	2.4	0.5
Other	0.6	3.6
Total employment (in thousand of workers)	1749.9	1689.3

Sources: IMF (1998: 100; 1999: 91).

Asia in general, and Uzbekistan and Kazakhstan in particular (Klugman, 1998: 67; Klugman and Scott, 1997: 130).

The employment share of the consumer service sector has also been expanding, from 6.6 per cent in 1990 to 9.3 per cent in 1996. As a result of these reallocations of labour, the industrial working class, which was not very numerous even before the reforms (compared to other republics in the FSU), shrunk, a process accelerated by the emigration of Russians (and other ethnicities of European origin) who formed the majority of urban industrial workers.[2] Within the industrial sector, jobs requiring higher qualification experienced larger cuts. Consequently, the share of highly-qualified workers and professionals declined relatively more rapidly than that of workers with fewer qualifications.

An important new development relative to the pre-transition period has been the extensive spread of self-employment. Self-employment embraces farmers, owners of small enterprises, persons engaged in individual economic activity and family workers. This type of (statistically accountable) employment accounted in 1996 for 14 per cent of the economically active population (MLSP, 1998: 71), and is a phenomenon closely interrelated with the informalization of the economy. A majority of the self-employed in Kyrgyzstan represent the subsistence sector, generating very low incomes barely sufficient for survival. Only a small fraction of this group are real entrepreneurs, but even those operate largely in the informal sector. There are an estimated 1 million workers (over half of the economically active population) outside the official employment statistics, consisting of 350,000 agricultural workers, 300,000 in the informal private sector, and 350,000 subsistence farmers (IMF, 1998: 12).

In addition to the observed decline in real wages, the *de facto* collapse of the wage economy and the considerable deterioration of the social position of the employed population, profound changes in wage formation have resulted in extremely diverse wage movements by sector, industry and occupation, contributing to the rise in wage inequality. The most striking phenomenon is that of the very low wages paid in the state budgetary sector, notably in education, research, social, cultural and healthcare services. The gap between wages in industry on the one hand, and wages in education, culture and healthcare on the other, increased from 1.5 times in 1990 to 3 times in 1997 (Table 11.4). At the other extreme, earnings in the banking and insurance sector – a rapidly expanding albeit very underdeveloped area of new private entrepreneurship – are quite high. Salaries there are 4 times higher than in education or health services and 2.8 times the economy-wide average. The income situation of low-paid workers is considerably worsened by massive wage arrears which persist despite attempts by the government to solve the problem.

Another striking development of the transition is that professionals and engineers (who were traditionally underpaid) have suffered even more.

Table 11.4 Kyrgyzstan: average wages by economic sector (as % of total average wage)

	1991	**1997**
Average wage	100.0	100.0
Industry	122.3	173.8
Agriculture	94.3	54.7
Forestry	59.4	46.6
Transport	97.7	112.5
Communications	106.3	145.5
Construction	120.6	140.6
Trade & communal catering	85.1	77.8
Supplies	–	118.5
Procurement	–	85.7
Computing services	102.0	139.5
Real estate	–	78.7
Commerce	–	118.0
Geology, meteorology	–	169.3
Other sectors of material production	–	76.9
Housing & communal services	80.0	95.8
Health & physical welfare services	76.0	56.6
Education	76.6	61.0
Culture	69.7	57.9
Art	71.4	53.3
Science & scientific services	109.7	114.4
Banking & insurance services	190.3	283.8
Government	112.6	131.5
Minimum monthly wage	43.1	12.1
Average pension	112.3	45.1

Source: IMF (1998, 1999).

Their wages have fallen to levels which are on average 1.2 to 1.3 times lower than those of low-skilled workers, due particularly to the very low earnings of teachers and medical staff. The majority of professionals are employed in the budgetary sector, which has the lowest pay levels. However, even in the private sector professionals do not earn much more than blue-collar workers, reflecting the tradition of underpayment for high skills. Top managers form a group which has considerably benefited from economic independence, granted by the new status of their enterprises, both state-owned and privatized. Managers' salaries are on average 2.5 to 4 times higher than the wages of their employees.

The generalized erosion of wages has stimulated the emergence of other sources of personal incomes, which have become available with the development of new forms of economic activity. Statistical information suggests that real per capita money incomes are increasing faster than real wages. The share of wages in overall personal incomes decreased from 55.1 per cent in 1994 to 33.4 per cent in 1997. Wage data does not reflect an accurate picture of the overall income situation since many workers supplement their earnings through secondary employment mainly in the informal sector. It is important to bear in mind that labour compensation in a form other than wages may be underestimated in statistics, as they are very difficult to monitor; their weight may be even higher than that suggested by the above figures. Furthermore, workers often receive substantial additional income from their primary employer, such as payments in-kind which are difficult to quantify but may account for up to 20 per cent of the base wage (IMF, 1998: 12).

Agricultural reforms

Over 65 per cent of the Kyrgyz population live in rural areas and most are engaged in farming and animal husbandry. Therefore development of the agricultural sector and agricultural reforms undertaken by the government have had a far-reaching impact on the social position of the majority of the population. Kyrgyzstan has embarked on the most radical market-oriented land reform in Central Asia. Beginning 1993, the government distributed long-term land-lease contracts, liberalized agricultural prices and privatized agro-industries. In 1995, land-use rights were distributed for more than half of all the land. Finally in 1998 a new law introduced private land ownership, a revolutionary step for the entire Central Asian region.

In 1996 there were over 38,000 individual farmers holding 13 per cent of the agricultural land, including 33.6 per cent of the total arable land, 9.3 per cent of pastures, 24 per cent of total cattle, 26.4 per cent of sheep and goat herds, 30.9 per cent of horses, 14.1 per cent of poultry and 3.1 per cent of pigs (UNDP, 1997: 6). The land that has not been allocated to individual farmers is generally under the control of state or collective farms of various forms. There were 48 state and 673 collective farms in 1997 producing about 17 per cent of total agricultural output. Two-thirds of farmers still work at state or collective farms and only one-third became individual farmers (IMF, 1998: 35). The new private farms faced serious difficulties in obtaining machinery, seeds and fertilizers, as well as access to credit and marketing channels. In addition, most of the individual land holdings distributed are too small for economically viable production. According to LSMS data, only 4.6 per cent of rural households have land holdings of over 5 hectares. The size of plots of one-third of households ranges between 0.2 and 1 hectare, which is hardly sufficient to produce marketable farm output.

Thus individual farmers produce less than one-third of agricultural output. The economic position of larger collective farms, however, is not much better. The economic crisis had a severe impact on agricultural production and the rural economy as a whole, and the agrarian sector has lost much of its state subsidies and preferential credits. All farms have faced a sharp rise in the prices for equipment, fertilizers, electric energy and fuel, and simultaneously acute marketing problems caused by depressed consumer demand and import competition. In some collective farms wages have not been paid for years.

Economic difficulties pushed a substantial number of the rural population into subsistence farming on their household plots (which should be distinguished from farmland distributed to farmers from former collective farms). This subsistence form of production has become the most typical form of activity for the bulk of the rural and a substantial part of the urban population. In 1997, it yielded 54 per cent of all agricultural output. However, the amount of income generated by this activity per household is generally so low that it only allows few rural families to get out of poverty. In 1997, 53 per cent of rural households were poor (Heinrich, 1999).

Changes in the social transfer system

The social transfer system has important repercussions for the income positions of an important share of the Kyrgyz population. In 1997, 13.2 per cent of all personal incomes derived from pensions and other social benefits. There are 544,300 pensioners in Kyrgyzstan, or 12 per cent of the population. In addition 829,800 people (18.1 per cent of the population) were receiving means-tested welfare benefits in 1997. Almost the entire population relies on publicly-provided education, healthcare, and subsidies for housing and utilities.

The share of social transfers in GDP in Kyrgyzstan is similar to that prevailing in other transitional economies. Annually, approximately 8 per cent of GDP is spent on pensions and unemployment, medical, disability and poverty relief benefits. This figure is higher than in developing countries with similar levels of GDP per capita, but lower than in East European transition economies. However, as a result of the economic crisis, inflation and budgetary problems, the real value of all social transfers has tumbled and eroded the livelihood of people depending on these benefits. The high burden of social expenditures imposed on the state budget did not leave room for much-needed increases in the level of social protection. The lack of financial resources was exacerbated by poor fiscal discipline and a poor collection record, particularly among the rural populations who, while remaining recipients of the bulk of benefits, have greatly reduced their contributions to the pension system, unemployment insurance and the general tax system.

The rise in inequality

As already mentioned, the pre-transition distribution of incomes in Kyrgyzstan was relatively egalitarian. This changed dramatically following the liberalization of prices and wages, the inflation-induced erosion of real wages and social transfers and the redistribution of assets from privatization. Kyrgyzstan witnessed an unprecedented polarization of incomes and

Table 11.5 Distribution of household expenditures, 1993–97

	1993		1997	
	per capita	equivalized*	per capita	equivalized
Gini coefficient	0.47	0.46	0.42	0.40
Percentile ratios				
P90/P10	15.3	14.6	6.2	5.7
P75/P25	3.8	3.8	2.7	2.6
Decile shares				
1st	0.72	0.76	2.21	2.67
2nd	2.03	2.16	3.30	3.64
3rd	3.49	3.57	3.47	4.35
4th	4.81	4.95	4.27	4.70
5th	6.26	6.43	5.22	5.95
6th	8.08	8.32	6.67	6.73
7th	10.27	10.39	7.70	8.53
8th	13.43	13.54	10.41	11.06
9th	18.62	18.54	15.18	14.88
10th	32.30	31.44	41.56	37.48

Note: * Equivalent expenditure is computed as: eq_exp = household expenditure / (nb_adults + 0.70 * nb_children)$^{0.90}$.

wealth: the spread of mass poverty on the one hand and the concentration of wealth in the hands of a small elite.

The Gini coefficient of household expenditure, which stood at only approximately 0.30 during the pre-transition period 1985–90, shot up to 0.47 in 1993 (Table 11.5). This is twice as high as in the most egalitarian Western economies (for example, Finland, Norway and Luxembourg) and is also substantially higher than the Gini in the least egalitarian Western societies (USA, UK) and Russia. In fact, the extent of inequality in Kyrgyzstan is comparable to that prevailing in some developing countries which are known to have the most uneven distributions of income in the world (for example, Argentina, Philippines). The spending of the very rich households was 15 times higher than that of the poorest households: the poorest 50 per cent in Kyrgyzstan accounted for only 17 per cent of all household expenditures in 1993, while the richest 10 per cent accounted for almost one-third of all expenditures. This is evidence of an extremely skewed distribution of resources and deprivation on a large scale for the poorest members of society.

By 1997, the Gini coefficient had fallen to 0.42, still one of the world's highest figures. There is evidence that the decrease in inequality was mainly driven by an improvement in the situation of the poorest households relative to their better off counterparts, while at the same time wealth became even more concentrated in the hands of the wealthiest. The relative improvement of the situation of households located at the bottom end of the expenditure and income distribution may be attributed to the introduction of the Unified Cash Benefit (UCB) system. Under this programme, a single welfare payment targeted at only poor households replaced several cash transfer payments with wide coverage but poor targeting.

The same factors that account for the initial upward surge in inequality are also responsible for the spread of mass poverty. A small segment of the population amassed considerable wealth through speculative intermediary commercial activities and profiteering from consumer price increases under monopoly conditions and initial scarcity of many goods. The redistribution of the former state property during privatization, large-scale tax evasion especially among the high-income groups engaged in private business activity and, last but not least, the criminalization of many aspects of economic life further contributed to the social stratification. Thus, the fact that the new opportunities offered by the emergence of the market economy were disproportionately seized upon by a select few, in the process leading to a polarization of the income structure, contributed far more to the rise in poverty in Kyrgyzstan than the fall in GDP. A similar phenomenon has been noticed in the case of Russia (Milanovic, 1998: 87–92). Under these conditions of very high income and asset inequality, poverty relief can only be successful if it is placed within a framework of effective income redistribution.

Emerging social structure

In this section, information from the 1993 KMPS and the 1997 LSMS is used to assess the determinants of and changes to the social structure in the Kyrgyz Republic during transition to the market. The 1993 KMPS and the series of LSMS surveys carried out between 1996 and 1998 represent the best available source of information about social change in Kyrgyzstan. However, caveats apply. The recorded income information typically suffers from measurement and recall error. Some income sources, like property incomes, are customarily underreported while income obtained from illegal or semi-legal activities may not be reported at all. For these and other reasons (Ackland and Falkingham, 1997) household expenditure is often preferred to income as a proxy for household wealth. Expenditure exhibits a more stable path over time than income, as households may save or dissave and the expenditure information is adjusted for auto-production and consumption by households, which is not a negligible consideration in the Kyrgyz context. For this reason, the information presented in this section is typically based on expenditure rather than income data.

Despite the greater constancy over time of household expenditure, it may still fluctuate considerably over time, especially in conditions of fundamental economic change. Membership in a certain social class, however, is not only acquired through position in the income distribution but also through the proprietorship of items symbolizing the belonging to this particular class like, for instance, the ownership of real estate and the possession of certain consumer durables. For this reason, a wealth index[3] has been created in order to complement the information derived on the basis of the household expenditure data.

Kyrgyzstan started the transition from a relatively egalitarian position but rapidly transformed into a highly polarized and stratified society with limited scope for social mobility. Asked in 1993 whether they expected to be better or worse off during the following 12 months, 23 per cent of households expected to be better off in the future, 39 per cent expected no significant change and 38 per cent expected to be worse off. Strikingly, the uncertainties surrounding the process of fundamental economic and social change appear to have been so pervasive that attitudes towards the future were undifferentiated by social position: similar proportions of rich and poor people expected to be better or worse off in the future.

The capital Bishkek is the centre of economic and commercial activity and the power-base of the Kyrgyz elite. This predominant position was cemented during the transition. Households living in Bishkek are significantly better off than households living elsewhere in the country; in 1993 the average expenditure of Bishkek households was 50 per cent higher than the national average and in 1997 it was a staggering 100 per cent higher. At the same time, the situation in rural areas, home to the bulk of the impoverished population, has become more desolate.

The composition of the Kyrgyz elite did not change very much relative to the pre-transition period, and some of its members, for reasons outlined earlier, even succeeded in increasing their wealth and consolidating their social status. In addition, education, which previously was bearing little relationship to social status, now became an important vehicle of social mobility and an important factor in determining social class. Table 11.6 traces the relationship between household spending and education of the household head. In the first column, the highest degree obtained by the head in described, column two provides the distribution of educational attainment of the head for all households, and columns three and four contain the relative expenditure levels by education group. In 1993, almost one-third of household heads had benefited from higher education. Higher education is not, however, associated with higher levels of household spending. Households with highly-educated heads spend, in fact, less than an average household and considerably less than households with lower-educated heads. This situation reversed in 1997. Households with heads who have received vocational education only, with no particular qualification, are significantly worse off than households where heads have received more education. Households with heads that have benefited from tertiary education collect a substantial expenditure premium, that is they spend almost 40 per cent more than an average household. Thus, while in 1993

Table 11.6 Education of household head and expenditures, 1993–97 (as % of total average household expenditure)

	Frequency	Per capita expenditure	Equivalized expenditure
1993, highest education obtained			
Vocational courses	18.51	108.5	108.1
Vocational school, no diploma	7.59	104.5	103.5
Vocational school, diploma	33.88	92.6	93.4
Technical school	8.66	101.4	101.4
Higher education	31.36	96.1	96.2
1997, highest education obtained			
No formal education	11.67	79.4	79.0
Incomplete secondary education	12.32	91.9	90.8
Complete secondary education	34.08	85.9	87.3
Professional/technical school	9.60	99.8	100.1
Technical college (*'technikum'*)	16.41	119.2	118.5
Higher education	15.92	140.7	139.1

high levels of education appeared to be a hindrance rather than an asset in providing social status to the bearer, the transition process appears to have significantly contributed to the valorization of human capital.

Accumulation of human capital significantly enhanced the earnings potential of highly educated young people who increasingly formed the new local business elites and the new professional middle class. This new class of young and dynamic entrepreneurs predominantly operating in the service industries is among the main winners from the transition to the market. Notice, however, that this form of upward mobility was observed on a much smaller scale than had been the case in, for example, Russia and Central Europe (CE). This may be explained by the oriental specificity of the society and in particular the strength of the clan organization.

In addition, despite its radical reform agenda, market distortions are still pervasive in Kyrgyzstan. For this reason, marketable skills, education and innovative thinking do not necessarily go hand in hand with business success and the ensuing status gains. Many business opportunities are created through the conditioning of personal networks and clan connections. Rent-seeking activities and monopolistic practices are pervasive, as are underground economic activities.

The social position of blue-collar workers, peasants and some professional groups who, for ideological reasons, had acquired social status and influence under communism has been eroded. Their loss of social status and influence was compounded by loss of income and many of them entered protracted spells of poverty. In addition, pensioners and the disabled, who previously received adequate protection against adverse contingencies, lost not only their income but also many of their privileges (for example, access to healthcare). These societal groups, along with the newly-created underclass of the unemployed, stand out as the main losers from the transition to the market.

On balance, the number of losers appears to clearly outweigh the number of winners from the market-oriented reforms. There are fewer winners in Kyrgyzstan than, for instance, in the CE transition economies. However, its radical reformist approach to manage economic change has provided a framework for rewarding ambition and entrepreneurial spirit and thus created a scope for social mobility and reranking – but also instability – unknown to its Central Asian neighbours. The large-scale migratory movements of the Russian and ethnic German population groups also substantially affected social mobility and reranking. These had previously formed the backbone of the professional and working classes and their replacement by ethnic Kyrgyz leads to further changes in occupational and social status.

Regrettably, as elsewhere in the Commonwealth of Independent States (CIS) criminalization of the society has interacted with social developments in Kyrgyzstan. While crime has flourished in general, a new threat stems from the proliferation of drug-related crime (Rumer, 1996a: 63). Kyrgyzstan has become a major drug transportation route from Afghanistan and Gorno-Badakhshan in Tajikistan to the city of Osh in the Fergana valley in southern Kyrgyzstan, and from there on to the CIS and Europe. For a considerable number of people involved, the drugs trade sustains their livelihood, rendering efforts by law-enforcement agencies to stomp out these crimes even more perilous, and in vain. Some observers have even suggested the emergence of a 'Colombian' pattern, where a substantial part of the local population specializes in the cultivation and transportation of opium as their only viable alternative for economic activity (Zhukov, 1996: 126).

Thus, despite the rapid modernization of Kyrgyz society, many traditional factors – personal networks, clan structure, rent-seeking, the informal sector – continue to influence the social stratification process, hampering the emergence of a liberal, democratic and culturally diversified market economy. Notwithstanding, the process of modernization is clearly visible, especially in the capital Bishkek, and certainly exerts a powerful demonstration effect thus forcing social change.

The upper class

Casual observation suggests that the Soviet nomenklatura has successfully defended, and even strengthened, its position at the top of the social pyramid. The chairmen and directors of most 'national companies', holdings and investment funds emanated from the Soviet bureaucracy and political elite; their power and resources were consolidated using their clan connections. Rumer observes that 'one gains the impression that the national wealth has been plundered during the process of privatization – and on a truly fantastic scale, spawning a whole new class of predatory "bourgeoisie"' (Rumer,

1996b: 56). Consequently, vast resources have accumulated in the hands of a tightly knit network of government officials, their relatives and close associates. This is confirmed by the information in Table 11.5 which already suggested that despite the overall reduction in inequalities in Kyrgyz society, the rich became considerably richer between 1993 and 1997.

The former nomenklatura is joined at the top by a small group of successful businessmen and entrepreneurs. Using the 1993 KMPS and the 1997 LSMS, one may trace the background and the sources of the new-found wealth of this latter group. They are usually well-educated, active in the manufacturing or service sectors – particularly trade and banking – of the economy, and they live in Bishkek. It is much more difficult, however, to identify observable characteristics – personal, labour force or other – of the old-established elite, but informal evidence, again, suggests that they are the high-level government bureaucrats, enterprise directors and bankers.

Estimates of the size of this group of extremely wealthy persons vary and depend on the definition employed. Under no circumstances does the elite, however, encompass more than 5 per cent of the population. In fact, while the richest 10 per cent of Kyrgyz households accounted for approximately 40 per cent of total household expenditures in Kyrgyzstan in 1997, the top 5 per cent alone accounted for over 30 per cent of all expenditures. In addition, they are the largest property holders in the form of equity shares and real estate. They enjoy high-quality housing and have access to a wide variety of luxury durable consumer goods. Despite its small numbers, evidence of the high-life led by Kyrgyzstan's elite is abounding in the streets of Bishkek with a noticeable number of luxury Western cars and mobile phones. And here and there springs up the occasional impressive house, in the midst of a general slump in construction, to offer a sharp contrast to the poverty-stricken surroundings.

The composition of the upper class has also been affected in other ways by the economic and social transformation. As a result of the emigration of ethnic Russians and Germans, the Kyrgyz elite has been consolidated. Those Russians who stayed on in Kyrgyzstan after independence generally suffered a substantial loss of status, regardless of their initial social position. At the same time, generational changes have occurred at the level of the elite. The transition to the market and the ensuing privatization of state property and the creation of business opportunities has promoted the upward mobility of the young descendants of the old-established nomenklatura. For them it became easier than under Soviet rule to reach high social positions and wealth, using their enterprise and human capital. Nomenklatura networks and family ties remain an essential precondition to enjoy a privileged position in society.

In a country where criminal activity thrives, security is a major concern for the elite. Their security is often guaranteed by pledging loyalty to government officials and sharing profits with them. All businesses, from small kiosks to large enterprises, depend on these informal links with state officials on matters of taxation and customs regime. Through this channel government officials acquire an active stake in the conduct of the general economic activity. An anti-corruption campaign that began in December 1998 has shed light on a substantial number of dubious deals involving government officials. According to Kyrgyz Prosecutor-General Asanbek Shirshenaliyev, in the past five years, 383 government officials were dismissed from their posts on corruption charges.

The middle class

Identification of the middle class in the Kyrgyz context is not a straightforward task. The middle class is typically an urban phenomenon, yet over 60 per cent of the Kyrgyz population live in rural areas. And, while poverty estimates vary, between 40 and 50 per cent of all households in Kyrgyzstan are thought to be poor. Thus, the middle class can be expected to be much smaller than is the case in Western countries and the European transition economies. In addition, it may be useful to distinguish between middle-income middle-class households and the upper middle class. The former group is composed of households that are not poor but remain in a precarious situation; small losses of income may result in them entering poverty. In the latter group, one finds households in secure income positions who are more likely to experience upwards rather than downwards social mobility.

On the basis of expenditure data and the previously introduced wealth index, one may conclude that about 30–35 per cent of Kyrgyz households belong to the middle class, of which approximately one-third make up the upper middle class. Middle-class households spend on average 70 per cent more than poorer households, and the upper middle class, in turn, spends an additional 30 per cent more than the middle-ranking middle class. Asset ownership and possession of durable goods provides additional support for this classification scheme.

The lower middle class is generally composed of households that became disenfranchised as a result of the transition but avoided a full-scale descent into poverty. They include families where the head of household has remained employed but where the head and other family members supplement their income through secondary activities, farmers with larger landplots and livestock holdings who achieve good levels of productivity as well as pensioners who returned to work. In this group, one also finds many employees in the budgetary sector who had to accept real wage cuts as a result of the government's austerity package. These include junior civil servants, teachers and doctors.

The middle class is on average well-educated. In 1997, over 50 per cent of middle-class household heads had received more than secondary education. This is unsurprising given the good average educational achievement record of Kyrgyzstan, a positive legacy of the Soviet period. However, the abundance of a well-educated labour force and the fact that the 'new economy' creates jobs at a slower rate than they are destroyed in the 'old economy' means that adequate employment opportunities do not exist for all of these highly qualified individuals. As a result, many of them accept jobs for which they are overqualified or they engage in subsistence self-employment activities, degrading their skills in the process and adversely affecting their potential for upward social mobility.

Upper-middle-class households are concentrated, just like the elite, in the manufacturing and the service sector. They work as professionals, managers or small entrepreneurs. They also concentrate more heavily in new enterprises, for example joint-stock companies, joint ventures or private enterprises rather than in state-owned enterprises. Approximately 15 per cent of the upper-middle-class households engage in non-agricultural self-employment or entrepreneurial activity. While this is a relatively high percentage, it is significantly less than for upper-class households (25 per cent). The spread of these activities appears to be hampered by the unwieldiness of the tax system, administrative harassment, crime and economic instability. The upper class, through their closeness to the political elite and their greater wealth, may indeed be better prepared to deal with the heavy regulation that is entailed by entrepreneurial activity.

Poverty and the poor

With a GDP per capita in the region of US$2000 per annum, Kyrgyzstan is a poor country. Resources are distributed very unequally, a process exacerbated by the transition to the market. As a result, large parts of the Kyrgyz population are impoverished. The elimination of widespread poverty arguably poses the greatest challenge to the pro-market reforms, while its existence may threaten the success and sustainability of the reform drive.

It is very difficult to assess the true extent of poverty in Kyrgyzstan, and the existing evidence is conflicting. In addition, measurement and methodological problems are pervasive (Ackland and Falkingham, 1997). In 1989, before the beginning of reforms, 33 per cent of households in the Kyrgyz Household Budget Survey received a monthly per capita income below 75 roubles, the official Soviet poverty line. In the 1993 KMPS, 45.5 per cent of households were identified as poor, a marked increase from the pre-transition poverty level. According to LSMS data, 51 per cent of households were poor in 1997, a further 5.5 per cent increase. The IMF estimated a 40 per cent poverty rate for 1993, and almost 50 per cent in 1996 (IMF, 1998: 12). These estimates were later revised upwards: a 54 per cent poverty rate in 1993 and 70 per cent in 1996 (IMF, 1999: 12). Thus, poverty in Kyrgyzstan appears to be high and rising.

This latter claim – that poverty is rising – is disputed by Heinrich (1999). Using several poverty lines while paying particular attention to the problem of intertemporal comparability of these poverty lines, and using a range of equivalence scales to adjust the expenditure information for economies of scale in consumption, strong evidence is put forward that poverty fell by approximately 5 per cent between 1993 and 1997 and that less than 50 per cent of households remained poor in 1997. The results also demonstrate the importance of correcting expenditure data for household composition. Average household sizes in Kyrgyzstan are very large relative to Western households and precluding the existence of economies of scale in consumption is clearly unreasonable, when the results show that even small adjustments may fundamentally alter the conclusions. In addition, the inequality analysis suggested that expenditure levels of the poorest households had increased in 1993–97 relative to their better-off counterparts, possibly as a result of the introduction of the UCB. For the assessment of poverty in Kyrgyzstan, this implies a decrease not only of the simple headcount of poverty but also of the severity or intensity of poverty.

Poverty in Kyrgyzstan is heavily concentrated in rural areas. In 1997, over 50 per cent of rural households were poor but less than 20 per cent of urban households. The mountain oblast of Narynskaya is the poorest region, with a poverty incidence of over 80 per cent. Poverty is also concentrated in agrarian regions of the southern part of the country; these are Osh and Djalal-Abad oblasts where the proportion of poor residents reaches 50 and 62 per cent respectively. The capital Bishkek exhibits the lowest poverty rate: less than 10 per cent of households living there are poor.

The spread of mass poverty to mountainous and remote areas is largely due to the limited opportunities for productive farming and a drastic decline in livestock holdings. Rural development is further hampered by the absence of productive and social infrastructure. Rural areas thus experience a mass outflow of population, primarily among the youngest and most industrious. Poverty alleviation in these areas requires large injections of state support, to date by far inadequate. Measures for the development of local infrastructure and social services need to be combined with cattle breeding and crop cultivation (vegetables) so as to satisfy the basic needs of the local population.

Poverty is typically correlated with unemployment and is high in areas where unemployment is high. Areas of high concentrations of poverty are often single-firm towns which developed around a single big but now defunct enterprise; thus the majority of the local population became unemployed. Poverty relief in these areas requires the restructuring of large enterprises and, more importantly, job-creation in the SME sector.

Poverty in Kyrgyzstan extends to all the major socio-demographic groups. This includes the traditionally vulnerable groups – for example the unemployed, pensioners and those unable to work – but also households of working-age, able-bodied persons who pursue an economic activity. Table 11.7 shows that households with a retired or unemployed head in 1997 spent

Table 11.7 Economic status of household head and expenditures, 1997 (as % of total average household expenditure)

Economic status	Frequency	Per capita expenditure	Equivalized expenditure
Working	58.80	101.9	103.0
Retired	24.66	91.7	89.2
Unemployed	11.13	91.2	92.5
Other	5.41	135.7	132.0

10 per cent less than an average household, as opposed to households with a working head who spent slightly more. This figure masks, however, the enormous dichotomy that exists between workers.

The erosion of state welfare support has negatively affected the livelihood of old-age pensioners – many of whom return to work in the informal subsistence sector of the economy – the disabled and families with large numbers of dependent children. As a result, the majority of children in Kyrgyzstan grow up in poverty and are unable to acquire adequate skills and levels of human capital, in the process adversely affecting the long-run growth potential of the economy.

While households depending on public transfers for their income are disproportionately at risk from poverty, many households engaged in gainful economic activity are also poor. Therefore, strategies to relieve poverty are much more complex than just to increase the number of working households.

In 1997, over 85 per cent of households derived substantial income from earnings and a further 40 per cent derived substantial income from farming activity. Yet, 35 per cent of households with earnings and over 50 per cent of households with agricultural income were poor (Heinrich, 1999).

In the absence of an effective social safety net, many households rely on help from friends and relatives. In 1997, 23 per cent of households received a significant amount of private transfers, up from 14 per cent in 1993. Many households – especially pensioners – rely on the farming of private plots in order to procure minimal amounts of food. In urban areas subsistence-oriented economic activities include petty trading of foodstuffs, fruit and vegetables or cigarettes in open markets or the street. However, such subsistence activities are inaccessible to the most vulnerable groups in society: urban female-headed households, rural pensioner-headed households, and households with many children (Ackland and Falkingham, 1997: 98). The inability of the transfer system to provide sufficient help to these households means that they form a socially immobile and severely deprived underclass.

The extent and possible implications of the poverty problem have now been correctly recognized by policy-makers, and poverty alleviation has risen to the top of the political agenda with the adoption in 1998 of the National Programme for Poverty Alleviation (ARAKET). The structure of poverty suggests that effective poverty alleviation can be achieved by a coherent set of labour market policies including wage policy and active labour market policies, the removal of administrative barriers to the creation of small enterprises and support for households in rural areas, mainly in the form of improved infrastructures.

Policy implications for social cohesion, stability and development

Kyrgyzstan has successfully overcome the inertia of central planning. It has stabilized the macroeconomy and initiated the development of a new institutional structure. However, radical economic reforms have failed in delivering higher living standards to the bulk of the population, and the transition has resulted in a large increase in poverty. Only a small segment of the population has managed to take full advantage of the new opportunities that the market economy offers. This had led to a considerable worsening of the distribution of income and wealth and has contributed to the rise in poverty. The reduction of inequality and poverty has become a key objective of economic and social policies while social integration and cohesion have become major preconditions for sustainable development.

The policies to fight poverty should primarily focus on promoting economic stability and developing the key sectors of the national economy. Particularly important is the development of the agricultural sector, which employs almost half of the labour force. As almost three-quarters of the poor live in rural areas, increased efficiency in agricultural production, aided by the development of rural infrastructures is likely to improve considerably the fate of the rural population. In the short-term, the consolidation of economic stabilization and the resumption of growth are priorities. Attention should therefore be paid to preventing poverty from spreading, and scarce transfers should be devoted to eradicate poverty under its most acute forms. Poverty reduction on a larger scale should commence in the medium term as the benefits from economic growth are shared out to all strata of the society.

Strategic goals to improve living standards and reduce poverty may be achieved by a combination of social policies aimed at improving labour productivity, and appeals to the personal responsibility of citizens for their well-being with social assistance targeted only at vulnerable groups. Active social policies should aim at providing economically gainful employment and improving the structure, quality and competitiveness of labour. These measures include employment programmes, mitigation of unemployment, fostering of entrepreneurial activity and support to small businesses and the farming community.

The promotion of gainful employment as the main source of welfare improvements requires corrections to the distorted wage structure. Employment should guarantee an adequate remuneration and particular attention should be drawn to the level of the minimum wage and the wages of employees in the budgetary sector, many of whom are very poor.

The creation of equal opportunities requires investment in human capital. This is especially true for the poor. A high priority should therefore been given to essential commodities and services such as housing, education and training, medical care, and basic cultural goods and services.

Notes

1 The Kyrgyz Republic National Committee on Statistics together with the World Bank and the Research Triangle Institute of North Carolina have designed and implemented a comprehensive representative survey for measuring the standard of living in the Republic. The first survey, the Kyrgyzstan Multipurpose Poverty Survey (KMPS) was carried out in 1993. This effort was followed up starting in spring 1996 by four rounds of the Living Standards Measurement Survey (LSMS) implemented in spring 1996, fall 1996, 1997 and 1998. The survey is based on a representative sample of approximately 2000 households and a very extensive questionnaire. This enormous source of information on various aspects of economic and social life has yet to be explored in depth by researchers. The analysis in this chapter represents one of the first efforts to rigorously examine the 1997 LSMS survey kindly provided by the Kyrgyz National Committee on Statistics. We also acknowledge assistance of the Poverty and Human Resources Division of the World Bank, which kindly provided the 1993 KMPS data.

2 During the period of 1990–93, net migration to Russia from Kyrgyzstan amounted to 175,400 or 4.1 per cent of the total population and 8.2 per cent of the labour force (Zhukov, 1996: 113). Subsequently, in 1994–96 net emigration totalled 81,700 people or another 2 per cent of the population and 4.5 per cent of the labour force. As a result, the Russian and other European (in the first place German, Ukrainian and Jewish) population decreased in 1990–97 from 1197.2 million to 848,300, or from 27.6 per cent to 18.5 per cent of the total country population. The most massive was emigration of ethnic Russians whose population in Kyrgyzstan decreased by one-quarter, from 917,600 to 698,100.

3 In order to create the wealth index, a subset of questions from the 1993 and 1997 surveys are identified that are typically positively correlated with household wealth. These items include housing quality (for example, access to hot water, access to an indoor toilet, access to a telephone), possession of durable goods (for example, car, colour TV, VCR), land ownership, ownership of real estate and ownership of financial instruments and savings (for example, bonds, stocks, bank account with commercial bank, foreign bank account). A point is awarded to the household for each affirmative answer and the wealth index is simply the unweighted sum of the points scored by each household. The obtained score is then transformed into a five-point index. One may interpret each point on this scale to represent a social group: deprived, poor, middle class, upper middle class and elite. Although this measure may be criticized for being too crude, the index provides a faithful predictor of social status and exhibits a high correlation with the expenditure-based social status measures.

References

Ackland, R. and J. Falkingham (1997) 'A Profile of Poverty in Kyrgyzstan', in Falkingham *et al.* (1997).

European Bank for Reconstruction and Development (EBRD) (1997) *Transition Report 1997*. London: EBRD.

Falkingham, J., J. Klugman, S. Marnie and J. Micklewright (eds) (1997) *Household Welfare in Central Asia*. Basingstoke: Macmillan – Palgrave.

Heinrich, G. (1999) *Dynamic Aspects of Poverty and the Distribution of Welfare in Kyrgyzstan, 1993–1997*, UNU/WIDER, mimeo.

International Monetary Fund (IMF) (1998, 1999) 'Kyrgyz Republic – Recent Economic Developments', *IMF Staff Country Report* 98/08. Washington DC: IMF.

Klugman, J. (1998) 'Uzbekistan: Institutional Continuity Helps Performance', *MOCT-MOST, Economic Policy in Transitional Economies*, 8(1): 63–82.

—— and K. Scott (1997) 'Measuring Labour Market Status in Kazakhstan', in Falkingham *et al.* (1997).

Koichuev, T. (1996) 'Kyrgyzstan: Economic Crisis and Transition Strategy', in Rumer (1996a).

Milanovic, B. (1998) *Income, Inequality, and Poverty during the Transition from Planned to Market Economy*. Washington DC: World Bank.

Ministry of Labour and Social Protection (MLSP) (1998) *Social Policy Strategy: Labour Market, Employment and Social Assistance*. Bishkek: MLSP.

PlanEcon Review (1997) *PlanEcon Review and Outlook for the Former Soviet Republic*, Washington DC, September.

Roberts, B., Y. Gorkov and J. Madigan (1998) *Is Privatisation a Free Lunch? New Evidence on Ownership Status and Firm Performance*, mimeo.

Rumer, B. (ed.) (1996a) *Central Asia in Transition: Dilemmas of Political and Economic Development*. Armonk: M. E. Sharp.

—— (1996b) 'Disintegration and Reintegration in Central Asia: Dynamics and Prospects', in Rumer (1996a).

United Nations Development Programme (UNDP) (1993, 1998) *Human Development Report*. New York: Oxford University Press.

—— (1997) *National Human Development Report of the Kyrgyz Republic, 1997*. Bishkek: UNDP.

World Bank (1999) *World Development Indicators, 1999*. Washington DC: World Bank.

Zhukov, S. (1996) 'Economic Development in the States of Central Asia', in Rumer (1996a).

Index